W9-CCQ-636

the knot

COMPLETE GUIDE TO WEDDINGS IN THE REAL WORLD

CARLEY RONEY

& the editors of The Knot

the knot

COMPLETE GUIDE TO WEDDINGS IN THE REAL WORLD

The Ultimate Source of Ideas, Advice, and Relief for the Bride and Groom and Those Who Love Them

Broadway Books New York

THE KNOT COMPLETE GUIDE TO WEDDINGS IN THE REAL WORLD.
Copyright © 2004 by The Knot, Inc. All rights reserved.
No part of this book may be reproduced or transmitted in any form or by any means, electronic or mechanical, including photocopying, recording, or by any information storage and retrieval system, without written permission from the publisher. For information, address Broadway Books, a division of Random House, Inc.

PRINTED IN THE UNITED STATES OF AMERICA

BROADWAY BOOKS and its logo, a letter B bisected on the diagonal, are trademarks of Random House, Inc.

Visit our website at www.broadwaybooks.com

First edition published 1999
Second edition published 2004

Design by Judith Stagnitto Abbate / Abbate Design
Illustrations by Brittany O'Neil

The Library of Congress has cataloged the first edition as follows:

Roney, Carley.
The Knot's complete guide to weddings in the real world :
the ultimate source of ideas, advice, and relief for the bride and groom
and those who love them / by Carley Roney.—1st ed.
p. cm.
Includes index.
1. Weddings—Planning. 2. Wedding etiquette. I. Title.
HQ745.R66 1998
395.2'2—dc21 98-11805
CIP

ISBN 0-7679-1642-5

5 7 9 10 8 6

Contents

Foreword xi
Acknowledgments xiii

Part One: Decisions, Decisions

1. THE ADVENTURE BEGINS
Engagement Length 3
Spilling the Beans 3
Engagement Announcements 5
Engaged Ups and Downs 7
Buying the Ring 8

2. ENVISIONING THE EVENT
Setting Your Priorities 13
Divining a Date and Time 14
Settling on Size 17
Finding a Site 19
Selecting a Wedding Style 20
Wedding Consultants 22

3. BUDGET AND BUSINESS
Setting Your Budget 25
Who's Paying and How? 26

Budgeting Basics 30
Working with Wedding Professionals 32

4. ATTENDANTS AND GUESTS
Attendants and Their Roles 39
Lining Up the Little Ones 44
Roles for Other Important People 45
Fitting in the Folks 47
Greeting Those Guests 50

5. PREWEDDING PARTIES
Engagement Parties 55
Showers 56
Bachelor/ette Bashes 60
The Rehearsal Dinner 62
The Parties You Throw 64

6. STANDING ON CEREMONY
Religious vs. Civil Ceremonies 67
Finding Your Officiant 69
Ceremony Basics 70
Ceremonies with Personal Style 78
Religious Ceremony Specifics 84
Interfaith Ceremonies 88
Second Weddings 90
Commitment Ceremonies 92

7. A ROUSING RECEPTION
What Happens When 95
The Receiving Line 96
Seating Your Guests 98
Reception Rituals 99

Part Two: Details, Details

8. TAKING IT PERSONALLY
Playing Up Your Passions 107
Using the Season 111
Adding Ethnic Traditions 113
Getting Married Away 117

9. THE PAPER TRAIL
Printing Techniques 123
Invitation Basics 125
Invitation Wording 127
Addressing the Envelopes 130
Selecting a Stationer 132
Other Wedding Stationery 134

10. LOCATION, LOCATION
Starting Your Search 145
What to Look For 146
Great Wedding Places 149
Meeting with Managers 155

11. YOUR LOOK
The Gown 161
Where to Get the Gown 169
Going Shopping 173
The Search Is Over 177
Preserving Your Dress 179
Dressing It Up: Accessories 180
Getting Gorgeous: Wedding Hair and Makeup 186

12. DRESSING THE REST
Men's Formalwear 101 193
Dressing the Bridesmaids 198
Clothing Your Wedding Kids 202
Fashion Tips for Mom and Pop 203

13. FLOWER POWER
Which Blooms to Use? 207
Ceremony Flowers 209
Reception Flowers 213
Finding a Fabulous Florist 215
Other Decorations 217

14. EAT, DRINK, AND BE MARRIED
Deciding Which Meal to Serve 221
Choosing a Caterer 224
Talking to Your Caterer 226
Making the Menu Memorable 227
Hot Menus from Cool Chefs 229
Serving Drinks 232

15. CUT TO THE CAKE
Confection Reflections 235
Finding a Baker 238
The Groom's Cake 239

16. PICTURE THIS
Photography 241
Focusing on a Style 241
Hiring a Hot Shot 244
Photo Types and Twists 247
Videography 250
Zooming In on a Genre 251
Hiring a Video Pro 252

17. FACE THE MUSIC
Ceremony Music 257
Music-Deserving Moments 257
Ceremony Music Options 260
Hiring Your Music Makers 262
Reception Music 263
Band vs. DJ 263
Hiring Your Reception Entertainers 266
Getting Everyone Groovin' 270

18. SOMETHING FAVORABLE
The Favor 411 273
Ways to Give 274
Sweet Charities 276

19. WHEELING AND DEALING
Setting the Budget 279
Making the Reservations 280
Getting to the Ceremony 281
Getting to the Party 281

20. GIVING AND GETTING
Signing Up for Stuff: Registering 285
Gift-Getting Dos and Don'ts 289
Expressing Your Gratitude 291

21. THE COUNTDOWN
Unfinished Wedding Business 297
It's All in the Timing 303

Last-Minute Craziness 304
Having a Ball 306
Where to Next? 307

Part Three: Sticky Subjects

22. LOVE PATROL
Fending Off Your Family 311
Managing Money Madness 313
Passion Patrol 315
Religious Rifts 316
The Challenge of Change 317
Fighting Right 318
Cures for Cold Feet 322

23. COMBINING CULTURES
Differences and Your Relationship 325
Different Worlds, One Address 326
Compromise 101 328
Family Friction 330
Fair-Weather Friends 332

24. IN-LAWS AND OUTLAWS
Dealing with Your Parents 335
Divorced Dilemmas 338
Interacting with the In-Laws 339
Why Friends Freak Out 344

Part Four: The Great Escape

25. HONEYMOON HIGHWAY
The Best Beaches 349
Adrenaline Adventures 352
Urban Escapes 356
Head Trips 358
Exotica 360
Classic Cruises 364

26. HONEYMOON HELPER
Making Some Decisions 369
Booking Your Trip 372

Getting Ready to Go 374
Tips from Experienced Travelers 377
Advice for a Harmonious Honeymoon 379

APPENDIX A: CHECKLISTS AND WORKSHEETS
Your To-Do List 385
Your Big-Day Budget 391
Your Phone Book 397
Your Wedding-Day Contact List 405
Bridesmaids' Measurements 409

APPENDIX B: RESOURCES
Your Wedding Clothes 413
For Your Wedding 417
For Your Honeymoon 419

INDEX 421

Foreword

When we launched The Knot website in 1996, we just knew there were people out there like us—modern, smart, in-love couples looking for an up-to-date, stylish, and real-world approach to planning their weddings. Within a year we had a huge online following of hundreds of thousands of to-be-weds from all over the country. Word spread fast. It seems that couples simply can't find anything out there that matches our tell-it-like-it-is advice, fresh ideas, practical etiquette, and stress-relieving sanity. (Besides that, we are the only real resource out there for *both* the bride and groom.)

We're thrilled to be able to put in print the best of The Knot opinions, exhaustive databases of information, and real people's experiences. You simply can't beat the completeness and portability of a book—never mind the fact you can snuggle down into bed with it (together).

Before you dig in, take a look at the table of contents. We've structured things in (sort of) chronological order. But don't think you have to sit down and read this book from start to finish. At the opening of each chapter you'll see what's covered. Scan and look for the headlines that address your current issues.

Since we know planning a wedding can be kind of intimidating, we've tried to make this book as user-friendly as possible. The sidebars offer easy nuggets of important info on saving money, resources, hot ideas, and more. If you're overwhelmed and don't have the vaguest idea where to begin, check out the "To-Do" list in Appendix A. It tells you what to worry about when and tells you which chapters in this book will guide you through each to-do.

This is a working book, not a bible. Feel free to mark things, tear out pages, dog-ear to your heart's content. There's a fun and fact-filled resource section in the back of the book with phone numbers, resources, checklists, and worksheets. Make it your own.

Finally, as far as we're concerned, there's only one thing that really matters: that you have the wedding you want, not a nervous breakdown. Don't get too caught up in the details. Your wedding will be mesmerizing—no matter how big or small the budget, no matter how much or how little time you can devote to making it happen. So whether your wedding is an over-the-top 400-person formal religious affair or an intimate backyard barbecue after eloping, you're in the right place. Read up. Make decisions. Trust your judgment. Let go. Enjoy.

Acknowledgments

Many extraordinary individuals and organizations were critical in making *The Knot Complete Guide to Weddings in the Real World* a reality. Here's my attempt to thank them all.

I cannot express enough my appreciation and respect for my executive editor and devoted teammate, Julie Raimondi. I'd also like to thank Joanna Saltz, Lisa Carse, and Maribeth Romslo for their fast, wonderful work on this updated edition. My gratitude goes as well to the many wonderful writers who have contributed to The Knot editorial work past and present, notably Tracy Guth, Wendy Paris, Hagar Scher, Allison Micarelli, Amy Nathanson, Robert Moritz, and Robin Sayers. On behalf of my team, I'd also like to thank everyone else at The Knot for putting up with everything from our stress-induced moods to our constant taking over of the conference rooms. Michael Wolfson, it was largely your dreaming that gave us the opportunity to do this book in the first place. For this, I am not sure whether to hit you or hug you. I guess we'll go with the latter.

Thanks to Broadway Books and our editors for your guidance on our book series. It has been such a treat to watch it be a success! We appreciate your continued support.

To our agents past and present, Chris Tomasino, Jonathan Diamond, and Jennifer Unter: we adore you and appreciate your devotion to bringing The Knot brand into books. You are true experts, and we feel lucky to have you on our team.

Many talented photographers donated the use of their wedding photographs, in particular Elizabeth Messina, Karen Zieff, Missy McLamb, and Elizabeth Grubb (see the photo credits page for the full list). Thank you—your stunning images make this book more beautiful. We also appreciate the time of all the couples who participated in putting together our real weddings. Your personal stories give this book an important added dimension.

Many friends and industry experts contributed their sage advice on subjects ranging from seating arrangements to wedding-night sex—as well as their support for this project and the work that went into it. We depend on your wisdom and experience to make our resources both on- and offline realistic and robust. So, many thanks to you all, most notably: JoAnn Gregoli, Maria McBride-Mellinger, Denis Reggie, Marcy Blum, Carolyn Hefner, Joyce Scardina Becker, Gerard Monaghan, Reem Acra, Melissa Sweet, and the many others who are always able to help out in a pinch. Last, but certainly not least, we have to acknowledge our amazing "knotties" on both AOL and TheKnot.com. It is from the brides and grooms who participate on The Knot every day and night that we learn the most. We admire your ideas, insights, and undying enthusiasm for your weddings.

Above all, my love to my sweet husband (and The Knot CEO), David Liu, to my darling daughter, Havana, and to my founding partners, Michael and Rob, you are the best of companions on this crazy roller-coaster ride.

—CARLEY RONEY

the knot

COMPLETE GUIDE TO WEDDINGS IN THE REAL WORLD

PART ONE

DECISIONS, DECISIONS

CHAPTER ONE

the adventure begins

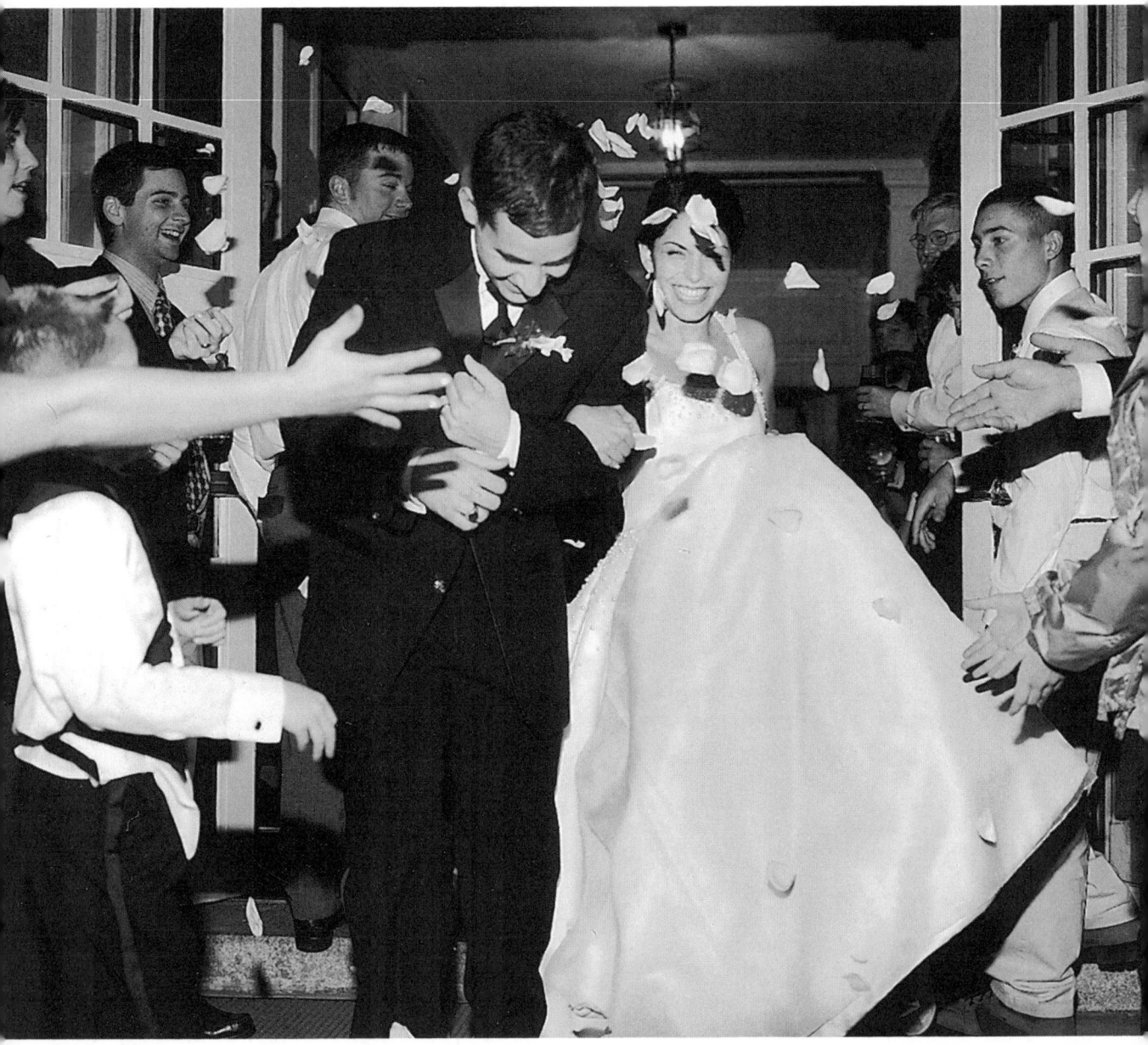

There's nothing more fun than the week you get engaged. Having a secret, practically exploding with excitement and anticipation, blurting out the news to your best pals, letting your families in on it all. There are a few details to attend to, but your biggest task right now is to linger on cloud nine!

Engagement Length

When your feet finally hit the ground again, the first thing to consider is how long your engagement will be. It'll depend on a couple of factors, such as your ideal wedding date and how much time you'll realistically need to prepare the wedding of the millennium. A typical engagement lasts from six months to a year, but many couples stray outside those boundaries—if you want to get married next Tuesday or two years from today, do it!

In any case, no matter how long your engagement is, build in some break time from all things wedding-related—you don't want to be drowning in wedding planning every single minute from right now until the big day itself. Granted, your nuptials are about the most exciting thing coming or going, but they're not the be-all, end-all, and you need to remind yourselves periodically that normal life is happening simultaneously. You'll be a lot less stressed out if you take your mind off all things canapé, carnation, and calypso from time to time. Your single friends, and those long-married, too, also will appreciate a respite from licking envelopes and hearing about the woes of finding the perfect wedding venue. It will make your life immensely more pleasurable and ensure that you remain healthily grounded in the real world—which is, after all, where you're going to be living once you descend gracefully from cloud nine.

Where the Words Come From

- Fiancé/e: Old French *fiancé,* a promise
- Betrothed: Be + the Old English *treowth,* truth
- Husband: Middle English *husbonde,* householder
- Wife: Old English *wif,* woman, or possibly based on Indo-European *weip,* "the hidden or veiled person"

Spilling the Beans

It's time to announce that you're taking the plunge. You could run buck naked together across the field during the live broadcast of the Super Bowl, with the words "We're getting hitched!" tattooed across your chests. That way everyone you've ever met will get the news. On second thought, a little decorum can go a long way (and your families will probably appreciate finding out a bit more privately, too).

Go to Chapter 2 for help figuring out when to do the deed.

Talking to Your Parents

Share the news with your immediate families first. Unless your folks are already great friends, your best bet is to tell each set of parents separately so that they (1) will be able to express their emotions freely and (2) won't have to deal with the surprise of the engagement and the possible discomfort of having to hug all their new in-laws simultaneously. Traditionally—if you must know—the bride's family gets first dibs on the news.

> "You're probably getting bombarded with questions from all directions. If people keep pressuring you about details, don't get intimidated. Whatever you do, don't forget to enjoy those first few weeks."
>
> **—Myrna Ruskin, New York therapist and marriage-stress expert**

The greatest way to let Mom and Dad in on your big secret is together, especially if they know and like your sweetie. Invite them over for dinner, or wait until your next planned get-together, and blurt it out. In your perfect universe, they'll leap from their chairs to squeeze you both, crying for joy. (Of course, if you get engaged on a trip or live far apart and you just *can't,* by all means, call!)

If your parents don't know your intended, this is the perfect time to organize a visit home. However, we don't recommend introducing your one-and-only *and* announcing your engagement on the same occasion. If you can, wait at least until the second visit. Otherwise, whether you're pressed for time or simply feeling awkward, it's A-OK to go solo when telling your parents about the engagement; in fact, they may appreciate your discretion.

Likewise, you may want to break the news *without* your partner if your parents:

- Have a problem with your mate-to-be
- Are over-the-top protective
- Have concerns about your religious or cultural differences
- Have seen you go through one (or two or three) messy divorces
- Are otherwise opposed to the concept of you getting married

If need be, telling them on your own means you'll be able to have it out openly with your folks without dragging your love through any unnecessary and unpleasant stress and strain.

If your parents live on another planet—metaphorically speaking—and you don't quite connect, send them a thoughtful letter. If your parents are divorced, make the time to personally let both sides in on your plans. The bottom line: Do whatever feels right to you.

> **Whom to Tell First**
>
> Don't share news of your engagement with your parents first if they've been negative about your relationship. Instead, turn to people you know will be thrilled. After they've showered you with love and approval, *then* tell your parents; you'll be fortified for the potential hostility.

Kids Come First

If you have children from a previous marriage, *they* should be your first priority—even before your mom and pop. They're the ones who are getting a new stepparent (and maybe a stepsibling or two), and they'll need some time to get comfortable with the idea of becoming the Brady Bunch. Give your kids lots of undivided attention: The two of you should have a one-on-one-on-one with each child. Also organize a fun stepfamily outing (picnic, bike trip, movie and dinner)—you might find that "the more, the merrier" rule is right on the mark. If not, it's probably just a matter of time.

Don't let your ex-spouse hear about your engagement from the dry cleaner you still share or, worse, Junior himself. If you have children together, letting him or her know is *not* optional. If you're not on speaking terms, drop a polite note with the news saying you're willing to discuss any worries or concerns, provided the skeletons in your relationship closet stay put.

BILL & EMILY

Proposed January 7, New York City

WHEN BILL WAS READY to propose to Emily, he wanted to do something creative and romantic, something that spoke to her. The solution was obvious: a crossword puzzle. A puzzle devotee, Emily did the *New York Times* crossword every day without fail. So Bill called Will Shortz, the crossword editor at the *Times*, hoping he would agree to play cupid. Shortz liked the idea, and the plan was a go.

On the day the puzzle appeared in the paper, Bill played hooky from work and took Emily out for a leisurely day on the town. They went to a café, and Emily, unsuspecting, started the puzzle. Soon Emily said, "Look, my name's in the puzzle." A few minutes later she exclaimed, "Look! *Your* name's in the puzzle, too!"

Emily says she was skipping around the puzzle, and "it seemed very relevant to our relationship." The giveaway clue was "1729 Jonathan Swift pamplet"—"A Modest Proposal." When she finally looked up at Bill, she just said, "This puzzle!" At that point, Bill got down on his knee and asked, "Will you marry me?" After such a memorable proposal, how could the answer be anything but "Yes"?

Engagement Announcements

You may choose to broadcast the news of your engagement to the masses through a published announcement. Or you may decide to wait and publicize the actual wedding later on. If you're recently widowed or divorced, definitely wait to make the announcement; there's no need to place yourself smack dab in the middle of the gossip circle. You also should hold off on the announcement if you don't know when you're actually going to take the plunge, or if you're already having second thoughts about the marriage. (Some couples' therapists specialize in premarital counseling—go now.)

A Family Tradition

A treasured betrothal custom: the European hope chest. The bride's parents would stock a beautifully crafted wooden chest with linens, knickknacks, and other cozy items for her to take to her new home.

Get the Announcement Ball Rolling

Call your local newspaper, your parents' hometown rag, your alumni magazine, and anywhere else you want your engagement announcement to appear and find out the name of the appropriate editor or department. Ask for writer's guidelines or a standardized form, if available. Also ask if there's a fee for publication.

Typically, announcements mention career details about the two of you, your parents' names and places of residence, and your educational credentials (space permitting). Don't include your wedding date if you haven't quite decided, or if you have decided but want to keep people in suspense. (You could include something like "A June wedding is planned.") Do list the date if you'd rather publicize it now than answer a million "So when's the big day?" questions later. If you're interested, ask if the publication accepts pictures. Some publications only print actual wedding portraits, but if they will accept an engagement photo, get an eight-by-ten or five-by-seven glossy taken of your adorable mugs.

Word Up! Sample Announcements

Engagements usually are announced officially by someone other than the Happy Couple (unless they have no close relatives to give the honor to). When composing your announcement, select the textual variations that best reflect *your* reality, including who will be "sponsoring" (read: "hosting") the wedding and how (dys)functional your family is. Feel free to freestyle, especially if the publication you're announcing it in is hip or humorous. For those of you who need a helping hand, here are some typical engagement announcement wordings:

First Photo Op

Take a photo of yourselves on the day you get engaged. It's a great way to remember that great day—and may come in handy if you decide on a formal announcement or to use pictures on your engagement party invites.

Standard, by the bride's parents. Mr. and Ms. John Doe of Little Rock announce the engagement of their daughter, Jane Annette, to Jack Smith, son of David and Beth Smith of Tishomingo, Oklahoma. Ms. Doe, a graduate of Vassar College, is a professor at Barnard College in New York City. Mr. Smith graduated magna cum laude from Princeton Law School and works at Smith, Golden, his mother's law firm, in Tishomingo. A June wedding is planned. (*Or:* No date has yet been set for the wedding.)

(The groom's family is also free to put an announcement in their hometown paper; it would follow the same format.)

Single parent sponsoring the wedding. Ms. Janet Jones announces the engagement of her daughter, Jane Doe, to Jack Smith . . . Ms. Doe is also the daughter of John Doe of Sioux City. *(This line is close to the end of the announcement.)*

(There's no need to mention the other biological parent if he or she wasn't involved in raising you.)

Remarried parent, sponsoring with new spouse. Ms. Janet Jones and Mr. Timothy Chapin announce the engagement of Ms. Jones' daughter, Jane Doe, to Jack Smith . . . Ms. Doe is also the daughter of John Doe of Sioux City.

If one parent is deceased. The engagement of Jane Annette Doe, daughter of Mrs. Janet Doe and the late Mr. John Doe, to Jack Smith, son of David and Beth Smith of Tishomingo, Oklahoma, is announced by the bride's mother. . . .

If your parents don't support your choice of partner, or are deceased, another close relative—or even a dear friend—can announce your engagement. Ms. Julia Doe announces the engagement of her sister, Jane Doe, to Jack Smith, son of . . . The bride is the daughter of (the late) John Doe and Ms. Janet Jones of Little Rock.

You're announcing/sponsoring the wedding yourselves (in the case of remarriage or just because). Jane Doe, a professor at Barnard College, is to be married to Jack Smith, a partner at the law firm of Smith, Golden in Fort Lee, New Jersey. Ms. Doe is the daughter of Mr. John Doe of Sioux City, Iowa, and Ms. Janet Jones of Little Rock, Arkansas. Mr. Smith is the son of David and Beth Smith of Tishomingo, Oklahoma. A June wedding is planned.

Engage Your Imagination: Party Ideas

Creativity and informality are the buzzwords when it comes to today's engagement parties. If you or your parents don't want to make this a formal dinner affair, here are some alternatives:

- Beach bash. Think sand between your toes and a breezy seaside mood. Serve a raw bar and summery cocktails as the sun sets.
- Cocktail soiree. Mix up some martinis, make trays of hors d'oeuvres, and have your favorite people over for a night of conversation.
- Sunday brunch. Champagne, decadent pastries, fruit, and a group of well wishers make for a mellow morning soiree with style.
- Chomp feast. Reserve a looooong table at your favorite restaurant.
- Surprise! We're engaged. Plan your own party, and when everyone has a champagne flute in hand, make your big announcement.

Engaged Ups and Downs

Now that you've made your announcements, it's time for engagement quandary number one: How to use diplomacy with friends and relatives. You've only just shared the news about your impending nuptials and already everybody wants to know when the big date is (their calendars are filling up), who your attendants are going to be, and whether you're serving chicken or beef.

Stop. Take a deep breath. Try to answer all inquiries with maximum coolness and your trademark sense of humor (one of the best tools for rebutting sticky questions without bruising egos). Keep in mind that the people who are drilling you with endless, aggravating, even sometimes insulting questions—"Aren't you too young to get married? Won't this interfere with your promotion at work? What about your handball team? Did you go see the florist I recommended?"—aren't *trying* to drive you nuts. They probably just want to be part of the excitement and help you avoid pitfalls. Or perhaps they're so gaga giddy with excitement and nerves that they don't realize that *you* might be feeling some stress here, too, and don't need this extra pressure.

In any case, the dominant emotion you'll be dealing with during your engagement is sheer glee. Our bet is that all of your friends, family, and coworkers are basking in the light of your love. Well, *almost* all of them. There will always be a few black sheep in the flock who, for one reason or another, just can't digest your good news. Friends may be jealous or feel like you're abandoning them, that they won't see you as often now (and they're probably right). Try your best to be aware of their concerns and reassure them.

Go to Chapter 24 for more help with dealing with friends displaying bizarre behavior patterns.

How do you handle evil-wishers like high-school enemies, your commitment-phobic squash partner, or that waiter with a crush from hell? Just ignore them, because:

1. Who cares what they think?
2. They'll get over it.
3. If all else fails, you can always slap 'em upside the head with your 3-carat diamond.

Buying the Ring

The most universal of engagement traditions, by far, is the groom-to-be presenting his bride-to-be with a ring. Customarily, there's a luscious diamond involved, perched atop a band of pretty damn expensive metal. We love the ice, of course, but it's great that some people select a different precious gem, or group of gems—such as aquamarine, topaz, or tourmaline. Others opt for Victorian-inspired posy rings (bands engraved with inscriptions of love) or elaborate tattoos. It's also not unheard of for a woman to reciprocate and purchase an engagement ring for her man or to chip in for her own sparkly bauble. Other couples also give engagement gifts to each other.

Let's assume that you're a classic guy (or gal). You're ready to contribute to the $18-billion-a-year world of the diamond business. If you've got the guts, go traditional and surprise your honey with a beautiful ring. But we like the idea of asking for her (or his) input—clear, or slightly colored? mounted low, or jutting out? round, square, or heart-shaped?—before you go diamond hunting. Even better: Go ring shopping together. Most couples do, and report no lack of romance in the "big moment." You can propose first (one groom used a candy-ring stand in); or you can choose the ring, then spring it on her when she least expects it.

Sneaky Ways to Get Her Ring Size

- Sneak away to the jeweler's with a ring she wears on her ring finger.
- Ask one of her friends to play detective. She should try on a ring of your honey's and say, "Oh, this is too loose (too tight, just right)—what size are you?"
- Measure the circumference of her ring finger with a piece of string and use a pen to mark the right spot. (This method is recommended only if she's a deep sleeper!)

Name Your Price

Before you embark on your ring quest, figure out how much you have to spend (literally, have in your budget, not "have to" as in must!). Generally, people set aside about two months' salary for the jewel, but you can spend as much or as little as you want (or, more realistically, can afford). A bigger diamond or swankier setting does *not* mean a better marriage.

Study Up

Once you've established a budget, ask friends and family to recommend a reputable jeweler. Make sure s/he's a member of the American Gem Corporation (212-762-0028) and offers stones that are in your price range. Be a savvy shopper; retailers will take you more seriously if you use professional lingo. Throw around a few of the buzzwords: clarity, carat, color, and cut (also known as the four Cs; we explain them next). However, don't act *overly* sophisticated if you aren't; your ignorance will betray you, and some jewelers who smell an easy kill won't hesitate to draw first blood.

Clarity: A stone's price tag is determined first and foremost by its clarity, or the degree to which it's free from internal flaws (professionally dubbed "inclusions"). The fewer the flaws, the more light reflected—and the more sparkle. Unless you're an oil tycoon, you'll probably have to settle for a diamond that falls between the VVS1 (very, very small inclusions) and the SI2 (small inclusions) categories. But don't worry about the inclusion rating too much. Slight inclusions may reduce a diamond's value, but they don't take anything away from its beauty.

Cut: The cut of a diamond also determines its brilliance. A skilled jeweler can make even an imperfect gem gleam like a cat's eye. The shape you select depends on your taste; the 58-facet round cut and the oval cut are today's most popular shapes, and the geometrical princess and emerald cuts are high up in the drama department. Ask your jeweler to show you the different stone shapes and explain how each cut will affect your diamond's shine.

Carat: The weight of a stone determines its size. One carat equals 100 points. A 0.5-carat diamond is the size of a very small pea; a 69-carat gem—like the one Richard Burton once gave to Liz Taylor—is the size of a golf ball. Don't get one this large—you'll snag it on *everything.* Of course, you'll pay more for a heavier diamond in the same clarity group. Size is a matter of preference when it comes to rings; by now you should know if your honey is the discreet or flashy type (or maybe she's made it crystal-clear to you how big a diamond she wants!).

Color: Most diamonds range from pure white to a faint yellow cast. Again, you'll have to exercise your aesthetic judgment here (or your judgment of your sweetie's aesthetic judgment). Most people prefer their rocks colorless. Your budget will come into play again; the more colorless a stone, the more expensive it is. (The exceptions to this rule are the extravagantly priced *fancies,* brightly colored diamonds in shades of blue, red, amber, and green.)

Your Diamond

Examine stones in their loose state—not mounted in a ring—under a magnifying glass and in sunlight. Put several diamonds in a row to get a sense of each one's uniqueness. If you find one you like, have the jeweler "plot" (draw) its flaws on a piece of paper, so it can be identified later when you're ready to close the deal.

ASK CARLEY

Conflict Diamonds

Q. My fiancé and I have discussed my engagement ring for weeks. He's ready to buy me one, but I've explained to him that because of my strong feelings about the human rights violations commited against victims in diamond-producing countries in wartorn Northern Africa, it's very important for me to not have a "blood diamond." How can I be sure my diamond is not a "blood diamond"?

A. As of this printing, there is no process that allows a consumer or a jeweler to definitively determine whether the diamond is a blood, or conflict, diamond. Legislation differentiating blood diamonds has not yet been put into practice. However, the diamond industry and other trade organizations have attempted to pass a law known as the Kimberley Process Certification Scheme. This law would forbid importation of diamonds from countries where human rights are violated. For consumers, a possible way to avoid purchasing a blood diamond is to consult a jeweler who belongs to the Jewelers of America organization. Every jeweler who is part of this organization has signed a code of ethics that states that he or she will not knowingly sell a blood diamond. Their website is www.jewelers.org.

Close the Deal

When you've found a diamond she'd die for, make sure the gem is appraised by an independent expert before you buy. (Check the International Gemological Institute at www.e-igi.com for references.) When you're sure the ice is what the jeweler says it is, try to negotiate a better price if it seems appropriate (it's generally expected—think car buying) before having it placed in a pretty little chic box.

You thought you were through with all the decision making, but there are a few more details to attend to:

- Choose the band you want the precious one mounted on. Generally, you're talking gold, silver, or platinum.
- Decide whether you want the diamond riding low or jutting out, or whether you want a more elaborate design option out. (This generally is referred to as the "setting.") These include the antiquelike *cluster* or *prong-solitaire*—jutting clusters—ring styles; the hill-and-valley geometric *bar;* the graduation ringlike *gypsy;* and the polka-dots-in-a-circle *channel* design. High-riding diamonds surrounded by several smallish gems and unique engravings in the metal band are also an increasingly popular option.

As we said, don't feel obligated to buy a diamond (unless you know you'll be in the doghouse if you don't). Gems like sapphires, rubies, and emeralds—long the preference of engaged European royalty—are now gracing the fingers of America's uncrowned princesses and dancing queens. Like diamonds (symbols of purity of heart and eternal love), these stones also bear messages of devotion. Sapphires connote sincerity; rubies suggest passion; and the emerald is the gem of Venus, goddess of l'amour. Another possibility is to choose a ring that sports your fiancée's birthstone as a way to say "I'm so glad you were born."

We told you getting engaged was fabulous—it's difficult not to get lost in the euphoria. Now, fresh from cloud nine time together and the shower of love from family and friends, you're ready to get down to the nitty-gritty of planning one of the best days of your life—your wedding.

CHAPTER TWO

envisioning the event

So there you are, staring at a blank piece of paper with the words "Our Wedding" scrawled across the top. What now? The first step in planning your celebration is answering the big questions: the who, what, where, when, and how of the event. These are the primary colors of any wedding composition; they'll narrow down the variations that are right for you and make the planning process feel less abstract.

We're going to help you draw the picture of *your* ideal wedding: Is it a candlelit evening ceremony in fall? A blue-sky spring garden luncheon? Do you want an intimate family gathering or an all-acquaintance extravaganza? It's time to think through the options and draw up a blueprint.

Setting Your Priorities

As in any other giant undertaking, you won't get anywhere with your wedding until you sit down and prioritize. What's important to you? Where should you start?

Talk About It

Close your eyes. When we say "fantasy wedding," what do you see? A $5,000 dress, shimmery and glam? Tons and tons of white roses? A floating reception on a yacht under a crayon-blue sky and yellow sun? Three hundred revelers waltzing in a regal ballroom? A spiritual ceremony and intimate dinner with only your inner circle in attendance?

This kind of free-form fantasizing will help you identify your dream scenario so that you'll be able to figure out your exact wedding priorities. These details will be at the foreground of the party you plan; if need be, you can make adjustments and cutbacks to the other elements.

Chances are, your dream wedding "drawing" is *different* from your betrothed's. (We said different, not *better.*) Part of this initial visualizing process is putting your visions side by side to see how they can work together. Compromise is reality—and good practice for a blissfully long marriage.

Plan to Pull It Off

No matter what priorities you've isolated as list-toppers, we believe it's possible to pull off a close approximation of your fantasy regardless of your finances or outside pressures. Say you decide that your number-one priority is a formal, medieval-theme dinner reception in an authentic castle. That may prove *way* too expensive. But how about a semiformal, midday, medieval buffet banquet in an outdoor tent? Conversely, if you just want to elope at the Church of Hunka-Hunka Love in Las Vegas but your parents really want you to have a hometown reception, there's a way to make everyone happy. Go to city hall with select family and friends to shower you with confetti, and then invite a larger group to a local funky lounge bar for the party. The point is to take your vision and try to break it down into realistic pieces—so it'll actually *happen*. Get inspiration from other couples' great ideas, and check out their tricks for making their own plans come together, by browsing through the hundreds of "Real Weddings" on The Knot (theknot.com). And be sure to pick the brains of your recently married pals—no one knows the drill like someone who has just walked down the aisle.

Get Organized

Buy a binder, plastic file box, or accordion file where you'll put everything wedding—magazine articles, printouts from The Knot (theknot.com), notes, pictures, vendor information, fabric swatches, etc.

Divining a Date and Time

Does your man need a green card so he won't be kicked out of the country? Did your best friend Paulo just tell you he's moving far, far away in a few days, and since your heart is set on having him be your best man, he needs to make that toast ASAP? Have you decided that your honeymoon will be a once-a-decade, hyperdemanding polar expedition that leaves next week? Your ideal wedding date is pretty darn obvious—tomorrow!

Your Time Constraints

For the rest of us, choosing the precise wedding date can be an elaborate production. The exact date you select will depend on several variables, including:

Planning Time: How much time will you need to prepare your dream wedding?

Family and Friends' Commitments: Check for possible conflicts like graduations, birthdays, or pregnancy due dates so that you can select a day when your loved ones *can* attend.

Significant Dates: You may want your wedding date to have sentimental value, commemorating your first kiss, your grandparents' anniversary, or Valentine's Day.

Site and Vendor Availability: Is there a church or caterer you've had your hearts set on *for years?* If so, their schedule is going to influence—and may even dictate—yours.

Budget: Certain times of the year are generally more expensive than others. (See "The Monster Months" later in the chapter.) Depending on how cost-conscious you need to be, this *may* be a factor in your decision.

Wedding Style: Certain kinds of weddings are more conducive to specific seasons and/or times. Formal clothing is much more fun when it's not 95 degrees outside; family affairs—with lots of wee ones—are best scheduled during the day.

Like everything in life, there will be pros and cons to virtually every date you consider.

To create your own personalized to-do list, go to The Knot Checklist at www.theknot.com/checklist.

While a Valentine's Day wedding—complete with gorgeous rose centerpieces, red velvet bridesmaids' dresses, and heart-shaped chocolate favors—sounds dreamy, getting a florist to give you great service at that time may be a nightmare better suited to Halloween. Scheduling your big day for a long weekend may seem like a great idea when it comes to accommodating your legions of long-distance guests, but your local pals may begrudge your interfering with three days of much-needed R&R. Once again, establish your priorities—and choose the date accordingly.

MELANI & HERB

May 17, Oracle, Arizona

FOR MELANI AND HERB, honoring the bride's grandparents became an integral part of planning their wedding. "My grandfather raised me as his own daughter; his life and death inspired our wedding and decision to have a family," Melani says. With this in mind, the couple chose to wed in Oracle, Arizona, in a house that had been built by the bride's great-grandfather—and where her grandfather, along with all of his brothers and sisters, had been born.

The date of their marriage was also significant—it was the fiftieth wedding anniversary of her grandparents. "We wanted to not only continue their love for each other but to also have our marriage certificate filed in the town where my grandfather's birth certificate is. It meant a lot that we were able to be married in the land that my grandfather loved and fought for—he was a major in World War II."

After the ceremony, Melani and Herb walked across the street to the cemetery where both her grandparents are buried. "We wanted them to share in our love and happiness as we shared in theirs."

After you've settled on your ideal date, choose two or three back-ups just in case the temple or Sicilian caterer of your dreams is otherwise committed. Flexibility is vital during the planning process.

Beware "Bummer" Dates

Don't schedule your wedding for "bummer" days—any day during the week before Tax Day (April 15), an important work deadline, on the anniversary of your father's death. Also steer clear of the major tourist season in your wedding area, especially if you're inviting a lot of out-of-towners who need hotel rooms.

Any Time Is Reception Time!

Arrival time indicated on your reception invite for:

- Breakfast: 10 a.m.–12 p.m.
- Brunch: 11 a.m.–1 p.m.
- Lunch: 1 p.m.–3 p.m.
- Tea: 3 p.m.–5 p.m.
- Cocktails: 4 p.m.–7 p.m.
- Dinner: 6 p.m.–8 p.m.
- Drinks and Dessert: 8 p.m.–10 p.m.
- Late-Night Fare: 8 p.m.–10 p.m.
- Midnight Madness: 9 p.m.–11 p.m.

Go to Chapter 6 for more on incorporating religion into your ceremony.

The Monster Months

These are the months when it seems like everybody and their cousin is getting hitched. The big three are June, August, and September, with May, July, October, and party-happy December hot on their heels. The more popular your wedding month, the less choice you'll have about the site, vendors, and exact timing. Competition for services may drive up your wedding expenses, too. By opting for an off-season month (November, January through April), you're bound to get more personalized service from your florist, baker, and officiant and have more control over the minutiae of your minutia-packed event. The flip side, of course, is that a romantic garden wedding in February is about as appropriate as stiletto heels in a bowling alley.

Days in Demand

Saturday is the crowned Queen of Weddings, with Friday and Sunday the ladies in waiting. The attractions of a Saturday wedding are obvious; out-of-towners have ample time to get to your wedding without missing work and guests have roughly twenty-four hours to nurse any hangover before heading back to the office. With Fridays and Sundays, it's more of a scramble to get, respectively, to and from your wedding, and there's no chill-out day—but they're still far more convenient than a weekday. A midweek affair is not advisable if you're inviting a lot of out-of-towners or are planning an all-night bash, but it's a great way to cut costs and get a better pick of vendors.

Power Hours

When deciding on the time of day for your ceremony and reception, remember that the earlier the festivities, the lower the cost of the reception; a brunch or afternoon tea will set you back substantially less than an evening dinner reception, and there probably will be less demand for that time slot, too. Lunch and teas are exceptionally good choices if you're inviting lots of children (and their frazzled parents). However, evening and night weddings are far more appropriate if you're thinking black-tie or boogie-woogie.

Blackout Periods

One more thing to consider: religious restrictions. Often there are blackout periods when it is *not* acceptable to tie the knot. For example, conservative rabbis will not perform weddings between Passover and Shavuot, and many ministers are reluctant to officiate ceremonies during Lent. Consult a clergyperson about traditions that might affect you.

Settling on Size

How many people to invite (not to mention who exactly) is one of the biggest decisions you need to make during this initial "sketching" period. This may sound like one of the most pleasurable aspects of your wedding preparation—the two of you, sitting down over a bottle of wine, taking stock of all the wonderful people you'll share this special day with. But the truth is, making the guest list is difficult, given all the forces (parental opinions, budgetary concerns, reception site considerations) pulling you in different directions.

The Guest List: What to Consider

There are five main considerations when figuring out how long you want your invite list to be.

Style: Is it more important for you to have one-on-one time with each beloved guest or to throw a bombastic, once-in-a-lifetime party for *all* your disparate friends and relatives? Is your fantasy wedding style more conducive to a small or large gathering?

Budget: There will be a per-head cost for food and liquor—more guests means more cash. There are many ways to cut expenses and still invite as many folks as you want, such as buying your own booze, opting for a buffet rather than seated meal, having relatives cater the affair as their wedding gift to you. But in general, you'll need to take monetary boundaries into account when deciding on a guest number.

Parents' Desires: If your mom and pop are adamant about inviting throngs of friends and extended family, you're going to have to hear them out—especially if they're footing a major part of the bill. Your mantra here: Compromise.

The Size of Your Extended Families: Obviously, the more relatives you simply *must* invite, the larger your guest list is going to be—unless you decide to make it a family-only affair and then throw a separate party for friends.

Logistical Constraints: If there's a dream ceremony or reception site in your vision, you're going to be limited by how many people it can accommodate. (You can't squeeze 500 people into a lighthouse.)

Who Gets to Invite How Many?

Once you've got your guest-list limit, it's time to decide who's in and who's out. Like limber limbo-ers, you and your wedding cosponsors have to slide everyone you love in under your quota. Traditionally, the bride and her family and the groom and his folks each invite half of the guests, with the parents on both sides—usually the major check-writers—calling most of the shots. But if you and your fiancé/e are underwriting the majority of the reception costs, it is definitely acceptable for you to determine the bulk of the guest list. Another arrangement that works especially well is to divide the invitee rations three ways: between the soon-to-be-weds, the bride's parents, and the groom's parents. If your parents are divorced, you're going to have to make even more divisions.

Making the Dreaded Cuts

If you're having trouble keeping the numbers under control, consider limiting invitations for dates. If your best buddy has been through more flames than a Burger King patty, send him or

The Kid Question

Children can be the heart and soul of a wedding, but they also can be a royal pain on the big day. Deciding whether to make your guest list adults-only is tough. Which profile best reflects your feelings?

With Children:

You and/or your babycake has a kid or other special tiny someone—a godchild, one you've "adopted" through the Big Brother program, an irresistible nephew—who is an important part of your lives. You want them to share in your big day.

Children epitomize family, which is what many weddings are all about. Their presence can be spiritually meaningful.

Your nephews and nieces live far away; you've never met your best friend's four-year-old twins. Weddings are a great opportunity to enjoy overdue introductions and infrequent reunions.

You're shy of the limelight. Cute kids may capture your guests' attention and take some of the pressure off of you (if only in your minds).

You don't want to force your guests with kids to leave home without them. You know it makes them nervous.

You don't want to ruffle any parental feathers.

Without Children:

Children are the epitome of chaos, which is what you *don't* want your wedding to be.

You're planning an intellectually challenging ceremony or a Dirty Dancing reception—kids would spoil the desired effect.

You'll save money with no kids there. Cold? Maybe, but it translates into a few less mouths to feed.

You'll be giving your friends with children a night off-duty.

You can't invite every kid you know—and you don't want to ruffle any parental feathers through omissions.

her a solo invitation. (Your wedding will be good place for a friend like this to ignite new sparks.) It's also okay to invite a group of acquaintances, such as your office mates or rugby team, *sans* significant others. Heavily monogamous, engaged, or married guests should be invited along with their honey-pies.

If your guest list is *still* seriously bloated, implement some across-the-board limitations, such as no children under sixteen or no coworkers. Remember, the key to making these kinds of boundaries work is not to make any exceptions. Otherwise, you're likely to get a fair share of wedding curses along with your blessings.

On that semisour note: *Never* invite anyone to your blessed event out of guilt. They're the ones being rude by practically demanding an invitation. If you have to give a great deal of thought as to whether to invite someone, that person probably doesn't belong on your list; your wedding guests should be the people you adore.

After each party has retreated to compile his or her wish list, you need

Leave Out the Little Ones?

If you decide not to invite kids, don't write it on your invites. Simply address the invite to the parents, omitting the little ones. Let word spread by mouth.

ASK CARLEY

Small-Wedding Blues

Q: My fiancé/e and I are having an intimate wedding and I'm afraid some people will be offended that they are not invited. What to do?

A: If it hasn't happened yet, it will. Everyone—from people you went to camp with to your nemesis from high school—will call with their congrats and fish around for that all-important invite. In the words of Nancy Reagan: "Just Say No." Be honest with people. Let them know that your wedding is going to be very, very, very small. (Honesty doesn't mean you can't exaggerate a little.) Explain that with two families to accommodate, it was simply impossible to invite everyone you wanted to. These might be difficult conversations to have, but most people will understand, and it's better than ducking into alleys to avoid non-invitees on the street.

to hammer out a more manageable master list. Compare notes, eliminate repeat names, and help each other make additional necessary cuts. Now that you have your final guest list (okay, there may still be some changes along the way—but it's pretty darn near finalized), don't forget to raise a glass of the bubbly. Completing this task is well worth toasting.

Figure Out Your Guest List First

You will want to choose your wedding location after you determine your guest list. Answers to questions like "Where are the majority of our guests from?" and "How many people are coming?" can help determine the right place for your wedding.

Finding a Site

It used to be a given that couples would say their vows in the bride's hometown. For many that's still true, but today's couples are just as likely to wed in the groom's hometown, in their college town, in the city they live in now, even at their honeymoon destination. Some couples are even hosting two or more receptions to facilitate the attendance of loved ones scattered across the country or around the globe.

If you want to throw a raucous dance party reception for all of your current friends, the city you now call home is the logical choice. If you're planning a cozy, family wedding, choose one of your hometowns, or head to your parents' current home. If you're planning everything, have the wedding in your proverbial backyard; if Mom and Dad are footing the entire bill, it's gracious to say "I do" in theirs.

Long-Distance Planning

Obviously, the big drawback of having a wedding away from *your* home is that you'll be coordinating everything from afar. That means that you have to take extra measures to get what you want. Fortunately, our wired world makes your task immensely easier. You can research your vendors online (we recommend checking out the hundreds of local vendors in dozens of cities on theknot.com). Use the web to check out photographer's portfolios, take virtual tours of reception sites, and see your cake designer's finest works of art. Finally, don't be afraid to zap those digital pics of things you like back and forth between your home base and wedding central. Other ways to get the long-distance thing done:

Go to Chapter 8 for more on destination and "progressive" weddings.

- Hire an on-site bridal consultant to be your right-hand man or woman when it comes to finding available services, negotiating with vendors, and supervising preparation details. (For more on these professionals, see "Wedding Consultants," later in the chapter.) Or you may have a good, reliable friend (like Mom) who can serve as your point person instead. Just make sure they know what they're getting into.
- Get and use vendors' e-mail addresses or fax numbers to keep long-distance calls (and costs) to a minimum.
- Plan at least one visit to the wedding location. Have your in-town wedding rep schedule meetings for you with all potential or actual vendors. Visit the reception site, set up a test hair and makeup session at the salon of your choice, and so on.
- Get all business arrangements in writing. This is always important, but never more so than when you've got the distance disadvantage.

Small Site? Separate

If you've selected a really intimate ceremony site, devise two lists: one for the select group who witness your vows, the other for those who will join in at your reception.

Inside or Out?

Once you've figured out what town or city is going to play host to your big bash, you'll need to answer another fundamental location, location, location question: inside or out-of-doors? Obviously, this depends on your wedding date. A beach party in January is nutso (unless you're wedding south of the border). Likewise, if the banquet hall you want for your reception isn't air-conditioned, shy away from a July or August wedding.

While outdoor weddings would *appear* to be the cheaper option—after all, you're not paying for a fancy reception hall—hidden costs, such as a permit (necessary at a public space like Yosemite or a state beach), a tent, a generator, and transportation can really add up. The main reasons to wed under the sheltering sky are beauty and drama, not dollars and cents. Whether you decide to go *au natural* or not, start thinking now about how you'll spruce up your site to fit the dream-wedding picture you've been painting in your head.

Budget-Friendly Black Tie

Want a formal wedding with tons of guests and chi-chi black tie but can't afford it? No problem. Make it a late-night champagne-and-cake (rather than a seated dinner), big-band affair at a formal location like a ballroom.

Selecting a Wedding Style

There may be six degrees of separation between any two people, but there are only four degrees of formality when it comes to getting married: ultra-formal, formal, semiformal, and informal.

The formality of your wedding will be reflected first and foremost in the location of the wedding (ballroom vs. bar, for example) and second in the outfits you choose and the dress code you establish for your guests. If you decide to go all out, you'll probably be expected to appear in a classic, long gown with a train (her) and a white-tie tail coat (him), with guests opting for evening dresses and tuxes. With an informal wedding, almost anything goes.

Go to Chapter 10 for lots more on ceremony and reception venues.

The most important aspect of deciding which degree of formality best suits your wedding is your personal preference, although your time of day and season may also come to bear. If you've decided on a beach wedding, for example, go informal, or at least semiformal. Black

The Inside Scoop on Outdoor Sites

Reservations: Do you need one?
Weather: When is rain, hurricane, or extreme temperature season?
Insects: If there's a problem, can an exterminator take care of it?
Allergies: Do you or your wedding party have them?
Accessibility: Will transportation be a problem?
Vendors: Will they be able to work there? What extra expenses would this locale entail?
Comfort: You may want to rent a tent, a portable dance floor, and wooden chairs (not temperature-absorbing metal seats, no matter how chic they look).
Port-a-Potties: If there are no bathroom facilities, you'll need to rent some.
Parking: Consider hiring a valet service or running a shuttle bus.
Backup plan: Make one in case Hurricane Zachary strikes.
Lighting: String lights between trees, rent some spotlights, or scatter scores of lanterns.
Equipment: Make arrangements early to rent everything you'll need, including tables, linens, an electricity generator, a dressing trailer, etc.
Attitude: Assign several pals to attitude detail. If it rains, they'll remind you that rain on your wedding day is good luck.

TARIKA & MICHAEL

March 30, Old Stony Hill, Jamaica

WHEN TARIKA AND MICHAEL became engaged, they knew they would be married in Jamaica. Although they both live and work in New York City, Tarika spent part of her childhood in Kingston, and her family still lives in the area where her mother owns a restaurant, The Fish Place.

Distance was not an issue for the 150 guests who attended. A website, designed by a friend, kept everyone up-to-date on the wedding plans. Friends and family were welcomed at their hotels with goodie bags of Jamaican treats and a list of organized activities to fill the prewedding days. "We wanted people to fall in love with Jamaica," says Tarika.

The ceremony took place on one of Villa Ronai's stone terraces late in the afternoon. The bridesmaids were dressed in various shades of Caribbean blue, and the bride wore an orchid tucked behind her ear. After the couple's first kiss, guests enjoyed colorful tropical cocktails and the music of a traditional Jamaican folk band while they munched appetizers prepared by The Fish Place (which provided all the food for the party), before sitting down for dinner. The menu featured Jamaican specialties, including ackee tarts, codfish fritters, Solomon Gundy (red herring pâté), jerk chicken, curried fish, and plantain and callaloo rolls.

At one point during the celebration, glasses were raised for toasts, and the bride's father welcomed everyone to the wedding. Says Tarika, "He captured the spirit of love and togetherness that we all felt throughout the wedding when he stated, 'We are all Jamaicans!' "

tie doesn't always mix well with sunshine and hot sand. If you must wear a tux or a diamond tiara, wait until dusk. The formality also can affect the number of guests, the food, the decorations, the entertainment—and the debits to your bank account.

Whatever you decide, here's our advice: While you're in the throes of planning, incorporate your chosen formality into every wedding detail. You want the overall vision of your nuptials to be a perfect composition—and knowing how formal a look you're going for probably will make your decisions easier.

Wedding Consultants

Looking for a Consultant?

Call for member referrals nationwide.

- Association of Bridal Consultants: www.bridalassn.com

Wedding consultants are professionals whose lives revolve around all things nuptial; they're part party planner, stage manager, financial adviser, vendor broker, shrink, and all-around wedding maniacs. Hire a full-time consultant to help you prepare your entire wedding, from announcement to Zurich honeymoon. Hire a part-time wedding consultant to devise a wedding blueprint—including budget, schedule, and lists of good vendor and site choices—before you launch solo into the preparations. Or you can hire one just to play ringleader on the actual day.

Critical Consultant Tip

We can't emphasize it enough—do *not* hire a consultant who doesn't listen, is bossy, tries to convince you what's best for you, has no references, won't sign a written agreement, or wears acid-washed jeans. Period.

Consultant Pros and Cons

There are many good reasons to hire a wedding consultant, not the least of which is reducing your stress level. S/he will do all the dirty work, starting with researching your options—given your budget and ideal scenario—and ending with supervising vendors during cleanup, ensuring they hit the road in a timely fashion and leave minimal mess. An ideal wedding consultant plays bad cop to your good cop.

The catch is that you'll pay for it. To the consultant, time is money, and depending on how long s/he thinks s/he's going to have to toil to make your wedding a smashing success, s/he'll quote you a fee. As a general rule of thumb, make sure that price does not exceed 10 to 15 percent of your total budget if you're hiring a consultant for the whole wedding. (So if your budget is $15,000, for example, $1,500 is a fair price to pay.) Since fees for blueprint preparation or wedding-day coordination vary, we say you better shop around.

Before you say yes to a particular consultant, make sure you've got a great rapport and that you feel confident s/he won't try to force any wedding vision other than your own on you. You're hiring this person to help you make your dream wedding a reality—don't lose sight of that. If you think you'd feel better doing it on your own, or with the help of your mom, maybe a consultant is not for you.

What a Wedding Consultant Can Do for You

Set up a realistic wedding budget.

Devise a wedding master plan that maps out all the little details, from ceremony music to favors.

Show you the best and most original locations in the area, considering your wedding size, budget, and vision.

Find the best florists, photographers, caterers, bands, and DJs in your price range. Consultants' Rolodexes are full of the names of wedding professionals.

Cut you choice deals. Consultants bring volume to favored vendors; often they'll reciprocate by slashing prices or throwing in extras.

Read over all your vendor contracts.

Create a timeline that tells everyone involved in the planning process—vendors, members of the wedding party, you soon-to-be-weds and your families—when to do what. Plus the consultant will make sure you *stick* to that schedule.

Handle the invitations, from the wording and ordering to the addressing and mailing.

Counsel you on proper etiquette and what's hot on the wedding front.

Coordinate with the photographer, florist, musicians, and caterer/banquet manager to determine realistic setup times and when they should arrive on wedding day.

Manage the wedding day, supervising vendors, handling emergencies, and soothing nerves.

Serve as your spokesperson, conveying your every whim and desire to vendors or family members when you just can't deal with doing it yourself.

Help plan and book your honeymoon.

CHAPTER THREE

budget and business

Enough fantasizing—on to the serious business of your wedding budget. We hate to admit it, but at the end of the day, dollars, not dreams, are the defining factor in what (and who) you'll have at your wedding. No budget, no matter how big, is ever big enough. Now that we've got that reality check out of the way, we can go on to tell you all you need to know to plan the perfect wedding—whatever the price tag.

Setting Your Budget

Before you buy anything—even that $5 garter—you've got to determine the dollar amount allotted for your big day. Where to begin? You have two options: (1) Figure out how much cash you (and/or your loving family) can spend, or (2) calculate how much the wedding you want will cost and then worry about where you'll get the bucks. For some perspective, the average American couple spends $25,000 on their wedding; in large cities like New York, Los Angeles, or Dallas, that average is at least double.

What Affects the Price Tag

Obviously, if you're planning on a formal candlelit dinner in the grand ballroom of that amazing hotel downtown, your budget is going to have to be much bigger than if you've sketched out a high-noon hoedown in your grandparents' backyard, catered by Dad. In general, several factors affect what you'll need to set aside:

Formality: The more formal the affair, the more expensive, because most ultra-formal weddings take place in the evening, and because you'll have to match the site, food, and musical entertainment to the overall upscale tone.

Date and Time: Certain months and times of day tend to be pricier.

Guest List: The more people you invite, the more money you'll spend—there's a per-head cost for food and liquor.

Food: The financial burden for a full meal is greater than for hors d'oeuvres; dinner is usually more expensive than breakfast or lunch; seated service is pricier than a buffet.

Reception Site: The use of some locales will set you back more than others. Some—such as your aunt's verandah or a city park—can be had at no (or low) cost.

Location: Some cities and towns are just more expensive than others. New York, Chicago, and Los Angeles are the obvious culprits, but small towns also can be pricey if things

Go to Chapter 2 for help mapping out scheduling considerations.

To create your own personalized wedding budget, go to The Knot Big-Day Budgeter at www.theknot.com/budgeter

like flowers, produce, and a DJ have to come from afar. Tourist towns can also up your wedding price tag, because of high demand.

How to Prioritize

If many of the wedding elements you're considering veer toward the amazingly expensive side of the scale, *don't* panic. It may require compromises, scheduling changes, or groveling for help from famly and friends, but even with a limited budget you can probably approximate your ideal wedding.

Prioritizing is paramount. Throughout the budgeting process you will need to coolly and calmly chip away at extraneous details that you can do without in order to have what's of tantamount importance to you. If there's no question in your mind that your florist bill is going to be huge, given your penchant for dramatic and lush arrangements (and lots of 'em), maybe it's not that important to wear a designer dress—your mother's gown will be a beauty once those rhinestone butterflies come off. You say your hearts are set on a nighttime party, when costs tend to be higher? Perhaps you can scale back your expenses by opting for a DJ instead of a live band, food stations as opposed to tableside service, and a basic photography package instead of a paparazzi extravaganza. We'll get into more specific cost-cutting strategies later in the chapter.

Organization Is Key!

Keep all your budget and business paperwork in one place. Get yourself a large folder or binder where you can keep track of all contracts, estimates, phone notes, and receipts.

Who's Paying and How?

In the days of yore (okay, as recently as the 1980s), it was the bride's family who paid for the wedding. Today, reflecting our ever-more-egalitarian society and ever-rising wedding costs, the division of financial duties is incredibly fluid. Our favorite? The communal model of wedding financing: Each family gives to the best of its ability and all come together for their collective happiness. Before you nail down your budget and begin allocating dollar amounts for different wedding elements, you need to know who will be doling out the dough. Why does it matter? you ask. Because those who pay have the say. Here are the options and our advice.

Three's Company: You Two and All Your Parents Pay

Our favorite wedding budget model is the one-third approach, in which the bride's family, the groom's family, and the couple—yeah, *you*—each contribute. You're getting the best of both worlds. You're not flying solo (and thus possibly dipping into your nest egg or saying bye-bye to your Christmas vacation), but you're also not completely relinquishing financial control, which often means that you're ceding creative authority, too. The three-way split is also a surefire way to make both families feel like significant partners in your wedding preparations, paving the way for a love-filled bash and years of extended-family happiness.

There are two ways to work out this arrangement. You can approximate the total dollar amount you're going to need and then split it three ways, or you can designate specific things that each party will pay for, based on how much they can contribute: your parents, rehearsal dinner, flowers, and music; your honey's parents, food, drink, and site fees; you guys, attire and photography.

However you decide to swing it, splitting things three ways is going to require lots of communication and teamwork. Asking your parents for cash and making sure everyone is happy with the budgetary decisions you make requires the grace of a ballerina, the communication skills of a preacher, and the diplomacy of, well, a diplomat. In all your interactions with your loved ones, remember these cardinal rules:

Be Informed: Your folks will feel a lot more comfortable about ponying up the cash if they know you're taking the budget seriously. Before you approach them about making a contribution, consult friends and relatives whose wedding styles were similar to the affair you're planning about *their* total budget. If you have time, get some definite price quotes from key vendors such as caterers, florists, and musicians. That way everyone involved will have a more realistic idea of the financial requirements—and you won't have to deal with the stress of dropping last-minute bombshells. ("Mom, Dad, the caterer's bill was $4,000 more than we thought it would be—sorry!")

Be Direct: Your parents will respect you more and feel less manipulated if you just tell them straight up how much money you think you're going to need from them as opposed to taking the "Well, I guess we'll never have the wedding of our dreams (sigh)" approach. Together, hammer out how close to your ideal budget you can get and then powwow on ways to cut your costs.

Be Sensitive: If your mother and stepfather have recently emptied their savings account to pay for an emergency heart operation, it's not such a good idea to ask them to make a major contribution. Likewise if your honey's parents are struggling financially right now. Instead, make them feel like an integral part of your wedding plans by asking if they're interested in helping with organizational tasks (picking up out-of-town guests, reading over vendor contracts), advice (coming along to the baker's, hosting an appetizer-tasting party), or contributing special skills (doing the floral arrangements themselves, sewing a veil, or baking the cake). Remember, time is money—and their contributions probably will cut your costs nicely.

Be Good Listeners: You can't just hit your parents up for money and run. Since they are making a financial sacrifice for this event, it's important that you make them feel appreciated. Solicit their advice on major decisions, such as where to have your ceremony and which caterer to use. Hear out any concerns they may have (the florist's bill is too high, the venue you've chosen is unrealistic cost-wise). You don't always have to go with their recommendations, but we guarantee they will be a lot happier—and thus more helpful—if you make them feel like business partners and not faceless investors.

Different Strokes?

If you foresee serious conflicts because of differing tastes, ask your folks to cover specific costs—flowers and transportation, say—as opposed to having them contribute to a general wedding pot. This way you'll be able to gracefully define what details they deserve input on.

Flying Solo: Paying for It Yourselves

Legions of modern couples are opting to pay for their weddings themselves. Their motivations are diverse. Some simply don't have families able (or around) to help out; others are making lots more money than their parents; still others are control freaks who simply don't want anyone else's input.

ASK CARLEY

How to Ask for $$$

Q: We're several months into planning our wedding and my future in-laws have not yet offered to make any contribution financially (or otherwise). I asked my fiancé to speak with them, but he seems very reluctant to do so. What can I do? They're nice people—I don't want to offend them. But we could use their help.

A: The way you interact with your brand-new family members while planning your wedding can really set the tone for how you'll get along once you're married, so it makes sense to be savvy and sensitive. First off, it's essential that you two talk honestly about the situation. Find out why your soon-to-be is hesitant about approaching his parents. If he knows they're broke, figure out some nonmonetary aid they can give you (calling vendors for prices, reserving hotel rooms, addressing and mailing invitations). If he's plain old nervous about their reaction, come up with a good strategy together. (If it's the bride's family who hasn't offered financial help, this same advice applies—we're not trying to make it family-specific. These days, any combination of financial contributions is possible, and there's no "right" way for it to work.)

Usually, it's best for your honey to approach his parents alone so they feel comfortable discussing a touchy issue. "Rehearse" the conversation with him to boost his confidence level, finding a light-but-direct opening line, such as "You know, Mom and Dad, Eva and I were talking about how great it would be if you could help us pay for the wedding so we can invite everyone on both our lists and not have to cut people that are important to you and us." If your honey is more comfortable approaching his folks hand in hand with you, as a team—oblige him. However you handle this anxiety-laden situation, make sure your expectations aren't *too* high; there are many good reasons why his parents may not be able to help out (college bills, approaching retirement, etc.). Then again, you might be pleasantly surprised with the results of your directness and initiative.

Who Pays for What?

In the old days, the bride's family paid for: invitations; announcements; wedding consultant; gown and accoutrements; the reception, including site, food, flowers, photographs, videographer, and music; transportation for the wedding party.

The groom's family paid for: marriage license; officiant; bride's bouquet; boutonnieres; the rehearsal dinner; the honeymoon.

The upside of this option is that you're going to be totally free to focus on those wedding elements that are most important to you and to do things *exactly* the way you want 'em. Who can argue with that?

You're probably wondering how you're going to be able to get the money you need before the curtain goes up. Good question. Of course, there is no pat answer, but we can offer you several pearls of wisdom.

Start Saving Early: The sooner you begin putting money away, the more you'll have come wedding day. As soon as your feet hit the ground after your engagement, set up a realistic savings plan. It's a good idea to set aside between 10 and 20 percent of every paycheck you get from now until the big day for wedding expenses, although your individual circumstances may make this difficult. Whatever your monthly savings target, remember that little cost-cutting tactics like brown-bagging lunch, snuggling in front of the VCR, entertaining friends at home, and postponing major purchases until after the big day go a long way.

Open a Wedding Account: It's a good idea to establish a separate bank account for your wedding fund. By putting whatever money you can save in one place, you'll have a clearer idea of how much you have to spend. It also will spare you the added stress of having to transfer funds from your personal accounts whenever you need to write a major check.

Maximize Your Savings: Putting some money you already have in a higher-interest-bearing account is a great way to make the most of your money. Look at short-term CDs (Certificates of Deposit) or money market accounts (often available with checking). Your savings should be earning more than the interest available in regular savings accounts, which are often below the rate of inflation!

Take the Do-It-Yourself Approach: Whenever possible, do wedding-related tasks yourselves to cut down on vendor costs. For example, be your own calligraphers, or buy the liquor yourselves. Ask (but don't expect) friends to help you accomplish certain tasks; have an invitation-preparing party or a favor-making fiesta.

Consider Hiring a Wedding Consultant: At first glance, this may seem like an *added* expense, but often a professional party planner can help you make the most of your budget—whatever it is.

Communicate and Compromise: Before you decide exactly how much money you'll be putting toward your bash, know what you are—and are not—willing to splurge on and ask your partner to speak her (or his) heart and mind. Find a middle road. For example, if your honey is willing to withdraw $10,000 from her mutual fund account to finance a gigantic rave with cage dancers, an all-night buffet, and an elaborate laser show, while you're adamant that the two of you purchase a house in less than five years, decide that each of you will contribute $2,000 of your savings toward a smaller (but just as wild) dance party at your favorite club. You don't want resentment to spoil this excellent adventure; make sure both of you are satisfied with the wedding budget you work out.

Be Realistic: You may be more in debt than your beloved is, which means the sum you can contribute is smaller; you can even things out by doing more of the time-consuming preparation tasks. Or perhaps you can't contribute *any* money, because you're in grad school or you've just quit your job. In this case, you'll probably have to scale back your wedding expenses considerably and do most of the wedding work on your own.

Your Savings Potential

My monthly income
x .20 = _____ (A1)

A1 x months of engagement
= _____ (B1)

My honey's monthly income
x .20 = _____ (A2)

A2 x months of engagement
= _____ (B2)

B1 + B2 = Total potential wedding budget

Go to Chapter 2 to see how a consultant can save you money and time.

When Your Parents Pay Your Way

If you are among the lucky few whose parents are footing the entire bill, you may have to deal with one potentially sleep-disturbing problem—those who pay for the wedding have a major say in the plans. Even if you trust your parents not to become wedding control freaks, it's important to set some ground rules early. Be frank with them about things you are absolutely not willing to budge on and areas where you're totally open to their input. Our bet is that they'll respect your deepest wishes. However, if your dad is adamant about his beer-and-bingo wedding vision, you're going to have to bring him around. Talk to your other parent and get him or her on your side; chances are he or she knows which strings to pull better than you do.

Even if they say they'll write you one big check, it's still a good idea to sit down with your parents and bang out the total budget number together. Come up with a realistic spending cap now, so you won't be put in the uncomfortable situation of having to ask for another check later.

Budgeting Basics

Now that you know how much money you have to work with and where it's all coming from, it's time to figure out how you're going to spend it. You've got to break the big number down, allocating each part of your wedding budget for items such as food, flowers, and clothes. This means considering things like whether you want imported orchids in your bouquet, color photographs or black and white, and how much each option will set you back. Yep, this is the tough part. Don't panic. Start by mapping out all the possible elements you may wish to include in your nuptials. Some—like the officiant's fee and refreshments—are mandatory; others—like a wedding video, limo, or string quartet for the ceremony—are optional.

Be Thankful

Never, ever, ever *expect* your parents to pay for your wedding. Accept their financial help graciously. Contrary to popular belief, it's not a birthright.

Breaking It Down

Your actual wedding ceremony will be a very small part of your total cost. Assume that about 50 percent of your total will go toward your reception, including the cost of your venue, food and drink, and service. Even if you're having a home-cooked backyard brunch, chances are that the cost of the ingredients, renting chairs and place settings, and hiring servers still will eat up half your budget. You're also likely to spend more on your reception flowers, decorations, and music than on those for your ceremony.

Before you spend a dime on anything, create a budget breakdown that you can stick to. (We will spend 40 percent of our budget—or $2,000—on food; 7 percent of our total on flowers. These are general guidelines; every couple's priorities are different.)

Go to Appendix A and use our handy worksheet, "Your Big-Day Budget."

Food: About 40 percent of your budget will go toward food (hors d'oeuvres and meal), beverages, the cake, and service.

Reception Venue: About 8 percent will go toward the reception-site rental plus any other rentals (chairs, tables, dinnerware, tent).

Attire: About 10 percent will go toward the bride's dress, headpiece/veil, hair/makeup, shoes, and lingerie, groom's attire, and going-away garb for two.

Flowers: About 8 percent will be needed to cover the bride's bouquet, bridesmaids' bouquets, boutonnieres, corsages, ceremony and reception arrangements. (If you're doing a floral headpiece, you can steal from your attire budget.)

Photography/Videography: About 12 percent will go toward the labor costs for photographer and/or videographer, plus the cost of the photography/videography package(s).

Music: About 8 percent will go toward ceremony music (vocalists, string quartet, organist, etc.) and reception music (band or DJ).

Stationery: About 3 percent will go toward invitations, announcements, and thank-you notes.

Gifts: About 3 percent will go toward attendants' gifts, favors.

Wedding Rings: About 3 percent will go toward bands for both bride and groom.

Ceremony Costs: About 3 percent will go toward ceremony-location fee, officiant fee, and programs.

HEATHER & GREG

January 3, North Caldwell, New Jersey

THE BRIDE'S FAMILY spared no expense for Heather and Greg's exquisite wedding. The ceremony was held in Notre Dame Church in North Caldwell, New Jersey; the reception site was the Pleasantdale Chateau. The wedding was elaborate, as were the extras. For example, all out-of-town guests who did not attend the rehearsal dinner were given Broadway show tickets, plus transportation into New York City for the evening.

Number of guests: 200
Total Budget: $80,000+
Flowers: $4,000 (5%)
Reception (food only): $33,000 (41%)
Fashion (bride's dress): $5,000 (6%)
Photography: $5,000 (6%)
Music (reception only): $7,500 (9%)
Invitations: $3,500 (4%)
Transportation: $2,000 (2%)

Transportation/Parking: About 2 percent will go toward bride and escort's ride to the ceremony, couple's ride to the reception, wedding-party transport and guest shuttle (both optional), and parking.

Miscellaneous: Try to set aside an additional 5 percent for extra and unforeseen costs like marriage license, overtime costs, tips, taxes, and last-minute purchases.

Note: If you choose to use a wedding consultant, his or her fee will cost you up to 10 percent of your total budget.

Asking for Help

While you're working on your budget, think of any shortcuts you might be able to take to get things done. Maybe Grandma would bake you a wedding cake or let you wear her heirloom veil. Perhaps your best friend is a DJ who would do your wedding at a discount. Be careful, though. Be polite and ask; don't declare or expect anything.

Let Us Manage Your Money

The Knot Big-Day Budgeter (www.theknot.com/budgeter) is an amazing resource for to-be-weds, if we may say so ourselves. Plug in how much money you can spend and it suggests how much to allocate to each wedding feature, with specific advice on how to get the most for your money.

Working with Wedding Professionals

If you haven't figured it out yet, you'll soon discover that weddings are a big business, generating $32 billion a year. Those profits are the combined efforts of the wedding professionals whom you'll soon work with and be billed by. They're vendors: bakers, caterers, florists, photographers, banquet-hall managers, bridal retailers. You need them to make your wedding a reality. To get the most out of your relationships with the pros, follow the advice below.

Protect Your Investment

Look into wedding and event insurance. First check with your own broker, but also check out www.wedsure.com and www.wedsafe.com. You're sinking a lot of money into your wedding—protect your investment. Depending on the policy you opt for, you'll be covered for vendor screw-ups, a natural disaster–inspired cancellation, stolen gifts, guest injuries, even the bride or groom's absence due to last-minute military duty.

The Ten Vendor Commandments

First Commandment: Vendors come good, bad, and ugly. Find good vendors through word-of-mouth (recently married friends are your best resource), an initial consultation with an in-the-know wedding consultant, and/or the advice of other (trusted) vendors.

Second Commandment: Shop around. Put aside ample time to call and visit a variety of vendors to get a sense of their price range, style, and expertise.

Third Commandment: Get *written* estimates from several vendors in each category (chosen because they suit your budget, your taste, and your timetable). Use these documents in future negotiations as a benchmark, adding or deleting elements to get the price you can afford.

Fourth Commandment: Ask for references of other couples who've used the vendor. But since no one's going to refer you to a couple who was unhappy with their service, also be sure to call your local better business bureau to see if any consumer complaints have been filed against any vendors you're considering.

Fifth Commandment: Schedule meetings with vendors you're interested in. Ask lots of little questions—hidden fees, size of staff available to you on the big day, how they'll make the site work for them—so you know exactly what you're going to get. (Each vendor chapter includes the specific questions you'll want to ask.)

Sixth Commandment: Haggle. Vendors want your business, especially during down months and on weekdays. Talk them down or get them to throw in extra perks. Vendors have needs, too—they'd rather make it work than see you walk away.

Seventh Commandment: Get a contract or written agreement—composed in easy-to-understand language—that spells out everything you've discussed. Have an expert eye (a lawyer friend, your detail-oriented aunt) look over the contract to make sure it's kosher and clear, and that nothing has been forgotten. (Each vendor chapter includes critical contract points.)

Eighth Commandment: Sign the contract only when you're completely comfortable with it. Keep two copies signed and dated by you and the vendor so it will be legally binding.

Ninth Commandment: Pay necessary deposits; always get a receipt.

Tenth Commandment: Your vendor is there to serve you. Call him/her periodically during the preparation period to make sure things are on schedule and that no details slip through the cracks. Never hesitate to speak your mind (as long as you're not simply being a paranoid maniac).

Crucial Contract Points

Each and every contract you draw up with a vendor should include these items. Don't sign until they are all in there.

- The date of the wedding.
- The length of service: exact start and finish time, including setup and breakdown periods.
- An hourly overtime rate. (Make sure the vendor will be available for overtime; you don't want wrap-up work interrupting the party if it's still in full swing.)

Tipping Tips

To tip or not to tip—that's another big question on your wedding day. You certainly don't want to stiff the people who are working to make your wedding dreams come true, but how do you know who to slip a few extra bucks for their hard work? Here are some guidelines.

Designate someone to be in charge of tipping—the host of the event or the wedding consultant usually handles this job.
Talk to the hotel or club manager directly if you are unsure of the tipping policy. S/he can let you know how tips have been handled in the past and make suggestions.
The gratuity is often included in the bill, so read it carefully to avoid double-tipping.
Remember, no one should *expect* tips; they're a bonus for a job well done.
Plan ahead. Have tips ready in sealed envelopes. Most likely you will want to go ahead and tip everyone who did a great job for you, but you won't want to have to think too hard when the time comes. (You'll be too busy kissing guests good-bye.)
At the same time, keep in mind that tips aren't doled out *automatically.* Most of these pros are providing a service for a previously determined fee. They've got to do their job first before you give 'em a penny extra. If you got what you paid for, offer a tip.

Here are guidelines for what to tip the people who make the reception run smoothly:

Maitre d'hotel: 15–20 percent of the reception bill.
Club manager/hotel banquet manager: 15–20 percent of the reception bill (less if there is a maitre d').
Waitstaff: At least $20 each (maitre d' will distribute the tips for you). Often the gratuity is added to the food bill, but ask before you sign your catering contract.
Bartenders: 10 percent of the total liquor bill.
Powder room and coatroom attendants: $1 per guest (because they shouldn't be hitting up guests).
Parking attendants: At least 50¢–$1 per car, or arrange a gratuity with the hotel or club management.
Limousine: 15–20 percent of the limo bill.
Delivery-truck drivers for florist, baker, etc.: At least $5–$10 each.
DJ, musicians: $20–$25 each.
Officiant: $100 and up usually as a donation to the church or temple.

- Details, details: a list of *everything* the vendor will be supplying, down to the minutest of minutiae.
- Exact prices, including tax. (A detailed list of gratuities is optional.)
- A staff dress code that's appropriate for your wedding's formality.
- Cancellation/refund policy.
- Contact numbers where you and the vendor can reach each other easily.
- Rental returns, if applicable. (Make sure it's clear when the vendor will deliver equipment and when you need to give it back.)

JESSA & JEFF

December 15, Deep Creek Lake, Maryland

JESSA AND JEFF chose a Christmastime motif for their December wedding. "But the underlying theme," says Jessa, "was that I couldn't stand to pay for things that were simple to make. We wanted to keep our budget down by doing as much as we could ourselves and finding discount sources for the things we wanted to buy for the wedding." With energy and talent, Jessa (and a staff of devoted family and friends) made the wedding invitations, the wedding cake, her veil, and many other wedding details.

Her headpiece came from a craft supply shop; the veil she made herself by sewing pearled lace onto a piece of tulle and then attaching a bit of Velcro to hold it to the headpiece.

For her bridesmaid dresses, Jessa bought a bolt of rich red velvet, then each of her maids selected a formal dress pattern. A sewing party was held at the bride's house and the bridal party made their own dresses. Jessa says, "We're no seamstresses, but we took Home Ec and know how to follow a basic sewing pattern."

"The invitations were the first major wedding project, and I went totally overboard," admits Jessa. Her creation involved Christmas-red cardstock, gold-paint pens, a heart-shaped logo with the couple's initials, a collage of childhood photos, a line drawing of the church, and vellum attached with gold ribbon.

Naturally, Jessa made her own wedding cake, taking a local cake-decorating class to get the hang of it first. Only the bottom and top layers of the six-tiered cake were real; the other layers were frosted Styrofoam "dummy" cakes. Jessa and her bridesmaids made a mess of the kitchen but perfected the basketweave frosting technique nonetheless. The cake was topped with the bride and groom dolls from Jessa's parents' wedding cake.

Jeff and buddies provided a sound system, and one of the groomsmen acted as emcee and DJ, playing several mixed CDs the bride and groom had burned for the occasion.

Twenty-five Cost-Cutting Tips

Think you can't have the wedding you want because you can't afford it? There are tons of easy ways to shave dollars off your wedding budget. We've put together our favorite twenty-five ideas that require the least amount of compromise (we know how you hate the "C" word).

1. Consider a night other than Saturday. There will probably be better availability for Friday and Sunday (or even Thursday) dates, and you may be able to get a lower rate on the space.
2. If you book the reception space far ahead (a year or more) or at the last minute (a month before), you may be able to negotiate a better price.
3. Stay in the season when choosing flowers and foods.
4. Trim huppahs, trellises, pews, and such with more greenery than actual blooms. They will still look lush.
5. Walk down the aisle carrying one or two large, stunning blooms like orchids, peonies, or sunflowers, tied with a ribbon.
6. Take ceremony flowers along to the reception site. Or arrange to share the cost of ceremony decorations with the couple marrying directly before or after you that day.
7. Use flowering plants on the tables as centerpieces.
8. Opt for local ingredients to save on importing costs.
9. Don't give guests a choice of entrées on the day of the wedding—either request meal preferences on your reply cards or select one entrée that appeals to all tastes.
10. A good wedding cake is often dessert enough—you don't need pastries and ice cream, too (maybe just some fresh fruit for the hard-core health nuts).
11. See if your caterer or baker offers a selection of standard cakes as opposed to ordering a customized design.
12. During cocktail hour, instead of an open bar, serve wine in passed glasses. Or serve a signature cocktail that uses less, or less expensive, liquor.
13. If your caterer and reception site allow, buy the alcohol yourselves; you may be able to return unopened cases, instead of paying your caterer or banquet manager a flat rate for a set amount of open-bar hours.
14. Close the bar an hour before the reception ends and provide soft drinks, sparkling water, and coffee. This should also reduce the risk of tipsy guests attempting to drive home.
15. Ask your DJ or band about cutting back on special effects like lighting and disco balls.
16. Hire students from local universities or music academies to play or sing during the ceremony.
17. Hire in-house musicians from your church or temple for your ceremony.
18. Ask bands about the minimum amount of time they will play at a reception. You might have them play for three hours, from the

Credit Cards to the Rescue

Pay all deposits with your credit cards. That way you'll have the law on your side if the vendor doesn't deliver on his/her promises; credit card companies are legally required to investigate any claim that a consumer has been wrongfully charged, and *they'll* get the vendor to cough up the dough if they find in your favor.

first dance to the cake cutting, with supplementary taped music for the cocktail hour and to wind down the party.

19. Find out if any of the musicians play another instrument; if the pianist also plays the guitar or violin, perhaps he or she can also provide cocktail-hour music and you won't have to hire another musician.
20. Ask stationers whether or not a discounted package price is available if you order all your stationery at once (invitations, thank-you notes, announcements, etc.).
21. Ask your photographer and videographer if they can limit their hours of participation; for example, can they only cover the first couple of hours of your reception instead of the whole thing?
22. Save on disposable camera costs by putting them at every other, instead of each, table and encourage guests to pass them around.
23. Buy a top-of-the-line bridesmaid dress—in white. While it may not look as impressive (or be cut as well) as a bridal gown, you can probably be outfitted for under $500.
24. Buy a sample dress. If you're lucky enough to fit into a dress right off the rack, as opposed to having it made for you, you can save money. Where you'll need to spend: You'll probably be on your own for the cost of alterations and cleaning that may be needed before the wedding.
25. Use limousines for the minimum amount of time—instead of having the driver wait, hire a limo to go to the ceremony and reception and a town car to pick you up at the end of the reception.

NOTES

CHAPTER FOUR

attendants and guests

From honor attendant to flower child, you have plenty of wedding roles to fill. This is good news: There's a place for all your favorite folks—best friends, childhood buddies, siblings, other relatives, a mentor, coach, even your dog. The one guideline? Ask the people you love the most to be part of your wedding. Not everyone has to stand at the altar; there are tons of ways to include everyone you want to. And don't forget that your guests are a big part of your big day, too—make sure they feel that way.

Attendants and Their Roles

While it's an honor for your attendants to be asked, it's also an honor for you that they accept! Keep in mind that your wedding party is agreeing to spend their hard-earned money and donate their hard-pressed time. Give them the consideration and kindness they're due. Keep them informed about all your plans and their roles in them, show them a good time, and make sure they know how much you appreciate them. Before you pop the attendant question, check out our rundown of attendant duties so you'll be able to let everyone know what to expect.

Be Clear and Be Kind

Don't assume the maid of honor knows what to do. Fill her in on exactly what tasks you'd like her to handle. And don't forget to thank her—early and often. This is voluntary service, not a full-time job.

The Honor Attendant

The maid or matron (a married woman) of honor is the bride's center—the person she feels closest to and wants by her side throughout the wedding preparations and at the altar. Traditionally your sister or best friend (though you can choose your mom, daughter, or even your closest guy pal—a man of honor), the honor attendant is responsible for overseeing a variety of essential minutiae as well as providing unflagging moral support. Even if she can't perform all the physical tasks (because she lives in a faraway city or is doing med-school rotations), make sure you choose someone who will be available to help you ride the emotional roller coaster of getting married. Specifically, she should:

- Offer to help with aspects of wedding planning.
- Help shop for dresses (yours and the bridesmaids'); pay for her own dress.
- Spread the news of where you two are registered.

- Host a bridal shower, tea, or luncheon (with help from maids or family).
- Work with the best man to organize a couple's shower (if you're having one).
- Assign someone to keep track of all those great gifts (enabling you to write personal thank-you notes).
- Organize a bachelorette party (if you're having one).
- Keep the bridesmaids abreast of all parties to attend and help host.
- Make sure all bridesmaids get their dresses, go to fittings, and find the right jewelry.
- Make sure all bridesmaids get to the rehearsal; coordinate transportation (and lodging, if necessary).
- Attend the rehearsal dinner.
- Make sure all maids get their hair and makeup done, get to the ceremony on time, and have correct flowers.

Double Duty

Two best friends? Have twice the fun with two maids (or matrons) of honor. If you're going with multiple honor attendants, just make sure to distribute the duties clearly among them. Don't leave it to them to figure it out—someone's sure to get stressed.

- Be with you before you walk down the aisle, assuring you that you look stunning; remind you to *breathe.*
- Walk down the aisle before you.
- Arrange your veil and train once you're at the altar; hold your bouquet during your vows.
- Hold the groom's ring until you're ready for it.
- Sign the marriage certificate as a witness.
- Stand in the receiving line, if you choose.
- Help you remove your headpiece and bustle your train so you can start partying.
- Sit at the head table (if you're having one).
- Pile the food on a plate for you (if it's a buffet) so you don't have to wait in line; make sure you sit down and eat something.
- Give a toast after the best man, or lead the toasting (if you want her to).
- Dance with the best man and the groom during a formal first-dance sequence (if you're having one).
- Serve as an auxiliary hostess during the reception, helping to introduce people and make everyone feel comfortable.
- Collect any gift envelopes guests bring to the reception and keep them for you. (She may deposit them in your bank account, along with the best man, or hang on to them until you return from Bora Bora.)

Go to Chapter 5 for the skinny on showers and bachelorette bashes.

ASK CARLEY

Uneven Attendants

Q: Help! I have four best friends and a sister, and I want them all to be in my wedding party. But my honey only has two friends on the whole planet. What should I do?

A: Easy—include them all. Scrap that old one-bridesmaid-for-one-groomsman "rule" and adapt your down-the-aisle approach to suit your reality. Have your maid of honor walk alone, while each groomsman escorts two bridesmaids, for example.

- Listen to your fears, complaints, and concerns; help smooth over any disputes (with family or bridesmaids); and keep your (and her) sense of humor intact.

The Best Man

Ahh, for the days when every man had a valet—a trusted servant always at his side to polish his shoes, pour his whiskey, and make wry, witty comments. Enter the best man. Usually your best male friend, dad, or bro (although you can choose a female friend or sister—a best maid), the best man serves as your personal aide and adviser throughout the planning and the wedding. You want someone reliable, who's not too busy to help you handle the details of doin' the deed, who's pro-marriage (or at least pro *your* marriage), and who's prepared to help keep your spirits up if you hit any emotional landmines. As leader of the groom's crew, he will:

- Work with maid of honor to organize a couple's shower (if you're having one).
- Organize the bachelor party (with help from the groomsmen).
- Help you choose and rent (or buy) your tux.
- Coordinate the groomsmen's rentals; pay for his own tux.
- Pay extra attention to groomsmen roles during the rehearsal (in case they're snoozing).
- Attend the rehearsal dinner.
- Coordinate groomsmen's wedding transportation (and lodging if necessary).
- Stand next to you at the altar.
- Hold the bride's ring until you need it.
- Sign the marriage certificate as a witness after the ceremony.
- Hand the officiant his or her fee after the ceremony.
- May stand in the receiving line at the reception.
- Sit at the head table (if you're having one).
- Kick off the reception-time toasting, traditionally.
- Dance with the maid of honor and the bride during a formal first-dance sequence (if you're having one).
- Collect any gift envelopes guests bring to the reception and keep them for you.
- Have cash in hand for anyone who needs tipping, paying, or bribing.
- May drive you to your wedding-night hotel or to the airport after the reception.
- Listen to your concerns, reassure you, and make you laugh throughout the planning and the wedding.

Not Up to the Task?

While asking someone to lead the toasting is an honor, giving him a nervous breakdown isn't. If your main man is a mouse in front of a mike, ask your bride's honor attendant, mom, or dad to lead the toasting. A joint toast with the maid of honor is also an option.

The Bridesmaids

This is your chance to surround yourself with a court of adoring attendants. In the distant past, bridesmaids escorted the bride as she traveled to the groom's village for the wedding, protecting her (and her dowry) from attack by highway robbers or scorned suitors. Today your maids probably won't have to do double duty as a defensive line, but they do have a variety of other challenging tasks. Choose considerate friends who work well with others. (Traditionally women, bridesmaids can be guys, too—bridesmen.) When you ask your friends to be maids, make sure they're clear on their responsibilities—and be realistic and understanding about how much time and money it will take. Here's what bridesmaids do:

- Help plan the bridal or couple's shower and bachelorette party (if you're having one).
- Offer to help with general wedding planning tasks—addressing invites, making favors, decorating the reception site, etc.
- Help scout out bridesmaids' dresses; pay for their own dresses, shoes, lingerie, and jewelry.
- Attend the rehearsal dinner.
- March on down that aisle before you and stand at the front during the ceremony.
- May dance with the groomsmen during a formal first-dance sequence.
- Serve as auxiliary hostesses at the reception, introducing people and making sure everyone's comfortable.

Go to Chapter 7 for more tips for great toasts.

Tips for Toasting

Traditionally, the best man's toast is an homage to the groom and his new bride. It should be sincere, *kind,* and sprinkled with lines that make the crowd laugh. If he's tongue-tied, give him a copy of our very own Best Man Toast Writer. He'll have the crowd weeping (and laughing) in no time.

Standard opening: Hello there. I'd like to take this opportunity to thank you from the bottom of my [body part] for joining us here tonight as we celebrate the union of [bride's name] and [embarrassing male nickname]. It would be difficult to imagine two more [adjective] people meeting one another, falling in love, and deciding to spend their lives together. I'm honored that they've asked me to say a few words tonight.

If he's known you since childhood, he can add: As you may know, [groom's first name] and I first met each other [number] years ago when we were [adjective] boys who liked nothing better than a day spent climbing [plural noun], playing with [animals] and shouting "[exclamation]!" as we [adverb] dove into his [relative]'s freezing swimming pool. Back then, girls were [adjective] and [sports figure] was God. Since then, we've shared a lot of good times together. . . .

If you've met more recently: I still remember the day [groom's name] and I first met. We were [fraternity brothers/coworkers/cell mates] with a mutual devotion to [television show] and [snack food]. Since [graduation/the downsizing/parole] we've remained close and have shared a lot of good times together. . . .

If he knows the bride well, he may add: And during these last few years, we've been lucky enough to have [bride's name] along to share more than a few of them.

If he barely knows her: And I look forward to sharing even more of them with both [groom's name] and [bride's name] in the days to come.

Time to pull the heartstrings: [Groom's name] has been more than just a [adjective] friend to me, he's been a inspiration. I can't say that I'd want to marry him (pause for laughter), but I envy the woman who did. So please raise your glass and join me in a toast to a very [adjective] couple and their many, many years of happiness to come.

Salut!/Cheers/L'chaim!

- Serve as dance starters, hitting the floor when the band kicks in and scanning the ranks for any toe-tapping guests eager to join them.
- Offer you emotional support during planning and on the wedding day.

The Groomsmen

Your groomsmen are the loyal, responsible friends who've been there when you needed them and will make you feel like the star you are on your wedding day. Back in the days when a groom would capture his bride—literally—and carry her away to be wed, the groomsmen were his trusty warrior buddies who helped fight off opposing forces (families, suitors) trying to get her back. Today your groomsmen probably won't engage in hand-to-hand combat. But they do more than just show up in a tux:

- Help plan bachelor party and/or couple's shower (if you're having one).
- Rent their own tuxes and shoes.
- Attend the rehearsal dinner.
- May serve as ushers, helping seat guests before the ceremony. (See "Roles for Other Important People: Ushers," later in the chapter.)
- Serve as information central during the wedding, directing wayward guests to the restroom, chapel, and/or reception site.
- Stand at the altar during the ceremony (may escort bridesmaids up the aisle first).
- May dance with the bridesmaids during a formal first-dance sequence.
- May serve as dance starters, surveying the room for any guests who are dying to disco.
- Decorate the getaway car, if there is one.
- Offer support and their unfailing sense of humor throughout the preparations and during the wedding.

You Can't Be Too Clear

Go over the list of everything you want your best man (and other attendants) to do before the big day—and one last time the night before. Better to be redundant than ringless.

Go to Chapter 12 for help outfitting all your attendants.

ASK CARLEY

Breaking the Bad News

Q: Help! I've chosen five bridesmaids and there just isn't room at the altar for more. But I don't know how to face the unchosen ones—I know they'll hate me for excluding them. What do I do?

A: You have an understandable reason for limiting your bridesmaids—the size of your ceremony space. Call each friend you didn't ask (or make a dinner date), tell her how excited you are about your wedding and how much you want her there. Let her know, straight up, that you were only able to choose a certain number of attendants and would love her to take another special role. Make her job a positive rather than a negative. "You're such a great singer (writer/speaker/baker), I would be honored if you'd sing at the wedding." While you don't want to lie, there's no harm in making up a good reason to help someone feel less slighted. ("I'm not having any out-of-town attendants; it's just such a pain for them. But I hope you will come and be an honored guest!")

Lining Up the Little Ones

So you have twenty-seven little cousins who are so cute, you have to include them? Great—there are plenty of roles for little folks. But keep in mind that part of kids' charm is the fact that you never know what they'll do—this sort of unpredictability tends to be more charming the less important the occasion! Generally, save the action parts for kids older than four, and make sure all tasks are age-appropriate.

Give 'Em a Break

If your wedding is costing your bridesmaids a bundle (the shower, the dress, etc.), let them know that their participation is the only wedding present you want.

Junior Groomsmen/Bridesmaids/Ushers

Include young friends and relatives (ages nine to sixteen) as junior ushers, bridesmaids, or groomsmen. Young guys can wear tuxes and do basically the same things as your older pals—seat guests, precede you down the aisle, snicker when you drop the ring. Young gals can wear less sexy versions of your bridesmaids' dress and walk down the aisle before you as junior members of the bride's squad. Girls can always seat guests, as well.

Introduce Your Crew

Get all your (local) attendants partying together early on in the planning process. By instigating some group-bonding activities, you'll help make it easier for them to work together—and ensure that they'll have more fun at the wedding.

Flower Children

Typically, these wee folks (ages four to eight) walk (skip, crawl) down the aisle before the bride, scattering flower petals. While flower *girls* are standard, there's no rule that says your adorable male cousins can't do flower duty, too. If you're having more than one flower child, have them hold hands, two by two, to give them courage. If you're afraid you'll slip on those slick blossoms and topple into your guests, skip the scattering part and have your flower child carry a basket or ball of flowers (a pomander), a single stem, or a bottle and wand to blow bubbles instead. Seat your flower children's parents up front to wave them in and seat them at the end of their march.

Ring Bearers

Traditionally a small boy (age four to eight), the ring bearer walks down the aisle either before or along with the flower child, holding a small, fancy pillow with your two rings tied to it. Afraid your rambunctious cousin Randy will run off with your new platinum bands? The ring

How to say "thanks" to your supporting cast? Buy 'em something super. For presents with pizzazz, go to Chapter 20.

ASK CARLEY

Who Pays for What?

Q: I'm having twelve bridesmaids, about half from out of town. Do I have to pay for their dresses *and* hotel rooms?

A: Generally, your attendants pay their own way for what they wear and their travel and lodging expenses. But you can help make it *a lot* easier by reserving a block of hotel rooms at a reduced group rate, or putting out-of-town attendants up with local bridesmaids or your nicest friends. If someone you really adore won't be able to make it/participate because of costs, it's your prerogative to offer financial help. (Just keep it low key so other maids don't get jealous or angry.)

ASK CARLEY

Sibling Rivalry?

Q: My fiancée wants me to ask her brother to be a groomsman. I don't hate him, *exactly.* But we've never been close, and I don't think he'll feel comfortable with my friends. Do I *have* to ask him?

A: No way, José. Your groomsmen are just that—*your* guys. Your sweetie can ask her bro to stand up for her. Or the two of you can create a special role for him. Of course, ultimately you might decide to ask him out of consideration for her and a personal desire to get in good with your soon-to-be in-laws (and pursue a better relationship with your brother-in-law). But it's your call completely.

bearer usually touts fake rings while the real ones wait safely with your honor attendants. If you don't like the artifice, have someone hand over the pillow with the real rings *just before* he starts his walk. Or skip the ring pillow and have your ring bearer carry something real, and less valuable, instead, such as a flower to hand to his mother when he meets her at the end of the aisle. The purpose of the ring bearer is to make your guests melt with affection—he can carry a Tonka Truck and still succeed.

Don't Count On It

Don't expect too much of young attendants. Even your very mature thirteen-year-old cousin might eat too many Sweet-tarts for breakfast and spin off into a sugar-induced mania during the ceremony. Kids will be kids—give any critical duties to adults.

Page/Train Bearer(s)

A pair of pages (ages six to nine) follow the bride down the aisle, carrying her long train. This English tradition usually is performed by two little boys, but girl pages are fine, too.

Candle Kids

Steady-handed preteens (ages nine to twelve) can light candles at the altar directly before the mother of the bride is seated (in a Christian ceremony). They can either dress like the junior attendants (to further highlight their roles) or come as they are. Your candle kids might stick around after the ceremony to snuff the flames.

Bored of Blossoms?

Your littlest attendant can carry:

- A little lantern
- Photo of special relative to remember
- Bible
- Basket of candy
- Arrangements for the altar
- Favorite toy

Roles for Other Important People

Maybe you were voted "Most Popular" by your high-school class, college dorm mates, and bowling league. Or perhaps you come from one of those families that considers everyone in the area code a cousin. Don't inflate your wedding party to a Rockettes-size line—make those VIPs into VIEs (Very Important Extras). You can acknowledge special people in a relatively passive way, by giving them corsages, seats of honor, or a place in the family pictures. Or you can make them part of the party by inventing entirely new roles for them. Your creativity is your only limit. Just make sure your honor roles are actually honorable—there's nothing particularly appealing about punch bowl duty or bathroom detail! Thank everyone with a small gift and/or a mention in the ceremony program. Below are some great ways to include VIEs.

Ushers

Ask special friends or relatives (male or female) to serve as ushers, walking your guests to their seats, rolling out the aisle runner (if you're having one), tying pew ribbons across the rows (if you're using them), and acting as general guest guides. Groomsmen often double as ushers, but if it's a huge wedding (you need one usher per fifty guests) or there are lots of people you want to include, go with the designated usher approach.

Go to Chapter 6 for more on ushering.

Huppah Holders

Ask four strong-armed friends to hold up your huppah (if you're having a Jewish wedding). They carry it down the aisle on four tall stakes before the wedding party enters and hold it steady throughout the ceremony. They might even help make it, if they have the time and creativity. Ask your rabbi for specs.

Attendants Wearing Tails

He's the love of your life (just after your honey). So what if he walks on all fours and drools? He's the person (all right, dog) second closest to your heart. Have him walk down the aisle in a flowered collar (led by a two-footed friend, of course).

Candle Lighters

If you're having a dramatic nighttime ceremony with candles along the aisle (or any other area), appoint a special friend to candle duty, asking her to light up directly before the ceremony begins. Or have her distribute candles to all the guests to be lit as a part of the ceremony. At a Jewish wedding, you can honor someone by asking her to light a candle during the reception.

Readers and Class Acts

Have a well-spoken, special friend do a reading during your ceremony. You can choose the text, or ask him to select something he loves. Alternately, you could ask a literary type to write something to read or to be printed in your program. Or ask a talented friend to be a featured performer during your ceremony or reception, singing a special song or playing an instrument.

Transportation Captain

If your Uncle Albert (or anyone else) is mad for all things mobile, has wallpapered his den with road maps, and considers clocking distances on the odometer a leisure-time activity, appoint him transportation captain and let him take charge of your guests' vehicular needs. He can check on the parking possibilities at your sites, chart the best course from the ceremony to the reception, keep abreast of any serious traffic problems on your wedding day, and—most important—create, copy, and distribute maps. He also may research the best place to rent a limo or a bus if you'll be routing guests to a remote or hard-to-find reception location.

Toast of the Table

Seat a special guest at each table—someone who had a major impact on your life or traveled from Siberia just for your wedding. Designate her place with a flower or card. Ask all special guests to stand up during the toasting and briefly explain their significance to you. Then toast them, along with all your guests, together.

Fitting in the Folks

You can't choose your parents, but you can decide what role they play in your wedding. While the bride's mother was the official hostess traditionally—meaning her hubby paid and she did all the work—parental involvement today is more a question of comfort and closeness than cash (especially since you two may be putting the whole wedding on your Gold Card, or the groom's parents may be paying more than the bride's). You can have your folks fill the traditional roles if it's appropriate and will make your wedding run more smoothly, but it's your call. No matter what you decide, keep in mind that the more they pay, the more they may want to play. If the idea of planning a wedding with Pop sounds about as fun as being stuck in an elevator with an unleashed crocodile, think seriously before accepting his generous offer of financial aid.

Advice on Volunteers

Beware of giving critical tasks to nonprofessionals. If your Aunt Esmeralda offers to make the bridesmaids' dresses, and she's a professional seamstress—bring on the pinking shears! But if she just happens to enjoy sewing, she may not have the facilities or experience to do the deed right. And, believe it or not, even the best people can flake out if they're not being paid. Assess the seriousness of your volunteer's skill and commitment *before* accepting a gift of catering, photography, flowers, clothing, or music.

Mother of the Bride

If you get along great with your mom (and she has plenty of time), feel free to ask her to help with just about everything, easing your burden and giving you some serious mother-daughter bonding opportunities. (If your mom is also your matron of honor, she'll be taking an even bigger part in your wedding planning; make sure she knows what she's getting into before she agrees.) You decide (or decide together) which of the following tasks you want Mom to tackle:

- Help scout out wedding and reception sites and ask friends for recommendations for caterers, florists, and so on.
- May serve as the main contact for wedding professionals.
- Help choose your wedding dress (and honeymoon bikini!).
- Compile her (and Dad's) guest list of family and friends.
- Talk to the groom's family about how many people they want to invite and deal with the difficult task of limiting the number of guests, if necessary.
- Help choose family or ethnic traditions to incorporate into your ceremony or reception.
- Coordinate with the groom's mom on clothing; they'll feel more comfortable if they're dressed equally elegantly.
- Attend most showers and the rehearsal dinner.
- May walk you down the aisle if Dad doesn't. (Both Mom and Dad accompany the bride in a Jewish wedding.)

- In a Christian wedding, be seated in the first pew directly before the ceremony and leave the chapel first afterward.
- Stand in the receiving line to greet guests—traditionally, as reception hostess, she heads up the line.
    - Sit at the parents' table (if you're having one).
    - Dance with your dad and your honey during a formal first-dance sequence.
    - Remind you often how special you are and that you'll be the most beautiful bride in the history of the universe.
    - Let you cry on her shoulder anytime, day or night (you know, be a mom).

Token Tasks

If you need a stiff drink to get up the nerve to call your mom (or dad)—or if she's too busy working on her Ph.D/latest novel/next divorce to pick up the phone—you're better off asking for help with small, specific tasks (if any at all).

Mother of the Groom

The groom's mom traditionally had only a shadow role—greeting guests in the receiving line and sitting at the parents' table. The unspoken assumption: This was the bride's family's party. But it's time for the groom's mom to step off the bench and get into the wedding action! By giving her a big role in the wedding planning, you not only make her feel important to both of you, but you also garner one more pair of capable hands. And believe us, there's plenty of work to go around. Your mom isn't losing a son, she's gaining a second career—wedding planner. She can:

- Host a dinner to introduce your bride to your side of the family.
- Help scout out wedding and reception sites and ask friends for recommendations for caterers, florists, etc.
- May serve as the main contact for wedding professionals.
- Draw up the guest list for your family.
- Attend showers.
- Help you choose family or ethnic traditions to incorporate into your ceremony or reception.
- Consult with the bride's mom on her wedding-day outfit, making sure that gold lamé jumpsuit will match the formality and style of the bride's mother's attire.

Go to Chapter 24 for help dealing with meddling mothers and infuriating fathers.

ASK CARLEY

Managing Two Moms?

Q: I'm close to my mom and my stepmom. Whom should I include in my wedding and how?

A: Include them both, but make sure you divide the duties. For example, if you ask Mom to walk you down the aisle, maybe your stepmother should be the last person seated before the procession begins. Try to keep their feelings in mind—your mother might feel her "Mom-ness" threatened by your stepmother; Stepmom might feel uncomfortable being involved because she's not your "real" mother. Wishy-washiness about who does what can create unnecessary friction. Have a heart-to-heart with each mom well before the wedding to let them know you're planning to include both of them and to see what they are comfortable (and uncomfortable) with. Decide together what roles they'll take on your wedding day.

- Traditionally, plan and host the rehearsal dinner along with your dad.
- In a Jewish ceremony, escort you down the aisle along with your dad.
- Stand in the receiving line after you two (along with your dad).
- Sit at the parents' table (if you're having one).
- Dance with your dad during a formal first dance.
- Bring down the house with you during the mother/son dance.
- Grow weepy periodically about how her baby has grown up.

Father of the Bride

The stereotypical father of the bride signs the checks and shows up in a tux. But there's no reason he can't participate as much as your mom. Don't assume your dad doesn't want to help just because he doesn't offer. Even if he's a tough guy at the office, he may be shy around all things wedding-related. Ask him for help on specific items. For example, Dad can:

- Help you come up with a budget.
- Pay for the wedding. (Be grateful if this is the case—it's not a given anymore.)
- Help with everything from scouting out reception sites to recommending dance tunes.
- Help your mom create their guest list.
- Find the perfect wardrobe for himself (tux? Scottish kilt?) and let the groom's dad know he should do the same.
- May attend the bachelor party and/or a couple's shower.
- Attend the rehearsal dinner and be prepared to toast the groom into the family (may also pay for/help plan this party).
- May ride with you to the ceremony.
- Walk you down the aisle and "give you away" or "support" you in marriage. (Both parents march in a Jewish ceremony.)
- May stand in the receiving line, next to your mother.
- At a Jewish wedding, may offer a blessing over the wine and bread.
- Sit at the parents' table (if you're having one).
- Dance with your mom during an official first-dance sequence.
- Kick up his heels for a special father/daughter dance with you.
- May make a toast after the best man.
- May help organize (and oversee) the bar.
- Stay until the bitter end of the party, possibly settling final bills.

Father of the Groom

No more sitting back and watching the bride's father squirm. The groom's father also plays a far bigger role these days, very likely shouldering some of the cost of the wedding. What your dad does depends a lot on his time and interest, and your relationship with him. The groom's father can:

- Contribute to wedding expenses (traditionally, the marriage license, officiant's fee, corsages, boutonnieres, the bride's bouquet, groomsmen's gifts, liquor, and/or music).
- Help with planning.
- Help create the groom's family guest list.
- May attend the bachelor party and/or a couple's shower.
- Host (read: pay for) the rehearsal dinner (with your mom).
- Buy or rent a new tux or other wedding attire.
- In a Jewish wedding, escort you down the aisle, along with your mom.
- May stand in the receiving line after your mom.
- At a Jewish wedding, may offer a blessing over the wine and bread.
- Sit at the parents' table (if you're having one).
- May give a toast (after bride's parents).
- Dance with your mom and the bride during a formal first-dance sequence.
- May help organize (and oversee) the bar.
- Stay until the bitter end of the party, possibly settling final bills.

Greeting Those Guests

If you've got scores of out-of-town guests, you have extra issues to think about—namely where they'll sleep, how they'll get around, and what they'll do with their spare time. This isn't just the biggest day of your life; it's also a party for your friends and family (who just doled out a lot of dough for a tux and that cappuccino maker you had to have). Take steps to ensure they have an awesome time.

Keep Them Informed

This is a party, not a game of Clue. Don't make your guests use super-sleuth skills to get to your wedding. Let them know early what the dress code is, when to R.S.V.P. by, where you're registered, how to get to the ceremony and reception, and the dates of any extra parties or activities they're invited to. You can include this info along with your invitation (except where you're registered—that's word of mouth). Appoint someone as Guest Services Coordinator, on hand to answer any questions. You might include this person's phone number in your invite. And think about setting up a web page with all the pertinent info.

Get Them There

Provide maps and directions for out-of-towners. In addition to including a small map in the invite, you may want to leave a packet of info in each hotel room for them. Your Transportation Captain (see "Roles for Other Important People," earlier) can handle the details.

While out-of-town guests often rent their own cars, you can welcome them in style (or ask your parents, friends, or relatives to do so) by greeting them at the airport and chauffeuring them to the hotel if they need you to. You also might arrange for a hotel shuttle to take a group of guests to and from the wedding. Talk to the hotel manager about options.

HEIDI & AARON

October 19, Miami Beach, Florida

HEIDI AND AARON worked hard not only to make their reception gorgeous, but, more important, to have their guests feel welcome and comfortable. The only lights in the room were pinpoint spotlights in the ceiling illuminating the centerpieces, which hung above the tables. Candles were placed on each table, giving the room an ethereal glow, and there was no wedding video—Aaron didn't want one, and Heidi didn't mind because the lighting involved would ruin the effect of her carefully chosen lighting scheme.

For the wedding cake, Heidi says, "Aaron and I have more books than anyone we know, so we thought, why not do one shaped like books?" Titles were written on the spine in frosting, including a joke title—*The Case of the Missing Ushers*—because Aaron had no ushers, only groom*swomen*. The groom's cake was made in the form of a chessboard with sugar chess pieces—in honor of Aaron, who plays chess.

Having no ushers clinched Heidi's decision not to do the garter thing, and that led to another twist on wedding tradition: "We had both boys and girls come out on the dance floor for the bouquet throw." And rather than letting the dancing peter out, Heidi and Aaron stayed until the end of the reception and planned a last dance—to the Beatles' "In My Life." Everyone formed a circle around them. "Everyone we loved was around us," Heidi says. "It was so emotional—the perfect ending."

Reserve Rooms

Contact a local hotel convenient to your wedding sites about six months before the big day to ask about a discounted group rate if you send all 50 to 200 of your guests their way. Reserve a block of rooms, then include the hotel info (address, phone number, directions, and special rate) on an invitation insert. Be considerate of your crowd's budget constraints; if appropriate, reserve rooms at two hotels—a super-luxe one for your flush friends and a less-expensive option for your budgeting buddies. (If you have close local friends or relatives with empty guest rooms, they may offer to house a guest or two for free.)

Keep Them Entertained

Appoint an outgoing, *very* loving friend or relative to play "cruise director" and arrange activities for your guests. Of course you'll have a rehearsal dinner and probably a brunch for out-of-

To keep your guests up-to-date on the wedding, go to www.theknot.com/weddingwebpage and create a free personal wedding web page.

towners. But your cruise director (or your attendants) might set up other activities, such as a golf game, a trip to the zoo, or a tour of the city. She should make sure that a local guidebook, a list of hot spots (with phone numbers, addresses, and hours), and a list of pertinent phone numbers (hers, the other guests staying in the hotel, the bride's and groom's families) make their way to each hotel room. You pay for the supplies; she donates her time.

The Buddy System

Out-of-town guests who are traveling alone? Create a buddy system. Appoint a kind, *willing* family member to welcome the guest to town and offer his phone number for questions. Your buddy probably won't get woken up at 4:00 A.M., but the knowledge that he's there should help nervous travelers relax.

Show Your Love

Make out-of-towners feel extra-wanted (and let them know that you appreciate the fact that they've used all their frequent-flier miles to see you wed). Welcome them with a basket of fresh fruit, local candy, or luxurious bath foam in their room. Attach a personal note, thanking them for coming, or make an announcement during the reception. Or get everyone coupons for dinner for two at your favorite local seafood shack, free skate rental at the area rink, or a manicure at the hotel salon.

NOTES

CHAPTER FIVE

prewedding parties

The period between your engagement and your wedding is busy, hectic, and stressful, but it's also a time for some serious partying. Some soirees are in your honor (showers, bachelor/bachelorette bashes), some are practice runs (the rehearsal dinner), but all provide important (and fun!) opportunities for your respective friends and families to get to know each other before the big day.

We thought we'd serve up some tips for organizing prewedding fiestas so you can pass them along to your fantastic hosts and hostesses. Do keep in mind that these parties cost your pals time and money—keep others' feelings and pocketbooks in mind before you go overboard with your suggestions, okay?

Engagement Parties

The Brits of yore used to celebrate a couple's engagement with a party they called a "flouncing." These days this bash—usually scheduled sometime during the first two months you're engaged—comes in all shapes and sizes, but, basically, it's a chance to whoop it up with close friends and family. Sounds great, right? Here's the lowdown.

Parent Parties

Anyone can host these events, but tradition dictates that it's the bride's parents' prerogative to host the first soiree. Then the groom's parents can throw their own party, or, maybe both sets of parents will come together to host the fete jointly. They'll invite their dearest friends and a bunch of your relatives as well as friends of yours whom they know are important to you. These fiestas usually take the form of an informal meal or cocktail hour at someone's home, or perhaps a dinner in a restaurant's party room; you'll be toasted, fed, pampered, and ogled until you can't take it any more (for now!).

If your parents have never met your honey's before, you might think about organizing a *pre*-engagement party get-together. This may very well already be at the top of your mother's

The Where and How of Engagement Gifts

Not every engagement-party guest will bring a gift—don't embarrass anyone who didn't by opening presents you do get in front of everyone. Wait until later or open each gift alone with the guest in another part of the house/restaurant. And don't forget to send thank-you notes.

to-do list, but if not, take charge! Suggest a meeting at your favorite restaurant or whip up your world-famous lasagna and have your families over. If your parents live far away, suggest you all come together for a weekend retreat in a convenient-for-everyone locale.

Host Your Own

Why not take charge and throw an engagement party for all your fab friends? More and more couples we know are jumping on this self-congratulatory bandwagon—and for good reason. Many of your crew may *not* be invited to your parent-hosted soiree, for lack of space or the fact that your mom and dad don't know them well, but you want to make them feel a part of your marriage not only from the start but *before* it. This is also a terrific opportunity to show your friends a great time before wedding planning kicks in full force and they're called upon to help you in all ways great and small—including hearing you rattle off the entire potential song list.

Showers

The prewedding shower's very purpose is to shower the bride (and more and more often, the groom) with gifts that will help her make the transition to married life. Here's the lowdown.

The Women-Only Affair

At a bridal shower, the bridesmaids and close female friends and family members come together to toast your soon-to-be-wed good fortune, bombard you with great gifts, make goo-goo eyes at your fabulous ring and glowing complexion (ahhhh, love), and take all the pressure of harried wedding preparations away for a few hours. Heaven! Historically, the shower was a way of decking out the bride-to-be with a decent dowry of all the things it was crucial for a woman to bring to her new home (and her man). Today it's simply a beautiful gesture on the part of your (female) loved ones. It's also a win-win situation—while the bride is feeling like a queen, her girl guests get in some good female bonding before the wedding.

Who Hosts? Usually the honor attendant, with help from the other bridesmaids, female friends of the bride, and family members. In some cases, a female member of the bride's family—sister, mother, daughter—will coordinate the festivities. Although etiquette says relatives should not throw this bash, claiming it looks like they're fishing for presents for the bride, we say go for it. In some regions (the Midwest, for example), it's standard. And if the honor attendant lives far away, is superbusy, or is clueless when it comes to party planning, it makes sense for the bride's mom or sis to pitch in.

Who's Invited? The guest list includes the bridesmaids, the bride's other close girlfriends and relatives, as well as her honey's tight women friends and family members. Important tip: *Only* women who will be invited to the wedding should be part of the shower. It's common sense, really. If Cousin Gina brings a comforter as a shower gift, Cousin Gina should receive full access to that fantastic all-you-can-eat buffet you're planning. Otherwise, she'll feel like she's only as good as her gift—and that's hurtful.

Keep Track

As the bride (or couple) opens shower gifts, the maid of honor or another willing attendant should record who gave them what, so it'll be easy to write thank-you notes.

In order to make sure that no mistakes are made, the bride may be consulted about the guest list; if it's a surprise party, your honor attendant or mother will probably spearhead the invitation committee. In terms of the actual size of the guest list, there are no hard-and-fast rules. While most showers are intimate affairs, we've been to a few that gave the actual wedding reception a run for its money.

When? Scheduling the shower depends on when all the core guests are free, when the hostess has ample preparation time, when the chosen venue is available (even if it's at the hostess's house, there may be conflicts), and, perhaps, when the bride-to-be is in town. A shower can take place six months before the wedding day or at two weeks and counting. The only fixed rule is that the shower should come sometime *after* the engagement parties but *before* the big day. (We don't recommend having the shower the same week as the wedding—there's going to be way too much going on.)

If a lot of shower guests will be traveling from afar, they should be consulted about days that are good for them—and given the final date at least two months ahead of time. If it's a surprise shower, a well-placed spy (the groom-to-be, perhaps?) should snoop through the bride's day planner so there will *be* a guest of honor.

Where? Many a valiant shower hostess has chosen to throw the fiesta in the comfort of her own home, but more and more women are getting far-out funky with the party site, getting together at a bar, hotel tearoom, restaurant, beach, or park. If it'll be a surprise party, consider the bride's fave pizza joint, her parents' or sister's living room, or even her own place. Decorations are advisable, if just a few floral bouquets and balloons; background music is a must.

How? The shower hostess delegates jobs (to bridesmaids and any willing friends)—inviting guests, preparing eats, making punch, hanging decorations. Written invitations are not obligatory for small parties, although it's always nice to send people a written reminder of the date. R.S.V.P.'s are crucial either way, however, so the hostess knows how big a refreshment spread to prepare.

What Happens? Noshing snacks, sipping drinks, and opening presents are the only mandatory ingredients for a shower. Then again, flour, eggs, milk, and sugar are the only necessary ingredients for a cake. If the bride will be into it, we say go wild with party protocol, incorporating games or a theme (see below), or anything else that will up the fun quotient.

What Else? A shower is not necessarily an isolated event. There probably will be one big bash hosted by the bride's closest pals, but she also may be "showered" by her coworkers, belly-dancing class, or volunteer group.

Shower Love

The first bridal shower took place in the Netherlands, where a young lass had made up her mind to marry a poor-but-hunky miller. Her father disapproved and refused to provide her with a dowry (necessary for the marriage to be legit). So the girl's friends came to her rescue by *showering* her with gifts.

The Couple's Shower

This increasingly popular variation on the classic bridal shower includes both male and female guests (friends, attendants, and possibly family members) in a coed gab-and-gift fest. Some refer to this prewedding bash as a Jack and Jill. No matter what you choose to call it, the who, what, where, and how of a couple's shower are similar to the bridal shower, except that both sexes help with planning and enjoy the festivities.

We love his 'n' her showers. For starters, they shatter the outdated notion that only women get excited about weddings. And they're an opportunity for *all* your favorite people to get friendly before the wedding, ensuring a smashing reception. Yes, a couple's shower is much more like a flat-out *party* than a traditional shower.

If you're really gung-ho about the idea, take aside your attendants soon after your engagement and tell them you two would *love* a coed shower. Chances are they, too, will relish the idea of mixing it up. If you think a bridal *and* a couple's shower sound cool, it's fine to have one of each—and who knows, maybe your wish will come true. Your pals might decide to throw you both. Or maybe your mom will take care of the bridal shower and your attendants will put together a coed party.

Registry FYI

Information about where the couple is registered can be included in the shower invitations. If you're not doing written invitations, spread the registry lowdown by word of mouth to simplify the present-buying process for guests.

Just Theme It! Great Shower Ideas

Whatever kind of shower it is, a sure-fire way to host a hit party is to theme it. Guests automatically will feel like integral parts of the festivities because they've bought a gift or dressed up accordingly. It's also a natural icebreaker

Games People Play

Games are great for bringing people together and upping the laugh quotient. Here are our top four picks:

Charades: Give each guest three slips of paper to write down three things that are characteristic of the bride-to-be or couple, like "Sailing," "Tandoori chicken," or "Fuzzy car dice," and let the good times roll by taking turns acting them out. (The correct guesser is the next one up.)

The To-Be-Wed Game: This riff on the popular TV game show will make the guests-of-honor blush, giggle, and laugh out loud. Split the soon-to-bes up and have them answer questions about each other—tap into close friends' and families' knowledge of the twosome when writing questions—and see if their respective answers mesh. Be prepared: It's only fair for the happy couple to put *other* couples on the spot after they've been through the ringer. For a bridal shower, get the groom's answers to the questions before the party and then put the bride on the spot.

Wedding Scattergories: Make up game cards using about eight wedding-related categories, such as Flower, Party Song, Site, and Honeymoon Destination. Put all the letters of the alphabet into a hat, draw one letter each round, and take a minute to fill in the categories with words that begin with that letter. (An hourglass would be perfect here.) For the letter D, for example, guests could write: Daisies; Disco Inferno (Burn, Baby, Burn); Dance Hall; and Disney World. Players get 1 point for every category filled appropriately (no newlyweds in history have honeymooned in Detroit) and 3 for an answer so original that no one else wrote it down.

Roast 'em: A couple's shower is a good opportunity to host a raunchy-but-friendly roast of the soon-to-be-weds in the company of their closest friends. Prepare strips of paper with situations in the couple's life together as well as those that *might* arise, such as "Jane tells John she can't go to the play with him because she made plans to play darts with the girls," or "Jane and John argue about baby names." Put John and Jane in front-row seats (with a nice bottle of wine to dull the pain) and have guests come up in twos, draw a slip, read it out loud, and then act out the scene. John and Jane get score cards—from 0 to 10—with which they will rate the accuracy of each skit after the curtain comes down.

when bringing together people who don't know each other well, because you'll all feel complicit in the outrageousness/goofiness/fabulousness.

An added bonus of a theme is that it makes the shower host(ess)'s life easier. He or she can delegate with less fear of screw-ups, since once friends hear the theme, they'll have a firm grasp on the party vision. Guests also benefit; gift-shopping is easier when there's a guiding principle.

If you're sold on the theme approach (and of course there are tons of fantastic *un*themed showers, so no pressure!), go hunting for a suitable one. Good starting points are the bride or couple's nationalities, honeymoon destination, occupation, or favorite leisure-time activities. Whatever the theme, it can be conducive to partying—for example, Disco Nights, Toga Trysts, Flapper Follies, Diner Days . . . but whatever the theme, make it run through all the party elements—from the invitations, food, and decor, to the gifts, music, and activities. More ideas:

Art: Invites on famous-painting postcards; art opening–like hors d'oeuvres (shrimp skewers, pâté on crackers, olives); jazz music; play Pictionary; give an easel or a subscription to a local museum as gifts.

High-School Sleepover: Girls only; boys are icky! Teddy-bear invites; junk food; '70s or '80s pop rock; Truth or Dare; give a certificate for a facial, rollerskates, or a party "outfit" as gifts.

This Is Your Life: Make a photo-montage invite; serve the guest(s) of honor's favorite foods; play their fave tunes; invite "mystery" guests from their pasts *(no* exes); show home videos and have people reminisce; gifts include a Polaroid camera, plane tickets to their first vacation spot, and compilation CDs.

Around the World: Globe invites; a spread of different "ethnic" foods; a mix of world music; Trivial Pursuit—just history and geography categories; gifts from around the world *or* a group gift of a getaway to a foreign country.

Twelve Months: Calendar invites; one dish from each season; Vivaldi's "Four Seasons"; the board game Life; assign each guest a month and ask them to get a related gift.

Stock the Bar: A martini-shaped invite for a late-evening shower; couples or girls only; retro cocktail music from the classic crooners; gifts include everything you need for future entertaining like glassware, wine rack, cocktail shaker, serving trays.

Around-the-Clock: Sun- or moon-shaped invites; each guest is assigned a time of day and brings a present that relates to the hour. For example: 6 A.M.—a coffeemaker, a juicer, an alarm clock, the tried-and-true toaster; noon—double showerhead, a series of yoga or fitness classes, manicure/pedicure passes, a comfy chair; 6 P.M.—dinner china, an Asian-inspired cookbook, or wine gear; 7 P.M.—movie or theater passes, a popcorn popper, or Web TV; 9 P.M.—fluffy towels, cuddly robes, an electric toothbrush; 11 P.M.—lingerie, linens, pillows, body massager.

Inventive Bridal Shower Gifts

They might not be on the registry, but that's what makes them more fun.

1. Stack of DVDs, popcorn, oversize candy—all in a big popcorn bowl
2. Gift certificate for ten yoga classes for prewedding stress reduction
3. Plush robe and a basket of home spa treatments
4. Three-year magazine subscription to a home magazine
5. Wine of the Month (or flower, or fruit, etc.) for a year
6. Scrapbook/photo album of your exploits together through the years
7. Games—from board games to video games
8. Airline miles
9. A commissioned portrait of the couple
10. A hand-knit blanket for snuggling

Bachelor/ette Bashes

In a way, the notorious bachelor party is the guys' version of the bridal shower. It's men only—the best man hosts, with the rest of the groomsmen, close male friends, and sometimes relatives on the guest list. (The bride's bros and buddies may come along, too.) It happens before the wedding (used to be the night before, but then some genius figured out hangovers and wedding days don't mix that well).

However, these two proud prewedding traditions differ on one essential point—and therein lies the problem. Whereas the girls' event usually is geared toward celebrating the bride's entrance into the wonderful world of marriage, the guys' party often focuses on giving the groom one last taste of "freedom" (read: $20 lap dances, tequila shots, and drunken antics), as if marriage were a punishment.

We don't need to tell you that the historical bachelor party—and the underlying ball-and-chain message—has been the source of friction in many a to-be-wed relationship. But we are here to offer two great solutions to the bachelor-party blues that should prove more effective than the usual: "Honey, I'm just not comfortable envisioning you with some scantily clad stranger gyrating on your lap." "But honey, I just wanna chill with the boys. Don't you trust me?"

The Bachelor Party: Good-bye Sleaze, Hello Creativity

Let's face it: Getting drunk at a strip club is not, how shall we say, the most *original* form of entertainment. Our favorite bachelor parties do not resemble the movies *Showgirls* or *Animal House.* They're studies in alternative thinking, outdoorsiness, and old-fashioned guyness instead. Come to think of it, these are all great bachelorette options, too. Consider these more creative (and more fun) options:

Surf and Turf: A day at an upscale gym or spa—relaxing in the pool and hot tub and on the massage table—followed by a visit to an A-list steakhouse.

Go Wild: White-water rafting, cross-country skiing, mountain biking, fishing, or camping with the boys for a long weekend.

ASK CARLEY

Who Plans the Bash?

Q: My best man and brother-in-law are putting together a bachelor party for me. Can I add my two cents? Am I supposed to be helping?

A: Yes—and no. While there aren't many etiquette rules about planning a bachelor party (after all, we're talking about an event that could take you anywhere from Hooters to a Hootie and the Blowfish concert), we suggest you take this opportunity to chill. (You won't have that many opportunities to just hang in the days before your knock-out nuptials.) Let your buddy and brother-in-law do most of the dirty work, but do get involved in the guest list. Clue the host(s) in to who would kill your mellow mood (testy relatives, overly obnoxious frat brothers, pompous coworkers). Your special night/weekend/week with the boys is too important to leave the human element to chance.

Show Him the Money: Forty-eight hours in Vegas or your favorite neighborhood casino.

Beach Bums: Volleyball, cold brews, sun, surfing, and harmless bikini-watching. Need we say more?

Extreme Pleasure: A group skydive or bungee-jumping session followed by a feast and lots o' cocktails.

ESPN Fun: Choice seats at a major sports event—or a grueling trip to the racetrack, bowling alley, or pool hall—and a hearty barbecue dinner.

Swingers: Eighteen holes or, preferably, a three-round weekend retreat. Get a Keg Caddie.

Puffers: A night at your favorite cigar bar—martinis, single-malt whiskey, and beef sold separately.

The Bachelorette Party: Evening the Score

If your honey and his crew just *gotta* go out for one last look at some T&A, we say two can play at this game—and should. If it's really that important for the groom to have that one last free-falling sleaze-fest, the bride should get one, too—but hers will be a "night out with the girls." Bridesmaids and/or girlfriends should plan the bachelorette party for the exact same night. Let the ladies don their skimpiest skirts and tightest tops (or coolest clubbing ensembles) and head for the all-nude male revue (or the bride's favorite place to dance the night away). Not only will dual parties help diffuse any feeling of one-sidedness, but they'll also greatly reduce morning-after friction. (It's pretty hard for the bride to chide the groom about staying out till dawn and smelling like a vodka refinery if they're both in exactly the same boat.)

Rules of the Game

Before you set out in a rented limo stocked with Riunite, take a look at our Rules of the Bachelor/ette Party Game:

The groom should . . .

- Talk to the best man in advance about how you'd like to limit the evening's raunch factor, giving specific examples of where to draw the line (nudie bars? strip-o-grams? mud wrestling? Swedish videos?).
- Shield your honey from guy friends' attacks. If they think she's the reason your bachelor bash is PG-13, set the record straight. Your future will be rosier if your pals treat your beloved with R-E-S-P-E-C-T.
- Ask the party host to let your honey in on his plans. Being in the know will put her mind at ease. Who knows? Maybe she can even contribute something to the bash—a raunchy audiotape saying what she's going to do to you come wedding night, perhaps?
- On the night of your bash, refuse to take part in anything that will make you uncomfortable (or will leave you with a grand secret to keep from your fiancée). But don't throw a public temper tantrum. Just graciously bow out.

- Reassure your honey when she expresses her fears; this isn't a good time to practice your eye-rolling skills.

The bride should . . .

- Chat with the hostess(es) about what craziness is thumbs-up and what's a no-go. Maybe you're just not into Chippendale's—maybe you'd rather go to a movie and then your favorite tapas bar.
- Ask the party planners not to invite anyone who has serious problems with your honey. You only want to party with people who think he's hot stuff!
- Excuse yourself elegantly from any debauchery that makes you uneasy. They're yelling for all the boys in the bar to French-kiss you; tell them you'd rather have some innocent pecks on the cheek.
- If he's getting queasy at the thought of turning you loose, ask your maid of honor to call your honey up and assure him there will be no wet-boxer contests involved. (It's nice to know he's worried, though, isn't it?)

Alternative Bachelorette Ideas

- Day-spa getaway
- Sailing jaunt
- All-night disco-hopping
- Comedy club
- Ski weekend
- Group scuba-diving lessons at a beach resort
- Salsa bar
- Helicopter ride
- Night of karaoke
- Concert
- Day hike

The Rehearsal Dinner

The rehearsal dinner is more than the kickoff to a huge celebration. For you, it's an opportunity to spend time with your nearest and dearest and give thanks for their support and help throughout the wedding-planning process. For your guests, it's a chance to bond over food, drinks, toasts, and roasts. And any way you throw it, the rehearsal dinner is another place to have fun and let your personalities shine through.

Who Comes

One of the toughest decisions when planning the rehearsal dinner is just how inclusive to make it. On the one hand, it's an opportunity to have an intimate gathering and a chance for both of your families to get to know one another better. On the other, it's a great excuse to have more face time with all of your friends and family.

Though rehearsal dinners often tend to be on the small side, you can certainly invite everyone, especially if you're having a modest-sized wedding. In general, the rehearsal dinner is definitely growing in size and scope as couples invite more friends and family. If you're keeping the guest list small, you'll want to simply include your immediate families (parents and siblings), members of the wedding party and their partners, the parents of any child attendants, and your officiant. It's also a nice gesture to invite guests who have traveled from out of town. For a small rehearsal dinner—under ten guests—word of mouth should suffice; if you're asking the whole gang, you should send out invitations.

Out-of-Towner Time

Schedule a welcome cocktail party or brunch if out-of-town guests are not invited to the rehearsal dinner. They're investing time and money to attend your wedding; the least you can do is make them feel included in the surrounding festivities. You'll also be giving them a chance to unwind from their trip and make it possible for them to get acquainted with some of the people they'll whoop it up with at the wedding. Ask a close friend or family member to host this soiree.

When to Have It

Ordinarily the rehearsal dinner is held the night before the wedding. It's long been a tradition that after the ceremony rehearsal, you, your parents, and your wedding party gather for a meal. But since the rehearsal dinner has become more of a celebration in its own right than just a formality, some couples are going really nontraditional and holding the event two nights prior. This way, there's more time to relax, recuperate, and get ready for the big day. For a Saturday wedding, a Thursday-night rehearsal dinner could also mean striking a better deal with a caterer or restaurant.

How to Plan It

Since the rehearsal dinner is more informal than the wedding reception, the food and atmosphere should reflect that. The goal here is to relieve some of the prewedding tension and make everyone invited comfortable with the impending nuptials, while still not usurping the big event the next day. While it might be the norm, there's no reason to feel hemmed in to a sit-down dinner. In fact, you can use the term "dinner" loosely. Work with the season or location of your wedding or your own heritage. However you organize the soiree, put your personal stamp on things. Use these ideas as launching pads:

Seasonal: Having a mid-winter wedding? Then invite guests to a ski lodge with a giant fireplace. Or if your aunt has a house with a rustic vibe, hold the gathering there. Decorate with snow lanterns, white holiday lights, and luminaries. Serve up thick soups and sandwiches and hot toddies.

Or if, like most couples, you're having a summer celebration, fire up the grill for an old-fashioned cookout. Serve unfussy grilled chicken and veggies and sliced watermelon for dessert. Hire an acoustic guitarist, and then sing and swap toasts around a bonfire.

Regional: Celebrate your roots, or show guests from home what's so great about where you've invited them. Tying the knot in New England? Treat guests to a classic clambake with chowder, lobster, mussels, and potatoes. Host it on the beach so you can build sand castles and toss a Frisbee.

Deep in the heart of Texas you might consider a classic barbecue. Some famous chefs we know have been doing lots of outdoor barbecues, offering up a mouth-watering menu that includes short ribs, kettle-baked beans, and homemade barbecue potato chips.

Ethnic: If you're from the Middle East, put on a nice spread in honor of your heritage. Break out the kebabs, couscous, and dolmas. Hire a belly dancer or henna tattoo artist. If your family is Chinese, host a giant dim sum brunch or traditional Chinese banquet.

Activities: You don't have to let food be the only guide to creating a memorable rehearsal dinner. Bring your sporty side to life with a party centered on a Wiffle-ball or kickball game. Divide the sides into "Bride" and "Groom" and put a keg of beer on second base—to encourage good batting, of course! Serve up hot dogs on the sidelines and finish the game with high-fives, whichever side wins.

If you're movie buffs or simply want to share old family footage, hold a movie night. Show home movies of you and your fiancé as cute little kids, and sit back with lots of pizza and popcorn.

In the end, the rehearsal dinner can be as loose or as formal as you want. But remember:

You don't want it to upstage the main event. The wedding should be the climax of the weekend; the rehearsal serves to whet guests' appetities. Besides, with all the stress of the weekend's activities, isn't it good to know there's one event that's meant to be completely mellow and easy?

ERRON & SCOTT

July 5, Moraga, California

OVER HALF OF THE GUESTS who attended Erron and Scott's wedding in Moraga were from out of state. There were large family contingents from Florida and from Texas; and a junior high school pal of Erron's arrived at the wedding directly from a year in Tanzania. One aunt, who is afraid to fly, spent three days (each way) on trains and buses to make it to the wedding.

Erron and Scott knew they needed to show such a loving and dedicated group of guests a good time, so they planned their celebration for the long Fourth of July weekend. The Golden Gate Bridge became a sort of wedding motif, with shades of yellow, red, and orange chosen to complement the bridge's coppery paint. The couple decided to kick off the wedding weekend with a Fourth of July barbecue in Golden Gate Park. Luckily, the weather cooperated—it was a crystal-clear, 70-degree evening—and by the time the last pyrotechnic blaze had faded, guests who had never met before had become as comfortable as old friends.

Ask Erron about the very best moment of her wedding day and her answer is decisive: "Seeing so many people who we love and who live in such disparate places getting along and having a great time."

The Parties You Throw

You may end up throwing a few bashes yourselves—attendants' get-togethers, working parties, a night-before chill-out, a morning-after breakfast. These informal get-togethers are optional, so don't feel obligated. But they're fun—and helpful, too.

Attendants' Parties

It's just plain-old good manners to celebrate your closest friends' and relatives' willingness to don those dresses and tuxes, keep the peace at the punch bowl, and dance with your single cousins at the reception. All you have to do is gather your wedding party in a hotel suite or your living room a few nights before the wedding (depending on when people are getting into town), drink a little bubbly, listen to some good music, and chat. You may opt to give your happy helpers their personalized presents in this intimate setting rather than at the rehearsal dinner.

Working Parties

A great way to tackle wedding-related tasks (like licking envelopes and preparing favors) without making your pals feel put-upon is to create a party out of the work. Don't get stuck in the gender trap; men are just as capable of test-tasting cheese puffs or preparing place cards as women are!

The Morning-After Breakfast

You and your honey may be in the clouds (literally) soon after your reception wraps up. But if you're not flying (or driving or sailing) away to your honeymoon right away, we think it's a great idea to gather your closest friends and family members—as well as out-of-town guests who made a colossal effort to come party with you—for one last wedding-related bash the morning after your big to-do.

Anyone can host this get-together (be it an adoring neighbor, an eager uncle, or a gracious friend), so definitely accept any offers—you'll have one less thing to worry about while you're trying to close that suitcase and dashing to the drugstore to buy sunscreen. You may, however, decide to do the honors yourselves, with or without the help of your ace parents, as one last thank-you to your excellent guests. It's also a chance to reminisce about last night's follies, talk about your plans for the future, divulge your honeymoon itinerary, and be up-close and personal.

Keep this party decidedly low key; it's an opportunity to talk and snack with your loved ones in an intimate, completely relaxed (finally!) setting. A buffet breakfast or brunch laid out in a living room is a perfect idea (have a nearby deli cater it), or invite everyone to the best little pancake house in town, where you've arranged for a mega-long table and pitchers and pitchers of maple syrup. You also could take the party outside, gathering in a public park for a cheese, crackers, and fruit picnic or even a noontime franks-and-burgers barbecue.

The Breakfast Club

Prewedding breakfasts/brunches are becoming a trend now that so many guests are coming from so many different places and making a two- or three-day deal out of weddings. A close relative or friend may offer to host this morning fiesta, or you, your honor attendant, or your parents can organize it. If you're feeling too stressed/overwhelmed/crazed/to attend, just make a quick appearance.

CHAPTER SIX

standing on ceremony

The ceremony *is* the wedding. It's the big event, that thrilling moment when the two of you stand face to face and share your most intimate, profound feelings for each other while your closest friends and family members look on. If anything from your wedding day is going to be permanently imprinted on your brains, it's bound to be the moment you look into each other's eyes and exchange your vows. Your ceremony is about who the two of you are, together. If you have to make small compromises on the reception, okay. But don't compromise on your ceremony (except with your sweetie, of course).

Religious vs. Civil Ceremonies

Religious or civil? That is the question. And it's one of the most important questions you'll ask yourselves during the ceremony-planning process. The answer will help determine who officiates, where you'll have it, and what elements you'll include. It may already be clear to you (a given, really) which way you two will go, but if not, read on.

Using Your Religion

While a civil ceremony is all that you *need* to be legally married, many people want their church (or congregation) to recognize their marriage, too.

What It Involves: A religious ceremony is officiated by a religious official and incorporates the wedding customs, traditions, and rules of that faith, along with the state's legal requirements. The wedding can be short and sweet or long and lavish, although it generally follows a specific format prescribed by the religion. The precise elements may depend on the branch and (sometimes) congregation.

A religious service can be held in a church, temple, mosque, or meeting room. Some clergy will officiate at nonreligious sites. You usually can wear whatever you like, although certain houses of worship may have restrictions against anything too revealing. (You'd simply wear a stole or shawl over your sleeveless dress.) You'll have several sessions of prewedding counseling with your officiant—a great time to talk about any wedding or relationship concerns. For more info on your religion's requirements, see "Religious Ceremony Specifics," later in the chapter.

Who Does It: If you're part of a religious congregation and your honey is of the same faith or a compatible one, you'll likely want to go religious. Even if you're not a member of a specific church or temple, you still may feel a strong spiritual or cultural connection to your faith. If your honey shares your feelings (or isn't opposed to them), you may decide on a religious ceremony. If your parents are very religious, you may go this route to show respect for them. Similarly, if you've been meaning to get back to religion, hope to raise your children with it, or want religion to be an important part of your married life, you may choose to make your ceremony the first step. If one of you plans to convert to the other's religion, the ceremony can be a great time to begin involvement with the new faith. If you plan to keep your separate faiths, you may want to create an interfaith ceremony as the first of a lifetime of blending rituals.

If you believe in God or some other spiritual force but not in organized religion, you may want to find an alternative, nondenominational clergy member (a Unitarian minister, for example). Look for someone who understands your religious sentiments, or a faith that is open to your beliefs.

Let's Be Civil

A civil ceremony isn't necessarily a drive-through Vegas-style affair. It can be a full production with attendants, rituals, and plenty of parental weeping. "Civil" merely means in accordance with the state's laws rather than in the eyes of the church or temple.

What It Involves: A civil ceremony is officiated by a legal official—a judge, magistrate, justice of the peace, county or court clerk, mayor, or notary public (not the *Love Boat*'s Captain Steubing, or any other boat captain, unless he also holds one of the above civil titles). The exact requirements vary state to state (and even county to county) but generally include a charge to the couple ("Do you, Tracy, take Todd to be your lawfully wedded husband . . ."), a ring exchange, and the pronouncement of marriage by the officiant.

After that, it's pretty much free-style. You can hold your service anywhere (providing your officiant agrees to come). And you can dress as you please—whether it's in white taffeta or blue jeans (unless your officiant requires something more formal). Call your county's marriage license bureau for the lowdown on the civil process in your area.

Who Does It: If neither of you is religious, or you're uncomfortable with the idea of a religious ceremony (and you're getting no profound opposition from your parents), you'll likely want to take the civil route. If your ideal ceremony is too creative for your clergy, you may go civil style, too. If you've both got religion, but not the same one, you may take the civil route to sidestep the interfaith headache. While some religious officials will tailor a service to include beliefs of both partners, others may refuse to do so, making that judge friend of yours an increasingly attractive option. (See "Interfaith Ceremonies," later in the chapter, for more.) Similarly, if this is a second wedding for one or both of you, you may take the civil path to avoid the obstacles your religion may present.

Other reasons you might choose a civil ceremony: Your dream wedding is a slip-out-and-do-it-during-lunch affair; you want to get married at an alternative venue (Jamaica, the top of the Empire State Building) and your religious official won't make the trip; you want to get married next Tuesday.

Reworking the Wording

The basic civil ceremony in the United States generally follows the wording from the Episcopalian *Book of Common Prayer* ("Dearly beloved, we are gathered here today . . ."). Many officiants use their own adaptation. Ask to see what your civil officiant plans to use and then see if you can adapt it to reflect your unique styles.

Finding Your Officiant

Once you decide what kind of ceremony to have, it's time to figure out who's going to officiate. This person will be more than just the ceremony director; he or she is the conductor of your wedding, spiritual or otherwise. All of the following guidelines apply for a civil or religious officiant.

What to Look For

Look for an officiant who understands you, your relationship, and your ceremony priorities. The officiant plays a *huge* part in shaping the ceremony; make sure he or she is open to any plans you have for writing your own vows or incorporating unique elements and ethnic traditions. If your potential officiant is inflexible, dismisses all your great ideas, or simply seems uninterested, keep looking.

If you know who you'd like to officiate, call and ask if s/he's available on your planned date (or on one of your alternate dates), then set up an initial meeting to discuss details.

Where to Look

If your ideal officiant is booked, or if you don't have one in mind, where do you find a fabulous officiant?

- Ask friends and family for recommendations.
- Call your city hall or the marriage license bureau for civil referrals.
- Ask consultants and other wedding professionals.
- Consider reconnecting with a childhood or college church, synagogue, or clergy member.
- Get married in the church or synagogue your parents belong to.
- Call that beautiful church or temple you love to drive by, and ask to make an appointment with a clergy member. Some churches may require you to join before hosting your wedding, while others will marry nonmembers or rent their spaces.

Talking to Potential Officiants

When you meet with an officiant, you'll discuss your wedding plans, find out if the officiant is open to your ideas, ask about the requirements, and decide if the three of you want to work on this wedding together. If s/he's clergy, don't say you just *love* the site and could take or leave the religion. You should be intrigued by more than just the architecture.

First Conversation

- Is the officiant available on your date?
- What documents should you bring to the first meeting?
- Are there any special rules or restrictions?
- Is the officiant open to personalized vows, readings, poems, or music?
- Will the officiant give a sermon or speech?

- What kind of prewedding counseling is required, if any?
- What is the ceremony fee?

The Do-It-Yourself Officiant

Convinced the therapist who saved your (spiritual) life should officiate at your wedding? Or maybe the friend who fixed you up? Ask that special person to be a legal officiant; he or she can become a minister by going to the California-based Universal Life Church at www.ulc.org and filling out a form. Call the marriage license bureau where you will get your license to make sure they will honor such an ordainment.

- Can you tour the sanctuary/ceremony room? (Check seating capacity, number of aisles, general layout; wheelchair accessibility, if that's a concern.)
- What does the church/temple/site provide and what would you provide yourselves (pew ribbons, runner, flowers, candles)?
- Are there any specific restrictions on the type of music you can play or on the readings?
- Will the officiant give you input on your vows and proposed readings?
- Will you have input on the sermon and/or hear it beforehand?
- Is there a dress code?
- Can the officiant help you deal with family conflicts connected to the ceremony?
- Do you bring your marriage license to the ceremony or will you all sign it together before the wedding?
- Can you have a videographer/photographer in the sanctuary/ceremony room?
- When would the rehearsal be?
- Would the officiant (and his/her spouse) like to come to the reception/rehearsal dinner?
- Would s/he play a role there (giving a blessing, etc.)?

Ceremony Basics

Before you begin cooking up the ceremony of the century, take a look at the ingredients. Whether your service is civil or religious, it will follow this general outline—a civil officiant will simply omit the religious rituals. Each state, religion, and sometimes congregation has its own approach. You'll probably start with your officiant's basic structure and then add custom details.

- Procession
- Officiant's opening remarks
- Charge to couple: ("Do you, James, take Ashley to be your lawfully wedded . . . ?")
- Vows
- Ring exchange and any other unity gestures
- Pronouncement (The "I now pronounce you . . ." part)
- The kiss (finally!)
- The officiant's closing remarks and final blessing
- Recession

Prewedding Counseling: What's Involved?

Generally, if you choose a religious officiant, you'll have about three sessions of counseling before the wedding. We asked two officiants to describe what happens.

"Couples should come prepared to discuss themselves, their feelings about their religion, and what marriage means to them. I might ask how they met, how the subject of marriage came up, whether or not their families support them in their decision to marry, even why they want to get married at all. I want to find out how the couple communicates. I want to see if they're talking about a marriage or a wedding day."

—Reverend Richard G. Francesco, a Catholic priest
and administrator of St. Benedict's Church, Newark, New Jersey

"The first meeting is usually all the logistics—date, time, and so forth. During the second meeting, I want to get to know the couple better. I ask how they deal with money issues, and sex, and how well they know each other. I ask what Judaism means to them, and what kind of Jewish home they want to create. I want them to open up to each other and be aware of issues they need to work on as a couple. During those first two meetings, I'll also discuss the details—for example, I'll ask if they're writing their vows and what kind of Ketubah they will have."

—Rabbi Judy Schindler,
Westchester Reform Temple, Scarsdale, New York

Now let's take a more detailed look at each part to help you get familiar with what a ceremony entails.

The Procession

The procession is like a flowchart of what's about to happen. You and your beloved each make your way to the altar separately, symbolizing the fact that you're coming from different backgrounds and families. You meet at the altar or stage and move closer to each other throughout the ceremony (holding hands, exchanging rings, planting the kiss), representing the merging of your lives into one new unit.

The doors of the church, synagogue, or Hyatt Grand Ballroom are thrown open, and your wedding party marches down the aisle. In a traditional Christian procession, the bride is escorted by her father; the groom waits for her up front. In a traditional Jewish procession, both parents escort both the bride and the groom. Or you can choose your escort based on your situation. If you're close to both your parents, it's fine to make the march a *pas-de-trois* (both parents) regardless of your religion. If your mother and stepfather raised you, you could acknowledge their support (emotional and otherwise) by walking with them. If your aunt raised you and is your closest confidante, ask her to be at your side. If you feel you've arrived at this moment on your own, you may want to go it alone.

Officiant Finances

The officiant fee probably won't make much of a dent in your wedding budget, but it's still something to factor in. Fees range from free to $800, depending on the congregation and/or individual officiant.

Also, make sure to thank your officiant, pay him or her (even if s/he accepts donation only; add a little extra to show your gratitude), and invite him/or her to your reception. (S/he may not come, but s/he'll appreciate the gesture.)

Who heads down the aisle when? If you're having a civil ceremony, you can improvise, or you might choose to follow the order of religious processions. Here are the basic plans:

Christian Procession

Aisle Runner Reasoning

The aisle runner, traditionally red or white, was believed to protect the couple from evil spirits lurking in the floorboards. A red runner also connotes a sense of honor (like rolling out the red carpet), while a white runner represents a pure pathway.

The officiant, groom, and best man wait up at the altar for the:

- Groomsmen (who walk in from the side or accompanying bridesmaids; also may wait at the altar with the other men)
- Bridesmaids (starting with the attendant who will stand farthest from the bride at the altar)
- Ring bearer and/or flower girl (child attendants can be seated with their parents once they reach the front)
- Honor attendant(s)
- The bride, walking to the left of her escort

Jewish Procession

- Rabbi and/or cantor
- Grandparents of the groom
- Grandparents of the bride (the grandparents are seated in the first rows; groom's on the left, bride's on the right)
- Groomsmen (in pairs)
- Best man
- The groom and his parents (dad on his left, mom on right)
- The bridesmaids (starting with the one who will stand farthest from the bride under the huppah)
- Honor attendant(s)
- Ring bearer and/or flower girl
- The bride and her parents (dad on left, mom on right)

The Officiant's Opening Remarks

Once you're up at the altar, the officiant calls things to order—welcoming the guests (and acknowledging God, if it's a religious ceremony). You've heard it a hundred times in the movies: "Dearly beloved, we are gathered here today . . ." By including your guests, the introduction reminds them that they are sharing this important event with you, acting as witnesses to it, and agreeing to support your marriage. The call to God is there to remind you and everyone else of the seriousness and solemnity of marriage, and to make this ceremony, and your marriage, holy. It gives you a minute to recognize that you're getting married not only in front of your friends and family but also before the Almighty One.

Charge to the Couple: Saying "I Do"

The "Do you, Mary, take John to be your lawfully wedded husband?" part, to which you each respond "I do" or "I will," verifies that you're marrying of your own free will. (This isn't an official part of a Jewish ceremony, though some rabbis will include it.)

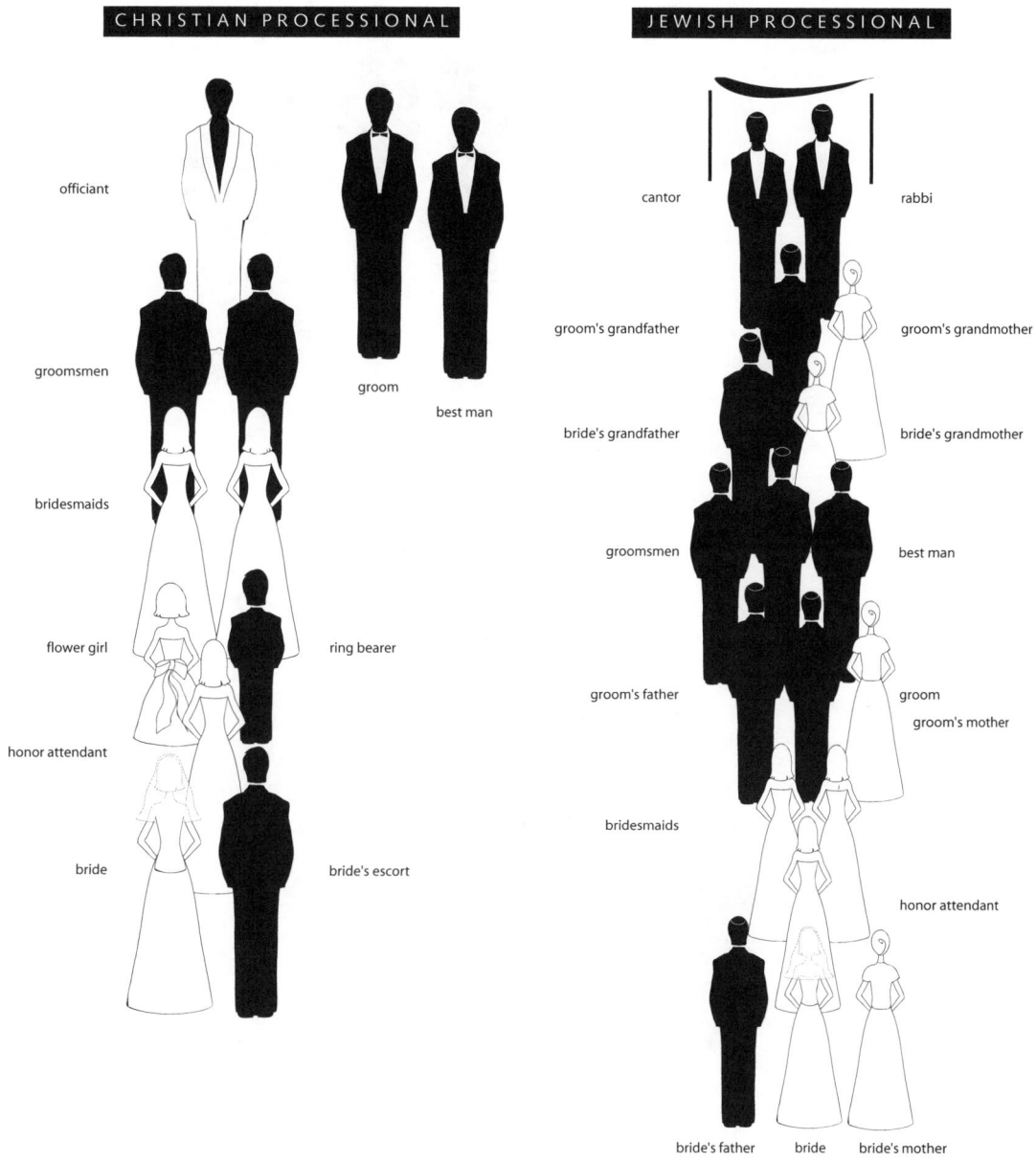

You need a license to wed. Go to Chapter 21 for marriage license how-tos.

CHRISTIAN CEREMONY POSITIONS

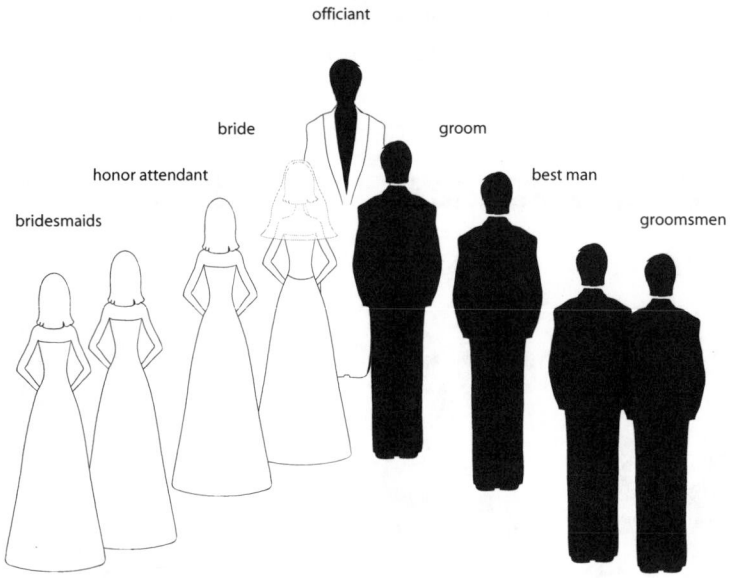

JEWISH CEREMONY POSITIONS

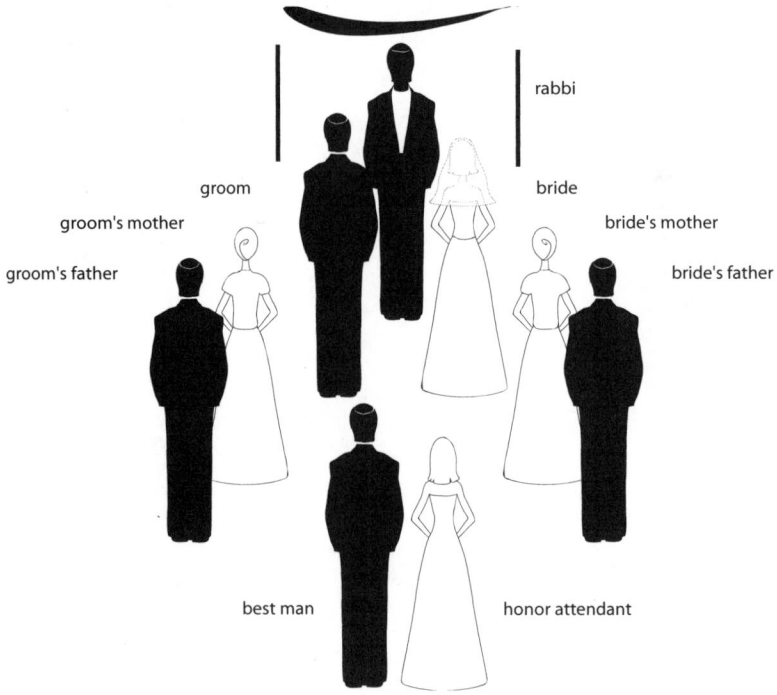

Take a Seat: Who Sits Where?

As a rule, the closer the person is to you emotionally, the nearer he or she sits to the action, and the later he or she takes a seat:

First and second rows: Immediate family, parents, siblings, grandparents
Third through fifth rows: Aunts, uncles, cousins, and godparents; stepfamily; other special guests

In Christian ceremonies, the bride's mother is *always* the last person to be seated (right after the groom's mother), signifying that the ceremony is about to begin.

Generally, in Christian ceremonies, the bride's family and guests sit on the left (when entering from the back) and the groom's side takes over the right. For Jewish services, it's reversed. A mixed marriage? Either choose a system that works for you, or make it a free-for-all. If you've invited 120 people, and your honey has, well . . . Mom and Dad, *don't* divide by family. Have your ushers direct people to the best seats available to create a balance.

Traditionally, an usher offers his right arm to a female guest, while her male escort follows them down the aisle. If that seems too formal for your crowd, the ushers can merely greet guests at the door and say, "Please follow me," or "Hello. Right this way." Plan to have one usher for every fifty guests to keep things flowing. Who's an usher? A groomsman on double duty, your teenage cousins, or good friends.

Altar Arrangements: Who Stands Where?

There isn't *one* correct altar arrangement, but several options from which to choose. Or design your own with your officiant. Here are the details on the traditional line-up.

Bride and groom: Traditionally, the bride stands on the left (with her back to the congregation), with her groom to the right (in a Jewish ceremony, this is reversed).

Attendants: Attendants generally divide by the sexes (ushers to the groom's side, bridesmaids to the bride's), or walk and stand in pairs (one usher/bridesmaid pair to the right, the next to the left, etc.). They either line up diagonally behind the spot where you'll stand or form a big semicircle around you. If you take the couple's approach, each usher/bridesmaid pair remains together in the line, or the bridesmaids stand on a step behind their escorts. In a Jewish wedding, your attendants stand under the huppah with you, honor attendants one diagonal step behind you, other attendants behind them.

Parents: Your parents' places depend on how much you want to include them in your ceremony. If both your parents walk both of you down the aisle, all four might remain standing with you for the entire service (as in a Jewish ceremony, where the parents remain under the huppah, on either side of the rabbi). Traditionally, if the bride's father walks her down the aisle, he either leaves her at the altar with her groom or remains standing between them until the officiant asks "Who supports this woman in marriage?" at which time he gives his blessing and takes his seat in the front pew with the bride's mother (as in a Protestant or Catholic service). The groom's parents traditionally sit in the front pew throughout a Christian ceremony. But again, if you prefer family closeness over tradition, they can stand with you.

Kids: Include pint-size attendants in the altar line-up only if they're old enough to stand still comfortably for the duration of your ceremony. Otherwise, stand them behind you, in front of your older attendants, or have them sit with their parents.

Readers/performers: They rise to do their bit, then retake their seat.

ASK CARLEY

With Whom Should I Walk?

Q. Whom should I have walk me down the aisle? I'm close to my mom, dad, and my stepdad.

A: If everyone gets along and they all agree to it, why not walk with all three (your dad on one side, your mom and stepdad on the other)? Or start out with Dad and do a parental hand-off halfway down the aisle, finishing with Mom and Stepdad. Just make sure you and your folks are comfortable with the format—and that the aisle is wide enough!

The Exchange of Vows

Your vows are your promises to each other—a statement of your intentions and expectations for your marriage. You may choose to use the familiar "To have and to hold, for better or for worse" vows; repeating words that have been worn smooth through years of use gives some couples a sense of permanence, a bigger-than-both-of-us feeling. Or you might decide to write your own vows. Make sure they express what's unique about your relationship and what you want your future together to be like. Some couples read prose or poetry passages that are meaningful to them. If you take the personalized approach, you'll probably need to run your plans by your officiant. S/he may check to make sure your vows clearly define your views on marriage and address the commitment seriously. (See "Vows That Wow," later in the chapter, for more.)

Face each other when saying your vows, not the officiant. And hold hands. You're marrying each other, after all, not the guy or gal in the robe.

About Face

Consider facing your guests, with your officiant's back to the congregation instead of yours, while you say your vows. This will allow everyone a good view of the exchange and make them feel more a part of the moment.

The Ring Ceremony

As you exchange rings, you generally say "With this ring, I thee wed." You may add something a bit more personal about what the ring (and your sweetie) means to you.

The Pronouncement of Marriage

The officiant makes it official ("I now pronounce you husband and wife").

The Kiss

It doesn't have to be a quick peck on the cheek—go ahead and show some emotion! Give each other a good, tight hug. Make it last as long as you like. Try to fix that moment in your mind to remember it.

Kissing Comes From . . .

The final ceremony kiss is an ancient Roman tradition. Contracts were sealed with a kiss. It was also believed that when you kissed, you exchanged a bit of your soul with your breath.

Closing Remarks

Your officiant wraps up the wedding with a few words to you and a blessing, if it's a religious ceremony. If it's a Jewish wedding, the groom—and sometimes the bride, too—will step on a glass wrapped in a napkin. When the glass shatters, the crowd shouts "Mazel Tov!" meaning "Good Luck!"

Ring in the Wedding

You'll be sporting a shiny "occupied" sign on your ring finger for the rest of your lives. So choose wedding bands you like. Any kind of ring can be a wedding band, but consider your choice carefully—this is the ultimate symbol of your union. If you're both getting bands, they don't have to match (unless you want them to). You can get them engraved on the inside (with your initials, wedding date, mushy sentiment, private joke) at the same store where you buy them. Here's our guide to all things shiny:

24k: 100 percent gold
18k: 74 percent gold
14k: 58.5 percent gold
Yellow gold: The higher the gold percentage, the richer the color and the softer the band. If you're active, go with 14k rather than 24k—its alloys (those nongold additives) help make it stronger than the pure stuff.
White gold: Karat for karat, white gold is stronger than yellow gold, although it's more brittle. It looks like silver and is a good choice if you like the look better or if you're allergic to yellow gold.
Platinum: Stronger than gold and more expensive.

The Recession

You're done—it's time to party! Here's how to leave the ceremony and get to the reception on time.

The Christian Recession

After the ceremony, the wedding party retraces its steps, the men escorting the women back down the aisle in this order:

- Bride and groom
- Flower girl and ring bearer (optional)
- Honor attendants (maid/matron of honor and best man)
- Bridesmaids and groomsmen, in pairs

(Parents leave the pews directly after the wedding party recesses, followed by the congregation.)

The Jewish Recession

Again, the procession is essentially reversed:

- Bride and groom
- Bride's parents
- Groom's parents
- Ring bearer and flower girl (optional)
- Honor attendants (maid/matron of honor and best man)
- Bridesmaids and groomsmen
- Cantor and/or rabbi

Places, Please: The Rehearsal

How are you supposed to remember all this stuff? Practice, practice, practice—at the ceremony rehearsal.

Who: Everyone who has a part in the ceremony—you two, your parents, your attendants, ushers, readers, singers.

When: Generally, the night before the wedding, though you can do it two or three days in advance. No earlier, or everyone will forget their lines!

Where: At the ceremony site, so everyone can see where they're supposed to stand, etc. It's followed by a celebratory dinner.

Why: Not everyone has your stage presence and nerves of steel! The rehearsal helps all the participants calm down and study up.

What: Attendants find out their entry and exit order and practice walking. Your special performers learn where and when to do their thing. You two practice your aisle style, along with your folks and/or escorts. You'll all do a ceremony run-through; you won't say your full vows, but you will go over the exact order of elements and any cues that inspire actions such as rising, sitting, kissing, or exiting.

Ring Lore

Brides in ancient Rome wore wedding rings on their thumbs; Puritan couples didn't wear any because they were considered frivolous jewelry or "relics of popery." In Colonial times, people started giving "marriage thimbles" (useful, and therefore accepted). After the marriage, the bottom of the thimble would be cut off to create a ring.

Ceremonies with Personal Style

Most ceremonies have a similar structure, but you can personalize yours with vows, readings, songs, speeches, unity symbols, free-verse Beat poetry, or a surprise performance of spiritual music—whatever elements help express your thoughts and feelings about your marriage. Discuss your ideas with your officiant to make sure they don't conflict with the requirements of your religion, church, synagogue, or hall.

Vows That Wow

This is the most important promise you'll ever make, so it should definitely reflect your hearts, minds, and voices. But before you get carried away and start spilling your heart out on the page, do your homework. Check with your officiant to make sure that it's okay to pen your own vows: some religions do not allow for variations on traditional vows. Even if you've gotten the go-ahead, it is imperative that you pass the vows by him or her once you've finished. He or she may raise faith-based questions or objections to your wording, or contribute a thought or quote that might make your vows even more emotive.

Go Solo? Decide whether you will take on writing the vows together or alone. If you go solo, you may want to take turns running them by each other before the big day. Make sure that both have approximately the same length of text so that one person isn't rambling on for five minutes while the other says ten words. If you don't mind hiding a stash of tissues behind the altar, saving your tribute for the ceremony can often be extremely moving. If you choose to make it a joint task, pen a mutual vow that you both take. Either way, run your finished product by a trustworthy friend or family member with polished editing skills just to make sure.

Talk It Out: A vow-writing "date" is a great way to get started. Over a romantic dinner or breakfast in bed, discuss what marriage means to you. With pen in hand, dish with your fiancé about important events and turning points in your relationship: how you met, when you fell in love, when and how you said "I love you," any breakups (and makeups) you've endured. List the qualities you most admire in your loved one and characteristics that he or she brings out in you. Recognize your goals and don't be afraid to confront the challenges you envision. Most important, take this alone time to laugh, cry, and divulge what *marrying* really means to you. You might not use everything you come up with, but it will be one of the most romantic dates you've had yet.

Gathering Ideas

Do you have a scrapbook of love letters and poems, "your" songs, romantic literature, spiritual texts, and your favorite movie lines that capture your feelings? Borrow freely from what you've gathered, and have fun picking and choosing just the rights words—even if they're someone else's. When it comes to the heat of passion, plagiarism is not crime. One hint: Try to avoid clichés; use unique phrases to express your truly unique love.

Movie Moments: Park yourself down in front of the American Movie Classics network armed with a tub of popcorn and take note of lines from timeless classics such as *Casablanca, Pal Joey,* and *An American in Paris.*

Sentimental Songs: Throw on the songsters of love for some unforgettable lyrics to add to your collection. Check out Frank Sinatra, Billie Holiday, and Ella Fitzgerald. For you free-loving spirits, try Richie Havens, Paul Simon, Janis Joplin, James Taylor, or Carole King. For more contemporary staples, opt for Elton John, Sting, Billy Joel, or Sade. Head to your local sheet-music dealer and comb through volumes of lyrics by classic composers such as Cole Porter, Ira and George Gershwin, Stephen Sondheim, and Andrew Lloyd Webber.

Wonderful Words: Go back and take a look at your favorite authors' works, including your childhood favorites like Winnie the Pooh. His musings may be simple, but they are always sentimental: "If you live to be a hundred, I want to live to be a hundred minus one day, so I never have to live without you." Read up on your religion's traditional passages and incorporate them into your own promise, or use them as a catalyst to get your juices flowing.

How to Do It

Make your vows funny and warm, but not cryptic or embarrassing; they should reflect the magnitude of the commitment you are about to make. Your vows should not drag on and on. Be concise and get to the core of what marrying that person means to you. Eliminate any redundancies or extra words. Save some words for the toast, and the honeymoon night, of course. Remember, less is often times more.

Yes, your vows are for your honey, but they are also for an audience, so be sure they sound good when spoken. Practice out loud, alone, or with a trusted friend. Also, watch out for tongue twisters and unruly sentences (you may run out of breath—you'll be nervous enough as it is). Make your final edits and consider copying your words onto stationery or in a beautiful card, so that you and your sweetie will have it in print for years to come.

If you think you can memorize your vows, go for it! If you're likely to draw a blank, we're giving you permission to cheat: have a copy ready to read from or have the officiant read them for you to repeat. Tip: You probably won't want to pull them out from the corset of your gown, so assign your maid of honor and/or best man the duty of holding the vows until the moment arrives. Set aside one to two months to work on them and have the final version ready at least a week before the wedding.

Real Vows

Here are a few of our favorite vows from real couples who penned their own promises.

Gregory & Danielle

Groom:

I love you for your beauty, your intelligence, your kindness . . . and for the way you always know how to make me feel so special. So on top of all the other vows that I will make to you on our wedding day, I also vow to always appreciate how lucky I am to have someone who makes me feel the way you do and to continue to try as hard as I can to make you feel as special as you make me feel, forever and ever.

Bride:

You have been my best friend, mentor, playmate, confidant, and my greatest challenge. But most important, you are the love of my life and you make me happier than I could ever imagine and more loved than I ever thought possible. . . . You have made me a better person as our love for one another is reflected in the way I live my life. So I am truly blessed to be a part of your life, which as of today becomes our life together.

Alex & Michelle

Groom:

I promise to encourage your compassion,
Because that is what makes you unique and wonderful.
I promise to nurture your dreams,
Because through them your soul shines.
I promise to help shoulder our challenges,
For there is nothing we cannot face if we stand together.
I promise to be your partner in all things,
Not possessing you, but working with you as a part of the whole.
Lastly, I promise to you perfect love and perfect trust,
For one lifetime with you could never be enough.
This is my sacred vow to you, my equal in all things.

Bride:
I promise to encourage your individuality,
Because that is what makes you unique and wonderful.
I promise to nurture your dreams,
Because through them your soul shines.
I promise to help shoulder our challenges,
Because through them we'll emerge stronger,
I promise to be your partner in all things,
Not possessing you, but working with you as a part of the whole,
I promise to share with you the joys of life,
Because with you they will be that much sweeter,
Lastly, I promise to you perfect love and perfect trust,
For one lifetime with you could never be enough.
This is my sacred vow to you, my equal in all things.

Russell & Amy

Groom and Bride:
You are my lover and my teacher,
You are my model and my accomplice,
And you are my true counterpart.
I will love you, hold you, and honor you,
I will respect you, encourage you, and cherish you,
In health and sickness,
Through sorrow and success,
For all the days of my life.

The Wedding Program

Wedding programs make great souvenirs, but they're also a gracious gesture. They help guests understand the ceremony and introduce them to the major players in your wedding. They can also help coordinate your wedding motif or theme.

What to Include. Wedding party members' names (and their relationships to you two), a list of the ceremony's traditions, the names of musical selections (and musicians, if they are friends or relatives), and the titles of the readings (and names of the readers). If you're including wedding traditions or customs from a culture many guests might find unfamiliar, provide explanations in the program. If you're including African-American traditions, explain why you're jumping the broom. If Jewish traditions are incorporated, explain why you break the glass. If you're lighting a Unity Candle, discuss why you've chosen to do so and what it symbolizes. If you wish to honor the memory of a lost relative on your wedding day, your program is the place to do it. Reserve a page where you can tell guests what the person meant to you, and include a favorite memory of or a poem for the departed loved one. You can also honor and thank your parents and grandparents in your program. Remember, as always, brief is best. Guests should be able to read the program between the time they sit down and the time the ceremony starts, then refer back during the ceremony if necessary.

Getting It Done. You can provide information to your stationer and have him or her print it for you, or you can assemble the program on your own computer. The size and shape can vary from a rolled scroll tied with a ribbon to a multipage square sewn together. But if you want to make it easy on yourself, 8½ by 11 sheets folded lengthwise make a perfectly appropriate size. Use embellishments like cool papers, ribbons, or other motifs that fit with your overall wedding style.

How to Distribute. Guests should get programs as they arrive for the ceremony. Ask a special cousin, favorite nephew, or just a gregarious high school friend to man the ceremony entrance to distribute them. You can also put them on a table and let guests pick them up themselves as long as the table won't be in the way of your big entrance.

SUZANNE & TRIPP

August 10, Lake Glenville, North Carolina

TRIPP AND SUZANNE often visited Tripp's dad's summer home in Cashiers on Lake Glenville before they got engaged. "Tripp always imagined getting married on the lake," says Suzanne, "and I couldn't think of a more appropriate place to say our vows."

The ceremony took place on a peninsula known as The Point. Tripp and his groomsmen built a huppah from fallen trees; and instead of chairs, bales of hay were arranged with an aisle down the center. Guests were ferried to The Point and back to the reception site, Trillium Landings, on deck boats.

In the early morning hours of their wedding day, Suzanne and Tripp paddled out to the very spot where he had proposed to her a year ago. There they privately shared their wedding vows with each other before they went their separate ways to prepare for the day to come.

The ceremony was performed by Tripp's sister and focused on the theme of union. The couple exchanged vows, promising to love each other and grow together. Tripp vowed to always love Suzanne's grilled cheese sandwiches, and she vowed always to make them for him. All the groomsmen were barefoot, as was Tripp, but when the ceremony was finished, the "boot boy" presented Tripp with a boot—and the groom smashed a glass with his heel to guests' cries of "mazel tov!"

Readings to Remember

A reading can be traditional, biblical, poetic, humorous, or serious—anything that elaborates on your ideas of marriage and your relationship. Just make sure you clear what you want read with your officiant first; some churches and temples may have restrictions.

The Bible is, of course, a great source for tried-and-true wedding readings, but there are many other places to look for ideas. Listen to your favorite CDs (or read the lyrics); peruse your best-loved poems, stories, essays, fables, Hallmark cards, romance novels, plays, operas, and self-help books. Ask recently married friends for suggestions; they've already done all this research and may have a pile of prescreened books you can borrow. See if your family or clergy member has any folktales or religious wedding texts you might be interested in, too.

Ask friends, relatives, stepparents, or mentors to read at your wedding. Or read yourselves, alternating verses of a poem or different paragraphs of the same story. A reading doesn't have to be formal; you might choose to talk (tactfully) about your relationship history, what specific challenges you face, and how you think this relationship will help you grow and flourish.

Include your guests by distributing copies of that great wedding poem, or print it in your program.

Say It with Song

You can march to music during the procession and recession, have musical accompaniment during a silent meditation, feature a special song (or songs), or use music to break up elements of the ceremony. Music is one of the most intense emotion conveyors—a perky tune will create an entirely different mood than a somber one. Pay attention to how your desired tunes make you feel. And check with your officiant *before* booking the band; there may be restrictions on the types of music you can use.

Procession, Recession, and Ambient Music: Ask the cantor (if you're Jewish), the church choir, or a talented friend to sing throughout the procession. Or go with a Gregorian chant group, a brass section, a classical trio, a harpist, pianist, flutist, Flamenco guitarist, or great harmonica player. If you have the interest but not the financial assets for marching music, choose great recorded tunes and assign someone to CD or tape-deck duty.

Featured Songs: If your best friend was an opera major in college, invite her to sing an aria as a featured act during your ceremony. Or ask someone to perform "your" song. If you're the one with the great voice, sing something yourself. (Do a romantic serenade.) Or ask a friend with a great voice to lead the entire congregation in song. (Distribute copies of the words, if necessary.)

Singer/Songwriter: Write your own song to sing to your sweetie, or to the crowd in general. If your dad is a basement composer, bring his best song to light at your wedding, or ask him to compose something new for the occasion. You could even hire a professional composer (or your favorite local band) to write you a wedding song.

Ethnic and Regional Options: Spice up your ceremony by including music from your families' countries of origin. Hire a twelve-piece mariachi band to play Mexican music for the procession. Go with the smooth sounds of steel drum band if you're from the Caribbean. Or have racy guitar music from Spain. You also can use regional sound stylings—a zydeco band from Louisiana, soulful blues from Chicago, bluegrass or Dixie from the Deep South.

Go to Chapter 17 for more on making your ceremony sing.

Unity Symbols

Incorporate visual representations of the marriage bond—two people becoming one while each retaining their own identities. You can include your families in the ritual to symbolize a broader blending of two clans.

Unity Candle: The bride and groom, each holding a candle, light a third, centrally located candle together. You may blow out the individual flames, or all three candles may remain lit throughout the rest of the ceremony. You could initiate the process by having your mothers each light a candle first; your mom uses hers to start up yours, and your sweetie's mom does the same on her side. Sometimes the entire congregation holds candles, which get lit from the final, unified flame.

Unity Cup: Each family fills its own cup with wine. The bride and groom each pour half of their "family" cup into one, shared cup. Then they each take a sip. The half-filled family cups represent their individuality, the shared cup their new union.

Other Options: For the vessel and rose rite—a recently created unity symbol—the groom gives the bride a rose during the ceremony. She gives him an earthen vase, and then puts the rose in the vase while the officiant comments on their union. You, too, can create your own unity symbol, drawing on an ethnic custom or just using your own vision. Your symbol might be a tree you plant together. It might be a food- or wine-sharing ritual. It could be religious—such as the figure-eight-style rosary that's draped over both partners' shoulders in a traditional Mexican ceremony. Ask your parents, grandparents, or a local cultural center about ethnic ceremony customs you could incorporate or adapt. Blend customs from both your heritages, or borrow those from other countries that you like. Then run your ideas by your officiant.

Honoring the Deceased

How can you pay a tribute to a special someone who's passed away?

- Write something about him and read it aloud.
- Read his favorite poem or a selection for his favorite author.
- Have everyone sing her favorite song.
- Have your musicians play his favorite song.
- Wear something belonging to her.
- Display a memory photo album.
- Leave your bouquet on his grave.

Religious Ceremony Specifics

If you're having a religious ceremony, that ceremony will be shaped, in large part, by the rituals and requirements of your faith. If you have different religions (or have been habitually nonobservant), this is a good time to choose a faith (or to decide how you'll handle religion once you're married). Below is a look at what major U.S. religions require for weddings. But rules may vary; check with your officiant for details.

Buddhist Ceremony

Buddhist customs differ depending on the sect, or "school," and there are very few hard-and-fast wedding "rules." Sometimes the wedding date is set by an astrologer, according to your birth dates. The ceremony might take place in a temple or at a special altar erected for your marriage somewhere else.

Here's how the Japanese-based "Jodo" Shin or "Pure Land" Shin Buddhist temple handles weddings in the United States: The ceremony opens with chanting by the priest and meditation by everyone else. The priest then reads some of the Buddha's words on marriage, followed by a charge to the couple ("Do you take this man . . ."), and a standard American-style ring exchange. Then bride and groom each take a pinch of incense and place it on the altar in front of the statue of Buddha (to show respect and gratitude to the Buddha and to each other). The officiant pronounces the couple husband and wife, gives the go-ahead for the kiss, and delivers a short closing message. He also may hand the newlyweds a set of meditation beads and a book on Buddhist teachings.

Islamic Ceremony

An American Islamic wedding tends to blend Muslim and American culture.

Before the Wedding: The bride and groom agree on a "meher," a specific sum of money he'll give her. The meher is considered the bride's security and guarantee of freedom within the marriage. The meher has two parts: The "prompt" is due before the groom has "conjugal rights"; the "deferred" is an amount he'll give his bride during the course of his life. The meher can be $1 or $20,000 (or as much as you two want). Before the ceremony, the groom proposes to the bride in front of at least two witnesses, giving the details of the meher agreement. The amount is officially recorded. Today a lot of couples make the ring the "prompt." (The groom hands it over during the ceremony.) The "deferred" can be anything you two decide on.

During the Ceremony: Both bride and groom must bring at least one witness. The ceremony generally follows the basic American style, but when the officiant says the "Do you take . . ." part, he mentions the names of the witnesses and the meher amount. And the sermon might be in Arabic rather than English. There isn't a class of clergy in Islam; any Muslim person can officiate your wedding. The marriage is considered a contract between the couple and Allah.

Jewish Ceremony

Minhag is the term used to describe the Jewish wedding customs. Jewish traditions may vary depending on the affiliation, the synagogue, and the individual rabbi. But here's a look at some of the minhag musts.

The Huppah: This canopy, held aloft over the bride and groom, dates to the tent of Abraham and those nomadic desert days when all Jewish wedding ceremonies were held outdoors. Back then the huppah was used to create an intimate, sanctified space. Today it represents your new home (with open sides, inviting friends and family in). While you don't technically *need* a huppah to have a wedding, many people feel it's mandatory (and it is nice!).

Wine: A Jewish wedding has two wine rituals, one at the beginning of the ceremony and one near the end. Each time you and your beloved drink from a shared cup.

Tangible Goods: To be valid, a Jewish wedding must contain an exchange of something of value. Today this generally means the ring ceremony.

Ketubah: After the ring exchange, the rabbi reads the Ketubah, or marriage contract. It's usually ornately decorated. The Ketubah belongs to

Jewish Wedding Wisdom

Check out *The New Jewish Wedding,* by Anita Diamant (Fireside, 2001).

the bride and lists her rights in the marriage. It's signed in the presence of a rabbi and two witnesses, usually directly before or during the ceremony. In Orthodox weddings, only the groom signs it; in Conservative or Reform ceremonies, the bride gets to sign, too.

Seven Blessings: This is the heart of the Jewish ceremony. The rabbi and other significant people in your lives recite the seven marriage blessings.

The Breaking of the Glass: Nothing says "Jewish wedding" more than the sound of a breaking glass. Depending on whom you ask, the breaking of the glass is, among other things, (1) a symbol of the destruction of the Temple in Jerusalem; (2) a representation of the fragility of human relationships; and/or (3), a reminder that marriage changes the lives of individuals forever. (Contrary to popular belief, the glass breaking has nothing to do with virginity!) It's also the official signal to shout "Mazel tov!" The glass is wrapped in a napkin and special pouch for safety. The groom smashes it with his foot, or bride and groom can stomp on it together.

The Yichud: The word means "seclusion," and it's a totally private affair. Immediately after the ceremony, the couple retreats to a private room for fifteen minutes of staring into each other's eyes. In the past, bride and groom would head to a nearby tent to consummate the marriage! This isn't done much these days, but it is customary for newlyweds to seize a Yichud moment and feed each other a bite of something.

Church of Latter-Day Saints (Mormon) Ceremony

There are two types of Church of Latter-Day Saints (Mormon) services: an official "temple wedding" or a standard church service. A temple wedding is always held within one of the world's fifty-three holy temples and is considered a marriage for life *and* afterlife. The wording is "for time and all eternity," *not* "until death do you part." The devout strive for a temple wedding, which requires advance permission.

Before the Ceremony: To get permission for a temple wedding (also called a "sealing ordinance"), you each set up a private interview with your own local bishop, during which you'll answer questions about your religious diligence. Basically, you attest that you believe in the church's teachings and that you're following the specific precepts. These include following the "Code of Health" (abstaining from alcohol, tobacco, coffee, and tea), being "Morally Clean" (abstaining from sex, or even heavy petting, according to some bishops), and following the law of tithing (paying 10 percent of your income to the church). If your bishop finds you diligent, he'll sign a "temple recommend," which gives you permission to enter a holy temple.

Then you take your temple recommend to the "stake president," a leader overseeing several bishops in a large region. He'll ask you the same basic questions, and, if he's satisfied with your answers, will sign your temple recommend, too. After that, you're ready to tie that eternal knot. Once you set up the interviews, you can complete the whole process within a week.

The Temple Ceremony: The ceremony itself is similar to a standard Protestant wedding, except that your guests must have a temple recommend to attend, as well, meaning it may be a *lot* smaller than a nontemple wedding. (Usually it's just family and close friends.) The temple president or a "temple sealer" (a clergy member with authority to officiate a wedding) will oversee. You need at least two witnesses.

A Nontemple Wedding: This is open to any member of the Church of Latter-Day Saints. You don't need a temple recommend, and your wedding can be overseen by your local bishop at any church. If you take this route or have a civil ceremony, you may be able to have a second ceremony later (after you've begun following the church's precepts), to "seal" the marriage for eternity.

Protestant Ceremony

The standard American wedding is basically Protestant in nature. Almost all Protestant weddings share the same procession, recession, and altar positions. The traditional call to worship, "We are gathered here today in the presence of God . . ." comes from the Episcopalian *Book of Common Prayer* (and it's almost identical to the Presbyterian opening, "We are gathered here today to witness the marriage of . . ."). Most Protestant services also include the giving away (or more modern "blessing") of the bride, your vows, the blessing and exchange of rings, prayers, and closing words.

Beyond those basics, each church will have a specific take on music, sermons, a unity candle, and audience participation. If you're Methodist, Lutheran, or Presbyterian, you'll probably follow the guidelines of your church's ceremony service book. If you're Unitarian, you'll work with your minister to create your ceremony. There's no set liturgy, meaning plenty of creative input for you. If you're Baptist, your church will set the rules regarding marriage specifics within it. Talk to your officiant about details.

Quaker Ceremony

If you want a Quaker wedding, you mail a "letter of intent to marry under the care of the monthly meeting" to the clerk of your meeting house. Though Quaker Sunday services are basically silent, each congregation has a monthly business meeting to discuss important issues such as marriages. The clerk will bring up your letter at the next business meeting, and the community will appoint a two- to three-member "marriage committee." Your marriage committee meets with you to decide if they think you're ready to tie the knot, based on their assessment of things such as your maturity, education, finances, plans for children, and the like.

If your marriage committee gives you the go-ahead, you'll then have a "wedding committee" assigned to you. The wedding committee is like an official honor attendant/helpful mom/supporting sponsor all rolled into one (actually, three to ten people). Your committee members will help you with wedding details, from reserving the meeting house to dealing with reception logistics.

The Ceremony: The most noticeable variation from the Protestant norm is the lack of an officiant. You two will be marrying each other before God, without any intermediary. During the wedding (usually held on a Saturday), you and your committee sit on "facing benches" before the rest of the congregation (your guests). Everyone worships silently until you two feel that it's time to say your vows. You stand up, face each other, hold hands, and deliver your promises (which you've written). Then you sit back down for

Ethnic Ceremony Ideas

At Egyptian weddings, a range of musicians plays the processional music on not-so-subtle instruments like drums, bagpipes, and horns. Belly dancers slink down the aisle, along with men carrying flaming swords—a far different effect from a string quartet!

The Apache mix colored sands in a crystal bowl as a symbol of unity.

For Hindus, red, not white, is the color of marriage. The bride might wear a red sari (or veil) and sport orange-red henna designs on her hands, feet, and along the part of her hair.

The sake-sharing ritual is the main bonding rite of a Shinto ceremony (an ancient religion, practiced primarily in Japan). The couple also honors ancestors with a food offering before family shrines.

In an Eastern Orthodox wedding (Russian and Greek), the bride and groom exchange their rings three times to represent marriage under the Holy Trinity. Then they slip them on the fourth finger of their *right* hands.

more silent worship. Congregants and guests will stand, if they want to, to say a few words or voice their support for you. The meeting usually ends with a nod from one of your committee members. Then it's on to the reception!

Roman Catholic Ceremony

Considered one of the Seven Sacraments, or channels to God's grace, the wedding ceremony is a serious affair in the Catholic church. Often the wedding includes a full mass (called a nuptial mass), including readings and communion. Your priest probably will help you choose prayers, hymns, and readings from the Scriptures to customize the service. After you exchange your vows, he blesses your rings before you slip them on each other's fingers. The procession, recession, and altar positions are identical to those of a standard Protestant wedding ceremony (although your attendants may sit for most of the mass and stand with you during the vows).

To marry in the Catholic church, one of you (or both, depending on the officiant) must be Catholic. If you want to marry in a church other than your home parish, you must get permission from your pastor. You'll have to show your baptism certificate and proof that any previous marriages were officially annulled.

Some churches still do a modified posting of the banns. In the past, banns (basically, a notice of your intention to wed) were physically tacked outside the church doors. Anyone in the community who knew of any reason why you *shouldn't* get married (another spouse already in the picture, for example) would see the notice and stop the wedding. Today your banns might be printed in the church bulletin or announced from the pulpit during a Sunday service.

Interfaith Weddings

Interfaith-accepting religions:

- Baha'i
- Buddhist
- Hindu
- Protestant
- Quaker
- Shinto

Somewhat interfaith-accepting religions:

- Catholic (more than ever these days)
- Eastern Orthodox (as long as the non-EO partner is Christian)
- Church of Latter-Day Saints (but not in one of the fifty-three holy temples)
- Muslim (man can marry a Christian or Jewish woman and still have an Islamic wedding; a woman can only marry a Muslim man)
- Reform Jewish

Interfaith Ceremonies

"Religion in a wedding is great," you say, "but, sadly, we don't share the same one." Rather than let this become a source of stress, rejoice in the fact that you have two great traditions from which to draw. We know many interfaith couples who had great weddings. (Some of our parents, for example!) In fact, more than 40,000 Jewish/Christian couples get engaged in the United States each year. Sure, arranging an interfaith ceremony can lead to disagreements and family pressure aplenty, but their increasing presence and acceptance means it should be easier than it's ever been for you to plan one.

Finding an Interfaith Officiant (or Two)

Each religion has its own view on interfaith unions, from "Go for it!" to "No way." Some religions and sects leave the decision up to individual clergy members. If both of your religions are somewhat flexible, you may look for an officiant from each to preside over a joint ceremony. This is the most complicated plan but also the most popular because it guarantees that each side's beliefs are included. It also reflects the meaning of marriage; you're joining your lives here. Think of your ceremony as the first of many blended rituals.

In some cities (including Chicago, San Francisco, and Washington, D.C.), you'll find Christian/Jewish "clergy teams." These ministers and rabbis have performed many interfaith ceremonies and will work together to help you plan yours.

If your religion is in the "no-way" camp (such as Orthodox Jewish), forget the dual-officiant approach—it's not gonna happen. You could hold two separate ceremonies instead—only one is legally binding; the other serves as a blessing over your union. A clergy member who won't officially oversee your wedding may be willing to bless it in a smaller, more private setting. Your other options include going with one of your religions; finding a third, neutral religion; or taking the civil route. To find interfaith officiants:

- Ask other interfaith couples you know for referrals. (It pays to get references!)
- Look in the society wedding pages of your local newspaper for names of clergy who have conducted interfaith ceremonies.
- Ask any clergy members who turn you down for names of officiants they know who are willing.

Planning an Interfaith Ceremony

You and your fiancé/e should sit down together to discuss your values and identify what is meaningful to you about the wedding ceremony in general. Then talk to your officiant(s) about which religious traditions you can use that won't conflict with the tenets of the other. Your officiant(s) should be able to help you choose appropriate customs that will enhance the ceremony without stepping on any religious toes.

For readings, consult texts from both religions. Consider each reading passages from the other's faith, or asking family members to do so. Create as many opportunities for family to participate as possible; it will make everyone feel included in this joining of two different backgrounds.

It's impossible to list what *exactly* you can incorporate in an interfaith wedding—the details depend entirely on the two of you, your officiant(s), and your house(s) of worship. But here are two samples of *possible* mixed ceremonies.

Finding an Officiant

Check out local college campuses for chaplains and other clergy likely to be comfortable with an interfaith wedding. Or try the Ethical Culture Society (www.aeu.org), the Unitarian-Universalists (www.uua.org), or your local marriage license bureau for a list of nonreligious officiants such as judges and justices of the peace.

Catholic/Jewish Ceremony: Hold it under a huppah in a nonreligious location; include the blessings over the wine, the reading of the Ketubah, the seven blessings (be sure to ask non-Jewish family members to recite a few), and the breaking of the glass. From the Catholic tradition, include prayers, hymns, a priest's sermon, and a closing peace-be-with-you handshake. And don't forget your personal vows, the rings, and readings, of course.

Buddhist/Christian Ceremony: Hold it in a neutral location and set up a Buddhist altar. After a standard Christian procession and officiant welcome, have a moment of silent meditation (during which time your Buddhist officiant might chant; Eastern music could be playing). After the pastor's sermon, your Buddhist officiant can share the Buddha's words on

Go to Chapter 23 for more help with interfaith angst and other relationship stumbling blocks.

marriage. Make your readings a combination of biblical passages and Eastern thoughts. In your vows, promise to respect both religions and religious traditions. After the ring ceremony, give an offering to the Buddha at the altar.

AKARI & SETH

June 16, Brooklyn, New York

WHEN AKARI SHIMIZU, who is Japanese, and Seth Werlinsky, who is Jewish, set out to plan their wedding, they began not by focusing on their differences, but on what they had in common. They both wanted to be married outdoors. And, at the time, they lived in Brooklyn, a place they both love. With these things in mind, they chose their setting: the Brooklyn Society for Ethical Culture, a short walk from their apartment. The proximity of the site gave Akari her first opportunity to practice a Japanese tradition. "A marriage for a Japanese bride means leaving her family to join a new family. She arrives on a horse at the groom's home with her furniture and her kimono. I wanted to experience that tradition my own way by walking to the site on our wedding day," she says.

The couple created what they describe as "a Japanese-influenced Jewish wedding officiated by a rabbi." Akari is not religious, so Seth's Jewish background became the religious element of their ceremony, while Akari's Japanese culture was woven in throughout.

The couple had no difficulty finding a rabbi to marry them (plans to include a Shinto priest fell through when the priest moved out of New York). The rabbi did have one request: "He wanted assurance that I intend to raise our children in the Jewish faith," says Seth.

The ceremony was almost perfectly balanced: for each Jewish tradition, there was a Japanese twist. Akari (in a white gown embroidered with Japanese cherry blossoms) walked down the aisle with her brother and her mother beside her, just as Jewish brides walk with their parents. When the three met Seth at the end of the aisle, they bowed. Akari had learned some Hebrew for the ceremony, which took place beneath a huppah (Jewish wedding canopy) made of Japanese shoji (wood and rice paper). Sips of kosher wine came from a sake cup.

The intercultural spirit continued at the reception, where 150 origami paper cranes, made mostly by Seth, hung from the tent. And when the best man made his toast, guests raised their masu, or wooden sake cups, on which the couple had engraved their names (in Japanese), as well as the character for happiness and long life and the wedding date.

Second Weddings

This is your chance to do it all over again, exactly the way you want to. Planning the wedding this time around just may be more fun—there's bound to be less pressure from parents or other well-meaning opinion-meisters. Since second-timers often foot the bill themselves, they have far more freedom to call the shots. And, having done it before, they know exactly what shots to call.

A second wedding can be a huge soiree with all the trimmings or an intimate, family-only affair. Brides, you can walk down the aisle with your parents again (or anyone else you choose) or go it alone. You both can wear anything you want—white, off-white, red-velvet jumpsuit. (But brides, you might want to skip the veil this time—you're going into it with your eyes open, and the veil is a first-time bride tradition, anyway.) Basically, a second wedding is just like a first wedding, except one (or both of) you has a bit more experience. And you'll probably feel less tied to tradition.

If you have kids, include them in the ceremony. Even if they're thrilled about your honey and your wedding (cake, presents, party!), they'll probably need reassurance about their continued importance in your life (particularly if they live with you). Your new status gives them new status, too—and it wasn't of their choosing. Don't expect them to do more at your wedding than they usually can—if your five-year-old refuses to stand still for ten minutes on an ordinary Saturday afternoon, he won't suddenly do it at your wedding. And if your kids don't want to participate, try to respect their feelings.

If you're still friendly with your ex-spouse and your ex-family-in-law, go ahead and invite them, if you want to. If your ex is the father of your children, including him shows your kids that they don't have to "take sides"; your new spouse doesn't mean they get a replacement parent. But consider the feelings of your partner, too. If he or she will be uncomfortable with your ex at the wedding, you might want to withhold that invite.

Be considerate of each other during the planning process, and respect the fact that your differing experiences may lead to different desires and expectations. If this is your second wedding and your fiancé/e's first, don't make too many comments like "Last time we used this

Major Religions on Second Marriages

Here's a brief look at religions' views of remarriage:

Buddhist: Divorce and remarriage are allowed, provided the priest has no reservations about the couple's commitment.

Mormon: You can remarry in a temple, providing you're both living according to the church's precepts (including reabstaining from sex until after your wedding).

Islamic: Divorce and remarriage are permitted, according to the Koran. You'll need legal documents proving your divorce is final, and there's a waiting period of about three months.

Jewish: You can remarry after a civil divorce if you're Reform. If you're Conservative or Orthodox, you need a *get*—a Jewish divorce decree from a rabbinical court.

Protestant: Views about divorce vary, but Lutheran, Methodist, and Presbyterian churches, in general, allow divorce. Baptist churches each have their own authority; some ministers permit second marriages, others don't. Episcopalian rectors review each case individually and make recommendations to the bishop about whether to grant a remarriage or not. The process takes about two months.

Roman Catholic: You must get an annulment to remarry within the Catholic church. Because marriage is considered a sacrament, you must get it officially declared null and void.

Unitarian-Universalist: Each minister sets his/her own criteria.

caterer," or "I know because I've done it before." You want the first-timer to know that *this* is the most important wedding in the history of the universe.

If you're the first-time partner, don't dwell on your to-be's past. Focus on *your* wedding. Don't ask about the first wedding or dig out old photo albums from your honey's basement. If s/he keeps bringing up last time, keep explaining that this is new to you and that you want to start from scratch.

Roles for Little Folks

How can your kids participate?

- Take vows accepting their new siblings or family.
- Be a flower girl, ring bearer, or usher.
- Be a junior bridesmaid or groomsman (teens).
- Escort you down the aisle and "give you away."
- Read a poem, biblical verse, or prose piece.
- Sing a song; play the guitar; accompany a singer on the banjo, guitar, violin, tap shoes.
- Create the program.
- Decorate the getaway car.
- Pass out candles, flower petals, birdseed.

Commitment Ceremonies

As of this printing, Vermont is still the only state that allows same sex couples to marry in the form of a civil union. Although no other state recognizes such a commitment, Hawaii and California are making strides to follow Vermont by offering a Domestic Partner Registration in California and a Reciprocal Beneficiaries Law in Hawaii. Both offer same sex couples some, but not all, of the benefits of marriage although none of these state laws are recognized on the federal level. Check out each state's website for further details.

Civil unions can be performed by judges, justices of the peace, and clergy. A great website that clarifies same sex union laws as well as the steps to filing such a union and finding someone to perform the ceremony is www.buddybuddy.com. Another website, www.unionoflove.com, lists resources state by state and incorporates everything from ceremony officiators, caterers, and reception halls. Having a commitment ceremony or Holy Union serves the same purposes as a traditional wedding.

- Makes a public proclamation of your love and intent to remain together.
- Brings your family and friends together to support your union.
- Gives you a sense of permanence, stability, and security.
- Helps you secure domestic partner status (in some states).

Gay Wedding Books

Check out *The Essential Guide to Gay and Lesbian Weddings* by Tess Ayers et al. for great ceremony planning advice. And try *Legal Guide for Gay and Lesbian Couples* by Hayden Curry et al. for info on everything from navigating the courts to dealing with issues such as inheritance, medical, finances, and children.

A wedding ceremony can have added significance for a gay or lesbian couple—since you're not always getting a legal document, the ceremony itself is *the* binding ritual (as it should be). A wedding ceremony—gay or straight—is about the two of you, your commitment to and belief in each other.

Finding an Officiant

A civil servant is somewhat gratuitous, since his/her primary role is to legalize the event—and that's not what's happening here. But you *can* ask a favorite judge or justice of the peace to symbolically sanction your ceremony. If you want your union to be blessed before God, you have a few choices. You can go with an officiant from a gay-friendly religion (Metropolitan Community Churches, Unitarian-Universalists, or the Universal Life Church). You could find an officiant from a religion that leaves the same-sex decision to the clergy

(Buddhist, some Protestant, Reform Jewish). Or, you could ask a sympathetic but congregationally restricted minister or rabbi to conduct an off-duty ceremony, lending his/her presence to the event without actually representing the church or synagogue.

Or ask someone you admire or no one at all. Since it's not legally sanctioned, you can ask a layperson whom you respect to conduct your ceremony. Or don't ask anyone—run the show yourselves. To find an officiant:

- Ask friends within the gay community for referrals.
- Call gay-friendly churches or other religious organizations.
- Look through gay newspapers and magazines.
- Check out the *Gayellow Pages* (www.gayellowpages.com).

Creating Your Commitment Ceremony

Your ceremony can incorporate any or all of the traditional wedding customs, but you may want to create some new traditions of your own. You're breaking ground for all the same-sex weddings that come after yours; you can help determine what elements will go into the developing "canon" of gay wedding rituals.

Focus on the vows, readings, and unity symbols; these are the areas most open to creative input. You could have a standard unity candle. Or create a new unity symbol, perhaps a unity bouquet. Each member of both your families (or close friends) holds a single rose (your family red, your partner's white, or go with rainbow hues). Participants in the unity bouquet ceremony approach the altar one at a time to give you the flowers and a blessing. Then the two of you combine your roses into one bouquet. The rose petals represent the tenderness of love; the thorns, the obstacles you may face; the fragrance, your joy in life and love.

For readings, you don't have to address gay issues; you could read something about love, friendship, companionship, trust, growth, or whatever you want to. By choosing something *not* specifically gay-related, you're focusing on your personal commitment, not on politics.

Now that you've got the basics, it's time to start planning the ceremony of the century. This is the most meaningful part of your wedding; don't get so wrapped up in reception details that you forget the reason that you're here in the first place. Do the deed right. Then party down!

Gay-Friendly Religions?

Friendly:

- Metropolitan Community Church
- Unitarian-Universalist Church
- The Universal Life Church

Sometimes Friendly:

- Buddhism
- Judaism
- Protestantism

Unfriendly:

- Mormonism
- Islam
- Roman Catholicism

CHAPTER SEVEN

a rousing reception

Your wedding reception may well be the biggest and best party you ever get to throw, so really think about what kind of event you want it to be. How do you want to mingle—quietly over canapés and caviar, a quartet in the background, or bumping and grinding on the dance floor after a five-course filet mignon dinner? The reception is the hardest part of your wedding to plan—there are so many details involved in setting the mood you want (and the next section of this book will take you through all of them). There are also a ton of reception rituals, like the bouquet toss and cake cutting, which you may choose to do or not. Don't feel obligated to include anything you're not comfortable with or that you feel doesn't work with the tone of your party.

What follows is a framework for the "classic" wedding reception—just so you know what to expect (and what's expected of *you),* plus some great twists.

What Happens When

What you do at your reception depends largely on the kind of party you're throwing. The more elaborate and traditional the reception, the more classic elements you may want to include.

If it's a simple champagne-and-cake reception or cocktail reception, the order of events goes something like this:

- The receiving line forms.
- Cocktails are served; guests mix and mingle.
- Champagne is served. If it's a Jewish wedding, the bride's father (and maybe grandfather) offers blessings over the bread and wine.
- Toasts are made.
- The bride and groom cut the cake.
- Guests enjoy a slice.
- The bride may toss her bouquet; the groom may toss her garter.
- The bride and groom make for the getaway car (or stay until the end of the party with guests).

If you're serving hors d'oeuvres and cocktails followed by a dinner accompanied by a fourteen-piece orchestra—or otherwise having a reception that includes a meal and dancing—the party will go more like this:

- Cocktail hour begins.
- You arrive and the receiving line forms.
- The cocktail party continues.
- It's meal time. The catering manager and waiters begin letting guests know they should take their seats and/or head to the buffet. You may decide to have dinner announced, by the DJ or bandleader if s/he will emcee, or by someone else you've designated—a friend, the banquet manager, whomever. You take your seats, or wait to be announced (along with your attendants and perhaps your parents). You may do your first dance before you sit to eat; father/daughter and mother/son dances also may happen now.
- Your officiant may offer a blessing. Your parents also might give a blessing over the about-to-be-served food and wine (a tradition at Jewish weddings). Waiters serve the first course, or guests make for the buffet. The band continues playing background music.
- Time for the toasts. The best man kicks them off, followed by the groom, the bride, and any other guests who want to say something.
- Dinner continues; you may do special dances after the salad course or after everyone's finished with the entree.
- Serious dancing begins, including any ethnic dances.
- Things get thrown (bouquet and garter toss).
- You cut the cake.
- Everyone does dessert.
- More dancing; the party starts winding down.
- You two head out to your car under a shower of flower petals, or stay until the bitter end to bid guests thank-you and adieu.

Don't Be Your Own Emcee

Don't even think about running your own reception. If you don't have a wedding consultant to handle the details, appoint someone as Reception Master. (This person can be a friend, relative, even the banquet manager or caterer.) Let your RM monitor the party and make sure everything happens on schedule.

Jewish Reception Blessing

At a Jewish reception, the rabbi, the couple's parents or grandparents, or another honored guest gives a formal blessing, called the *hamotzi,* over a loaf of shiny egg bread called challah. Hunks then are passed around to all the guests.

The Receiving Line

Say it's not your wedding. It's just an ordinary party—a summer backyard picnic, for example. As all your guests arrive, do you: (1) rudely ignore them and hope they find the potato salad, or (2) hurry over as soon as you can and say "Oh, Sylvan! I'm so happy to see you! Would you like a drink?" Survey says: Option B. These are your friends and relatives. You've got to welcome them to your wedding celebration, and let them know you're glad they came.

Should You Have a Receiving Line?

This formalized greeting allows you to welcome every guest in an organized manner and guarantees your guests a minute of face-to-face time with you on yours. With the greet-them-as-you-see-them, casual approach, you may spend the whole party ducking out in the middle of conversations to say hello to people you haven't greeted yet. If there are fewer than fifty guests, you could make the entire cocktail hour a meet-and-greet instead of doing a formal receiving line. You and your receiving team form a big, amorphous shape in the center of the room; guests get their drinks and then head over to say hello. The amoeba approach creates a more casual atmosphere and lets you introduce your guests more easily to more people. (You're not limited to the two on either side of you.)

How to Receive

Here's everything you must know about your receiving line.

When: Directly after the ceremony or at the beginning of the reception.

Where: Outside the ceremony site's doors—in the vestibule, hallway, or on the front porch—or somewhere near the reception party room—by the doors, in the cocktail lounge, or in the lobby.

Who Stands in It: Traditionally, the bride's parents head the receiving line and are the first to greet guests. You and your honey stand next to them, with the groom's parents filing in after you. If you choose to include them, the honor attendant and the bridesmaids line up after the groom's parents. If most of the guests are your friends (not your parents'), you can head the line yourselves and be the first greeters.

What You Do: Introduce your sweetie and your parents to all guests they haven't met. ("Honey, this is Rob, whom I used to work with at the ad agency," or, "Dad, I'd like you to meet Sally, my next-door neighbor.") Your

Reception Timetable

For a formal, seated meal reception, hours break down pretty much like this:

- Beginning: Receiving line, cocktails.
- First hour: Cocktails and hors d'oeuvres continue. (You may do photos.)
- Second hour: Everyone is seated for the meal, blessings, and toasts; first dance and other special dances.
- Third hour: Bouquet and garter toss; more dancing.
- Fourth hour: Cake cutting, other desserts and coffee; party winds down.

ASK CARLEY

Stepparents in Line

Q: My stepdaughter is getting married next year and I would like to know if I should be in the receiving line—and how do I introduce myself? Her father and I have been married for thirteen years. Her brother was married four years ago and I was in the receiving line but felt as if I didn't belong there.

A: Comfort is key for all the family members at the wedding. First, talk to your stepdaughter—she and her groom are really the ones who should make the decision about which parents are in the receiving line. Let her know that it felt awkward for you to be in her brother's, but if she wants you there, you would love to be there (assuming you would). There's no clear-cut answer about whether stepparents *should* be in the line—it really does all depend on the family and how comfortable everyone is with it. But rest assured that it's completely appropriate for you to be there, especially since you've played such a significant role in the bride's life. You didn't say whether the bride's mother is planning on standing in the line—that may also be a factor in your discomfort. If you both are in the line, you should be standing next to your husband, and the bride's mother should not be standing next to either of you, so guests will understand what the relationships are. If you are in the line, simply introduce yourself as the bride's stepmother. If you're not in the line, start to circulate with the guests, greet and thank people—and introduce yourself as the bride's proud stepmom.

new husband or wife will introduce you to guests you don't know as well. Accept their congrats, hugs, and kisses, and thank everyone for coming. It's that easy!

Seating Your Guests

You remember the seating chart from grade school. Having a personalized place to sit each day gave every student a feeling of stability and security, and it also helped the teacher organize the class; she could position problem kids near the front, scatter strong students throughout. The reception seating chart does essentially the same thing. You decide who sits at which table, taking the confusion, hassle, and fear of choosing the wrong spot out of your guests' hands. And you can shape how much fun everyone has, too, since you can choose wise positions for volatile divorced parents or guests who hate each other and sprinkle good conversationalists and great wits throughout the room.

Why Seating Is Important

Your goals, of course, are different from the teacher's in a critical way—you *want* people to talk to each other. Unlike the grade-school plan, your seating chart should designate only the tables where guests sit, not the specific chairs they'll take (unless you're having an ultra-formal affair). Have *some* faith in your guests' social skills.

ADELA & NATHAN

June 13, Denver, Colorado

ADELA'S ASIAN ROOTS were an important part of the wedding-day details when she and Nathan wed at Denver's Grant Humphreys Mansion. She and her parents made their invitations by hand from ecru Italian cardstock and a Nepalese sand-and-gold overlay, which were closed with gold sealing wax and stamped with the Uchida name in Japanese script. Adela asked her bridesmaids to don different-colored kimonos, from deep peaches to pale blues, all of which were owned by her family. (The groomsmen's attire set off the look with modern tuxedos worn over vests with Nehru collars.) The ceremony featured Shinto details: the bride and groom sipped sake three times from three cups (three being good luck in Japan). Rice-paper fans on which Adela's eighty-nine-year-old grandfather had calligraphically inscribed Japanese poetry were given as favors. (Nathan also led a traditional banzai toast during the reception.) In a display of their ethnic versatility, Adela's parents, celebrating their anniversary the same day, took a spin on the dance floor to show off their tango moves.

The wedding was not without touches from many other nationalities. In honor of Nathan's Irish heritage, a kilt-wearing bagpiper was added to the ceremony, along with a traditional Irish wedding blessing before the two were pronounced man and wife. Even their getaway vehicle—the Irish Rose Carriage—carried a Celtic theme.

You don't need a seating chart for a cocktail- or dessert-only reception. If it's a very casual or very small party, it's fine to skip it, too. But we highly recommend it for a seated meal, whether buffet or waiter-served.

Reception Rituals

So you've greeted your guests and everyone's found their seat. Now what? The majority of reception time (that is, time when people aren't eating) is spent dancing and carrying out reception customs. Here's the lowdown on each.

Here Comes the Couple: Being Announced

Many couples choose to be "announced," along with their wedding party and sometimes their parents, once guests are seated. You all assemble outside the reception room. The banquet manager, DJ, or someone else you've designated then takes the mike and announces everyone by name—"Please welcome the bride's parents, Jane and John Smith"—and everyone walks in as couples. After the bride's and groom's parents comes the wedding party, walking with the partners they had at the ceremony. You two, "for the first time as husband and wife," come in last.

Waltzing into Marriage: The First Dance

The first dance physically reiterates what the ceremony just stated: You and your honey are a unit now. The first dance is a way of bonding to the beat. (Of course, if you rate dancing in public up there with standing naked on a table at an office party, it's fine to skip the spotlight first dance and open up the floor to everyone instead.) You'll probably also want to plan a father/

Classic First-Dance Order

- Bride and groom
- Bride and her father; groom and his mother-in-law
- Bride and father-in law; groom and mother
- Bride and best man; groom and honor attendant
- Everyone else!

Tips for Talkative Tables

Put people with similar interests together.
Put people of similar ages together.
Put family who live in opposite corners of the country together (if they like each other) so they can squeeze in some quality time during your wedding.
Seat your officiant at a table with family members (usually your parents).
Generally, let divorced parents host their own tables, or seat one with your honey's parents and the other with the officiant, family members, or other special guests.
If you're using place cards, we recommend the boy-girl-boy-girl approach; it's more exciting for your guests. (And for you—few things beat the thrill of playing matchmaker for your single friends.)
Put an even number of guests at each table; people tend to pair off in conversation, and if you have five, seven, or nine people at each table, someone is *always* the fifth (or seventh, or ninth) wheel.
Try to make sure every guest will have at least one person at the table s/he'll be thrilled to talk to.
Put dance lovers near the dance floor—they'll get the party rocking.

daughter dance (bride and dad) and/or a mother/son dance (groom and mom), which will come later in the reception.

When: Your first dance as newlyweds can happen right when the band starts playing, after the toasting, after the first course has been served, even after everyone finishes eating. The point is, it's not necessarily the first dance of the evening, just the first time you and your sweetie hit the dance floor as newlyweds.

Who Does What: You could dance the entire song together while everyone watches, or do a formal first-dance sequence; after you've made a few laps around the floor, you switch partners—the bride dances with her father while the groom dances with his mother-in-law. After another few turns, it's switch time again—the bride dances with her father-in-law and the groom kicks it up with his mom. Then switch once more—the bride spins about with the best man and the groom twirls the maid of honor. You'll probably want to ask your emcee to act as a guide so no one gets confused.

A Twist on Tradition: Rather than dancing to a traditional first-dance song, consider using something more unusual—a swing, tango, salsa, lambada, or flamenco song, perhaps!

Go Ethnic: Make the first dance a traditional ethnic one that represents your backgrounds. Do the Jewish horah and invite everyone to join in. (You two can dance in the center of the circle.) Or do an Italian tarantella. Take lessons ahead of time, or ask your grandparents or parents to lead the dance. It's a great way to tap into your heritage, and to pay respect to your family.

Go Period: If you're doing a '20s-style party, make it a Charleston. If it's a '50s malt-shop party, do the jitterbug. If it's a '70s night, do the hustle.

Go Family-Style: You can personalize the father/daughter and mother/son dance, too. Brides, if you and your dad are known for your fabulous Lindy hop, do it! Grooms, if your mom taught you to hand-jive back in fifth grade (to impress the ten-year-old girls), hand-jive with mom.

Control Your Emcee

If you want your bandleader or DJ to serve as announcer during your reception, give the person specific instructions about how much talking you actually want him or her to do. If you *don't* want this person announcing things, make that very clear.

Get into the Groove

Afraid people won't dance? Appoint a few friends as "dance starters"—the delegated first group on the floor whenever the band (or DJ or boom box) kicks in. Or resort to group dances that everyone will do—the limbo, hokey pokey, electric slide, a conga line.

Here's to You Two: Getting Toasted

Toasting is a way of stopping in the middle of some fabulous event to acknowledge your good fortune and say, "Hey! This is a truly fabulous event!" It lets everyone take stock *now* of just how good things really are, rather than waiting twenty years from now to say "Boy, those were the good old days!" Toasting also lets you thank those around you for sharing in your happiness (and in the work it took to celebrate it). Toasting is *not* meant to be another painful rite of passage. If you'd rather ski the North Pole in a bikini than speak in public, just say a quick word. ("Thanks for coming, everyone!")

When: Toasting usually begins after everyone has found a seat and gone through the buffet line (or been served the first course). You also can toast during cocktails, after everyone has been served champagne.

Who Does What: Traditionally, the best man leads the toasting, offering one up to the bride and groom. Then the groom takes the floor, followed by the bride. (This doesn't happen nearly enough. Brides, take that mike!) Thank your guests, your parents, each other. Then parents, other relatives, and other members of the wedding party may speak. After that, it's a free-for-all. The toasters stand up and speak from their places, or head to the dance floor and take the microphone. Everyone else remains seated (even the toastees—you don't have to stand when you're being toasted.)

Toasting Hints: Ask friends and family to talk about when they first knew you were in love or when they knew you'd be getting married. Or invite them to share some funny memory from your mutual past. But they should make it a story *everyone* will enjoy hearing. If you suspect your old single-days gal pal intends to give a detailed list of all the guys you dated before finding your honey, ask her to share that story at your bachelorette party instead.

For your part, say something you mean. You may want to thank your parents for their support and your honey for—everything. You may thank members of your wedding party for their help, and tell everyone how much their presence at the wedding means to you. Or share some hilarious story about how you two met.

It's a Toss-Up: The Bouquet and Garter

The bouquet and garter toss traditions are modern takes on old superstitions. These days they're designed to help hurry single friends to the altar—the woman who catches the bouquet and the man who snags the garter will be the next to get married (though not necessarily to each other!). Some couples wouldn't dream of omitting these entertaining traditions, but others are known for retreating to the bathroom when they came up at past weddings. If the mere thought of these traditions makes you cringe, it's okay to skip them. Or skip the one you don't like and do the other.

When: Toward the end of the party; usually before the cake cutting, but they could happen right before the couple make their getaway (if they're doing so).

The Bouquet Toss: The single female guests gather on the dance floor. The bride either faces them or turns her back and lobs her bouquet over her head. According to tradition, whoever catches it will be next to marry.

The Garter Toss: The single men gather in the same area. The bride sits on a chair while the groom lifts her skirt up to remove her garter, slipping it off her leg with his hands (or teeth!), and then whips it at the crowd of single men. Whoever catches the garter poses for a photo, dances with the winner of the bouquet toss, or slips the garter on her leg.

Tossing Alternatives: If you'd rather present your bouquet to a close friend or female relative, you can do so privately. Or make an announcement about the meaning of your hand-off. Another idea: Have both women and men try to catch the bouquet.

It's a Toss-Up

Historically, different cultures have thrown different things at couples as they left their wedding. In Italy, guests threw coins, dried fruit, and little pieces of candy (the original *confetti*). Today your guests may throw birdseed or flower petals, blow bubbles, ring miniature bells, or even release birds, to symbolize a life of plenty.

Breakaway Bouquet

If you want to save your bouquet but still do the flower toss, ask your florist to create a smaller piece that can be separated and tossed. Or just have a separate smaller bouquet made.

SALLIE & JASON

November 30, Cliffside Park, New Jersey

JUST ABOUT ANY COUPLE can tell you about the swingin' music or scrumptious seven-layer cake they had at their wedding. But how many people can say they also ate kimchi or wore the matrimonial robes of Korean royalty?

By choosing to serve Korean cuisine, wear traditional costumes, and incorporate Korean customs into her otherwise all-American wedding, Sallie was able to share something that is important to her—her heritage—with some of the people who are most important to her. "That includes my new husband, Jason, who is not Korean—although now we like to joke that he is, at least by marriage," Sallie says.

For the reception, held at a fancy Korean restaurant, the couple served traditional Korean foods like kimchi (a spicy pickle made of Napa cabbage, red pepper, and garlic that's practically Korea's national dish) alongside the American fare. But perhaps one of the highlights of the wedding was the Korean p'yebaek ceremony that Jason and Sallie did for their parents as all of their guests looked on. "Back in the old days, p'yebaek marked the first time a bride greeted her husband's family as his wife," Sallie explains. "Dressed in bright silk clothes, the newlyweds would perform a series of elaborate bows to the husband's family, to whom the bride now belonged. In turn, the groom's parents tossed handfuls of dates and chestnuts into the bride's skirt—the more she caught, the more children she was supposed to bear." Jason and Sallie recreated this ritual at their unforgettable wedding.

ASK CARLEY

Which Dad to Dance With?

Q: I don't know if I should do the father/daughter dance with my dad or stepdad. I grew up with my stepdad and feel closer to him. But I don't want to offend my real dad. Help!

A: You could handle it in a few ways. Start the dance with your dad and then switch halfway to your stepdad, or vice-versa. (Let them know your plans so they won't be surprised.) Or do a complete dance with each one. You don't have to do an emotional "Daddy's Little Girl"–type song if it feels fake. Dance with Dad to something fun, like the Twist. Or choose an instrumental piece. Or skip the entire father/daughter dance sequence and show respect by including them in the receiving line instead.

So Sweet: Cutting the Cake

Wedding cake serves two purposes—it taps into the ancient ritual of sharing a bite of food to seal the marriage bond, and it's *cake,* for God's sake! Cutting the cake is one of the tastiest wedding traditions.

When: Near the end of the reception—the cake cutting is often guests' signal that it's okay to leave now. Or after the receiving line or ceremony at a champagne-and-cake-only affair.

Who Does What: The groom puts his hand over the bride's and they slice through the bottom layer of their cake together, feeding each other from the slice—whether or not to smash each other in the face with it is up to you. Often they use some special silver cake cutting knife that they've registered for or that has been bequeathed by their parents. Cameras flash. Then the couple may each serve slices to their in-laws.

Go to Chapter 15 for more on cake.

Great Cake Tip: You can include others in the bonding tradition by asking your married and as-good-as-married guests to do the feed-each-other's-face routine along with you. Wait until everyone has a slice of cake and then lead a group first-taste. You also could add a dessert-time version of an ethnic food-bonding ritual: Sip dessert wine from a two-handled cup, like the traditional *coupe de mariage* used at French receptions. Or do an after-dinner take on the Japanese sake-sharing ritual.

Where Do These Traditions Come From?

- The term "toast" stems from the sixteenth-century custom of placing a piece of toast at the bottom of a wine cup.
- The garter toss comes from two different Old English traditions. After the wedding, friends crowded into the honeymoon suite, the women to throw the groom's stockings backward over their heads at him, the men to do the same with the bride's. Whoever hit the mark was believed to be the next to marry. Guests also used to rip pieces from the bride's gown for luck; women began offering up their garters to keep the rest of their outfits intact!
- The bouquet toss comes from an ancient belief that certain herbs are lucky. A bride would give her bouquet to a friend for luck.

The Getaway

While not all couples leave their receptions in a blaze of glory, it certainly makes a nice ending to a spectacular event. We love the idea of a "last dance" song to cap the night on a high note, then, once everyone stumbles outside to line up for a fond farewell, the glamorous couple makes their way through the applauding crowd and into the car. This is the time to again be showered with bubbles or birdseed or have onlookers hold sparklers aloft. (We feel the need to point out that this will not work indoors or under a covered porch—you must be outside or else your "blaze of glory" will be a "smoky haze of chaos.")

While fewer and fewer couples are "allowing" their getaway cars to be decorated, it's still a cute, kitchy gesture. Traditionally, people tied cans and other loud objects to the back bumper of the newlyweds' car because they believed that the cacophony would drive away any evil spirits chasing after the couple. Today members of the wedding party, family, or friends might decorate your car as a way to salute (or embarrass) you. Usually someone with a cheerleading background and concurrent spirit-raising experience will volunteer to head up the decorating squad. If no one thought of it ahead of time, members of a self-appointed decorating team may sneak out near the end of the reception and hit the nearest drugstore in search of supplies.

If you don't have a car (or don't want it decorated), your friends might sneak into your honeymoon suite and loose their creativity there instead. They could scatter rose petals on the bed, pile sex toys on the nightstand, and write encouraging words on the mirror. Or maybe they'll just call your honeymoon love nest in Niagara Falls and request a bottle of champagne or welcoming sign to greet you there.

Not all couples make an official getaway from their reception these days—many stay and visit with guests until the end of the party. Especially because couples increasingly wait until the next day to leave for their honeymoon, they figure they'll spend more time with loved ones. Very nice, we think!

PART TWO

DETAILS, DETAILS

CHAPTER EIGHT

taking it personally

So you've made your decision. You want a laid-back afternoon affair on a summer Sunday. Or maybe it's going to be a dressed-to-the-nines occasion on a Saturday evening smack-dab in the middle of June. Now the key is making it *your* casual summer-day soiree, *your* black-tie ballroom affair. Create a wedding that's uniquely yours, a party that only you could have thrown, one people will remember long after they walk out the reception-hall door.

No matter what you do, just the fact that it's *your* wedding is going to make it personal. But if you're dying to be different, this chapter is for you—it's simply hundreds of ideas, some serious, some silly. Our aim is purely to inspire.

Wedding Colors

Favorite colors can be reception themes all by themselves. If you love purple, you can incorporate various shades of it into your invitations, flowers, decorations, and (of course) bridesmaids' dresses. Likewise, a cherished bloom such as a daisy or tulip can inspire an entire wedding plan.

Playing Up Your Passions

What passions, interests, or (healthy) obsessions really say who you are? What do you two do on weekends, during the evenings, whenever else you have some spare time? What do you love about your work? Would any of these things make a great party theme? You don't have to go all out to the point of kitsch—you might just choose to personalize a detail, such as favors or decorations. No matter what your passion is, chances are there's something about it that you can use to uniquely accent your big day. Here are our picks for a personal wedding, passion-style.

Going Green

Whether you're fervent activists or just Earth-loving nature buffs, infuse your wedding with your passion for the planet. Print your invitations and programs on recycled paper. Wear a secondhand dress and tux. Use flowering plants as centerpieces and a variety of live plants and trees as decorations. (They'll be easy to replant later.) Recycle all disposable cups, bottles, and paper items (or better yet, use real plates, flatware, and linen napkins). Ask guests to donate money to an eco-organization instead of buying you pres-

Do a Good Deed

A great green idea: Donate any leftover reception food to a food bank or shelter; give flowers to a shelter or retirement house.

ents. Give tree seedlings or flower seed packets as favors. Escape on a bicycle built for two or in-line skates. Take an ecotourism honeymoon.

Mad for Movies

If you two have seen every movie ever made (most of them twice) and have your own parking space at Blockbuster, incorporate your love of film into your wedding. Do up your reception room like a movie set—hang huge lights from the ceiling, put director's chairs everywhere, and stack old film-reel canisters on the tables as centerpieces. Or rent an elegant, landmark theater for the event—guests can sit in movie seats to watch the ceremony. Run silent films on the screen throughout the reception. Old theaters often have great lobbies (for the receiving line) and large areas or even a stage in front of the screen (for dancing and/or dining).

A Bibliophile Bash

Do you spend romantic Friday evenings together each with a book in your lap and Sunday mornings fighting over the *Book Review*? You're perfect candidates for a literary wedding. Have the invitations read like a story ("Once upon a time, two fabulously interesting people fell in love . . ."), or steal some lines from a treasured book or poem you both adore. Ask a loved one to read some of your favorite prose or verse during the ceremony. Have the wedding in a grand library hall or a used bookstore. Give favorite paperbacks or funky vintage bookmarks as favors. Take a literary honeymoon—head to the site of your favorite novel or visit the stomping grounds of your favorite author—Jane Austen's England, a Mississippi River cruise à la Mark Twain.

Old-Fashioned Romantics: Period Weddings

If you long for a bygone era, wrap your wedding around your favorite time. Research will be fun (and probably right up your alley). Rent your favorite period films from the era and hole yourselves up for a long weekend of armchair time travel. Pay attention to the clothes—cut, color, fabric, frills, gloves, hats, scarves, and jewelry—as well as to the music and decor. If you're mad for all things medieval, for example, hold your wedding in a Tudor-style mansion, English cottage, or period castle. Or rent the special-events pavilion at a Renaissance fair or medieval joust. Send invitations done in calligraphy on heavy parchment paper and tied with ribbon. Toast with pewter goblets. If you're more of a Gothic couple, take your cue from the *darkest* part of the Middle Ages and have a midnight gala in a castle illuminated with dozens of flickering candles. Have a fortune teller on hand.

Too dreary for you? Maybe you'd prefer an elegant Civil War–era lawn party. The bride can dress the part with a huge hoop skirt; the groom can don linen tails. Hold the wedding outside in the spring or summer, under a huge old magnolia tree. If you live in the South, take advantage of all those beautiful, historic antebellum mansions and rent one for your reception.

Period Wedding Wear

Wondering what to wear for your period wedding? Check out *What People Wore: 1800 Illustrations from Ancient Times to the Early Twentieth Century,* by Douglas Gorsline (Dover Publications, 1994).

Going Victorian

Roses, lace, harpsichord music—few historical periods are as romantic as the Victorian era (1837–1901), or as popular for period weddings.

Invites: Go formal, the norm in the Victorian era. Use script-style engraved letters on pure white or ivory paper. Slip dried rose petals into your envelopes.

Where: Rent a Victorian-style inn, a ballroom done in Victorian colors (pinks, golds, and greens), an elegant room in a history museum, a botanical garden, or a nineteenth-century estate. Or have your wedding at your parents' home, a popular choice in the Victorian era.

Style: Decorate with roses, the quintessential Victorian (and wedding!) bloom. Make liberal use of candles, flowers, and old black-and-white family portraits in silver frames.

Food: The tea reception is classic Victorian.

Music: Hire a string quartet for the ceremony and/or cocktail hour. Go with harps, harpsichords, or chamber music for the reception. Learn (and then teach guests) a popular Victorian dance, such as a reel, waltz, or quadrille.

Favors: Give engraved lockets, ivory hair combs, or soft kid gloves to bridesmaids; chocolate truffles, ornate silver frames, romantic fans, or brocade-covered boxes to guests.

Resources:

- The Victorian Paper Company is a great resource not only for invitations but for all things Victorian; www.victoriantrading.com
- The Victorian Society in America, www.victoriansociety.org
- The Victorian Yellow Pages, www.teapotpress.com

Travel Buffs

Perhaps it's not a time but a *place* that excites you. Whether you're frequent fliers or armchair enthusiasts, your wedding can reflect your love for a faraway locale. For example, if your heart is set on Spain, rent a Spanish-style hacienda or mission and hold the wedding in the central courtyard. Think wrought iron, balconies, stucco walls, and red-tile roofs. (If you live in the Southwest or California, you should have no problem finding the perfect locale.) Serve tapas (appetizer-size dishes) during cocktails and paella for the main meal. Hire Spanish classical guitar musicians for the ceremony and a flamenco performance for the reception. For favors, give Picasso-print notecards.

Career Couple

Maybe you live for the thrill of going to the office (or recording studio, or theater, or courtroom, or trading floor). If work is your passion, enhance your wedding with it. You're stockbrokers? Name the reception tables after hot commodities. If you're journalists, have your videographer and a reporter friend "interview" guests during the reception, about how they met you, when they knew you were in love, any tips they have for marital bliss. Lawyers? Maybe your favorite judge would marry you two. If one of you is a teacher—or a doctor—be sure to put an apple at every place setting!

CARA & CHRIS

August 10, Belle Isle, Michigan

WHEN CARA AND CHRIS got married, their wedding came complete with cootie catchers, a disco-era first dance, a Barry Manilow impersonator, and a gaggle of nieces and nephews cutting the rug. Like all engaged couples, Cara and Chris wanted a wedding that reflected who they are as a couple. Cara, a teacher, says, "We like to have fun—it's a must when you teach kindergarten—and we wanted our wedding to have a fun element to it." With that goal in mind, they created an event that took place in the midst of the Mardi Gras mood during the Venetian Festival at the Detroit Yacht Club.

And so two hours before the ceremony started, the two met at the end of the main dock at the yacht club, where the carnival's events were in full swing all around them. After a big hug and lots of whispered sweet nothings, the couple walked back up the dock to the club. "Lots of the people thought we were in bride and groom costumes for the festival," laughs Cara. The couple was invited to play games, taste snowcones, and carry balloons. A Barry Mainlow impersonator, hired to sing on the docks, stopped by to introduce himself and ask if he could sing for the bride. "Of course, I told him he could!" says Cara. "My sisters and I used to sing 'The Copacabana' all the time when we were little."

The wedding ceremony took place in the Starlight Circle, a manicured stretch of lawn between two trees near the water. Cara walked down the aisle with her mother and her father, to a recording of the tune "Bridal Dancing Queen." "I always loved 'Dancing Queen' by ABBA," says Cara, "and when I heard the 'Bridal' version in the movie *Muriel's Wedding,* I knew I would walk down the aisle to it someday." After a big first kiss and a round of applause from the crowd that had gathered on the docks, the newlyweds headed back up the aisle to ABBA's "I Do, I Do, I Do, I Do, I Do."

A square motif had evolved over the course of the wedding plans, starting with the princess-cut diamond in Cara's engagement ring. Cara requested an ice sculpture in the shape of three dramatic cubes, chose square invitations, ordered a square wedding cake, made square cootie catchers (Chinese fortune tellers) for the tables, used square place cards, and put the centerpiece flowers in square vases.

Cara and Chris's wedding was as much for the kids as it was for the adults. Gift bags for the youngsters included Matchbox cars, bridal Barbies, diaries, Play-Doh, ring pops, coloring books, and Barnum's Animals crackers. After dinner, the bride and groom opened the dance floor (to a choreographed dance to Tavares's "More Than a Woman"). Later, guests wandered down to the docks to play games, eat cotton candy, and enjoy the carnival. A late-night snack of brownies, cookies, and coffee was served before the last dance to Donna Summers's "Last Dance."

Using the Season

What's your ultimate romantic moment? A winter afternoon in the country. Pine trees and roaring hearth fires, crisp air against your skin, snowdrifts, and delicate flurries that transform the land into a misty netherworld. Or maybe summer is more your time of year—beach parties, bare legs, tropical drinks, romantic evening strolls. But then there's fall—the changing leaves, that smell in the air, delicious sweater weather. And spring's not too shabby, either—new beginnings, rose gardens, the most perfect temperatures. The season can help you decide on wedding food, music, flowers, favors, decorations, even your wardrobe. And the holiday wedding takes the idea one step further. It also lets you tap into the sentiment of the occasion—romance on Valentine's Day, eerieness (and fun!) on Halloween. Here are some of our favorite seasonal wedding ideas.

A New Year's bash. Ring in the new year with the ultimate resolution. Start late on New Year's Eve—the reception might not begin until around 8:00 or 9:00 P.M. Consider partying first and saying your vows at the stroke of midnight. (Imagine the anniversary celebrations!) Have your best man toast the two of you soon after the witching hour. Invite guests to wear their glitziest clothes. You, too, can dress in sparkly style; a bridal gown with silver or gold trim; bridesmaids' dresses shot through with silver thread; groom's and groomsmen's cummerbunds or vests in metallic shades.

A Valentine's party. For a February wedding, send invites that look like Valentine's Day cards. Or go with Victorian-style invitations embossed with hearts and flowers. The flowers should be roses, of course. Use a pink or red color scheme, with blush-hued bridesmaids' dresses and groomsmen accents. For a cute, clever touch, attendants might all wear heart-shaped sunglasses down the aisle. (You could, too!) Have the flower girl drop heart-shaped confetti. Decorate with cupids, and scatter candy conversation hearts on all the tables. Choose songs for the playlist that always mention love.

Music Makes the Mood

One of the best ways to get a theme across is music. Use songs from your era of choice—be it 1970s, 1980s, Baroque, or Victorian—to set a reception mood.

Spring fling. For a springtime wedding, think growth and green. Spring is the season of renewal. (And *rain*—unless you're gamblers, you might not want to plan an outside wedding for this season—at least make sure you secure an indoor alternate.) Decorate with spring colors—watery blue, light purple, pale yellow, new-shoot green. Use a flower motif for the centerpieces and room decor. Give bulbs or pastel umbrellas as favors. Have classical music playing during the ceremony and reception. (How about Vivaldi's "Spring"?)

Easter affair. For the site, think garden, tearoom, or a greenhouse. Brides, wear a dress with pastel touches or simple lace details. Grooms, go for a light-colored linen suit and pastel tie. Serve a traditional Easter meal (ham, potatoes, eggs, pound cake for dessert) on tables topped with pretty pastel umbrellas; have your officiant do a traditional Easter blessing over the food before you eat. Decorate with plenty of lilies. Have an Easter egg hunt.

Summer lovin'. Make your June, July, or August wedding the essence of endless summer. Cover tables with red-and-white picnic tablecloths. Or go with limeade-green cloth and serve food on thick, matte-plastic plates in jewel tones. Serve upscale picnic food (grilled chicken, fish, and steak, along with tons of fresh fruit and vegetables). Use sand pails full of flowers as centerpieces. Dance together to Gershwin's "Summertime" (from *Porgy and Bess).* Or throw a pool party and give guests their own pool towels as favors, embroidered with your names and the wedding date. If you live near a beach, have a late-afternoon wedding on the shore. Start the ceremony around 6:00 P.M., with the crashing ocean and the sunset as your backdrop. Light a bonfire later and have the band kick in. The bride might wear a short white dress; bridesmaids, flirty sun dresses. The groom could appear in a linen suit or linen pants and shirt with no jacket.

Fourth of July. Want to express some national pride? Rent a Colonial-era mansion and hang a huge flag out front. Or plan your party at a site with a great view of your city or town's annual fireworks extravaganza. Make the meal an Independence Day picnic—grilled or barbecued chicken, potato salad, watermelon, Bomb Pops (those big red, white, and blue Popsicles). Hand out sparklers wrapped with ribbon as favors, or use them to top off your wedding cake.

Location Salvation

Fall weather can turn at the drop of a leaf—and so can spring weather, for that matter. If you're planning an outdoor wedding in October or November or during the rainy months of March or April, make sure to have a location backup.

Fall fest. Fall offers great wedding weather. Choose a location with windows that look out on a valley of red, orange, and burnt umber trees. Or wed in a park, forest preserve, apple orchard, or vineyard (if it's not too chilly where you live). Include a pressed leaf with each invitation (available at craft stores), or go with a leafy border. Dress bridesmaids in velvet, jacquard, or brocade in rich colors such as magenta, hunter, bronze, and gold. Decorate with piles of leaves, bales of hay, pots of mums, and pumpkins. Hang gold netting with leaves woven into it over the cake table. Have hayrides available for guests, or set up a dunking-for-apples station. Serve turkey, stuffing, potatoes, cranberry sauce, pumpkin pie, caramel apples, and mulled cider. Decorate the cake with fresh leaves.

Monster mash. A Halloween wedding? Invite guests to come in costume. Or make it a black-tie (and orange accent) affair. Use jack o' lanterns as centerpieces, or opt for bouquets of dried or fresh flowers with sheaves of wheat and cattails surrounded by mini-pumpkins and gourds. Put bowls of candy corn on every table. Give Halloween masks, little pumpkins with your names and the date inscribed on them, or bags of Halloween candy for favors. Be sure to dance to the "Monster Mash."

Winter wonderland. Want to create that cozy, romantic feeling? Rent an estate or hall with a working fireplace. Decorate with huge silver, gold, and white pillar candles. Hang sparkly snowflakes from the ceiling, and put fresh pine or fir trees in the corners. Spray the windows with snow-in-a can, give snow globes as favors, and give snowflake pendants and faux-fur mufflers to your bridesmaids. Serve hot cocoa (spiked with Peppermint Schnapps for the big kids). Arrive at the wedding in a horse-drawn sleigh (or carriage). Or make it a decadent pre-Russian Revolution winter party. Choose a room with gorgeous chandeliers. Crown an overflowing buffet table with a swanky ice sculpture. Serve champagne, vodka, caviar, and smoked salmon. Hire strolling violinists to play during dinner. The bride can wear a white, fur-trimmed cape over velvet, taffeta, or silk. The groom might come in tails and a fur cap. Arrive and depart in a white limo.

White Christmas. If your ceremony's in a church, chances are quite good that it will already be decked out for the Christmas season. For your reception, decorate Christmas trees with white lights, silver balls, and red ribbons. Stack huge piles of oversized "presents"—boxes wrapped in holiday paper. Hang mistletoe *everywhere.* Serve eggnog, plum pudding, ham, and turkey. Have a cake decorated like a candy cane, and serve Christmas cookies along with it. Hire Christmas carolers or a barbershop quartet to lead guests in singing favorite holiday songs. Lots of young guests? Have Santa drop in!

Adding Ethnic Traditions

Show respect for your ancestors and your families—and get in touch with your cultures, too—by incorporating ethnic traditions. Blend rituals from both your backgrounds, making your wedding a mélange of customs. And keep in mind that there's no rule that says you have to stick to your own heritage. If you love the sentiment or meaning behind another culture's custom, add it to the brew.

African-American broom jumping. This custom dates back to nineteenth-century slave weddings in the United States. Slaves' marriages weren't legally binding—even if a minister conducted the ceremony—so many couples jumped over a broom together to symbolize their entrance into married life. (A broom represents the home in certain parts of Africa.) Some believed that whoever jumped higher or cleared the handle first would rule the roost!

More African-American Wedding Advice

The best African-American wedding-planning book is *Jumping the Broom: The African-American Wedding Planner,* by Harriette Cole (Henry Holt, 1995).

Chinese red. In China, red is the color of luck and joy. Chinese and Chinese-American couples often incorporate red into their wedding decor with red candles, favors, tablecloths, napkins. Guests present the couple with money or jewelry in red envelopes. Brides may change into several dresses throughout the ceremony and reception, the last one usually red. You might insert a sheet of red tissue paper into your invitations, choose red wedding flowers, walk down a red aisle runner, and/or tie red ribbons around your favors. Check out local Asian stores for Chinese party decorations or a red silk dress. Or wear white but have the bridesmaids wear red. The groom and groomsmen might wear red cummerbunds and ties.

More Asian Wedding Advice

An excellent book: *Wild Geese and Tea: An Asian-American Wedding Planner,* by Shu Shu Costa (Riverhead Books, 1998).

You don't have to wear red to incorporate the Chinese tradition of changing gowns into your wedding. Some brides change from a white Western-style dress for the ceremony into a less-restrictive gown (such as a bone-colored slip dress) for the reception.

Chinese tea ceremony. Chinese couples traditionally honor their ancestors with a tea ceremony—the couple kneels before older relatives and family friends and offers a cup of tea as a gesture of respect. Each honoree hands the couple an envelope of money or gold jewelry, then gives the chair to the next relative in line. You can follow the tradition or honor your ancestors in your own way: Dance to your grandparents' first-dance wedding song, or give thanks to your parents or other relatives and toast them with tea.

English wedding walk. In English villages, the bride and her wedding party traditionally walk together from her home to the church, led by a young girl throwing flower blossoms in their path. The wedding walk is perfect if your celebration will be in your small, close-knit hometown where you can parade down Main Street, or if you're having your ceremony in the same site as your reception. Consider having the entire wedding party and all of your guests join the procession to the party area after you exchange your vows.

Indian henna. Having your hands and feet painted with henna—a popular prewedding ritual in India, Pakistan, and many Muslim countries (including some in Africa)—originated as a way to replace or augment the precious dynastic jewelry worn by fabulously rich Muslim brides. Typically, a hired henna professional visits the bride about a week before the wedding to draw elaborate, flowery scrolls on her hands and feet. Thicker than the henna used to dye hair auburn, hand and foot henna stains the skin for a couple of weeks. Henna has become a fashion accessory in the hipper enclaves of some large urban areas.

Hire a professional to decorate you, or ask one of your friends to do it. (Choose carefully; there's no washing off a wobbly henna job.) Look through a few photo books for design inspiration. Or call an Indian or Pakistani cultural center for a recommendation.

An Irish Ring Thing

Named after a fishing village in western Ireland, the Claddagh ring is worn with the crown facing inward, toward the wrist, upon betrothal, and outward, toward the nails, to symbolize marriage.

Irish toasts. Toasting is an art in Ireland. Here are some traditional toasts:

- "May your hearts be as warm as your hearthstone."
- "May God sleep on your pillow."
- "May you be poor in misfortune, rich in blessings."
- "May you know nothing but happiness from this day forward."
- "A generation of children on the children of your children."
- "If you're lucky enough to be Irish, you're lucky enough."

At the end of the reception, the wedding party may gather around the bride and groom; everyone is poured a glass of mead. The newlyweds recite an Irish toast: "Friends and relatives, so fond and dear, 'tis our greatest pleasure to have you here. When many years this day has passed, fondest memories will always last. So we drink a cup of Irish mead and ask God's blessing in your hour of need." The guests respond: "On this special day, our wish to you, the goodness of the old, the best of the new. God bless you both who drink this mead, may it always fill your every need."

Japanese sake ritual. Japanese weddings include a sake-sharing tradition, popularly called *san-san-kudos (san* means "three," *ku* means "to deliver," and *do* means "nine.") Using three flat sake cups stacked on top of one another, the bride and groom take three sips each from the cups. Then their parents also take sips (for a total of nine), cementing the bond between the families. You can incorporate a sake-sharing ritual into your ceremony or do it at the reception. Ask your guests to join in after the last sip; you might give them sake cups as favors.

Latin American sponsors. In Latin American countries, a group of sponsors (usually married couples who are friends of the couple's parents) sometimes help host the wedding. Each couple (or person—there's no rule against a supportive single) hosts a different part of the celebration. If your parents have a tight group of close friends, include them in the wedding preparations. Let each sponsor choose which part to be involved in—the flowers, the food, the alcohol, the music, and so on. Thank them officially in your ceremony program.

If you're uncomfortable with financial help, include these special people in your wedding planning to create a sense of community *without* asking for money. Have sponsors to help organize or oversee various elements rather than foot the bills for them. Your aunt's a great cook? Ask her to help with the menu. Your uncle's a music buff? Ask him to listen to bands and narrow them down. Seat all the sponsors in places of honor at the ceremony and reception.

Kids Will Go Crazy For . . .

In Mexico, a candy-filled piñata can be part of a wedding. Guests take turns whacking the papier-mâché creation until it bursts open and spills onto the floor. This is a great after-dinner tradition to incorporate if you'll have lots of child guests.

Native American corn. Navajos use that crop of all crops, maize (that's corn to you), to symbolize the marriage union. Families combine yellow corn (ground by the bride's family)

More Intriguing Cultural Traditions

More wedding traditions we're intrigued with:

For Polish village weddings, brides traditionally wore a crown or head wreath of rosemary woven by their friends. (Rosemary symbolizes remembrance.)

In Dutch tradition, a pine tree is planted outside the newlyweds' home as a symbol of fertility and luck.

Czech newlyweds are showered with peas—not rice—after the ceremony.

A Japanese groom crushes a raw egg with his bare foot during the wedding ceremony. One meaning: to symbolize the delicacy of the marriage bond.

German brides carry salt and bread on their wedding day to symbolize wealth and good fortune.

Egyptian women pinch the bride for good luck.

and white corn (ground by the groom's side) in a pudding, which is brought to the reception. The couple tastes the pudding together, the first of many married meals.

You can tap into your Native American heritage by adapting the grind-and-taste ritual to suit your style. Serve a two-tone pudding (corn or otherwise) as a special dessert. Or offer marbled bread along with the wedding feast. If your mother makes a special dessert—such as pineapple pudding—and your honey's father is known for his chocolate cake, consider serving both. Let your guests in on the tradition by including a line about the special dish on a printed menu.

Norwegian night life. Nomadic Norwegian tribes traditionally held their weddings late at night. For your own midnight wedding, light the room with countless votives and candlesticks. Bridesmaids can carry candles instead of bouquets. Or set them on stands illuminating the aisle. Start your all-night wedding no earlier than 8:00 P.M. Have cocktails, dinner, dancing, and a breakfast buffet in the wee hours. Make sure to brew plenty of coffee! Serve Norwegian food—salmon, herring, vodka to drink. Use upturned Viking-style helmets full of flowers as centerpieces.

Educate Your Audience

Explain cultural traditions you include in your ceremony in the program; at the reception, announce the meanings of any rituals that are performed, or put little cards on the tables that note the symbolism.

Russian road trip. In Russia, newlyweds take a tour of their hometown's sites—snapping photos of themselves at various locations—before heading off on the honeymoon. You, too, can spend an afternoon of local appreciation before catching that flight to Bali. By taking stock of your hometown's own offerings, you're establishing a pattern of valuing what you already have.

Scottish fling. In Scotland, the reception includes a Highland Fling dance, a high-spirited performance with lots of kicking. Ask your Scottish uncle to give you a tutorial, or hire professional Scottish dancers—kilts and all—to perform during your reception.

Destination Wedding Paperwork

You'll probably do less planning for a wedding away, but there might be a few more documents to deal with:

If you're marrying in the United States, call the county marriage license department for the town in which you'll have the ceremony; ask for explicit guidelines regarding birth certificates, health tests, and proof of divorce (if applicable).

If marrying overseas, ask the country's U.S. embassy or tourism bureau about residency requirements, documentation, medical tests, paperwork processing time, proof of divorce, witnesses, and the requirements for a religious ceremony vs. a civil ceremony.

Getting Married Away

The Destination Wedding

Before you plan a faraway affair, ask yourself if your essential friends and family will be up for the trip. Grandma may not want to fly to Italy for the week. Many couples compromise by hosting a postwedding celebration back home for those who could not attend the actual event.

Keep in mind that if you're hosting a wedding in a distant locale, you will need to entrust at least part of the planning to someone else's capable hands. An on-location wedding coordinator (many resorts include a coordinator in their wedding packages) can shoulder the burden of researching and securing vendors, arranging airport transportation, and locating all those last-minute things, from dry cleaners to hiking tours, that may come up. Depending on your temperament, this can be a welcome reprieve or a scary proposition.

See "Destination Wedding Requirements" on The Knot (theknot.com/destination weddings) for the rules in some of the most popular wedding-away countries.

The affordability of many destination weddings—especially at a beach resort—has many couples speeding off to the airport faster than you can say "I do." For instance, a couple can fly to an all-inclusive in Jamaica, get married, and stay for a deluxe weeklong honeymoon for as little as $3,000 to $4,000. Napa Valley and Nantucket won't be as budget friendly, but the close proximity allows for easier access. Keep in mind you can spend as much or as little as you want on a destination wedding, just as you can at home; there are no steadfast rules about which is less expensive. But don't forget to factor in at least a couple of prewedding research trips into your budget, even if the coordinator is doing the bulk of the work for you.

LEE & JEFF

July 7, Orcas Island, Washington

WHEN JEFF WAS FIVE YEARS OLD, his family spent their summers on Orcas Island, in Washington's Puget Sound. One summer, he built himself a little bench and set it on a point overlooking the water near the family cabin. Decades later, back on Orcas with not only his family but also his girlfriend's family, Jeff took some time to make sure his bench was sturdy. Then he walked his girlfriend, Lee, out to the point, sat on the bench with her, and presented her with a diamond ring and a marriage proposal.

Deciding where to set their wedding was a challenge for the couple. "My family is from Chicago, Jeff's is from San Francisco, and we were living in L.A.," Lee reports. "But we kept coming back to, 'Oh, I really wish we could be married on Orcas.' " When they finally decided to have the wedding in the place that meant so much to both of them, Lee says, "It took a bit of convincing to get my parents to accept that I was not going to be married at the Four Seasons in Chicago. But they love Orcas Island, too."

Planning the wedding involved lots of long-distance research since the couple lived in California, but they got help from the staff at Rosario Resort.

The days before the wedding were filled with celebrations. Jeff's uncle hosted a fireworks-filled Fourth of July party for about 50 people; the next night there was a crab-fest party at Jeff's family's cabin, this time with 125 guests. Friday was the rehearsal dinner, limited to about 45, while 150 guests attended the wedding.

The Wedding Weekend

Your mom lives in San Francisco, your dad in Boston. Your sweetie's parents are in Tulsa, you two live in Houston, and other friends and family are scattered all over the country. You're the perfect candidates for a weekend wedding—a three-day affair that'll make everyone glad they used their frequent-flier miles to come see you get hitched.

Don't Be Demanding

Make weekend wedding activities optional—you don't want to force everyone to climb aboard a tour bus every day. Some guests may prefer to just hang out around the hotel pool and catch up.

A weekend wedding requires a bit of "cruise directing" on your part; you'll want to have some preplanned activities set up. Definitely include a dinner for out-of-town guests the night before the wedding (or just invite everyone to the rehearsal dinner) as well as a pre- or postwedding brunch, as casual or formal as you like. You also might schedule a barbecue, picnic, or another organized activity, such as a round of golf or museum trip during the several days before the ceremony. For free-time activities, provide your guests with the information they'll need, whether it's a list of events from the hotel concierge, tourist brochures, or a "hot sheet" of fun activities you write yourselves. You don't have to stay at every event the entire time—ask close friends and family to oversee things, and be sure to make an appearance at everything.

The usual course of events goes something like this:

- The day that guests will be arriving in town, welcome them with an open house–style party. A friend or family member might offer to host an all-day barbecue; guests can trickle in, grab a hot dog and a drink, and shake off jet fatigue while they mingle.
- If most of your out-of-town loved ones are staying at one hotel, check out the options for hosting a hospitality suite. This lounge, usually stocked with drinks, snacks, television, and games, is a place for your guests to kick back and catch up without having to sit on their beds.
- The night before the big day should be marked by an all-invited dinner (often, this will be the rehearsal dinner). Most couples like to keep this final prewedding fête on the casual side (a beach party, a feast at your favorite ethnic restaurant), so guests are ready for a more formal feel on w-day.
- On the day of your wedding, plan a couple of activities to keep people busy (especially if the wedding is late in the day). Perhaps offer a tour, a hike, a golf outing, or a shopping expedition. No need for the bride and groom to show up (you two will have plenty to do)—ask members of the wedding party to play host for you.
- The morning after should bring everyone together for one last time for a breakfast or brunch gathering. Most couples love the day-after brunch; it's a chance to relive that day before and spend more time with guests in a less-pressured environment. You can host a brunch at the hotel or have a friend or family member do the deed for you.

With such a hot list of social opportunities on the weekend's schedule, you've got to keep the folks informed. One option is a newsletter. This can be fun for your guests, and you can probably create a cool newsletter on your computer. List the schedule of parties and events, important phone numbers (the hosts of the parties, the hotel concierge), fun places to eat, tourist sites you think are cool, and so on. Many couples also use the newsletter to list their wedding party along with cute bios. Mail this a month or so before the big day if you can; otherwise, tuck it into the guests' hotel rooms.

A cooler option, for those with the skill, is a website. If you're not totally tech-savvy, you can follow the super-simple directions for creating a wedding web page at theknot.com. a website or web page is handy because you can update it constantly and get guests the info they need about directions and activities without packing your invites with twenty pieces of paper. It's also okay to put your registry information here, but don't make that the point. Add photographs of yourselves and, if you can, the wedding party and your families along with bios. One drawback: Some of your guests may not be Internet-savvy, so make sure you have a backup plan for getting pertinent information out to everyone who needs it.

Action! The Extreme Wedding

You need action; you crave excitement. Your lives are intense, and you want your wedding to measure up. For an active twist on the destination wedding, make it a high-adventure affair. Have your ceremony on a mountaintop and ask select guests to don hiking shoes to make the trip up with you. Say your vows in midair—while skydiving—with your most daring guests floating with you (and the rest waiting safely on the ground).

If you're set on a specific locale (a cliff, raging rapids, a bridge off which to bungee-jump), call the tourism office or chamber of commerce in that area to see how you can make your wedding dream come true. If you'd like an active wedding that's not *too* over the top, call companies that offer various degrees of adventure travel. Check with several to see where they can take you and how they'll get you all there, plus what arrangements they can make for the ceremony and accommodations. (Just how rustic are those rooms?) Some good places to start with include Backroads (camping or hike-and-bike trips; www.backroads.com) and Butterfield & Robinson (bike tours throughout Europe and Canada; www.butterfield.com).

Just Do It: Elopement

You can just picture it—the two of you racing out of town in a borrowed Mustang convertible, the wind whipping through your hair. You're eloping! You can elope far away—make it a destination wedding you don't tell anyone about (how utterly romantic!)—or head over to city hall, then meet family and friends at a restaurant to celebrate (or simply take yourselves out and tell everyone else later).

Some couples even get parental consent to wed this way. Here's how it works: Offer to elope, saving your parents the $20,000 they'd spend on a big wedding. They see the brilliance of your thinking, slip you a check for $10,000 as a gift, and act shocked, surprised, and hurt about your decision (to save face before their friends). You wed at the courthouse and use the $10,000 as a down payment on your dream house.

More Info for Elopers

Caribbean Tourism Organization: www.ct-cto.com
Fiji: www.bulafiji.com
Hawaii Visitors and Convention Bureau: www.gohawaii.com
Jamaica Tourist Board: www.jamaicatravel.com
Las Vegas Convention and Visitors Authority: www.lasvegas24hours.com
Mexican Tourism Board: www.visitmexico.com
Puerto Rico Tourism Company: www.gotopuertorico.com
United States Virgin Islands Department of Tourism: www.usvitourism.vi

Before you go, there are a few details to check on. Every state has its own rules for the waiting period between when you apply for your marriage license and when you actually can wed. Call the courthouse to find out the local law. If you want to elope abroad, call your dream country's tourist office, consulate, or embassy for rules and legal requirements.

NOTES

CHAPTER NINE

the paper trail

Invitations are the first tangible evidence your guests have of your wedding—they can go a long way toward setting the tone. Think of them as a grand direct-marketing opportunity. Besides just letting guests know when and where the festivities will take place, invites provide clues as to the formality of the affair (which will tip them off to the dress code) and a sneak peek at your wedding vision. Ideally, you should get busy with invite investigating at least six months before the wedding.

Printing Techniques

Probably the most important factor in an invitation's character (and certainly price tag) is not the paper but the print. There are four main printing techniques, each with its own distinct charm and price range, and one fancy extra called embossing. Depending on the formality of your wedding style and, of course, your budget, here are the options.

Engraving

This is the most expensive of print methods, used for all ultra-formal wedding invites (and hoity-toity party invitations in general). The printer uses a metal plate engraved with the text you've provided to stamp the words onto the paper from behind. The final product is textured, with raised letters in the front and "cavities" in the back.

Choose this if: you have a generous invitation budget; can find a retailer that does this (mass-market shops sometimes don't); can wait up to eight weeks for the job to be completed (high style hurries for no one); are having an ultra-formal affair with a *huge* guest list (the engraving will tip guests off that you mean formal business; also, the larger the order, the more cost-effective engraving is).

Paper Prices

What a hundred invitations with standard text at Kate's Paperie in New York City cost:

With Printed Envelopes
Engraving: $375
Thermography: $244

Without Printed Envelopes
Engraving: $284
Thermography: $204

Thermography

This is the most popular method, used by most large stationery printers and mail-order companies. A heat-based process fuses ink and resinous powder to create raised lettering; it's virtually indistinguishable from engraving work unless you feel the back of the invitation, which remains smooth.

Choose this if: you have a less-than-gigantic budget but still want formal invitations; you're not concerned with having the absolute crème de la crème when it comes to the invites; you want an off-the-wall ink color (often not available with engraving); you don't have the two months you'd need to wait for an engraved order.

A Grave Decision

Don't stress over choosing thermography over engraving. Most people won't know the difference, and you'll shave up to 50 percent off your invitation costs.

Offset Printing

This is the flat printing that's used on most every flier, letterhead, or birthday card the world 'round. A rubber cylinder is used to press ink onto the paper. Many ready-made invitations, thank-you notes, and R.S.V.P. cards are made using this technique, but not all retailers offer this option for wedding stationery (thermography being all the rage these days).

Choose this if: you need all the cost-busting you can get; you want to play with different colors of ink (with both thermography and engraving you are pretty much limited to one color); you want to use highly textured paper (pressed with flowers, say) that won't work with raised lettering; you want to put a photograph on your mail-outs; you're having a theme wedding and want invitation art that will reflect it (with this method, specially crafted stamps can be used to create, for example, a rose garden for an English tea wedding, lovey-dovey giraffes for a safari wedding, or a heart-shaped baseball diamond for a sports-related weekend wedding).

Letterpress

A beautiful printing alternative to engraving (but more expensive). The labor-intensive method dates back to the fifteenth century and involves inking an image to produce an impression; the impression is then transferred by placing paper against the image and manually applying pressure. The images and typeface appear precise—individually "stamped into" the paper—and very rich in color. Choose this if: you're using unusual paper, motifs, typeface, or want to play around with pigments. Comparatively, engraving and thermography restrict the possibilities.

Embossing

A raised printing method usually used for large initials or borders; because of its high price tag, hardly anyone has an entire invitation embossed. Upscale stationers usually will be able to oblige, however.

Choose this if: you want spectacular-looking initials on your thank-you notes or formal couple's stationery; your wedding is formal and you want a border or other raised detail on your posh invites; you're a sucker when it comes to "extra" touches.

Calligraphy

The ancient art of gorgeous, curvy, curly handwriting. You should be able to locate calligraphers through your local phone book. (Be sure to get references and check out samples before you hire.) You'll spend a *very* pretty penny for this hand-crafted look, but—thanks to technol-

Paper and Printing Glossary

The type of paper you use is as important as your actual design in terms of establishing a "mood" with your invite. The lingo to know:

100% Cotton: Elegant, understated, and pure.
Blind-embossing: A printing process that employs a die (see below) to yield colorless letters and images with a raised "relief" surface.
Corrugated: Thick, folded stock that says "urban chic."
Deckle edge: The irregular, feathered, "torn" edge of handmade paper.
Die-cutting: The process of cutting various paper shapes, particularly with envelopes.
Glassine: A very thin, waxy paper. Thinner than vellum (see below), its surface is slick and shiny, whereas vellum is more translucent. Glassine is best suited for envelope use, while vellum is sturdy enough to be printed on directly for invitation use.
Handmade papers: Made from natural organic materials including cotton, rag, hemp, and plant fibers, uneven or "rough" in texture.
Industrial papers: Made from chipboard or newsprint, often from recycled fibers, industrial papers have a rugged, hip look about them. Corrugated cardboard and brown kraft paper (think brown grocery bags) are examples.
Jacquard: Screen-printed paper that creates an illusion of layering; for example, paper that looks like it's overlaid with a swatch of lace.
Laid: Like Vellum except with a rougher, "bumpy" finish.
Linen: Another classic choice. Linen papers are grainier than pure cotton stocks.
Marbled paper: Decorative paper marked by swirling, abstract patterns that resemble the surface of marble.
Matte: Paper with an opaque, nonreflective finish.
Moiré: Named after the fabric, this stock bears subtle watermarks.
Mylar: Shiny, mirrorlike paper that's highly modern.
Parchment: Cloudy, translucent paper that creates an airy, dreamy effect.
Rice paper: A thin, soft paper, that is actually *not* made from rice. It's nontraditional, but beautiful and elegant. It can only accept the letterpress printing mode; cream and ivory are the most common colors used in the design of rice paper wedding invitations.
Vellum: A cotton blend (thus, somewhat less expensive) with a smooth finish.

ogy—you can get a similar effect for less by using calligraphy software, available at many stationery shops.

Choose this if: you're having a small wedding and want handwritten, intimate invites to match; you're planning a Victorian or other suitably themed wedding; price is no object, or calligraphy is important enough to you that you're willing to pay for it.

Invitation Basics

You can have the most gorgeous invitations on Earth (and we're sure you will!), but when it comes right down to it, this handy-dandy piece of paper is a functional item, spelling out the essential wedding info—it tells guests who's getting married, who's hosting the wedding, and where, when, and what time the festivities will take place. So it's important that they are not only attractive but easy to read and understand. Just about every wedding invite includes the names of the wedding hosts/sponsors (that usually means your parents), your names, the day of the week, the date, time, and address of the ceremony and/or reception, and R.S.V.P. information (unless you're sending separate response cards). See "Invitation Wording," below, for specific examples.

Ordering Your Invites

Order invitations as soon as you have your guest list nailed down—shoot for five months before your wedding day. You'll have time to choose the exact invitations you want, have them printed, fix any printing mistakes—and still get them out six to eight weeks before the big day.

How Many?

Order enough invitations for your entire guest list (that includes the wedding party), plus twenty-five extra for the inevitable boo-boos and last-minute changes (such as replacement guests for nonacceptances). We also think giving your parents a few invitations as keepsakes to place in their wedding albums is a nice idea—and you'll want to keep a few for yourselves, too.

What Style?

There are thousands of invitation designs—and millions of custom-made possibilities. When selecting yours, consider:

The Formality of Your Wedding: From engraved block or script print on ecru, ivory, or white paper (for a super-formal affair) to a beach ball imprinted with text (for an informal seaside bash), your invitation should clue guests in to what to expect—and wear.

Your Personal Style: If you're not buttoned-down types, people aren't going to expect a hoity-toity invite, so go nuts! Conversely, if Class is your middle name, go the whole nine yards—with tissue paper, lined envelopes, embossed seals, and all.

How Many Invitation Inserts You'll Have: If you need to include a map, separate response cards for five different weekend events, and hotel information, keep the design simple so that your invitations don't weigh a ton (and thus cost a bundle to mail).

The Size of Your Wedding: If you're inviting fewer than fifty guests, it's fine to handwrite your invites on pretty paper—a great money-saver (and time-saver if you're marrying quickly). If your handwriting is less than wonderful, get someone else (Mom? a bridesmaid?) to do the dirty work. Bribe them with your undying devotion.

Prepare for Postage

Go to the post office and weigh a complete invitation so you know *exactly* how much postage to put on each one; your mailing costs might be relatively high if you have lots of inserts. Having your invites returned for insufficient postage can throw your wedding-planning schedule for quite a loop!

The Envelope, Please

Don't forget to order your envelopes. Get fifty to one hundred more than the number of people on your guest list. (Wedding invite envelopes have to be handwritten, and that means mistakes—if you know you'll make many, get yourself lots of extras.) If you'll have inner envelopes (most invitations, and definitely formal ones, are assembled with an inner and outer envelope; see "Assembling the Invites," below), get fifty to one hundred more than double your guest list.

Invitation Wording

As far as what to actually print on your invitations, the must-haves are who is getting married, who is hosting the party, when the ceremony will begin, and where. Beyond that, it's up to you, although most people go with the formal, polite wordings we're about to spell out. You can add your own personal flair, but in general, it's a good idea to keep the text simple. If you are having your ceremony or reception on the beach, or at a park, or any other place that does not have an adjacent indoor location, make sure to list where guests should go in case of bad weather.

The wording of the invitation should reflect who's hosting the party. Typically, the phrase "request the honor of your presence" is used formally; "request the pleasure of your company" is a bit more familiar.

Below are sample wordings for typical family/hosting situations. Ask your stationer for help and advice, as well, and don't be afraid to adapt these based on your families' circumstances.

When the Bride's Parents Are Hosting the Wedding

(Adapt for groom's parents if they're sponsoring.)

MR. AND MRS. PETER JOHNSON
(or Peter and Miranda Johnson)
REQUEST THE HONOR OF YOUR PRESENCE
AT THE MARRIAGE OF THEIR DAUGHTER
HEATHER AMANDA
AND
JEFFREY MICHAEL HARRIS
SON OF
MR. AND MRS. BRADLEY HARRIS
(or Bradley and Wendy Harris)
THURSDAY, THE THIRTEENTH OF MAY
AT SIX O'CLOCK (*"in the evening"* IS OPTIONAL)
CHIP OF HEAVEN CHURCH
111 YUMA AVENUE
KIRKWOOD, MISSOURI

If the bride's parents are primarily paying for the wedding, the names of the groom's parents traditionally are left off the invite, but we like adding the "son of" line and acknowledging the groom's parents, too. Be forewarned, though—if one set of parents is putting out lots of money for the wedding, they may object to this "equal" treatment.

More Intimate Invites

Add a personal touch to your wording. Suggestions:

- "Sara Amanda Ferrari and Todd Alan Springer invite you to join them in a celebration of their union."
- "We ask those closest to our hearts to help us celebrate our marriage . . . (where, when info goes here) . . . Sara Ferrari and Todd Springer."
- "Sara Ferrari and Todd Springer are getting married! Come dance till dawn and raise a glass (or two or three). . . ."
- "Love is in the air—and you're cordially invited to come smell the roses at the wedding of Sara Amanda Ferrari and Todd Alan Springer. . . ."
- "Sara Amanda Ferrari and Todd Alan Springer request the pleasure of your company at their wedding reception" (if you're using separate ceremony cards).

When Both Sets of Parents Are Hosting

MR. AND MRS. PETER JOHNSON
AND
MR. AND MRS. BRADLEY HARRIS
REQUEST THE PLEASURE OF YOUR COMPANY
AT THE MARRIAGE OF THEIR CHILDREN
HEATHER AMANDA
AND
JEFFREY MICHAEL
THURSDAY, THE THIRTEENTH OF MAY
ETC.

When the Couple Is Hosting Their Own Wedding

MS. HEATHER AMANDA JOHNSON
AND
MR. JEFFREY MICHAEL HARRIS
REQUEST THE HONOR OF YOUR PRESENCE
AT THEIR MARRIAGE
THURSDAY, THE THIRTEENTH OF MAY
ETC.

RECEPTION AFTERWARD AT
THE ROSELAND BALLROOM
222 GROVE STREET
ST. LOUIS, MISSOURI

The reception info can go in the lower right- or left-hand corner of the ceremony invite, or you can have separate reception enclosure cards printed. If the reception is in the same location, put "Reception immediately afterward" on the ceremony invite.

When a Single Parent Is Hosting Alone

MR. PETER JOHNSON
REQUESTS THE HONOR OF YOUR PRESENCE
AT THE MARRIAGE OF HIS DAUGHTER
HEATHER AMANDA
TO
JEFFREY MICHAEL HARRIS
THURSDAY, THE THIRTEENTH OF MAY
ETC.

KINDLY RESPOND
MR. PETER JOHNSON
44 LEAF WAY
KIRKWOOD, MISSOURI

R.S.V.P. information can be included on the invite in lieu of separate response cards—this is the formal way to request a handwritten response.

When a Divorced or Widowed Parent Is Hosting with Spouse/Bride's or Groom's Stepparent

JOHN AND MIRANDA PECK
REQUEST THE PLEASURE OF YOUR COMPANY
AT THE MARRIAGE OF MRS. PECK'S DAUGHTER
HEATHER AMANDA JOHNSON
TO
JEFFREY MICHAEL HARRIS
SON OF
MR. AND MRS. BRADLEY HARRIS
THURSDAY, THE THIRTEENTH OF MAY
ETC.

When Divorced Parents Are Hosting Jointly

(Stepparents can be included on the same line as their spouses if everyone agrees to it.)

MR. PETER JOHNSON
AND
MRS. MIRANDA PECK
REQUEST THE PLEASURE OF YOUR COMPANY
AT THE MARRIAGE OF THEIR DAUGHTER
HEATHER AMANDA JOHNSON
TO
JEFFREY MICHAEL HARRIS
SON OF
MR. AND MRS. BRADLEY HARRIS
THURSDAY, THE THIRTEENTH OF MAY
ETC.

Never put divorced parents on the same line on an invite; it may confuse guests as to their relationship. Only the names of couples who are married should go on the same line.

Addressing the Envelopes

You've got a stack of invites on your kitchen table, and you're staring at a bunch of blank envelopes. Here's what to do next.

The Outer Envelope

The outer envelope is where you write the recipients' full names, official titles, first names, and all. It's where tradition is upheld, decorum celebrated; that means no cutting corners with abbreviations such as Dr., NY, or St. (Mrs., Mr., Ms., and Jr. are the only okey-dokey shorthands). Some examples:

Single Recipient

MS. ABIGAIL ANSCH
44 ACORN DRIVE
HOUSTON, TEXAS 77380 *(Zip is very, very important)*

If the single guy or girl is bringing a date, get the individual's address and send a separate invitation. "& Guest" on an outer envelope is too impersonal. Roommates who aren't honeys also should each receive their own invite.

Assembling the Invites

1. Depending on the style of your invite, it will be left flat or folded in half or in fourths, with the text on the front of the "booklet," the fold on the left, and all other "pages" blank.
2. Tuck any enclosures inside, or set them on top of the card.
3. Place all the paperwork in an unsealed (inner) envelope, if you have one, with the print facing the back so that it's immediately visible upon opening. (Note: A high-end printer probably will place a piece of tissue paper on your invites to prevent smudging. It's your call if it stays in or not.) Leave the inner envelope unsealed.
4. Handwrite the guests' names on the inner envelopes. The formal way is with titles only: "Mr. and Mrs. Smith" (or "Ms. Jones and Mr. Smith," alphabetically, if a couple has different last names). If your wedding is more casual and intimate, you can use just first names or familiar titles ("Aunt Zoe"). Check out "Addressing the Envelopes" for more.
5. Place the inner envelope inside the outer envelope, with the guest's name facing the back.
6. Handwrite guests' full names and mailing address on the outer envelope, or have a calligrapher do it. See "Addressing the Envelopes" for guidelines. Your stationer probably will have a booklet all about titles that will help you with other specific questions you have.
7. Go to the post office and have the finished products weighed. Opt for some of those "Love" stamps—they're a nice touch. Presto! Let the U.S. Postal Service do its magic.

Married Couple, Traditional

MR. AND MRS. HAROLD PARIS
92 PACIFIC AVENUE
ETC.

Married Couple, Modern

HAROLD AND EMMA PARIS
92 PACIFIC AVENUE
ETC.

Married Couple, Different Names, or Unmarried Couple, Living Together

PROFESSOR CONNIE CHIDEYA
DOCTOR DARREN DUNCAN *(list the names in alphabetical order)*
18 BLUEBERRY ROAD
ETC.

With Kids

Names of children under eighteen need not appear on the outer envelope (phew—you were afraid you'd run out of space), but over eighteen-ers who live at home should either appear on their parents' envelope or, preferably, be sent their own invitation. Examples:

MR. AND MRS. EBERT ESTONIA
FARRAH ESTONIA
195 OAK STREET
CHICAGO, ILLINOIS 60010
or
FARRAH ESTONIA
MAILBOX 13301
HARVARD UNIVERSITY
ETC.

Common Titles

Here are how titles should appear on the outer and inner envelopes, respectively:

- **Lawyer:** Ms. Ingrid Innsbruck, Esq.; Ms. Innsbruck
- **Physician:** Jill Jamal, M.D. or Doctor Jill Jamal; Dr. Jamal
- **Professor:** Professor Kirk Kant or Kirk Kant, Ph.D.; Prof. Kant
- **Judge:** The Honorable Lucy Lindqvist; Judge Lindqvist
- **Mayor:** The Honorable Marion Myrtle Missioni, Mayor of Grand Forks; Mayor Missioni
- **Captain:** Captain Neville North, U.S. Army; Captain North
- **Minister:** The Reverend Olivia Orton; The Reverend Orton (Roman Catholics use Father)
- **Rabbi:** Rabbi Pinkus Pressman; Rabbi Pressman

The Inner Envelope

Formal invitations always are slipped into an unsealed inner envelope that is placed inside the outer envelope. They are addressed in a more informal fashion—typically only title abbreviations and last name—and include the names of all invitees at the address, including children.

Single Recipient, Traditional

MS. ANSCH

Single Recipient, Casual/Intimate Wedding

ABIGAIL
or
AUNT CAROL

Married Couple

MR. AND MRS. BAILEY
or
BEN AND TAMIKA

Married Couple with Different Names, or Unmarried Couple, Living Together

PROF. CHIDEYA AND DR. DUNCAN
or
DARREN AND CONNIE

A Family

MR. AND MRS. ESTONIA
FARRAH, GILBERT, AND HARRIET

Order in Bulk

Think about your wedding-related stationery needs (invites, thank-you notes, etc.) *before* you find a stationer. You'll have more leverage in terms of getting a price break (bulk customers rule the retail world), and you'll save yourselves time and energy by placing all your orders at once. Always order extras to save yourself time and money having to print more later.

Selecting a Stationer

Now you're ready to find yourself a stationer—there are almost as many options as invitation styles.

A Large Stationery Store

This is the most popular option. You browse through scores of stationery catalogs, pick out the style you like best, submit the wording you want, indicate special requests (like extra artwork), and wait anywhere from a few days to a couple of months to pick up your order, depending on the complexity.

Pros: Mainstream stationers work with major-league printers (who deal with gazillions of customers), so prices most likely will be lower than those of mom-and-pop printers or upscale retailers.

Cons: You're confined to the catalogs they carry, in most cases. Some

Early Addressing

When you order your invitations, see if you can take the envelopes home immediately—or at least request that they be delivered ASAP if you're having a return address printed on them—so that you can start addressing while your invitations are being printed.

shops may be willing to special order, but the above-mentioned cost advantage might thus be offset. If you're thinking Picasso-esque creativity, you may want to look elsewhere.

An Independent Printer/Stationer

In our big business–dominated world, small print shops are following the fate of the dodo bird, but you should be able to find a great independent stationer through friends' referrals or online. Instead of looking for your perfect invitation (and other stationery) in a thick catalog, you sit down with the owner or a salesperson and design your own, or peruse a book of original designs.

Pros: You have more stylistic leeway. That means multicolored invitations, several ink colors, or weird shapes are all available. (Plus, you're supporting the small-business economy that makes this country great.)

Cons: Customized work is always more expensive. Also, it usually takes longer for a small operation to fill your order, so don't go this route if you're pressed for time.

The Internet

As with most businesses, the stationers have gone online, saving you hours of running around town flipping through books of invites. You can now order your invites over the Internet. For those of you who bank, shop, and live online this is a great advancement, but if you need someone to hold your hand through the process you'll miss the human interaction. Most companies will send you paper and color samples so you can touch what you see.

Pros: You aren't limited to what the stationer has on hand and can view the portfolios of multiple stationers in one fell swoop—a big time saver. You will also be able to see what the invite will look like with your wording instantaneously as opposed to waiting a few weeks.

Cons: Having to order samples is kind of a drag, and there won't be anyone sitting next to you to help you through the ordering process. Plus, your ability to customize will be limited, as will access to the ideas of a professional stationer.

A Department Store

Many upscale stores have wedding-stationery services to augment their registry programs. The idea is the same as with a large stationer; you choose from ready-made designs.

Pros: One-stop shopping; order your stationery and register for gifts on the same day. Often you can get a good deal if you're registering at the store; after all, you're bringing in a lot of business. In addition, upscale department stores tend to be choosy about the stationery they carry (with a penchant for classic designs), so if you know you want mainstream-highbrow, they've already made the first cut for you.

Cons: As impersonal as the large stationer, but with less selection.

Mail-Order Catalogs

Bypass the retailer and go directly to the printing company from the comfort of your own home. Catalogs come in all shapes and sizes, so there are thousands of styles to choose from.

Go to Appendix B for a list of our favorite mail-order invitation catalogs.

Pros: Unbeatable prices, convenience, and quick turnover (sometimes within a week of placing your order). If you're having a theme wedding, often you'll find quirky (or kitschy) invitation designs to match, which will be much cheaper than custom-ordering.

Cons: High screw-up potential; spelling mistakes are not uncommon when dealing with a printer over the phone. Even though many reputable catalogs will fix their errors at no extra charge, the time advantage may be eaten up. Also, excellent designs are fewer and further between, and paper quality may not be great—you're going to have to do a lot of browsing and checking of samples.

A Graphic Designer

Find a talented pro by word of mouth, or ask a designer friend to create your stationery in lieu of a wedding present; he or she will design super-duper, one-of-a-kind stationery for you and probably hook you up with a trustworthy print shop.

Pros: Artistic flair; originality; the good deed of feeding a freelancer.

Cons: Unless the design work is, in fact, a present, you'll have to pay two people—the graphic artist and the printer—which could wind up being more expensive than the other options. This process can also take a while, so get started early.

Doing It Yourselves

If you have good desktop publishing software (like QuarkXPress or PageMaker) and a creative streak (maybe one of *you* is an artist or graphics guru), design your own invites, notes, cards, even stationery. After you've perfected your creations, get the job done on a laser printer on high-quality paper; this may mean taking a trip to your local copy shop or output service.

Pros: Total creative freedom; one-of-a-kind specimens; quality time together (albeit in front of the computer).

Cons: This method is the most time-consuming for you two.

Other Wedding Stationery

Save-the-Date Cards

People have very busy lives and the need to plan in advance has become critical. That's why save-the-date cards are sent to guests long before the invitation arrives. The cards are especially helpful for out-of-town guests, or if the wedding will happen over a holiday weekend or in a seasonally busy locale (such as Nantucket in June) when guests will need to book travel accommodations far in advance. While save-the-dates are not mandatory, they've become the norm. Order them as soon as you know your wedding date and locale, and mail them out six months before your wedding.

What Should They Say? You guessed it: The date. Information on area hotels—and contact information for a travel agent if one is coordinating guest arrivals and securing discounts—are often included.

How Many? Same number as invites.

Choices? These cards can be on more casual stationery and include illustrations or graphics, but ideally they should play off the theme or color scheme of your wedding. If it's too

MARGARET & RICHARD

October 19, New York City

THE 120 GUESTS invited to Margaret and Richard's wedding each received a handmade, one-of-a-kind invitation that could only have come from Margaret. Why? They were made from sugar. A cake designer, Margaret also sculpts with sugar. For the invitations she decorated the paper with sugar designs. "They were so great." Margaret laughs. "When they went through the mail, some of the sugar would fall off, so the envelope made this nice sound when you shook it."

Margaret's creations were featured at the event, as well. Instead of flowers, her table centerpieces were sugar chalices, goblets, and bowls. She also designed her cake, of course—but then enlisted the help of various smaller folk: "I wanted to take some of the focus off my own work, so instead of decorating the cake myself, I got my friend's kids and my new nieces and nephews to come over and make the decorations. They loved it, and it let them be a real part of the celebration."

soon for you to decide on anything besides the date and locale, try to link the cards to either of those aspects; guests informed of a wedding held over Independence Day weekend, for example, could receive cards with a flag, fireworks, or a red, white, and blue motif. Or, if you're marrying in the city where you live but most of your guests are from out of town, fun city facts and hand-drawn maps are great ideas.

Reception or Ceremony Cards

If your ceremony and reception will be at two different places, *or* if you have separate guest lists for each event, you'll need a small card to add to your invitation. (*Don't* invite to the ceremony but not the reception; if you want a very intimate ceremony, however, vice versa is fine.) Wedding invitations generally give the ceremony lowdown; however, if you're inviting *many* more people to the reception than to the ceremony, you may want to simplify your life by printing up smaller ceremony cards instead and giving the reception information on your main invites.

What Should They Say?

Formal Reception Invitation

MR. AND MRS. PETER JOHNSON
REQUEST THE PLEASURE OF YOUR COMPANY
AT A RECEPTION TO CELEBRATE THE MARRIAGE
OF THEIR DAUGHTER
HEATHER AMANDA
TO
JEFFREY MICHAEL HARRIS
THURSDAY, THE THIRTEENTH OF MAY
AT SIX O'CLOCK
THE ROSELAND BALLROOM
222 GROVE STREET
ST. LOUIS

Ceremony Enclosure Card to Go with a Reception Invitation

CEREMONY
AT FOUR O'CLOCK
CHIP OF HEAVEN CHURCH
111 YUMA AVENUE
KIRKLAND, MISSOURI

If the Invitation Gives the Ceremony Information, Include a Reception Enclosure Card

RECEPTION
AT SIX O'CLOCK
THE ROSELAND BALLROOM
222 GROVE STREET
ST. LOUIS

How Many? The number of guests at the event plus twenty-five extra.

Choices? If you are inviting only a handful of people to the ceremony, use reception invitations, and handwrite personal notes to the select vow-observing crew instead of printing up ceremony cards.

What Else? Save paper—and money—by printing a map on the back.

Response Cards

We are big believers in spontaneity, but *not* when it comes to how many people are going to show up at your wedding. That's where the response card comes in. Unless you're including telephone or e-mail R.S.V.P. info on your invites, this is an *essential* bit of wedding stationery. By returning the card, guests are letting you know that they understand all the details of your wedding and that they'll be there (or not).

What Should They Say? There are a few possibilities:

- Blank Cards. All that *you* write is the response deadline; the guest composes her own message. Example: "Kindly respond by March 1" *or* "The favor of your reply is requested by the first of March." This is our favorite option because guests can get creative and wacky on you, turning the response cards into keepsakes.
- Fill-in-the-Blanks. Easy to use, for you and your guests; all they need to do is write a few words and draw a few circles.
- Checklist. This is a great option for long weekend or extended activity weddings. Have a check-off box for each nuptial-related fiesta (prewedding picnic, late-night beach party, post-wedding brunch, etc.) so you'll know how many people the hosts should prepare for at each event.

How Many? Print enough for all your guests plus twenty-some extras for replacment guests.

Choices? Ask for responses on your invite. (This may mean more work for you, however, because people are less likely to sit down and compose and mail their own note than check off a box on a ready-made card; they may forget, meaning you'll have to make follow-up calls.)

What Else? Include a stamped response-card envelope addressed to the person in charge of the guest list (you, Mom and Dad). You also can use a small stamped postcard.

Map-Hotel Info Cards

If you're inviting a lot of out-of-town guests to your wedding or are getting hitched in an out-of-the-way place, order map cards to insert in your initial invitation mailing. If you've also re-

The Write Stuff: Talking to Your Vendor

No matter whom you choose to rock your stationery world, roll out the usual consumer caution. If possible, find your vendor through recommendations from people whose own party invitations or personal stationery have caught your eye. Then ask to see examples of the stationer's work and, when possible, contact other references. It's also always a good idea to visit at least three stationery retailers, so that you get a general sense of available styles and price ranges. In addition, never forget to:

1. Get in writing the vendor's liability for printing mistakes.
2. Predetermine a reasonable price for extra orders if the need arises.
3. Carefully proofread all master texts *before* placing the order and again when you pick it up.

served a block of rooms at local hotels for far-out guests, include that info on the same or a separate card.

What Should They Say?

Map Information: Sometimes you can get a map from the venue itself (ask the site manager), which you can have printed onto your cards (or just fold the pieces of paper into fourths). Or you can do a hand-drawn map; get someone who knows what they're doing to help you out. It should clearly spell out road names and major orientation points.

Hotel Information: Some hotels will provide printed materials; otherwise, call up the hotel manager and get the reservation line number and the going rate for your rooms. Those are the essential tidbits you'll need to include for each of the hotels you've made arrangements with, as well as maps of how to get there from major ports (airport, train station, bus terminal).

How Many? Number of guests plus twenty.

Choices? Instead of getting this info printed up on hefty cards, photocopy it onto regular pieces of paper that match your invitation colors.

What Else? You may want to put this information in a letter that you mail out long before the invites (four to six months before the wedding, say) so that guests can get a head start on making travel plans and reserving rooms. This is especially important if the wedding is in a popular tourist destination or is scheduled for the same weekend as another big event in town.

When Do You Need R.S.V.P.s?

Set your R.S.V.P. deadline for no later than two weeks before wedding day (after that point, you need to call nonresponders so you can get a final head count), leaving you ample time to make last-minute arrangements for seating and catering orders.

Ceremony Programs

Programs are a wonderful way to make your guests feel a part of your ceremony, especially if you're incorporating original readings or special ethnic traditions. Instead of having your guests whisper among themselves to try to figure out what's going on, why not spell it out?

What Should They Say? Include the names of everyone in your wedding party—and perhaps their relationship to you. There should also be a ceremony itinerary so guests know what's coming next. Include any original texts or literary passages you'll be reading so people can follow along more easily, and explain any special rituals.

How Many? Guests plus thirty. You'll want to keep a few as keepsakes and so will your guests of honor.

Choices? Have some historical pictures of the religious practices you're incorporating printed in your programs to heighten the sense of tradition. Some couples include family or childhood pictures of the couple if the service is not particularly religious. While photographs are not essential, including your invitation motif in the program's aesthetic is.

What Else? The program is the place to include any special tributes or thank-yous you want to make to close friends, relatives (especially deceased ones), even each other.

Secure Honored Guests' Seats

If you're having a very large ceremony, consider printing up pew cards to include in the invites of your closest relatives and friends. Pew cards tell the usher that these guests of honor are to be seated in specially reserved pews close to the altar. Or just have a trusted friend or relative brief ushers on who should get white-glove treatment.

Escort Cards & Place Cards

Both are small cards that help guests find their dinner tables and seats. Usually escort cards are laid out alphabetically on a table outside the dining space and include each guest's name. Guests find their name and the card tells them their table number or table name. Once they find their table, place cards set at each guest's plate tells them specifically where to sit. You can order these with your invitations, but you won't be able to have guests' names printed. But don't worry, these cards look just fine with hand-printing or calligraphy.

What Should They Say? The name of each guest and the table number or table name.

How Many? Number of guests plus twenty for last-minute switcharoos.

Choices? Add a unique thread to carry out a theme on your reception cards. If you're marrying on the shore and naming your tables after islands or beaches, navy blue lighthouses would be appropriate. Or stamp the cards with a red rose if that's a primary bloom in your bouquet.

Menu Cards

As reception menus take on personal significance by incorporating traditional ethnic dishes and favorite family recipes, more and more couples are providing menu cards at each place setting, a few for each table, one at every station, or along the buffet table. Lots of couples having standard fare have caught on, too. After all, an informed guest is a happy guest. Obviously, you'll have to define your menu and wine offerings before you get these printed. So start your tastings early and order these no later than six to eight weeks before the wedding.

Earth-Friendly Stationery Suggestions

All this talk about paper, paper, and more paper has got you bummed out about your complicity in this ecological fiasco? Cheer up. These environmentally sound tips will have you, your guests, *and* Mother Nature smiling:

Use recycled paper. There are many great options for your invitations, thank-you notes, and envelopes (napkins, too!), including handmade sheets with flowers and ribbons mixed into the pulp or corrugated heavy stock—perfect for a rustic wedding.

Concentrate information. Instead of a separate R.S.V.P. card for each wedding-related event, mail out a one-stop checklist.

Reuse materials. Wrap attendants' gifts in recycled brown packing paper.

Think small. The smaller your invites and thank-you cards, the fewer trees suffer—and the more you cut down on waste.

Double-side it. Put that map on the back of the actual invitation. Put hotel information on the same sheet as the itinerary.

Find a stationer who uses nontoxic inks and dyes.

Skip the frills. Don't use inner envelopes; ask the printer to skip the tissue paper; don't get layered invites.

Instead of having people send you their R.S.V.P.'s, have them phone or e-mail.

What Should They Say? List each course and what will be served along with drink options. If at a buffet line, explain the dish in a bit more detail. If you've created a menu to reflect your heritage, explain why you are serving *limoncello* as a dessert drink. If your dessert table includes a family member's specialty, share the recipe on the back of the card.

How Many? One for each guest, two to three per table, one for each station, or one in front of each dish on the buffet table.

Choices? If you're putting them at each place setting, tall and thin on a medium to heavy card stock works best. You don't want a piece of paper covering your plate. If there are a few at each table you can use a size like 4x6 or 5x7—these fit nicely into a frame. Buffets menu cards will need larger type, and 8x10 would even be appropriate here. Carry your wedding motif through the menu cards or add your new couple monogram.

What Else? If you have traditions or other events that will be taking place at the reception, you can turn the menu card into an "Evening Events" card and list everything in store for your guests, including specifics of the meal.

A Weekend Itinerary

Since more and more couples are opting to have weekend weddings, it's a great idea to put together event programs that serve as an easy reminder of all the planned events. Leave them in guests' hotel rooms or mail them out several weeks before the giant get-together.

Wedding Announcements

There are going to be people you're fond of whom you simply couldn't invite to the wedding. It's a common practice to share your happiness with these individuals—and to let them know that they're on your mind—by sending a wedding announcement, typically mailed immediately after your ceremony. (Some say on the way to the reception, but we'll allow you the next day; you're only human, after all.)

What Should They Say?

Traditional

MR. AND MRS. PETER JOHNSON
AND
MR. AND MRS. BRADLEY HARRIS
HAVE THE HONOR TO ANNOUNCE
THE MARRIAGE OF THEIR CHILDREN
HEATHER AMANDA
AND
JEFFREY MICHAEL
ON THURSDAY, THE THIRTEENTH OF MAY
ONE THOUSAND, NINE HUNDRED AND NINETY NINE
KIRKWOOD, MISSOURI

HEATHER AMANDA JOHNSON
AND
JEFFREY MICHAEL HARRIS
(OR JEFFREY AND HEATHER HARRIS)
ANNOUNCE THEIR MARRIAGE
ETC.

How Many? This will vary depending on the size of your wedding and, thus, how many people are not receiving invitations.

Choices? Personalize the announcement by sending the same favor your reception guests received. If you feel uncomfortable telling people about your wedding via mail, pick up the phone and spread the good news verbally.

What Else? Don't expect gifts! If you receive them, though, be sure to send a thank-you note.

ASK CARLEY

Recalling Invitations

Q: What is the proper way to inform guests that a wedding has been canceled when your invitations have already gone out?

A: When a wedding is canceled or rescheduled, you can let guests know with printed cards, personal notes, or even by phone if you don't have much time. If possible, a written mailer is preferable; that way you don't have to explain the sad circumstances over and over and over, which can be painful whether the wedding was called off because of a sick parent or because of cold feet.

An official card is generally worded like an invite:

Mr. and Mrs. Ray Ronco
announce that the marriage of
their daughter
Talula Justina Ronco
to
Javier Terzo
will not take place/has been postponed
or
Mr. Ray Ronco
regrets that the death of his wife
obliges him to recall the invitations
to the wedding of his daughter

A personal note generally should give the same information, just not as formally. In any case, specific reasons for the cancellation need not be included. Typically, only a death or illness is mentioned.

Great Guest Books

Put a guest book for people to sign somewhere very visible, such as on a table in the entranceway or on a stand near the receiving line. You don't have to use a traditional, leather-bound keepsake book. Here are some other ideas:

A silver platter with your names and the wedding date engraved on it; have an engraving pen on hand for guests to sign their names.

A book with blank pages in which guests attach a Polaroid of themselves arriving at your wedding (snapped by a photographer). Guests write their greetings next to their photos.

A handmade book with photos from your childhood to give guests creative inspiration.

A wedding "yearbook," which the bridesmaids or you make and get professionally bound, with photos of the two of you during your dating years, head shots of your wedding party, "guest appearance" shots of your caterer, officiant, dressmaker, ceremony site, and anything else you want to include.

A memory book in which guests paste pictures of themselves with one (or both) of you. Don't forget to ask them ahead of time to bring a photo. (You could include the request on an invitation insert.) Guests write comments next to their photos.

Blank sheets of colored paper on which guests write or draw whatever they want to. You bind them together after the wedding.

Have them say their wishes to your videographer for an electronic memory "book."

Go to Chapter 20 for more on thank-you notes.

Thank-You Notes

Rules of etiquette dictate that every gift deserves a thank-you note. This means that between the gifts you'll receive before, on the day of, and after your wedding, you two will be doing a lot of writing. A thank-you note is traditionally a simple ecru sheet or folded card. You might add a monogram, choose ready-made cards, or design something original with your stationer.

Hello, My Name Is . . .

Couples have long sent out at-home cards with word of their new address. In recent years, with all the new name-changing scenarios, name-change cards have become the new thing, a way of letting others know what to call you besides "the couple formerly known as Sunil and Anne." Or order new letterhead to do the talking; it'll show people where you live *and* what your (new) names are.

What Should They Say? How grateful you are for the gift. Whatever you do, personalize each note to reflect your relationship to the addressee and the specific gift s/he gave. For example: Dear Aunt Joan, thank you so much for the barbecue grill. We can't wait to throw our first July 4 party and hope you'll be able to join us." It doesn't have to be a work of genius; a dash of humor and a sprinkle of loving sentiment are the essential ingredients.

How Many? Lots and lots. Many people will be giving you more than one gift (for your engagement, your shower, etc.). You're going to get a lot of stuff, and thank-you notes never go bad. Stock up.

Choices? This is your opportunity to continue your wedding theme or motif, or simply create a new one for yourselves as a couple. It's also nice to include a wedding photo, but remember that your professional prints will not be back in time, so you'll have to use a snapshot. We also love the idea of using postcards from your honeymoon destination.

The paper trail has come to an end. You've dealt with one of the biggest items on your planning schedule—getting invites, which should be ordered six months before the big day, ideally—and taken care of countless other details, such as place cards, ceremony programs, and thank-you notes. One more page of your wedding book has been written. Let's bandage up those paper cuts and move on.

CHAPTER TEN

location, location

Your first big planning task to tackle is deciding where to do the deed—where to have your reception and, if it won't be in a church or temple, your ceremony, too. Your location is the backdrop for your wedding—a grand ballroom plays host to an affair far different from an intimate, bucolic garden.

If you're set on a wedding style, you'll be able to focus your location search. If you're not sure yet, surveying sites can help. That crumbling castle may finally get you in touch with your long-lost dreams of a medieval marriage. Unfortunately, you don't have too much time for dreaming here—the hottest spots go quickly. So get going!

Starting Your Search

Whether you have an exact, general, or just a vague and sketchy sense of where you want to wed (okay, you have no idea), your next question is "Where the heck do we start looking?" This is where all those research skills you learned in school will come in handy.

Internet. As with most things, the Internet can give you a wide and thorough look at what places are available for your wedding. Everybody has a website; whether they are a small historic inn or a hotel chain, you should be able to see images online. It's now a question of sorting. Don't expect price info and never make a decision based on what you see online. We of course would recommend heading straight to theknot.com/cities, where you can look through hundreds of listings for reception sites all around the country. Looking for something off the beaten path? Check the website for the chamber of commerce in the town where you're marrying for some alternative ideas, like the zoo or a sculpture garden owned by the city.

Local magazines and papers. City magazines and bridal guides published by local newspapers can be good places to find out about party rooms and/or bona fide wedding-reception places. Call your newspaper and ask when (and if) they're planning a special wedding issue, or track down a past one at the library (maybe the paper even has some extras).

Historical societies. If you're thinking about a historic mansion, castle, or estate, get in touch with the historical society in your wedding area. They'll be able to give you a list of all the local historic landmarks, plus let you in on which ones allow special events on their grounds.

Tourism bureaus. Even if you've lived in the same city or town all your life, chances are there are great places nearby that you don't even know about. Call the tourism bureau for location ideas close to home—you may discover something fabulous, such as the fact that you can have your wedding party at certain museums, civic buildings, bed and breakfasts, state or national parks, historic areas, farms, or orchards. State and local bureaus of parks and recreation are also good places to contact.

Chambers of commerce. Local business organizations are great resources for hotels, banquet and catering halls, country clubs, and other party locations. Call the chamber of commerce, an entrepreneurs' association, the Realtors association, and any similar groups you can find.

Wedding professionals. Wedding consultants, caterers, photographers, DJs, and other people who make a living on weddings likely have been to more receptions than Liz Taylor's closest pals. Consequently, they've probably seen and worked at every location within a fifty-mile radius. Call them up and pick their brains. Make it part of your vendor-selection process. When you ask a photographer about his style, for example, also ask him where he's shot local weddings and which venues he liked best. Not only might you get some good location ideas, you'll also find out how experienced he is—a factor you'll want to consider when hiring a shutterbug.

Other couples. No one's more willing to talk weddings than freshly married couples (the fresher the better). Ask newlywed friends about great sites they saw. Inquire about other weddings they attended. Ask coworkers for ideas. Ask the guy who repairs your shoes, people at the gym, the salesperson at your favorite clothing store. Okay, ask anyone who'll listen. You never know whose brother owns a really cool downtown gallery where he'd love to start hosting special events. Firsthand accounts of the success (and failure) of various venues can give you invaluable tips.

Sites A to Z

- Aquarium, Aboretum, Airplane Hangar
- Boardwalk, Bed & Breakfast, Bowling Alley
- Castle, Cave, Covered Bridge, Casino
- Disco, Disneyland, Dock on a Bay, Dunes
- Empire State Building
- Farmhouse, Football Field
- Gallery, Greenhouse, Golf Course
- Harley-Davidson Convention, Historic Estate, Hot Tub
- Ice Skating Rink, Inn
- Jazz Club, Japanese Gardens
- Koi pond

(continued)

What to Look For

Okay, now that you know where to look for the greatest locations, you need to know what you should be looking for (aside from that sense of rightness you know you'll have the moment you see the perfect spot). Shopping for a site is a lot like finding a mate, a test you've obviously aced. You should be looking for the same sorts of things—charm, personality, depth, more than just a pretty face (although looks do count!). Take this list of what to look for with you—in your head or on paper—when you're ready to go scouting.

Wide open spaces. First, make sure the room is large enough. It may look like Yankee Stadium when it's empty, but wedding essentials—tables, chairs, a buffet, a bar, the band or DJ setup, the dance floor—can take up a lot of space. Not to mention your guests, who'll need some elbow room. Even if you choose an outdoor site, you'll need ample room on the lawn, in the arboretum, or poolside. The best way to assess size? Ask to check the place out when another wedding is being set up. Space is one of the biggest reasons to have an idea of how many guests you're thinking about inviting before you start your site scouting. Of course, if you decide you *must* have your wedding at your favorite bar (the one with one bathroom, two booths, and three feet of floor space), you always can work backward and tailor your guest list to match.

A place to park. Make sure the site is near a good parking lot, garage, or big, empty (safe) street that's okay to park on. If parking is a problem, look for other ways to get everyone there. Can a shuttle bus or vans take guests from the ceremony to the reception? Inadequate parking isn't necessarily a deal killer, but it may mean spending more time and money figuring out a viable vehicular alternative.

Privacy, please! Privacy varies widely from place to place, as does the importance couples place on it. If you're having a daytime bash in a public spot, such as a park or botanical garden, be prepared for strangers to trek past your party. They may even smile and wave and come by to offer their good wishes. If this is okay with you (the more the merrier!), go for the park. If not, opt for a lovely lawn on a private estate. Or hold the reception at a restaurant or gallery that will post a "closed for private party" sign.

But don't think you're safe just because you're indoors. Banquet halls and hotels often hold more than one affair at a time. If there'll be other events going on simultaneously in rooms close to yours, you may hear karaoke-loving guests singing their hearts out to Madonna through the walls, or meet them over the hot-air dryers in the bathroom. If this bothers you, try to schedule your wedding when there won't be another one next door. If this is impossible, visit the site on a dual-party night and see how the sound carries, and whether there really are any major people problems, before you make a decision.

Seeing the light. Light can make—or break—the mood. If you're marrying during the day, make sure your hall has plenty of windows. Who wants to spend six hours in a dark room when the sun is shining? If it's an evening affair, make sure the room's not *too* dim—or that the lighting can be controlled for the big entrance, dinner, and dancing. If you're marrying outside, say at dusk, will you be able to set up candles if necessary?

Sites A to Z (continued)

- Lighthouse, Library
- Museum, Mountaintop, Mission
- Nature Reserve, National Park
- Oceanside, Orange Grove
- Poolside, Parade
- Quarry, Quebec
- Rodeo, Roller Coaster
- Ski Slope, Stables, South of the Border
- Train Station, Toy Store, Theater
- Under the Stars, Underwater (scuba vows?)
- Vineyard
- Waterfall, Windmill, in the Woods
- X . . . um, ahhhh . . . ?
- Yacht, Yard
- Zoo

Try to see the site at the same time of day as your wedding is planned for. Even if the space looks swell by candelight, you may be surprised by the sight of that twenty-year-old carpet during the day. You'll also miss a chance to see how sunlight streaming from floor-to-ceiling windows completely transforms the room if you check it out only in the evening.

The right color. If you're having a party that necessitates a certain color palette—say a Victorian tea done in pink, green, and gold—that brown shag carpet is really going to wreck the effect. The place doesn't have to be done in the *exact* colors as your planned decorations, but the walls, carpets, chairs, and curtains shouldn't clash or conflict with your party's mood or theme. If you want a spring wedding brunch, look for a space that's done in light (perhaps pastel) colors or florals; black walls and red leather booths just don't say "spring." But they'll look great if you're going medieval (or 1980s, for that matter). For classic elegance, consider a room done in neutrals or black and white.

A great view. What will your guests look at (when they're not gazing at you or smiling for the videographer)? Whether it's a stunning vista of rolling mountains beyond the windows, the crashing sea on the sand behind you, Picasso prints on the walls, fine Persian rugs on the floors, period furniture in the corners, or an amazing crystal chandelier as the room's centerpiece, exceptional locations always have something fantastic to see.

Eating, drinking, and partying areas. There should be logical places within the space where guests can eat, drink, talk, and dance. See if you can envision where each activity would happen (especially if your ceremony will be there, too). If a room is too small to separate into sections accordingly, you may feel cramped. If it's shaped like an S or other oddball figure, that could compromise your party's flow, as well. Also note the locations of columns or other obstructions in the room—will they block people's views?

Ample outlets. Make sure your room has lots of places to plug things in—especially if you're partying in a place that's not used to hosting weddings. Your main outlet user will be the entertainment crew. Take note of where the outlets are; if their location will force your DJ to spin records in the bathroom, make sure s/he has plenty of extension cords.

Good vibrations. If the place is too echo-ey, it could give some weird reverb to the band, not to mention making it difficult for guests to hear each other talking. A tile or wood floor, for example, will amplify sounds, while a thick carpet will tend to muffle them. Try to take a listen to the room during an event. And tailor your music to the acoustic conditions. A jazz combo will sound better at an intimate art gallery than a fourteen-piece orchestra would (not to mention taking up less floor space).

JEANNETTE & DEMARCO

July 6, Atlanta, Georgia

HIGH SCHOOL SWEETHEARTS

Jeannette and DeMarco had two words in mind when they started planning their wedding: classy and cool. "We wanted an urban wedding that was very unqiue, with an emphasis on the nontraditional." The venue—the Block Candy Company Building—was the perfect fit. Built in 1912 as a candy factory, it has a very sparse, funky industrial loft and a rooftop with spectacular views of the Atlanta city skyline. "I wanted the event to be informal and fun," says Jeannette, who chose punchy colors like pink, green, yellow, and orange as her wedding-day colors.

The rooftop ceremony opened with a Miles Davis tune before the wedding; participants walked down the aisle to Bach. More Miles Davis filtered through the air at the conclusion of the ceremony as guests were encouraged to linger, mingle, and enjoy the 360-degree views.

The reception that followed was held in the lobby of the building, where summer afternoon light poured in through tall windows, warming the open space and creating a welcoming glow. "I specifically asked my decorator to keep the decorations sparse," says the bride. "I wanted the drama of the space to shine through the unadorned room that was already striking in its industrial, yet rather elegant, simplicity."

Great Wedding Places

It used to seem like every wedding ceremony was held in a church or temple, every reception in a hotel ballroom. Of course, many people still take this route—it's quintessential wedding! But since the first hippies tied the knot barefoot on the beach in the 1960s, the idea of the alternative wedding location has become so popular, it's downright mainstream.

Don't just look for the trendiest or prettiest place. The best weddings are the ones guests walk away from saying "That was so *them.*" Maybe your first date was in a funky Mexican restaurant—that might be a perfect reception venue. If you're both animal lovers, consider the zoo. That little hotel on the bluff overlooking the beach—come on, the one where you got engaged!—has that beautiful party room, remember? If you studied together and then fell in love at the college library, wed on the university's gorgeous grounds. If you're into feng shui (the Chinese art of harmony in placement), choose your wedding spot based on the size, shape, location, and spirituality of an area—a perfectly circular clearing in the woods, a hilltop

Location Contract Points

Here's what should be in your *written* contract.

- ☐ Total cost and a line-item breakdown of what's included.
- ☐ Amount of deposit and when it was paid.
- ☐ Balance and when it's due/payment schedule.
- ☐ Exact date and time of your wedding.
- ☐ Exactly where it will be (e.g., "In Main Gallery," "In Presidential Ballroom").
- ☐ A detailed list of everything the place is providing (tables, chairs, linens, amplifiers, whatever).
- ☐ The name of the site representative who will be on hand on your wedding day, as well as the name of an acceptable substitute.
- ☐ Cancellation/refund policy.
- ☐ Anything else you agree about orally that you want to ensure happens.

cliff overlooking a leafy valley. Unless you're having a Catholic ceremony (the majority of Catholic priests will not officiate at a wedding ceremony outside of a church), chances are you can exchange vows in most of these places too.

The Old Standbys: Hotels, Banquet Halls, Country Clubs, and Restaurants

If these traditional reception locations have one thing, it's experience. Weddings are their business. They know what's supposed to happen at a reception; they know how long one typically lasts. They've set up dessert buffets and band lighting a million times. They can offer suggestions on things you're unsure about. Conveniently, they'll often have an in-house caterer (in a restaurant, obviously, the chef will do your food) and maybe even a florist. This can make everything incredibly easy for you—but it also can be a hassle if you want to bring in vendors from the outside or decide that you don't jibe with the style or philosophy of one of the in-house professionals.

At a hotel or banquet/catering hall (or anyplace else that has a special events staff), you'll probably deal with (surprise) a banquet or catering manager. The most important thing to find out from him/her is exactly what the establishment will take care of. Will food, drinks, and the cake be handled in-house? If you want to bring your own cake, say, are they going to charge you extra to slice it? Be very specific when you first sit down to talk about what the place will (or can) provide. For example, many catering halls will give you arches, votive candles, or potted trees to use free of charge, while most hotels won't—you'll have to go through your florist or rent stuff. Knowing up front what you need to get yourselves will make it clear what you're in for—and how much extra money you'll spend (or save) if you settle on this locale.

Home-Grown Weddings

Marrying at home sounds perfect, especially if you or your parents have a gorgeous, big house with a beautiful backyard. Think about a ceremony under the old oak tree you climbed as a

EMILY & SEAN

September 1, Austin, Texas

GUESTS AT Emily and Sean's wedding were treated to an effortlessly beautiful celebration that was as warm and stylish as the bride and groom. The setting, the Trois Estate in Austin, might have been vaguely familiar to some guests (it was featured in the movie *Spy Kids),* and the Spanish Colonial limestone buildings, with courtyards, pools, and fountains, has been featured in *Architectural Digest.*

But "we had a terrible time finding the right spot for our wedding," admits Emily. "It was a major fiasco." Like so many couples, Emily and Sean did not have a solid connection with any one place. The couple lives in Waco; their families have lived in Chicago, Wisconsin, Florida, Nebraska, and El Paso. Rather than try to choose one of these locales, they decided at first to focus on a destination wedding. "After reviewing every upscale resort in the country, we realized that any place that we could be excited about for our wedding, none of our friends could afford," laments Emily. "Travel and lodging would be way too much to ask."

They then found the Trois Estate and completely switched gears. "Having the wedding in Texas meant we were able to invite a lot more people," points out Emily, "and it was close enough that it was easy for our friends to come."

Dinner was served family-style at long banquet tables in several different rooms. The tables were each named after places that the couple almost chose for their wedding, like "Hotel del Coronado" and "Litchfield Plantation."

kid, dinner in a tent in the yard, or even an intimate family meal in the living room. This is about the most personal wedding place there is.

But don't think it's just that easy—home weddings come with a set of considerations all their own. And contrary to popular opinion, they aren't necessarily cheaper. Where will you put everyone? Where will they sit and what will they eat off of? We're talking rentals. Tables, chairs, dinnerware (you may be able to find a caterer who will bring this stuff along), a tent—it can add up fast, and you may end up spending just as much as you would to rent a hotel banquet room. You also need to think about the nitty-gritty of infrastructure: Will electrical power be able to handle the load? Are the caterers cooking in your kitchen? What about bathrooms? You might need to rent some port-a-potties. (Don't worry, you can rent some that are much better than the ones at the local fairground.) You also have to make sure your neighborhood (and the city) will allow for such a

Raring to Rent?

Visit the American Rental Association at www.ararental.org for referrals to local rental stores and companies.

raucous good time; there could be some noise ordinances that would prohibit that seven-piece cover band you're planning on. We have heard stories of police arriving to disband a few very classy weddings. Oh, the horror! Of course, you'll be marrying on very familiar turf, instead of being wedding number 4,623 of the day at Your City Hotel. And most of your guests already will know how to get there. But there may be a serious parking issue so you might have to ask for carpooling or hire valets to park cars in a local lot. Again, you're going to need permission for that one. And you really should tell the neighbors what's going on. (Easier yet, invite them!) Oh—and one more thing—the weather. If you rent a tent, make sure it's equipped to keep everyone dry if it rains. Also have an inside game plan—will everyone fit inside the house if they have to? Home is an amazing wedding place, but there's lots to think about.

The Great Outdoors

Getting married outside is the ultimate for many couples. From the quintessential outdoor celebration on the beach to a pretty garden (botanic or grandma's), poolside at a ritzy resort or smack dab in the middle of a National Park, outdoor weddings are fantastic.

Of course, utter perfection comes with a price—even though it usually costs less to rent the great outdoors than to rent a room with a roof over it. The most critical step: Find out if you need a permit to party in a public area. If you're thinking beach, public park, or forest preserve, you can't just congregate—you'll need to reserve the area with the local parks and recreation department. Find out when you apply whether you'll also need permission to have cooking fires on the grounds, and if it's okay to have a band or DJ. Like home weddings, outdoor weddings may require you to rent tables, chairs, a tent, maybe even portable toilets. Also think about lighting—if it's an evening reception, do you need lights? Then there's bug control—light citronella candles and tie ribbons around mini-bottles of insect repellent as favors.

In Case of Rain . . .

Be sure to have an alternative *indoor* site in mind. You can't control the weather—the possibility of a torrential downpour is the riskiest part of choosing an outdoor wedding site.

Mansions, Castles, and Other Great Old Buildings

The biggest advantage to renting a landmark location? Major photo ops. The place is going to be gorgeous! Many historic mansions and estates also come complete with beautiful grounds—perfect for romantic walks. You might even employ a strolling chamber orchestra for the cocktail hour. Castles may come with cool period relics and/or instruments, though they'll probably be off-limits for use. Find out if you're renting a look-but-don't-touch museum (not necessarily a bad thing)—will you have to pay a security deposit to ensure that no period furniture, priceless artwork, or Persian rugs get damaged during the party? Make sure to find out exactly what the restrictions are: Which rooms of the house you can use, what parts of the grounds are off-limits, which precious porcelain vases can't you touch? Otherwise, just enjoy—often these sites are so picturesque, not much extra decoration is necessary!

Boats, Trains, and Trolleys: Weddings on the Move

Cruising through New York Harbor on your wedding night, riding around Chicago in a double-decker bus with all your guests, or saying your vows on a New Orleans trolley are pretty dang romantic options. What is it about modes of transportation that we love so much?

Ten Great Cities, Ten Great Locations

Austin

Classic: The Trois Estate. www.thetroisestate.com. Gorgeous grounds and a Spanish-style limestone castle offer loads of options.

Romantic: Umlauf Sculpture Garden. www.umlaufsculpture.org. An outdoor sculpture garden features a majestic lily pond and waterfall.

Unique: Old Glory Ranch (Wimberley, Texas). www.oldgloryranch.com/weddings.html. Enjoy old-country style amid the Texas hills when you say "I do" in the oak grove or by the Blanco River.

Boston

Classic: Boston Harbor Hotel. www.bhh.com. Invite up to three hundred of your nearest and dearest to this classic Boston venue with a breathtaking view of the historic harbor.

Romantic: The Mansion at Glen Magna Farms, Danvers, Massachusetts. www.glenmagnafarms.org. Exchange vows in one of this mansion's lush gardens and have an elegant celebration in colonial revival style.

Unique: Boston Harbor Cruises (Boston). www.bostonharborfunctions.com. Take to the seas for your celebration—at night, there's no more spectacular backdrop for your wedding than the Boston skyline reflected in the water.

Chicago

Classic: John Hancock Building Signature Room. www.signatureroom.com. Primo 360-degree views of Chicago from the ninety-fifth floor of the city's third tallest building.

Romantic: Francis J. Dewes Mansion. www.dewesmansion.com. Bursting with sophistication and grandeur, this four-story mansion was modeled after the Chateau of Versailles in France.

Unique: Brookfield Zoo (Brookfield, Illinois). www.brookfieldzoo.org. You can have cocktails with the animals, take a Sunset Safari motor tour, and dine in the Discovery Center.

Miami

Classic: The Palms Hotel (Miami Beach). www.thepalmshotel.com. Poolside cocktails, an exchange of vows in a bougainvillea garden, and a ballroom reception are just a few of the elegant options at this seaside resort.

Romantic: Ancient Spanish Monastery (North Miami Beach). www.spanishmonastery.com. Filled with history, this ancient stone-walled monastery offers seven distinct areas for weddings, both indoor and outdoor.

Unique: Vizcaya Museum & Gardens. www.vizcayamuseum.org. From the gardens to the European art and furnishings, this is the perfect setting for a fairy-tale wedding. Modeled after an Italian villa.

Minneapolis

Classic: Nicollet Island Inn. www.nicolletislandinn.com. A historic landmark right on the river, known for its excellent hospitality and spectacular view of the Mississippi.

Romantic: Washington County Courthouse (Stillwater, Minnesota). www.co.washington.mn.us/hstcrths.htm. It's the oldest courthouse in Minnesota—and it's an architectural gem.

Unique: Minneapolis Sculpture Garden. A mix of art and blooms makes for a truly unique ceremony. Have your reception in the Palm Room at the nearby conservatory.

New Orleans

Classic: Elms Mansion. www.elmsmansion.com. You and your guests can enjoy classic Creole cuisine and the southern charm of this nineteenth-century mansion, located in the Garden District.

Romantic: Degas House. www.degashouse.com. Make an impression on your guests with the colorful Victorian charm of this restored nineteenth-century house, where the French impressionist painter once lived.

Unique: New Orleans Paddlewheels. www.neworleanspaddlewheels.com/weddings.html. Charter an old-fashioned paddlewheel boat for your day. Take the plunge on the promenade deck and enjoy seaworthy cuisine in a Victorian dining room.

New York

Classic: Tavern on the Green. www.tavernonthegreen.com. Just pick one of this NYC landmarks' distinctive reception rooms—they're all dazzling.

Romantic: Brooklyn Botanic Gardens. www.bbg.org. Each of the distinctive gardens, which include a Japanese garden with waterfalls or a fragrant rose garden, are an oasis in a frenzied city.

Unique: Angel Orensanz Foundation. www.orensanz.org. This former synagogue became a hot spot after Sarah Jessica Parker and Matthew Broderick married there. The neo-Gothic space creates a dramatic backdrop for your big day.

Seattle

Classic: Seattle Space Needle. www.spaceneedle.com/groups.htm. Your guests will feel like they're on top of the world with the 360-degree view of the city at the SkyLine Level.

Romantic: Rosario Resort. http://rosario.rockresorts.com/. A romantic panoramic view of Puget Sound can be the backdrop for your wedding at this Orcas Island mansion–turned–resort and spa.

Unique: Pickering Barn. www.ci.issaquah.wa.us/pickering_barn/. For the ultimate rustic wedding, this barn, built in the 1800s, has been fully restored and can accommodate up to four hundred people.

Southern California

Classic: Tijeras Creek Golf Club, Rancho Santa Mararita, California. www.tijerascreek.com. With Tijeras Creek's outdoor ceremony location and Spanish motif, weddings here are quintessentially California.

Romantic: Mission Inn, Riverside, California. www.missioninn.com. Have a fairy-tale ceremony in an ornate mission-style chapel and celebrate in a high-ceilinged banquet room overlooking the Atrio courtyard.

Unique: Bacara Resort, Santa Barbara, California. www.bacararesort.com. Do it up in sunny California style! Everything is clean and fresh here, and your guests will want to stay the week at this uber-luxury resort and spa.

Washington, D.C.

Classic: Reception Rooms at the International Trade Center. Say "I do" steps away from the White House in the Atrium (capacity 800 people) or the more intimate rotunda (up to 120).

Romantic: Woodrow Wilson House. www.woodrowwilsonhouse.org/rentals.htm. This Georgian revival town house creates an elegant atmosphere for a wedding—incidentally, it's the only presidential museum in D.C.

Unique: D.C. Union Station. www.unionstationdc.com. Have a lavish reception with thousands of guests in the East or Main hall—or something more intimate in one of this landmark's fine restaurants.

Maybe it's the moving forward aspect—a perfect marriage metaphor. You may have to do some digging to find train, bus, or trolley lines in your city. A wedding on water floats your boat? Any town with a decent-size body of water nearby will have boat lines, from yachts to riverboats. But keep in mind that when it comes to water transport, you can't exactly get off until it docks—you and your guests are stuck until the reception's officially over. Have some Dramamine on hand (just make sure it doesn't get mixed with champagne), serve light foods (good with waves) and, perhaps most important, make sure that boat's big enough to keep people who don't get along on opposite ends.

Great Party Rooms in Not-So-Typical Places

If you're not into hotels or banquet halls but you like the idea of celebrating in a party room, think about other places, public or private, that host special events—museums, aquariums, train stations, nightclubs, university buildings. Some will have special-events staff ready and willing to help you plan the event. Others won't, so you'll be bringing in your own caterer and other wedding professionals. Price will vary. If you want to use the private party room at New York's Metropolitan Museum of Art, it's going to cost you a pretty penny, while your favorite nightclub may give you a great deal. And if one (or both) of you is an alum of the college whose space you're looking at, you may get a break on the price.

Meeting with Managers

Okay, you've narrowed down your list and you're armed with the knowledge of what you need in a location. You're ready to go out there and meet the owners and managers. Call the places that interest you, ask to speak to the person in charge of weddings or special events, find out if the date you have in mind is available, and make an appointment.

Your Contact

Don't just head to the site and look around. Make sure to meet the person you'd work with if you had your wedding there. Is s/he enthusiastic about the space and about working with you? When you ask questions or make comments about wanting something specific or different, does s/he say, "That sounds great. Let me see what I can do." Or do you get "No. We don't do that here. No. No, no, no"? You're going to be dealing with this person for a while and you want to feel comfortable with him or her. And you want him or her to *understand* you and what you're trying to do with your wedding.

Keep in mind that this person is working for you—not vice versa. Don't let yourself be talked into (or out of) anything. If the place seems like a possibility, ask your contact for references and then actually call them and see what they have to say about the place.

Check the Place Out

Even if you fall in love with a site and the references are glowing, keep in mind that most establishments aren't about to give you the names of people who hated the service they got. The best way to make sure a place is reputable is to call the local better business bureau. Ask how the place is rated and whether any complaints have been filed against it.

Ways to Save Location $$$

If you're getting married in the off-season—say January, instead of June or September—you're likely to finagle a much better rate. Plus you'll probably have your pick of rooms or dates.

The day of the week can make a difference, too. Saturday nights are the hottest. You may pay less for a Friday night or Sunday afternoon.

If you're celebrating in a hotel or club with guest rooms, have your out-of-town guests check in there. Not only will they avoid annoying transportation issues, but they'll also save money, because you'll be able to get a discounted group rate for them. And you may even get your wedding-night room free.

How Much It'll Cost

The location fee is likely to be one of your largest wedding expenses, especially when you combine it with catering costs. Of course, this isn't always true—if you have a beach bonfire wedding, you may have to pay only for a permit. But generally your location will run you from $500 to $3,000 (more in larger cities, less if it's an unconventional site or someone's doing you a favor). Usually you will pay a flat fee; some places may charge by the hour. And you're going to be asked to put down a deposit of 10 to 25 percent.

Say you think you want to move forward on a specific place. You've checked off all the great location factors, and all of your questions have been answered to your satisfaction. Can you negotiate on the price? Of course you can, and you should. But first, find out what's being offered at competing establishments nearby. If you can get a better deal at another place but you like this place better, see if it can match or beat the price.

A big, expensive reception may help you negotiate for lower costs on small things. If you're having a huge party, for example, with a lot of overnight guests, you may be able to get some of the smaller fees waived—like charges for napkins, microphone stands, or cake cutting. Similarly, a less-popular date may lead to some super savings. If you're getting married smack dab in the middle of June, your chances of getting a deal are much slimmer than if you're marrying on the first of February. (In June, there'll be a line of couples behind you waiting to take

When to Walk Away

They want more than 50 percent of the rental cost up front.

The place is downright dirty.

You just don't like the person you'd have to deal with.

The place refuses to draw up and sign a written contract—or refuses to add your specific requests onto the standard contract it uses.

Your celebration is being squeezed in between two others in the same space and it seems too tight time-wise.

The references you call tell you the place treated them horribly. (Pretty amazing, because if the establishment gave you the reference's name, *they* must have thought things went pretty well!)

You feel like you're "settling."

your place and pay full price.) Make sure you know what you've agreed to pay for and that you get everything in writing—in a detailed contract.

Questions to Ask

There are a lot of points to talk through before you make your final decision to reserve a reception site. Here's what you need to find out before you sign anything on the dotted line.

- How much will it cost to use this site? What's the payment plan?
- Is there a reception "package"? Exactly what is included?
- Does the place have liability insurance? (In case someone gets injured during the party, you don't want to be held responsible—or if you are going to be, you want to know about it.)
- How many hours will you have the site? Is there an overtime fee if you stay longer? Is there a *minimum* amount of time you have to rent it for?
- Will there be another party right before or right after yours (or both)? Will there be enough time to decorate and take stuff down before the next wedding begins? Is there any chance of an awkward overlap?
- Will you be required to leave everything "as is," or can you move things around and/or decorate to suit your purposes?
- Are tables, chairs, plates, glasses, and so on available, or will you have to provide (rent) those yourselves? (This can jack your costs way up.)
- Is there an in-house caterer, or can you bring in your own? Can you use an outside caterer instead of the in-house person?
- Are there kitchen/cooking facilities? (Caterers will charge you extra if they have to haul in things like refrigerators and stoves.)
- If there's parking, is it free? If not, what are the rates and/or gratuities for valets? (You can and should pay this up front so your guests don't have to tip.)
- Will there be, or can you set up, a coat room? Are there bathrooms nearby? (Look at them to make sure they're nice!)
- If there's no bar—can you set one up? More important, does the place have a liquor license?
- Is there a private room off the main room where you two can change or just be alone for a few minutes? This is a nice perk.
- Is there a dress code that you'll need to inform guests of—coat and tie after 6 P.M., for example?
- Does the site have any restrictions or regulations about what kind of music you can play and/or a time by which it must be turned off? Are there guidelines about what kinds of decorations you can use?
- Will someone who works at the location be there to supervise during your wedding? This really should be the person you make all your plans with, *not* someone you've never met until that day.
- What about security? Will you have to hire your own security guards, or does the place hire them or have them on staff? (The point is to find out

Cancellation Happens

Don't assume there's no chance you'll cancel—you never know. You may *have* to change the date or postpone things due to unforeseen circumstances (a bad illness, a death in your family, a great new job in Europe, etc.). Protect your investment.

just how safe the place is and to decide whether you're comfortable with its level of security.)

- What's the cancellation policy? (This is important to know, because some places will give you most of your deposit back if you cancel far enough in advance since there's still a chance they can rent the space for another party. But after a certain date you may *not* be able to get your deposit back, or at least not all of it.)

Rental Rules

You can rent everything from a yellow-and-white tent for your circus reception to the tables, chairs, plates, parquet dance floor, disco ball, and smoke machine for your all-night dance party. Begin the search for your perfect rental company early—you'll want three to six months' lead time. Ask around for catalogs and prices. And assign someone to return duty—getting that elephant back to EZ Rent will be the last thing on your mind as you head off on your honeymoon!

Know Your Needs

Visit potential rental companies with the following info in hand:

- Date, time, location, and approximate number of people
- Reception budget
- Event style (Medieval? Flapper '20s?)
- Event type (Lawn party with kids? Formal dinner?)
- Site specifics (Underground sprinklers, wires, cables, or sewer easements that would interfere with an outdoor tent? Enough electric outlets for five cotton-candy machines?)

Choose Your Crew

Whether you go to Paul's Party Shop or the local branch of a huge chain, make sure you're working with pros. Your ideal rent-a-center will:

- Be a member of a business or trade group like the American Rental Association. (Call 800–334–2177 for members in your area.)
- Show you the inventory. If the china is cracked and caked with mashed potatoes from the last party, keep looking.
- Send staff to help with setup.
- Accommodate last-minute changes (additional tables for unexpected guests or extra tents if it rains).
- Offer names of past customers as references.

Check the Contract

After you've chosen your source and tagged your goods, get the details in writing. Your rental agreement should specify that all goods will be in great condition, plus:

- When and where your products will be delivered (or picked up).
- The exact length of your rental agreement.
- The store's rental rates, hours, and return policy.
- The fact that the store will replace equipment that breaks down.

NOTES

CHAPTER ELEVEN

your look

From head to toe, every piece of your overall bridal look plays an important role. The wedding gown is just a scoop of vanilla ice cream—albeit the most delicious scoop you've ever eaten. Your accessories are the sprinkles and the hot fudge (looking better already, right?). Your hair and makeup are like the whipped cream and the cherry. See? All of those pieces to your style puzzle should fit together and complement each other, just like a totally decadent sundae, only less fattening and even more tasteful. So let's break it down piece by piece.

The Gown

As what-to-wear occasions go, your wedding tops the list. Maybe you've wanted to wear a big, poofy ball gown since the first time you saw *Cinderella*. Or maybe your tastes have changed, and these days you're into more modern styles and shapes. Maybe you'd never be caught dead in one of those confections they call bridal gowns, and you've got a smashing suit in mind. Well, you're in luck: bridal fashion now includes all of the above. Whatever your dream or preference, what you wear on your wedding day is completely up to you. That goes for first-time, second-time, even third-time brides (and up!). The only requirement is that you feel great in whatever you choose to wear—because if you feel great, you'll look great.

Buying your wedding dress is going to be an unforgettable—and quite possibly, harrowing—experience. This dress has a special significance, and besides that, it's got an entire industry attached to it. Your goal—to purchase the dress of your dreams and remain a savvy consumer. Since buying a wedding gown is not something most of us do very often, there's a lot you probably don't know at this point. But never fear. As usual, our job is to fill you in.

Before you even step out the door to the store, read up on the lingo that'll get thrown your way when you set foot in a bridal salon. Wedding-dress shopping comes with its own language, and the more you know about what types of silhouettes, necklines, and shades of white might flatter you, the easier shopping for your dress will be.

The Shape's the Thing: Silhouettes

As with suits, skirts, and other dresses, the silhouette of a wedding dress can make or break how it looks on you. Here's our guide to who looks especially great in which wedding-dress

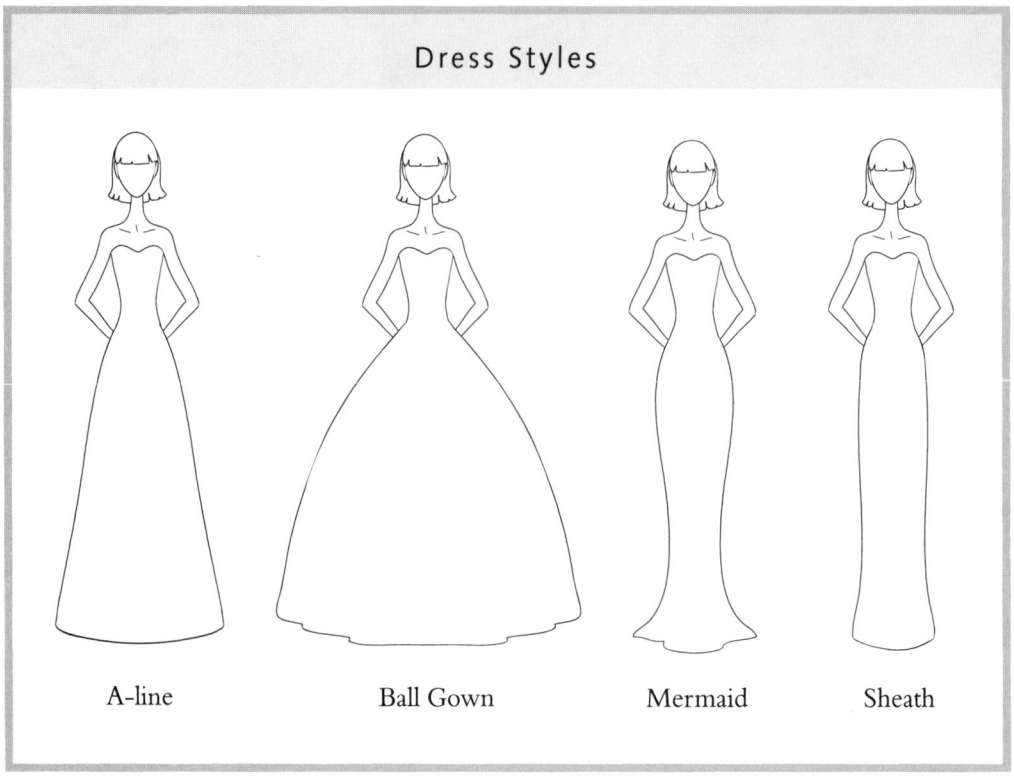

shape. No, we don't mean Christy Turlington vs. Cindy Crawford. We're talking body shape here. As with everything else in life, it's all about proportion.

A-line: As its name implies, the A-line cut is narrow at the top, cut close to the rib cage, and extends out along the body in the shape of a triangle (or "A") in a smooth, elongated line. It is perhaps the most popular skirt option, as it looks wonderful on a variety of body types. The lines of the skirt are always clean and ungathered.

Ball Gown: The classic ball gown has a fitted bodice, a natural waist, and a full skirt. It's truly feminine (that "Cinderella" connection), and looks particularly good on women with boyish figures (narrow hips), because it'll make you look more curvy.

Basque Waist: Are you full-figured or hourglass-shaped? Think about a dress with a basque waist, which comes to a V in the front at your stomach. It has a slimming effect on your waist and deemphasizes hips. Like ball gowns, basque-waist dresses usually have full skirts and fitted bodices.

Empire: This is that tiny-bodice dress with a high waist and a skirt that falls in a slight A-line from right below the bustline. (Did you see the movie *Emma*?) This silhouette lets you minimize your waist, because it really *has* no waistline. If you have a large chest or full hips, you probably want to stay away from this one—but it depends on the dress. Some come with fabric overlays that flatter.

Mermaid: A slim, tapered, curve-hugging skirt that follows the line of the hips and

A Question of Formality

Brides are lucky—they've got more flexibility when it comes to what's appropriate for a "formal" vs. "semiformal" vs. "informal" wedding than grooms do. (See the next chapter for groom guidelines.) Basically you should just use common sense. A sequined, long-sleeved gown wouldn't be appropriate for a daytime garden wedding, right? Velvet isn't really a summer fabric, and a floaty chiffon number with spaghetti straps might not work in a blizzard. (That isn't to say you can't wear a sleeveless gown from November to April—you most certainly can.) As a rule of thumb, consider the typical temperature on your wedding day when selecting a fabric, and save the shiny stuff for evening. Otherwise, the bride gets to wear what she wants, when she wants.

thighs and flares out below the knee. This dress is always a sheath, and is sometimes refered to as a "trumpet" skirt.

Modified A-line: Somewhere between a mermaid silhouette and an A-line, this shape is roomier in the hips (unlike a sheath) and slightly flairs out at the bottom, giving the gown movement as you walk. It's a flattering fit for someone who wants more shape than a simple A-line.

Princess: This shape flatters just about everyone. With seams running from the shoulders or bust straight down the skirt, with no seams at the waist, it elongates your torso (great if you're short-waisted). For the most part, princess-seamed dresses fall into an A-line shape (described above).

Sheath: If you're petite or just have a fabulously sleek figure, consider this form-fitting style, which follows the body's natural line. A slim silhouette adds length, and it won't overwhelm a small woman like a big, elaborate gown could (anything too poofy might look as if it's wearing you)!

If you're short, keep it simple. Stay away from anything with tons of beading or lace—look for something with detail around the shoulders (this also holds true if you have a small chest) to bring the focus up to your face.

Neck and Neck: Bodices

Although the neckline's main duty is to frame your neck and face, the best one for you also depends on body shape—arms and especially bust. You'll see most necklines on all different dress shapes, so they are in large part independent from silhouettes, but the combination of a specific dress shape and neckline probably will hit a home run on you. Think about the length of your neck when you're considering necklines. The lower the neckline, the longer your neck will look; the higher the neckline, the shorter it will seem.

Asymetrical: This neckline appears different on either side of the center front; one example is a one-shoulder design.

Bateau: This wide-necked shape gently follows the curve of the collarbone, almost to the tip of the shoulders. The Sabrina version—made popular by actress Audrey Hepburn—is always sleeveless; the front and back panels of fabric just touch at the shoulders, sometimes with thin straps. This look does wonders for the lesser endowed.

Necklines

Asymmetrical

Bateau

Halter

High-Neck

Jewel

Off-the-Shoulder

Portrait

Scoop

Spaghetti-Strap

Square

Strapless

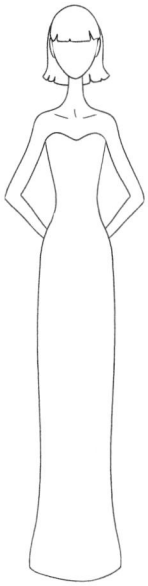
Sweetheart

Tank

V-neck

Halter: The halter features straps that wrap around the neck, or a high neck with deep armholes. The shape can often be backless, and works perfectly for someone with great shoulders. It does not, however, allow for much bra support.

High-Neck: A band collar that extends up the neck. The mandarin version of this style is taken from traditional Asian dress, and doesn't quite meet at the center front. It works for anyone desiring an elongated affect and is very flattering with an updo.

Jewel: Also known as the "T-shirt neckline," this is a round neckline that sits at the base of the throat. If you're full-chested you already know the effect a T-shirt has on your bust—this may not be the best choice for you. But for petite or flat-chested women, this neck can enhance you on top.

Off-the-Shoulder: This one is self-explanatory—the neckline sits below the shoulders, with sleeves that cover part of the upper arm, and just about everyone can wear it. Especially when combined with a sweetheart shape in front (see below), this neckline is super-flattering to medium or full-chested women. (If you've got fuller arms and are a bit uncomfortable with baring your shoulders, think about a portrait neckline, which is similar, but with extra fabric framing the neck and/or a bit of on-the-shoulder material.) The prettiest thing about the off-the-shoulder neckline? It exposes your collarbone, which looks beautiful *and* a bit sexy.

Portrait: Characterized by a wide, soft scoop from the tip of one shoulder to the tip of the other. If you've got super-plush or very bony collarbones steer clear.

Scoop: The scoop, a square neckline with rounded edges (or a variation on that shape) is practically retro now—it's associated with Jackie O. It can be low cut, but not uncomfortably low. Often the scoop continues on the back of the dress. Just about everyone can wear this one, too.

Spaghetti-Strap: This neckline is nearly strapless, save for the presence of thin, delicate straps. It's great for someone with a smaller bust, as the show of the décolleté can be very flattering.

Square: The neckline is cut straight across the front. This universally flattering cut is especially great for the bust-endowed (cuts low but is not revealing).

Strapless: This bodice is usually cut straight across, but it can also peak on the sides or have a slight dip in the center. Good for: broad or thick shoulders.

Sweetheart: This neckline is shaped like the top half of the heart, and full-chested women look great in it, because it really accentuates the décolletage. (Don't be shy—if you've got it, flaunt it!) If you don't dare to bare, the sweetheart often is done with an overlay of lace or sheer material that rises higher than the heart shape.

Tank: Similar to a men's undershirt, with a U-shaped neckline and deep armholes under the shoulders and narrow straps. It can accentuate a great pair of arms.

V-Neck: The neckline dips down in the front in a flattering V shape, elongating the neckline and deemphasizing the bustline.

The Long and the Short of It: Sleeves

Are you comfortable with baring your arms? Kind of baring them? Or not at all? Remember, too, that you also can wear a shawl or little jacket over your dress. Sleeves in a nutshell:

Spaghetti Straps: Thin straps that come straight up from the bodice and go over your shoulders.

Off-the-Shoulder: With this type of neckline, the sleeves may simply be bands of fabric that cover part of your upper arms. This coverage may be all you need to feel comfortable.

Go to Appendix B for dress designer phone numbers.

Cap Sleeve: Little sleeves that pretty much just cover your shoulders, but at least make you feel like you're not going sleeveless.

T-shirt Sleeve: Longer than cap; about as long as your average T-shirt, strangely enough.

Three-quarter: Straight sleeves that end midway between your elbow and wrist. A very elegant look.

Long: Sleeves that come all the way to your wrist, often with cuffs banded in lace, satin, even velvet. Also in this category is the unfortunately named leg-of-mutton sleeve, which tapers to the wrist to further deemphasize full upper arms.

Fabulous Fabrics

Most wedding dresses are made from one or a combination of the following fabrics. Why is it important to know this? Because different fabrics will hang differently on your body; the same style of dress may look (and feel) quite different on you in a different fabric. They're different weights and thus may be appropriate for different kinds of weather. And, of course, there are price differences, too—silk is the most expensive material.

Brocade: Jacquard-woven fabric with raised designs. A popular fall and winter fabric that has started to sneak its way into warmer-season dresses, as well.

Charmeuse: Lightweight, semilustrous satinlike fabric.

Chiffon: Delicate, sheer, and transparent—made from silk or rayon, with a soft finish. Popular for overskirts, sheer sleeves, and wraps.

Silk: The most sought-after and cherished wedding-dress fabric (and fabric in general!). There are different types, with different textures and weights. Raw silk and silk mikado are two examples.

Organza: Crisp and sheer like chiffon, but with a stiffer texture. It's popular in skirts these days—it has an effect similar to tulle, but it's more flowing. It's also popular on sleeves and bodice or back overlays.

Satin: A heavy, smooth fabric with a lustrous face and dull back. There's some satin on just about every wedding dress.

Silk Gazar: A four-ply silk organza.

Silk-faced Satin: Smooth silk with a glossy front and a matte back.

Shantung: Similar to a raw silk, with a rough, slubbed texture.

Taffeta: Crisp and smooth, with a slight rib. You probably remember it best from high-school prom dresses; it's not used as frequently on wedding dresses as it once was.

Tulle: Netting of silk, nylon, or rayon, it's used primarily for skirts and veils (think ballerina tutus).

Velvet: This fabric is being used more and more, for details at sleeve cuffs, on bodices, even for the dress itself.

Hot- vs. Cold-Weather Fabrics

Hot-Weather fabrics:
- Chiffon
- Linen
- Organza

Cold-Weather fabrics:
- Brocade
- Faux fur
- Velvet

All-Weather fabrics:
- Satin
- Shantung
- Silk
- Tulle

Extra Embellishments

Silks and satins are just, well, silks and satins without the intricate embellishments that turn them into masterpieces. Here are a few of the most popular kinds:

Appliqués: Fabric elements like flowers, ribbons, or cutouts stitched or embroidered onto a gown; sometimes raised.

Beading: Pieces of glass, crystal, gems, or other material sewn onto lace or fabric.

Boning: Stays used in corset and strapless bodices for shaping and stiffening.

Border Trim: Braided, ribboned, ruffled, or scalloped edging that provides a decorative effect.

Bows: Used in various lengths and sizes, from one giant butterfly bow to a tiny shoestring tie.

Corset: A tight, figure-enhancing bodice that laces up the back.

Edging: A narrow decorative border of lace, embroidery, braid, or ribbon used for trim.

Embroidery: Fancy needlework patterns of various fine threads done by hand or machine.

Fringe: Ornamental trim consisting of loose strands of thread or beads fastened to a band.

Insert: A piece of fabric, usually of contrasting texture, inserted between pieces of the main fabric of the gown.

Keyhole: A wedge- or keyhole-shaped cutout in the center of a high, round neckline.

Laser Cut: Clean-edged intricate patterns cut into fabric via a laser.

Overlay: A piece of fabric, usually sheer, layered on top of the main fabric of a garment.

Paillettes: Larger versions of sequins (see below), these shiny or matte plastic disks with a hole at one end are sewn onto the gown at one end to provide movement.

Quilting: A sandwich of two layers of fabric and batting, which is then stitched in a pattern; offers subtle surface interest.

Ruching: Fabric that is gathered at two ends via concealed strings on those ends.

Sequins: Tiny shiny, iridescent plastic disks sewn into place on a gown to add twinkle.

Why White?

Queen Victoria turned the wedding-fashion world on its ear when she wore white to marry Prince Albert in 1840. Before that brides simply wore their "best dress" to marry, no matter what the color.

Made in the Shade: Color

These days, white is simply a color of celebration—it no longer symbolizes purity or virginity. No need to worry about guests gasping in horror if you choose a wedding dress in ivory or eggshell—or one in pink, for that matter! What's important is choosing the shade of white that looks best on you.

Many wedding dresses are available in multiple shades, so color is not necessarily tied to style. But it *is* tied to fabric. For example, organza, because it is a lighter, sheerer fabric than most others, is a softer white, and it reflects the color of the lining. A stark white dress can be lined in an off-white fabric to create a softer white. A wearable option for many skin tones: lining a white organza gown in soft pink or coral.

Stark White: The brightest, crispest white you can get. This whitest white is best achieved with synthetic fabrics (satins, taffetas, polyester blends). Looks stunning against dark skin. Fair-skinned beauties should stay far away—it'll wash you out.

Silk, Diamond, or Natural White: The whitest white for natural fibers, like silk (hence the name)—a shade off of stark white. It looks pretty much the same in photos but is much more flattering to most skin tones (especially skin with yellow undertones). Just about anyone can get away with this shade.

Ivory: Also referred to as "eggshell" or "candlelight." Some ivory dresses have yellow undertones, making them look creamy; some are just a "quiet" white. Fairer skin tones look best in a yellow-ivories and warmer natural colors. Women with pink undertones in their skin also should stick to these creamier colors. If you're not sure of your skin tone, avoid yellow-whites; they can make you look sickly if they don't complement you.

Not Quite White

The samples in bridal salons may be less than spotless—all those brides trying 'em on—so while the fabric is "white," it may appear a shade off from its actual color and more flattering than it really is against your skin. Be sure to look at a clean fabric swatch—put it up to your face—before making your final decision.

Rum or Champagne: Has pink undertones but looks nearly white in photos. Great for dark complexions or yellow/olive undertones.

Other Colors: There's no rule that says you *must* wear white! In recent seasons designers have created dresses in soft shades of lavender, rose, even blue. Also more and more dresses are being designed with color in the details: embroidery, lace, bands of satin. If your complexion gets totally washed out by white—no matter what shade—send up the white flag and try a color.

Do the Locomotion: Trains

The train is that extension of your wedding dress that starts at the waist, trails out behind you, and demands your maid of honor to readjust it constantly so it fans out perfectly at the altar. Generally, the more formal your wedding is, the longer of a train you'd wear; some dresses don't have a train at all. If your dress doesn't have a detachable train, you'll want to "bustle" it after the ceremony so you can move around freely at the reception. This entails pulling the train up and attaching it to your dress by tiny hooks, buttons, or snaps sewn onto the back of your gown and the train.

Sweep: This is the shortest train, extending back a foot or less after the fabric hits the floor.

Chapel: Extends three and one-half to four and a one-half feet from the waist.

Semicathedral: Four and one-half to five and one-half feet from the waist.

Cathedral: Six and one-half to seven and a one-half feet from the waist.

Extended Cathedral/Monarch: Flows to twelve feet (or more) from the waist.

Do the Bustle

You can't bustle your dress by yourself! Make sure your maid of honor and/or another attendant learns how to do it and that they practice a few times before the wedding.

Where to Get the Gown

Okay, now that you're so well versed in bridal-speak that you'll amaze and impress every salesperson you ever meet (as well as your mother, sister, bridesmaids, and even your fiancé, who's a little scared at this point), you're ready to go out and use it. But where? The following are your options for acquiring the dress of all dresses.

Bridal Salons

These stores sell custom-made, designer wedding dresses and are the most traditional places to shop. You'll find boutiquey salons in upscale urban shopping districts, suburban downtown areas, strip malls, real malls, and also in some larger department stores. Check online for local bridal salons near you (or head to theknot.com/local for a complete list). Then call stores you're interested in—you may need an appointment—and check out "Going Shopping," later in the chapter, for in-depth advice before you go. You also can buy bridal accessories such as

Period Costumes

Having an antebellum, Renaissance, medieval, or Victorian wedding? Here's where to look for clothes:

The Society for Creative Anachronism is a medieval re-creation group that holds medieval and renaissance fairs around the county; they'll send you tons of information as well as put you in touch with a local chapter of the organization, which will help you find not only the right clothes, but local sites appropriate to your theme; www.sca.org.

Designs by Jane Wilson-Marquis are decidedly (and beautifully) medieval; 212–477–4408.

Amazon Dry Goods catalogs, from a company known as a "purveyor of items for the nineteenth-century impression." Merchandise includes lace fans, high-laced shoes, dainty parasols, corsets, ready-made vintage dresses, and dress patterns. Visit www.amazondrygoods.com for more information.

Museum Replicas Ltd. offers an extensive line of products, which includes period clothing and jewelry. Call 800-883-8838, or look on the Web at www.museumreplicas.com.

Ethnic Options

Want to celebrate your heritage with what you're wearing?

African: Kente cloth details, gold thread, headdress/crown

Chinese: Red silk details or a red *cheung sam* (a form-fitting dress with intricate designs)

Japanese: A traditional kimono

Indian: A colorful sari, a bindi on your forehead

Scottish: Tartan details or sash, lace

Spanish: A mantilla veil, black lace, colorful silk flower details

veils, lingerie, shoes, and gloves at most salons. Besides the day-to-day business of selling dresses, salons also hold special wedding-dress events:

Trunk shows are shows to which a specific designer (or a representative of a bridal manufacturer) brings his or her entire latest line of dresses for brides to try on. The advantage—you get to see *every* dress in the line of a designer you really like, not just the styles that store chose to sell. And you also may get the small thrill of chatting with the designer herself and even having her check out what her dress looks like on you.

Sample sales are sales at which dresses usually used only for brides to try on are sold. Some stores have sample dresses in an array of sizes, but the general sample sizes are 6, 8, and 10. Wedding dresses run small—see "Just Your (Wedding Dress) Size," below—so if your regular dress size is a 2, 4, 6, or 8, you may be in luck. The dresses may not be super-clean, but you may get a great price, and you can put some of the savings toward a good dry-cleaning. (Designers also hold sample sales—so if you live in or near New York, where most are based, call around to see when these are happening!)

Shopping in a bridal salon is not cheap. These are dresses made by top bridal designers in the finest fabrics, you're getting full service (a salesperson well versed in the world of wedding gowns helping you, fittings), and your dress is going to be custom-ordered and altered for you. Expect to pay at least $1,000 and up to $6,000 or $7,000 for a really amazing designer or dress. But even if you don't end up buying your dress at one, a salon is a good place to try on a lot of dresses and get some expert feedback on what looks best on you.

Warehouses/Outlets

Inside these sometimes huge, more often cramped, stores is row upon row of racks of wedding gowns. Some are top designers' past designs that have had their run in the salons; others are designed by lesser-known (or not-known) companies whose names you may not recognize.

But shopping here can save you some money. It's kind of like shopping at TJ Maxx or Marshall's—if you look through enough racks, who knows? You just may find something you love for a to-die-for price. (We must warn you, though, diamonds in the rough are sometimes few, and prices aren't always that low—you'll find dresses that cost $1,000 or more at warehouses, too.)

Some warehouse stores have salespeople that are assigned to you when you walk in the door; this person may or may not be as knowledgeable about wedding dresses as someone in a bridal salon. In others, you get to just wander (which isn't such a bad thing). Alterations usually can be done by the store. As in a bridal salon, often you can also buy veils, headpieces, shoes, gloves, and other accessories here, as well. Our take on warehouses and outlets? If there's one near you, it's worth taking a look. You never can tell. And if you're not very caught up in name-brand wedding dresses but you *are* into getting a good price on a traditional style, this may be for you.

Rent the Dress

If you're not the type to get particularly attached to a piece of clothing (even a special one), the logic of buying a multithousand-dollar dress to wear for one day may be lost on you. Some clothing-rental stores have wedding dresses in stock—you might even find a store near you that just rents wedding dresses. In a good one, you should be able to find a dress in wedding-picture-perfect condition. You won't have to worry about dry-cleaning or storing the dress after the wedding—you just take it back to the store. Some shops may be willing to order a brand-new dress like the used one you find in the store—you still rent it, but it's never been worn before. On the downside, you probably won't find the selection you'd find at a bridal salon or even a warehouse or outlet; you'll be able to choose among only the dresses that the rental shop has, which may not be in the latest styles. If you do find the *perfect* style, just hope you don't get too attached to it on your big day! To find a bridal dress rental shop in your area, look in the Yellow Pages under "Bridal Shops" or "Wedding Services."

Looking for the perfect dress—in your price range? Go to The Knot Bridal Search at www.theknot.com/gowns to view thousands of choices.Go to Appendix B for dress designer websites.

Direct from Designers

Each spring and fall, wedding-dress designers come together in New York, Chicago, Las Vegas, and Dallas for bridal markets, biannual fashion shows during which they present their new lines to the media and to bridal-shop owners—so they'll buy them and sell them to you. A majority of the designers and manufacturers are based in New York City, many in the Bridal Building (1385 Broadway, in the Garment District) and in the building next door (1375 Broadway). If you're planning to visit New York, you might want to check out the Saturday sales, when sample and new dresses are offered direct to the public. You can save 50 percent on sample dresses and 20 to 25 percent on orders. You'll probably find the largest selection of sample dresses in the months directly after the markets.

Not everyone is in the Bridal Building, though—be sure to check some of the many individual New York design studios. You may want to get on the mailing lists of designers you really like so you'll be among the first to hear about sample sales.

Just One of the Girls

Want to really save a bundle on your wedding dress? If you're looking for something straight and simple, consider a stylish bridesmaid dress in white or cream.

TIMBERLY & ROBERT

August 16, New York City

TIMBERLY KNEW exactly what she wanted her wedding dress to look like but didn't want to spend a fortune to get it. Her vision of the perfect dress was simple and elegant, which she found out translated to outrageously expensive. But as Timberly soon discovered, who needs a fashion designer when you have friends like hers?

"My sister-in-law and roommate are both excellent seamstresses. They both offered to help make my dress," Timberly says. The bride picked out an ecru material and a Ralph Lauren pattern, and the two seamstresses got to work. The two didn't know each other well before the project, but they turned out to be an exceptional team: after three fittings, the dress was perfect. "It turned out exactly the way I pictured it, and it only cost me $400," says the grateful bride.

Test Your Seamstress

Think you've found someone to create your wedding gown? Have her make you another dress—a shift for work, maybe—so you can see her work and how you work together before you entrust your wedding dress to her.

Getting a Dress Made

You loved several of the gowns you tried on in salons, but you have such amazing taste that they all cost more than $5,000. Or maybe you can't seem to find the dream dress you can see in your head in any store, anywhere. Find yourself a good seamstress and have her create your vision. Show her pictures of dresses with features you like (sleeves, waistline, etc.). She'll probably be able to create a "test" dress in muslin first, so you'll be able to see what it will look like.

You pay for the material, which you can pick out yourself and bring to the seamstress. Or you can talk to her about what you want or bring her a swatch and have her buy the fabric for you, if that makes you more comfortable. Fabric can be expensive—for example, good silk may run you $40 to $50 a yard, and you'll need eight to ten yards for the full dress—but it's still less than you'd pay in the salon. The other expense, of course, it paying the seamstress to design and create your dress. Cost can vary; for example, a simpler design will cost you less than a complicated one. Still, you probably won't pay much more than $1,000—if anywhere near that. Extra bonus—since the seamstress is making the dress for you, she'll probably alter as she goes along. At any rate, you won't have to take the dress elsewhere if it needs to be taken in or let out when it's finished.

Wearing Mom's (or a Vintage Gown)

You love the sentiment behind wearing the same dress your mom wore when she married dear old dad, and you know it would mean a lot to her if you chose to wear it. And just your luck—you *love* the style, and it just about fits! Not only will this save you money, it's a great way to personalize your wedding wear (and make your mom cry). Or maybe Mom's gown doesn't quite fit or look right on you, but you're into the idea of a vintage dress, and you've found a gorgeous one in the bowels of a thrift store.

Wearing an old dress often means restoration is in order. Maybe the dress needs updating, or a little brightening and mending. Take it to someone who specializes in restoring old wedding gowns. Consult your local dry cleaners to see if they specialize in that type of care (it takes a special kind of cleaners). If your Mom preserved her dress properly (see "Preserving Your Dress," later in the chapter), it's a plus—if the fabric is torn or weakened from moisture or mildew, the chances of successful restoration are not as good, unless the affected areas are small. If the dress is made of polyester, you're in luck—it's the easiest material to restore. (Silk is one of the most difficult.)

If restoring the dress is a go—or if it's in great shape as is—you can update it by getting it altered to fit differently, adding different sleeves, cutting it short, or putting on beading or other appliqués. Seek out a seamstress (see above) to get it wedding-day perfect.

Going Shopping

Okay, this is definitely not like going to the mall for a pair of jeans. Shopping for a wedding dress is overwhelming. Salespeople know this. They also know you've never done this before. The key is to do your homework before you go so you're not a clueless customer. You wouldn't buy a car without researching what you need and want first, right? Don't buy your wedding dress that way, either. Read our shopping tips and you'll be in the know.

Simplicity Is In

"I try to be sophisticated and elegant at the same time. I like simplicity—clean lines, touches of embroidery or lace. Not a lot of details. Definitely not ruffles and flowers everywhere."

—Dress designer Carolina Herrera

When to Begin

Be prepared to shop early—as in nine to twelve months before the wedding. That's right. Unless you buy a ready-to-wear dress or a sample gown right off the floor, wedding dresses are custom-made, which means they need to be ordered well before the wedding day so the manufacturer or designer has time to create the dress and you have time for multiple fittings. (See "The Perfect Fit," which follows.) If all goes well, the right dress will arrive on time—but the earlier you start, the better (and the less stress)! We're not saying you won't be able to do it in less time—just make sure your salesperson is aware of your schedule.

Before You Go

Before browsing in a salon, do a little research. Read "The Gown" so you'll know what's out there and how to talk about what you like. Look at pictures of different designers' dresses online and in magazines to get an idea of the latest styles and shapes, colors, necklines, and so on. At least you'll have a shopping starting point. Then call and make appointments at salon(s) where you want to start.

Who to Take with You

Mom, your sister(s), your honor attendant, your bridesmaids, and close friends or relatives whose advice you trust top the who-gets-to-go list. But try to maintain crowd control: Limit your shopping entourage to no more than three friends or family members at once. Otherwise, you'll feel overwhelmed (and so will your salesperson). There will be more than one shopping trip—trust us—so everyone will get a turn.

Also shop on your own at least once. It sounds like the exact opposite of what you'd expect wedding-dress shopping to be like, right? But chances are that after you've gone a few times and you get into the swing of how the process works and what you like, you'll be the most focused on what dresses feel right on you when you're alone in the dressing room. Maybe you'll narrow down the choices on your own and then invite Mom and sis to help pick the winner.

What to Take with You

When you're trying on dresses, you want to get an idea of how the entire package will look on you. This means bringing along some accessories.

- A strapless bra or bustier, for trying on strapless gowns or those with corset-style bodices.
- Control-top panty hose (sometimes a dress goes on more smoothly with them on, and you'll be wearing them on wedding day).
- A slip.
- Shoes with the same heel height as what you want to wear on wedding day (obviously you don't need the exact pair yet).

Many salons have bras, petticoats, and shoes available for your use while trying on dresses, so you may not have to bring your own. Ask when you call to make your appointment.

Dealing with Salespeople

At a bridal salon, a specific salesperson (sometimes called a "bridal consultant," not to be confused with those wedding professionals you can hire to plan your entire wedding) will be assigned to help you. You will work with this person every time you come into the store and after you buy the dress (for alterations, etc.). A good salesperson will ask you what kind of wedding you're having (i.e., style and formality), how you envision yourself looking on your wedding day, and what kinds of dresses you're drawn to. She also will probably check you out and decide for herself what kinds of dresses will look good on you (based on your body type, height, weight). Then she'll bring you dresses to try on.

At some salons and shops, you'll be able to look through the sample dresses and choose what you like. (This is definitely true at a warehouse or outlet.) At others, it's "closed stock"—you don't get to see *all* the dresses, only the ones the salesperson finds it in her heart to bring you. If you're uncomfortable with this, try to find a store where you're free to look through everything.

If you find a dress you love in a magazine ad, bring it with you. Make sure you have all the information the store will need—don't rip out a picture without the designer's name and other information. If the store doesn't carry the particular style you liked, ask whether it's willing to order a sample for you to try on. (If so, make sure you're not obligated to buy it!)

Notice how you're treated and how the salespeople make you feel. Are they treating you respectfully, as every good retailer knows you should treat a customer? Or are you feeling like a little girl who couldn't possibly know the first thing about buying a wedding dress? This is where all the knowledge you've armed yourself with comes in—if you can talk expertly about silhouettes, laces, and shades of white, the salesperson will know she's dealing with an informed consumer.

Take advantage of a salesperson's expertise. She works with brides every day—if anyone knows anything about dresses, she does. Bounce ideas off of her and consider her advice if you think it's given in good faith. But if anyone tries to talk you out of or into something, or makes you feel uncomfortable about your decisions, remember: A good salesperson will never pressure you to buy something you're unsure about.

What to Wear?

"The bride needs to identify the personality she wants to project on her wedding day. Some brides go into the shopping process thinking they want to be a glamour queen, and then they backpedal and say, well, I actually want to be pretty and romantic—a very different look."

—Dress designer Helen Morley

Authorized Dealers

Some stores cut the tags out of their sample dresses, so that on first glance you won't know who the designer is. If you ask the salesperson who designed the dress and she won't tell you, ask why. If you don't get a satisfactory answer (and you won't, because there isn't one), don't shop there. Why? Well, first of all, you have a right to know whose merchandise you're spending money on. And it's important to know which designer's dresses a salon is *authorized* to sell. You know how sometimes store names are listed on a dress ad? Those stores are authorized to sell that dress. (They're not the only ones, but if their names are there, they are among the authorized stores.) If you buy your dress at a salon that's not authorized to carry that designer, there is *no guarantee* that you're going to get the dress you ordered in a timely fashion—or at all. If you're unsure, use the list in Appendix B to contact the manufacturer and find an authorized dealer near you.

Important Shopping Tips

Read our crucial shopping advice and you'll be ready for some stress-free dress shopping.

Avoid Shopping on Weekends. And evenings, if you can swing it. Bridal salons can get insanely busy. Especially if you're marrying in a popular wedding month, there are going to be a lot of other brides shopping along with you.

Take Along an Open Mind. You may think you already know exactly what kind of dress you want—or at least what shape and color are best, which neckline will suit you, and so on. But even if you think you want a scoop neckline, for example, try on an off-the-shoulder and halter, too. Something that looked great in a picture might not look so great on you—and something you thought you didn't like might be perfect.

Don't Eliminate Anything on First Glance. If the salesperson brings you something she says you *must* try—hell, try it, even if you detest the way it looks on the hanger. We know lots of brides who ended up walking down the aisle in a dress the salesperson persuaded them to try on.

Try a Range of Styles. One of the hardest things about wedding-dress shopping is that you're probably a virgin when it comes to long, white dresses. (Sorry, we couldn't resist!) Even though certain styles are best on certain body types, don't let those "rules" narrow your search too much. It helps to try on all different kinds of dresses—full skirt, A-line, sheath, long-sleeved, off-the-shoulder—and then decide what shape and style you look and feel best in.

Keep Your Dress Budget Flexible. (If you can, of course.) Don't tell anyone your price range unless it's so strict that you absolutely *have* to restrict it—otherwise you may inadvertently limit the types of dresses you're shown. On the other hand, you may want to look at dresses only in your specific range, so there's no chance you'll fall in love with a dress out of your financial league. Remember, though: If you realize that to afford the wedding dress you want you'll have to cut back in other wedding line items, cutting back is an option.

Look in Various Kinds of Stores. You may find you prefer shopping in a small boutique or designer's studio to navigating a large, bustling bridal salon or warehouse. Or vice versa.

Trust Yourself. If you have to be reassured that the dress looks great on you, ask yourself how much—or even if—you really like it. Even the most well-intentioned people may project their own dress fantasies onto you.

Don't Buy on the First Day Out. You didn't get engaged on your first date, right? Of course, it's happened that brides go back later and buy the first dress they tried on. But no matter how much you love it, give yourself all the options and the time to think by shopping more—and elsewhere—before you buy.

Sleep on It. Even after you think you've found it. Since dresses are custom-made, most salons put a no-return policy into their contracts; if you can get any money back, it probably won't be more than 50 percent of the total cost. So you should be absolutely sure that this is the one for you.

Dress Contract Points

Make sure all of the following are listed on your dress receipt:

- ☐ Manufacturer/designer name and style number
- ☐ Color ordered (white, candlelight, champagne, etc.)
- ☐ Full price quoted
- ☐ Size ordered
- ☐ Date the dress will be in
- ☐ Deposit amount required and paid
- ☐ Special-order requests and costs (taper sleeves, change bodice, etc.)
- ☐ Other costs (pressing, etc.)
- ☐ Alterations estimate, specifying exactly what type of alterations it covers
- ☐ Future payments schedule/when balance is due
- ☐ Cancellation/refund policies (most stores will refund 50 percent tops if you change your mind)

The Search Is Over

It's happened! ("Hallelujah Chorus" starts playing in the background.) You've found the perfect dress, and now that it's been on your body (maybe it still is because you won't allow the saleswoman or your mother to even come near you—she might try to unzip it), you're never letting it go. Okay. So it's a go. What now?

Before You Buy: Ordering Tips

Don't be shy—ask questions. This is an important investment you're making. If you don't get the "right" answers (or don't feel comfortable for any other reason), you may want to take your business elsewhere.

- If you don't know already, find out who designed the dress and make sure the store is authorized to sell it.
- If you love the dress but are thinking you'd adore it with slightly different sleeves or another neckline, find out if it's possible to make those changes and how much extra it will cost. If you think you might decide you want something like that done *after* the dress is in, will they do it then? Will it cost more?
- Ask how long the dress will take to come in and whether it can be rushed if you're shopping late (or you didn't find The One until the last minute).
- Ask to see fabric samples, so you'll know the exact color you're ordering the dress in; sample dresses can get worn and dirty. (See "Color" in "The Gown.")
- If you're planning to sit for a bridal portrait (see "Picture This," Chapter 16), will the store let you borrow the dress for pictures and return it to the store to be pressed so it looks fresh for the wedding?

Staying Spotless

Ask the salon for quick cleaning advice for the fabric your gown is made of. A wedding-day spill will be less of an emergency, more of a momentary hassle.

- Ask how much alterations will cost and get a written estimate before you buy the dress. This usually is not included in the price of the dress; some stores will charge a flat fee and others bill according to the work needed. (See "The Perfect Fit," below, for more fittings info.)
- Make sure the store accepts credit cards—and use one. For such a big and important purchase, you want to be able to dispute a payment (which you can with the credit-card company) if something goes wrong.

You're So Vain

Do not, we repeat, do *not,* insist on ordering a smaller size than fits you because you're planning to lose a lot of weight before the wedding. It costs less to take a dress in than to let it out.

Just Your (Wedding-Dress) Size

Wedding dresses run small—which means you probably will need to order a size or two larger than your regular dress size. Don't let this bum you out! Even though you'd think if *any* kind of dress would run large, just for the buyer's mental health (don't you love when you get to buy a dress in a *smaller* size than usual?), it'd be wedding dresses, the fact is they don't.

When you're ready to order your dress, the store will take your measurements—the typical bust, waist, and hips. Each manufacturer has its own measurements chart, and that's what the store will use to determine which size to order for you. Ask to see this chart so you'll have a better understanding of how it works—and to make sure the correct size gets ordered.

The Perfect Fit: Alterations

Go to Appendix B for contact information for accessory manufacturers.

So you ordered the dress and it reached the store intact. It's the right dress, the right size. Yay! But wait, there's more. Every wedding dress needs alterations. That's because the size generally is ordered based on your largest measurement. For example, if you've got a large bust and fairly narrow waist, it makes more sense (and costs less) to order the size large enough to comfortably fit your bust and then take the waist in. Get it?

You'll probably have at least two fittings, which you'll schedule with the store when you buy the dress; more may be necessary, so leave ample time before the wedding. Alterations can

Clothes Call: The Dressing Checklist

The Bride

- ☐ Dress
- ☐ Veil/headpiece
- ☐ Shoes and hose
- ☐ Strapless bra or bustier
- ☐ Slip/petticoat
- ☐ Slimmer/underwear
- ☐ Garter
- ☐ Gloves
- ☐ Jewelry
- ☐ Purse

The Groom

- ☐ Tux/Suit
- ☐ Bow tie, long tie, or ascot
- ☐ Shirt
- ☐ Vest or cummerbund
- ☐ Socks
- ☐ Shoes
- ☐ Undershirt/boxers
- ☐ Cuff links
- ☐ Studs
- ☐ Suspenders
- ☐ Tie tack

be as simple as just taking in the waist a bit and hemming the dress to shortening sleeves, taking in the bodice, or even adding beading or lace if that's what you request. (If the store doesn't do its own alterations, chances are the salesperson you've been working with can recommend a tailor or seamstress that the salon does a lot of business with. But most bridal salons do it in-house.)

Preserving Your Dress

After countless hours spent searching for your dream wedding gown (not to mention the dollars spent), you're not going to say good-bye to it as it lays crumpled on the floor of the honeymoon suite, right? Take a moment to remember why you chose this dress in the first place: the daring neckline, the fur-trimmed cuffs, the perfectly plump bustle—all reasons to save it for posterity so your daughter can enjoy it when *she* struts down the aisle.

What Is Gown Preservation?

The quality and appearance of your gown is maintained through special cleaning and packaging techniques called gown preservation. A professional preservationist will look over your gown: the materials used, ornamentation, and various stains, then formulate a specialized cleaning procedure. After cleaning, your gown is wrapped and placed in a box. Preservationists recommend having your gown cleaned as soon as possible after your wedding because if you wait too long, some stains can set permanently. Materials, ornamentation, and degree of stain damage usually determine the price. Costs vary across the country, but the national average ranges from around $200 to $500, but can be as much as $1,000, depending on the gown and location.

Finding a Preservationist

A few weeks before your wedding, you'll need to investigate where to take your gown for cleaning. Ask your bridal salon, family and friends, and your wedding consultant for preservationist referrals, or check out theknot.com/local to find a specialist in your area. Though many dry cleaners claim to clean wedding gowns, many are not specialists. Unless the dry cleaner you are thinking about using processes more than a hundred wedding gowns a year, keep looking for a pro.

How It Works: Some gown specialists use the wet-cleaning method, which consists of gently washing the gown by hand with gentle cleaners that remove noticeable stains and unseen stains, such as champagne and sugar, as well. If left untreated, unseen stains can oxidize and turn yellow over time. Other companies use a more traditional dry-cleaning method, which involves pretreating the stains and then placing the garment in a dry-cleaning machine.

Wrapping It Up: The correct packaging materials are key for guaranteeing the gown. Plastic is out. White acid-free tissue paper or unbleached muslin are ideal packaging materials and an acid-free or pH-neutral box are ideal holding materials. You can open the box again, just make sure you have clean hands to prevent body oils from invisibly transferring to the gown and cause yellowing over time. Store your gown out of the light, heat, moisture, or cold.

Basically, your gown wants to be in the same kind of environment you'd be comfortable in—no attics or basements.

Do I Really Need This? It all depends on what is important to you. If you'd rather DIY, you can get instructions for cleaning your gown online at theknot.com. But the same concepts of preservation: acid-free papers and boxes and comfortable surrounds hold true.

Dressing It Up: Accessories

A wedding dress by its very nature is gorgeous, but that doesn't mean you shouldn't accessorize. From the top of your head to the tips of your toes, there are plenty of enhancing extras that really do the job of transforming you into The Bride: your veil and headpiece, the right lingerie, the perfect shoes, and—optional—glamorous gloves and a wedding-day purse.

Bare That Back

If your dress has beautiful back details, don't choose a veil so long that they're hidden!

Topping It Off: Headpieces

The bride originally wore veiling because the groom wasn't supposed to see her before the wedding—not just in the hours before the wedding, but *ever* before the wedding. These days veils and headpieces are about celebrating rather than cloaking your identity.

Some dresses are made with matching headpieces, which can make it easy for you—you may even be able to get your bridal salon to alter a headpiece if it doesn't sit quite right with you. You'll probably choose your headpiece at your first dress fitting (if your salon sells headpieces; if not, bring your chosen headpiece and veil with you to the fitting), although you may try some on while you're shopping for your dress. The options and combinations are many. Here's a glossary to ease your way:

Veils: Veils usually are made of tulle or organza, either plain or embellished with lace, sprinkled with crystals, or bordered with satin.

- Blusher: A short veil worn over the face down the aisle and turned back over the headpiece when the groom kisses the bride. Often it's attached to a longer veil or a hat.
- Elbow: Extends twenty-five inches in length to your elbow.
- Fly-away: Multiple layers of veiling that brush the shoulders.
- Fingertip: Several layers of veiling that extend to the fingertips. This is probably the most popular veil length.
- Waterfall: This one, all the rage in the '60s, has made a 1990s comeback. It sits on the top of the head with tulle cascading down, usually held in place by a satin headband. Look for one with more than one tier of tulle, which gives the veil its shape and fullness.
- Mantilla: A Spanish-inspired lace veil that is worn without a headpiece, draped right over the head with a pretty lace border framing the face.

Veils

Blusher

Elbow

Fly-away

Fingertip

Waterfall

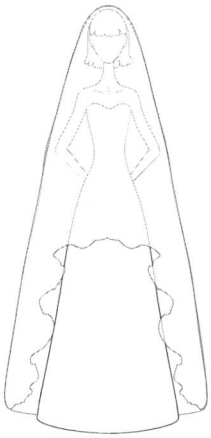

Mantilla

Ballet/Waltz

- Ballet/Waltz: Falls to the ankles, often in simple, multiple layers. A luxurious look that's once again making an impression; it can practically double as a train.

Headpieces: Some headpieces look better with either long or short hair—read on to decide what will look best on you.

- Headbands: These look great with any hairstyle and are perfect for prettily pulling hair away from your face, so everyone can see that bridal glow in your eyes and cheeks. For short hair, choose something narrow, maybe jeweled; longer-haired brides can opt for a wider band of satin or silk, or something decorated with beads or stones.
- Tiaras: Tiaras are a wedding mainstay—and they made their way into high fashion in general during the '90s, as well. These days they are not as tall and more delicately made—more like 3-D headbands than queenly crowns. Rhinestones are always popular—they catch the light so beautifully—but metal fashioned into different shapes, beads, or jewel-toned stones, are popular, too. Long- or short-haired brides can wear tiaras; they look equally as gorgeous in long hair worn down or in a simple updo.
- Headpieces: Some headpieces are made out of plastic or another sturdy material and decorated with rhinestones, lace, embroidered appliqués, pearls, crystals, silk flowers, even sequins. Often they're built onto a comb or series of small combs so you can attach them to your hair, or they're attached to a band. Depending on the style of the headpiece, these can work on either long or short hair. Backpieces, which sit at the back or crown of the head where they can be attached to a veil, can add a lot to your look without having to be an integral part of your hairstyle. Backpieces work best for those with shoulder-length hair or longer.
- Barrettes: Who says you *have* to wear a headpiece? Pull long hair back with one pretty barrette—in white satin, with beading, or decorated with lace, maybe—and attach veiling with Velcro (so you can take the veil off at the reception); a comb can serve the same purpose. If you have a short cut, think about holding bangs to the side with a pretty little jeweled or plain barrette or two.
- Hats: They look best on short-haired brides—but hey, try a few on and see! Choose from a pillbox to a dramatic, wide-brimmed hat—you even can tie veiling around it. Are you a second-time bride who's not comfortable in a veil again? A hat may be for you.
- Hairpins: Like little headpieces-on-a-stick, hairpins are great for the bride who just wants a touch of sparkle in her hair (not a band of it). These jewels, which can come in the form of flowers, bows, or even little starbursts, are attached to bobby pins. The pins are then dotted throughout the head—either in an updo, or placed along the crown of the head or behind the ear (for just an elegant splash of glamour).

- Fresh Flowers: Who said flowers are just for the girls getting married in Hawaii? Fresh blossoms, tucked behind the ear, into a chignon, a formal updo, or even in a French twist, is a great look that can go from the ballroom to the backyard with ease. Check with your florist before choosing a flower, as some hold up better than others after a long day out of water.

Your Jewelry

Remember the theoretical sundae we built before? Jewelry is where things get really tasty. The great thing about wedding-day jewelry is that you don't have to wear a lot to make a big impression. Here is a quick rundown of the pieces you already know:

Earrings: Whether just a simple stud or a dramatic drop, no bride should be without a pair of earrings. Much of your earring decision will be based on your hairstyle. That means, if you're planning on covering your ears, there's no reason to go for the big pair; if you intend to wear your hair up and put your ears center stage, you can afford to go for something with a little more zing. Choose earrings that are comfortable, as the last thing you want to deal with on your wedding day is that nagging pulling feeling and seriously sore earlobes.

Necklace: With so many options to choose from, necklaces have come a long way from your grandmother's strand of pearls (although pearls do look fabulous). Consult the neckline of your dress: strapless and low, décolleté-baring necklines are perfect for bigger pieces, like a strong choker. If the neckline is higher, however, chose a piece that's either smaller, like a single stone or a thin chain, or skip the necklace altogether.

Something Old, Something New . . .

This wedding tradition (old, new, borrowed, blue) is from an old English rhyme. This is possibly one of the most-fun last-minute wedding tasks—especially because you usually get help from your parents and attendants.

Something Old: The idea is to carry a token of the past into this new phase of your life. Go for: a locket with a childhood photo or your parents' wedding portrait; an antique necklace, bracelet, or pair of earrings that's been handed down in your family; an inherited book of prayers or poems (read from it during the ceremony); a piece of your security blanket or a family quilt sewn into the hem of your dress.

Something New: You're being reborn as a married chick—the idea is to celebrate the novelty. Go for: brand-new lingerie; a sparkly tiara or pair of barrettes; a daring new haircut or color (one that you've tested out, of course).

Something Borrowed: Marriage is about community, both your tight family unit and your wide support circle. Give it a nod by wearing something that belongs to a loved one. Go for: your mom's or sister's veil; your best friend's earrings; your niece's charm bracelet; gloves made from lace from your grandmother's wedding gown.

Something Blue: The color of fidelity, blue Curaçao, and other good stuff. Go for: blue toenail polish; baby-blue heels; bluebells scattered in your bouquet or tresses; a navy satin purse; sapphire earrings.

Bracelet: A great bracelet can tie a whole look together with just the flick of the wrist (pun intended). Unless you plan on wearing long sleeves, in which case the perfect piece will never be seen and will just look out-of-place, a bracelet is a great finishing touch. Slip on a simple chain or, if you dare to be bold and bohemian, a thicker dangling piece that jingles as you party. This type of piece works best with just a great pair of earrings and no necklace.

Your Lingerie

What you wear under the dress is just as important to looking good and feeling great as the gown itself. Here're some quick tips on the various bridal undergarments.

The Bra: Many of the bras and bustiers sold at bridal boutiques, while sometimes pricey, have wedding-dress-specific proportions that are quite useful with the right dress. But you should make comfort your priority—you don't want insufficient support or annoying wires cutting into your sides on wedding day, so take note of these things when you're trying pieces on.

If your dress has a low- or wide-cut neckline or skinny little straps, you'll want a strapless bra. The most versatile style is one with removable straps, which also will let you create a criss-cross or halter back. For a completely backless dress, get a backless bra that hooks at the waist. Or consider an "Unbra"—flesh-colored, tape-on support that you actually stick right to your skin. While an Unbra doesn't offer the same support as a full bra (it's probably not a good choice if you're full-chested, either), you can dance assured you've no straps to show. Want to pump up the volume on your cleavage? It's Wonderbra time.

It's smart to begin by looking for the correct style and type of support from your usual brand's offerings—you're already used to how that brand fits you. Take home a handful of styles and try them on with the dress. Move around a bit, do some dance moves—test the bra for comfort and to make sure it stays hidden.

Slimmers: While old-fashioned girdles went out of style after your mother's wedding, a number of contemporary slimming undergarments that use Lycra or Spandex rather than stiff stays or ancient whalebone are available. If you plan to use a slimmer, make sure to take it with you to your fittings; a body-support garment will give a slightly different shape than just sucking in your gut. And consider wearing it before your wedding day for practice. You want to make sure this is a type of support garment that you can wear for the duration.

Underwear: As with the bra and slimmer, choose panties that offer comfort over sex appeal. (There's just no way to discreetly rearrange a pair of creeping underwear through a wedding dress!) If your dress has an unusually slinky cut, you may want to go with a pantyhose/underwear combo; your guests don't need to know what style panty you chose.

Hose: If you want to wear a fancy garter belt with hooks to hold up thigh-high hose, make sure you choose one that fits snugly around your waist (and that won't be seen through your dress!). The pressure of the hose can pull an inexpensive elastic garter belt right over your hips, leading to wrinkly knees and an endless evening of trying to hitch up your hose (a task nearly as hard to hide as tugging at underwear). If you think you'll kick off your heels as the

There's the Run

Be sure to buy a few extra pairs of hose so that when you accidentally shred one leg on wedding morning, you can continue dressing without missing a beat.

ASK CARLEY

Glove Etiquette

Q: I want to wear gloves during the ceremony but I'm not sure what I'm supposed to do when we exchange rings. Should I take the left glove off and put it back on after, or take both of them off at that point and leave them off?

A: Here's what you do: Carefully unstitch the seam of the ring finger on the left glove so you have a small opening. During the ring swap, slip your finger out, and once the wedding band is in place, slip it back in—no taking on and off of gloves! You could take the glove off and hand it to your honor attendant during the exchange, but if the gloves are long, you may be left struggling and fumbling at the altar, so practice beforehand. (And since it would probably be too much trouble to put it back on again at that point, prepare to be asymmetrical for the rest of the ceremony.)

evening progresses, you might want to choose tights rather than sheer hose to avoid holes in your toes. Or go with knee highs that you can slide off along with your shoes.

Give 'Em a Hand: Gloves

Gloves are a Victorian artifact that had a resurgence in the 1930s and '40s, when they were worn for just about every formal occasion. Not only that, they're totally glamorous. They come in all kinds of fabrics—silk, satin, lace, cotton eyelet, knit, even kid leather. Some have trims that you can match to the details on your dress. Some handling tips:

- Wear wrist-length gloves with short-sleeved gowns, elbow length with cap-sleeve gowns, and over-the-elbow gloves with strapless gowns.
- If you're wearing a long-sleeved dress, skip them altogether (or wear wrist gloves, if you absolutely must).
- If you have full upper arms, avoid over-the-elbow gloves; wear a pair that stops at the elbow.
- Over-the-elbow gloves don't do much for short brides, either, who have shorter arms. Keep the glove length to a minimum if you're of less than average height.
- Take gloves off in the receiving line and while eating and drinking during the reception (you'll end up wearing them mostly during the ceremony and for formal photographs).

Walking on Air: Shoes

Of course you want a gorgeous pair of wedding-day shoes, but you also want them to feel good on your feet. Let's face it, this is not a day on which you're going to be spending a lot of time sitting. If you opt for heels, don't go too high (or too stiletto-like): Two inches is enough. Many styles are available in different shades of white or are dyable, so you can match them to the hue of your dress. (You don't have to buy "bridal" shoes, but do if you want them to match your dress exactly.) The options:

It's a Shoe-In

Wear your wedding shoes before the big day to get used to them and to scuff the soles so you don't slip.

- Silk or satin pumps with square or round toes—plain or decorated with appliqués
- Mary Janes
- Strappy sandals (We love gold or silver ones for the wedding day!)
- Slingbacks with closed or open toes
- Satin ballet slippers
- Bridal boots with ribbons for laces—very Victorian
- Decorative, pearl-studded, sequined, or beaded sneakers, or Keds with lace laces
- White Doc Martens

Your Big-Day Makeup Bag

- Lipstick, lip liner, mascara, eyeliner, blush—for touchups
- Pressed powder (to maintain perfection)
- Blotting tissues (to minimize shine)
- Lip gloss
- Moist towelettes
- Perfume (and some of your honey's cologne, if he asks nicely)
- Hair spritz or moisture mist

Getting Gorgeous: Wedding Hair and Makeup

Yeah, yeah, beauty is only skin deep. But on your wedding day, your skin—and your hair, for that matter—has to look darn good. Getting that "don't hate me because I'm beautiful" hair and a "maybe she's born with it" face is easy when you know how to find a good beauty professional. We have the tips you need on how to hire a great hairstylist and makeup artist, so you can get the best beauty bang for your buck.

First you'll need to answer some questions: What's our budget? Will you go to the professional or will the professional come to you? How long do you want your stylist to stick around? (Just for prewedding styling or for whole-day touchups?) Once you have your answers, get ready to roll.

Tips for a Perfect Face

"If you don't wear a lot of makeup on a regular basis, don't show up with a full face of makeup on your wedding day. Your wedding makeup has to last all day, but that doesn't mean that you should apply *more*—it actually means that you need to take your time applying it. Use powders—easier to use than pencils—and concentrate on defining the lines: your lip line, your eyelids, your brows."

—Mitchell Behr, New York City bridal stylist

Starting the Search

As with any wedding vendor, you'll want to do your research before choosing your professional. Look online, talk to the ladies at your bridal salon (or your reception venue), speak with local brides and friends—basically cover all your bases.

Hair: There are a few ways to hire a stylist, but the most reputable is through a salon. The plus-side: reliability. The salon will ensure that the stylist is where he is supposed to be when he's supposed to be there—because it's *the salon's* reputation on the line. The downside: price. If the wedding will require the stylist to be out of the salon for a whole working day, you may be asked to pay what he would normally bring in if he were in the salon (because they'll be losing all of that business).

You can also find a good person through a salon but chose to hire him privately. The plus side: price. If your wedding is on a day that the salon is closed, the stylist may cost less because he or she wouldn't be earning any money on that day anyway. The downside: reliability. Unless you have a signed contract, you're relying on the integrity of the stylist to be there when he says he will.

Makeup: Nowadays, you can hire a makeup artist through the same salons that offer hair specialists. Many salons offer makeup applications, often with their own line of cosmetics, which is a big help for a bride with limited cosmetic resources. Some salons even offer a discount if you book both professionals there—how sweet is that?

You can also find a great makeup artist through your local department store. If you have a favorite makeup counter, head there for a free makeover (or head to twenty different counters and pick your favorite). If you like what you see, ask the salesperson if she does any outside makeup work. (Who doesn't like extra cash?) She may be willing to come to you on your wedding day. If not, set aside an appointment at the counter for the morning of the wedding.

Finally, if you are marrying near a big city, you can find hairstylists and makeup artists through agents (the same folks who represent models and photographers). Check the pages of your favorite magazines to find big names, or scour the Internet for reps. While these folks will cost a pretty penny, you might find it worth the extra dough.

Next, you'll need to set up a consultation. Many salons or professionals will charge a consultation fee—anywhere from $25 to $100—and then a separate wedding-day fee (which can run as high as $1,200). Others will charge only one price up front, slightly higher than a wedding-day fee, and offer a free consultation as part of the package. Take caution: The problem with the latter option is that you sign on with the stylist before you have a chance to critique him—so don't be lured by the prospect of a free consultation (it's not "free" if you hate how you look and need to find someone else).

A word of advice: When it comes to a hairstylist, you may have a favorite to whom you've been going for years. Don't think about skipping the consultation step just because you have a history; getting yor hair trimmed or a getting a blowout isn't the same as having your hair done for your wedding.

Beauty and Hair Questions

You've got a long list of questions to ask both beauty professionals.

- Does she have a portfolio of her work you can examine?
- Does she have a list of references you can call? (You'll be able to get the inside info on things like promptness, attitude, and professionalism.)
- Will she bring her own products—a hair dryer, her own makeup brushes, curling iron, and other necessities, or will you be responsible for supplying the extras?
- How does she charge—by the hour? by the head?
- How many weddings does she do in one day? (Will yours be the only one, or will she be rushed to get to another wedding?)

Pulling It Together

You'll want to plan a consultation at least three weeks prior to the big day (giving you plenty of time to find someone new if things don't go as planned). Gather every photo that represents the look you're going for (from magazines, real weddings, and so on). Your hairstylist will also need a snapshot of your dress so he knows what kind of neckline he's dealing with.

What many brides don't realize about a consultation is that this is a trial run, which means that most professionals will want to give you only an *idea* of the look you're after, not an exact replica of what's to be expected on the big day. They do this for one main reason: It's hard to replicate a style or a look exactly the same way twice, so it's better to do it slightly under par on the first try.

What this means for your hairstyle is that an updo might not have as many pins (or be sprayed with as much hairspray) as you'll need on the big day. This also allows more movement if your stylist is trying a few different looks in one afternoon. (*Note:* You must buy your headpiece and veil *before* your consultation, since every tiara, hairpin, and veil will lend itself to a

ASK CARLEY

Hiring Hairstylists

Q: I think my whole wedding party, my mother, and my grandmother all want to have their hair and makeup done. How many people do I need to hire?

A: We say the more, the better. Plan on one hairstylist for every three heads, and one makeup artist for every five. (Since hair tends to take longer, the hairstylist will need more time with each person.) It's better to have too many hands than too few—you don't want Mom's hair mishap to cause everyone to be late for the ceremony.

different hairstyle. The idea here is to give the hairstylist the fewest number of surprises on the big day.) For makeup, your artist might do the left eye with one color combination and the right with another, so you can compare which works better for you.

Now smile, beautiful. You'll need to take photos—from every angle—once you get the look you're after. The more visual reminders your professional has, the more he or she will be able to re-create that look. Bonus: You'll also be able to judge how it all comes together in photographs, and you might find that a look you love in the mirror doesn't translate well on film.

The All-in-One Pro

Consider hiring one pro who does both hair and makeup, which many do. It's a great way to save money and get a cohesive look.

Wedding Emergency Kit

Put together a bag of "tools" to keep you two fresh and gorgeous, help you solve potential predicaments, and generally keep things together. (After pulling everything together, entrust it to your attendants.)

Breath mints/spray (or a small toothbrush and tube of toothpaste)
Safety pins
White masking tape (for wayward hems)
Small brush/comb
Clear nail polish (for inevitable stocking runs)
Krazy Glue (for shoe heels, decorations, even jewels)
Tissues
Aspirin
Smelling salts
Ponytail holder/bobby pins/butterfly clip (in case your hair does a double take)
Cellular phone (borrow one if you don't have your own—it's essential for tracking down vendors, guests, or other lost parties)
Tampons/sanitary napkins
Static-cling spray
Power Bar/Fig Newtons/bag of pretzels (even to-be-weds get hunger pangs)

Beauty Countdown

This step-by-step beauty schedule will have you looking fabulous come wedding day:

Six Months Before

- Want to grow your hair out or try a new color or cut? Experiment now.
- Get serious about your skin care. Start a good cleansing, nutrition, and stress-relief regimen.
- If you don't already, start exercising! A few sessions with a trainer may help to jump-start your routine.

One to Two Months Before

- Find and meet with a makeup artist for a trial run.
- Or get a makeover at a department-store counter and purchase any products you need now (so you have time to practice).
- Take your veil to your hairstylist to try out big-day 'dos.
- Have your eyebrows professionally shaped. Why not? It's your wedding!
- Test out at-home masks or a salon facial. (Don't risk an allergic reaction on your wedding day.)
- Moisturize! Soft and silky elbows, hands, and feet are a marriage must.
- Want a sparkling smile? Cut down on tea and coffee and try a whitening toothpaste.

Two Weeks Before

- Eat right. Load up on fruits and veggies; nix the salt and fat.
- Drink lots of water and exercise, exercise, exercise.
- Get your final haircut or trim.
- Touch up your haircolor or perm.
- Do a full big-day hair trial before your final dress fitting. (If you're not happy, now's the time to speak up!)

One Week Before

- Avoid overindulging in salty snacks and alcohol at those fab prewedding parties.
- Have a bikini wax and a final eyebrow shaping.
- Remind your man to get his final trim.
- Get a massage (if you can afford it; if not, ask him to do the deed, and give him one, too).
- Get a final facial. (Do not wait until the day before to do this!)

One Day and Counting

- Drink lots of water! (Have we made ourselves perfectly clear?)
- Deep-condition your hair.
- Have a professional manicure and pedicure.
- Take a long, relaxing bath.

Beauty Emergencies

It's true: sometimes good faces or hair can go bad. But that doesn't mean that those problems aren't fixable. Here are a few, shall we say, issues that might arise, and the best ways to save the day.

Chipped Nail Polish: With this type of problem, less fussing is definitely more. Don't try to pull off those magic nail fixes they do at the salon—with a drop of nail polish remover and a light touch. Simply apply a dab of polish on just the chipped area and wait two minutes for it to dry. Then apply one coat of polish over entire nail area, and add some quick-dry topcoat.

Puffy Eyes: The tried-and-true beauty trick is tea bags—green tea works best (the caffeine is a natural shrinker). Dip the tea bags in water, lie down, and place them over your eyes for ten to twenty minutes. Another DIY cure: frozen spoons on each of your eyelids. Combine these two tricks for double the de-puffing power.

Zit: If you wake up the day before with a new neighbor on your face, a dermatalogist can give your face a quick injection of cortisone, which will bring down any blemish-swelling and make it practically disappear by the following morning. But on the day of, you'll have to zap it with a touch of blemish ointment (there are great companies that make them with a built-in concealer), or a drop of Visine (seriously), which will take any redness out of the area. The more you try to hide it, the more prominent it will become—so go easy on the pasty cover-ups. We promise that the only person who'll notice it will be you.

NOTES

CHAPTER TWELVE

dressing the rest

To-be-weds spend so much time stressing over what everyone should wear—the cummerbunds have to match the bridesmaid dresses; the maids' ensembles (and hairstyles) must be identical; it's mandatory for the moms to plan their coordinating wedding-day wardrobes carefully. We say—lighten up! The goal here is to get everyone looking good and feeling great. Let go of your ideas of how you think everyone *should* look and concentrate on making every individual look fabulous. Here's all you need to know to do just that.

Men's Formalwear 101

The land of formalwear is confusing territory for pretty much anyone who's never been a maitre d' for a living, so to help you make sense of all your wedding fashion choices—and the cryptic jargon tux salesmen love to ramble on about—here's our handy groom's formalwear glossary:

Jackets and Coats

Tuxedo Jacket: The basic tux coat can be single- or double-breasted with your choice of three lapels: peaked (a cut in the lapel points upward, giving a broad, V-line look), notched (a triangular piece in the lapel is cut at the collar line and points outward), or shawl (there is no cut in the lapel, creating a retro rounded look). It's worn with black satin-striped trousers.

Tail Coat: Short in front and long in the back, it tapers from the waist into one or two tails down the back. Usually black, but sometimes you see it in white.

Cutaway/Morning Coat: Also short in front and long in the back, it tapers from the waistline button to one broad tail in the back, with a vent. Usually in pinstriped charcoal gray.

Stroller Coat: A semiformal jacket cut like a tuxedo, it's usually gray and often has pinstripes.

Dinner Jacket: Tuxedo-cut jacket in white or ivory (think James Bond). You also can get it in other colors or funky fabrics. It's worn with black satin-striped trousers.

Spencer Coat: An open coat without buttons, cut right at the waistline. Worn in the evening or daytime, depending on color (black for evening).

Men's Jackets and Coats

Tail Coat

Cutaway

3/4 Coat

Mandarin

Tuxedo Peaked Lapel

Tuxedo Notched Lapel

Tuxedo Shawl Lapel

Dinner Jacket

Shirt Collars

Wing Collar: A stand-up collar with downward points. The most formal style.

Turndown or Point Collar: Similar to a business-shirt collar, but in a more formal fabric.

Spread: Similar to a turndown collar but less pointy.

Mandarin Collar: Narrow banded stand-up collar without points. Can be worn with a button cover but not a tie.

Accessories

Ascot: A wide, usually patterned, scarf looped under the chin and fastened with a tie tack or a stick pin (very British) and worn with a wing collar, usually with a cutaway/morning coat.

Euro Tie: A long tie with a square bottom and a thin strap so that it can be worn with both spread-collar and wing-collar shirts.

Formal Tie: A typical necktie in a black or dark gray, usually silk.

Bow Tie: It's, uh, you know, a bow tie. Comes in multiple colors. Wear it with any collar.

Cummerbund: A pleated sash made of brocade, silk, or satin worn to cover the trouser waistline with pleats facing up. The color may or may not match your jacket, but it usually matches your tie.

Vest: Worn instead of a cummerbund or suspenders under the coat. In black, white, or any other color or pattern, they're great under tuxedo or dinner jackets; they come in full or backless versions.

Waistcoat: Like a vest except usually cut lower in front, it's a more formal look, especially appropriate with a cutaway/morning coat or tailcoat.

Finishing Touches: Cuff links, studs, tie tacks, stick pins, pocket squares, suspenders.

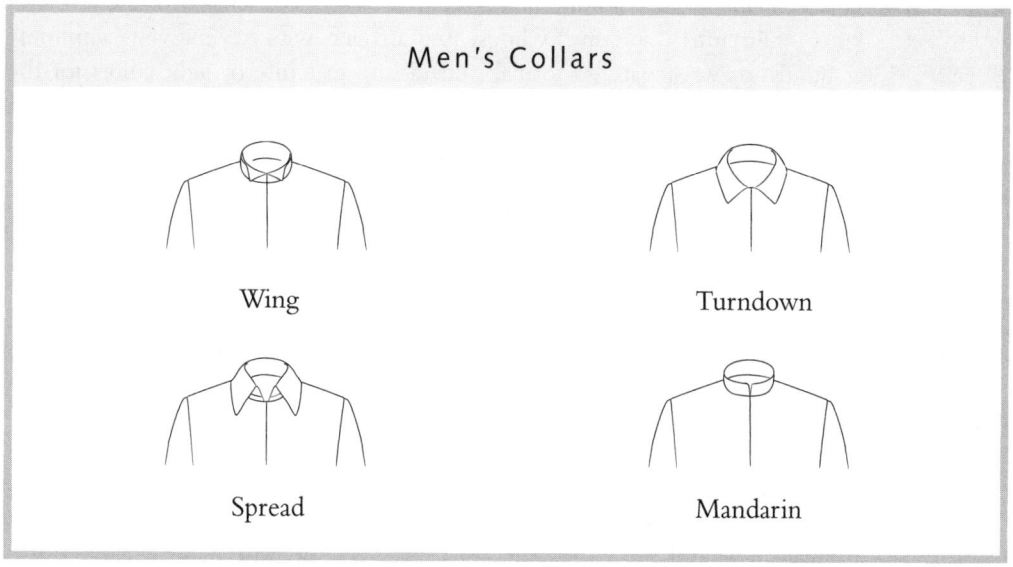

Feel free to drop some extra cash for a special pair of links—dice, rainbow trout, ball and chain—that will always remind you of your big day.

What to Wear When?

Rumor has it that at a wedding, the only person people pay attention to is the babe in the white dress. Not true! Grooms get noticed, too—especially if they're dressed wrong. But what could be so "wrong" about a tux—aren't they all the same? Think about it. James Bond wears a tuxedo—and so does the maitre d' at your favorite restaurant. So . . . no. There are a few guidelines.

Most of the rules about what kind of tux to wear have to do with whether you're getting hitched before or after the sun goes down and how formal or casual the festivities are going to be. The best resource for picking the right style of tux to match your occasion? The salesperson who helps you at the formalwear store. Let him in on the time of day you're getting married and how formal the wedding will be (describing where it is and what's in store will tell him all he needs to know), and then try on as many different outfits as he's willing to show you. Here's a quick lesson in some of the standard wedding dress requirements.

Semiformal Daytime: The groom and groomsmen wear suits (navy or charcoal are great year-round; reserve khaki or white linen for the warmer seasons) with nice shirts and four-in-hand ties (like the kind worn with business suits).

Semiformal Evening: The groom and groomsmen can wear black tuxedos with bow ties and cummerbunds or vests (or simply nice dark suits if they prefer). Their shirts may have wing-tipped or turned-down collars and are either white or ivory to match the bride's gown. Not required (unless your bride insists): cummerbunds that match the bridesmaids' dresses.

Formal Daytime: Choose gray strollers with ties and vests, cummerbunds, or waistcoats, or formal suits (again, in white or light colors for the summer—darker shades in the winter).

Formal Evening: In the evening, formal usually means black tie: The groom and groomsmen wear black tuxedos with white or ivory shirts and black ties, cummerbunds or vests. (It's totally legit to inject some color into things, however.) Another option for formal evening: white or ivory dinner jackets (the 007 look).

Ultra-formal Daytime: The groom and groomsmen traditionally wear cutaway coats with charcoal-colored striped trousers, gray waistcoats (sometimes available with a print), wing-collared shirts, and ascots or striped ties. It's a very dapper look that you're not going to get away with at any other occasion—and your bride will love it, trust us.

Ultra-formal Evening: White tie (also known as "tails full dress") is reserved for the most elaborate evening weddings. The groom and groomsmen wear black tail coats with white waistcoats or vests, wing-collared shirts,

What Renting Costs You

Approximate cost of renting specific formalwear styles.

- Classic tuxedo: $100
- Evening tails: $120
- Designer tux: $125

Time for Tuxes

The old rule: No tuxedos before 6:00 P.M. The new school: If your *reception* starts at 6:00 or later, it's okay to wear a tux for a late-afternoon ceremony. Tuxes for morning or early afternoon are still a no-no—so go for a morning coat, stroller, or great daytime suit instead.

Get the Guide

For a copy of the American Formalwear Association's free pamphlet, "Your Formalwear Guide." Send a self-addressed, stamped envelope to: The American Formalwear Association, 401 North Michigan Avenue, Suite 2400, Chicago, IL 60611–4267.

and white bow ties. They also may wear fancy studs and cuff links, and their shoes are black patent leather. (You can skip the top hats and canes.)

Going Shopping

For most grooms, renting a tuxedo probably will suffice. But if you think you'll have reason to wear a tux in the future, it may be worth buying one. Look at it this way: Renting costs about 25 to 30 percent of the price of a new tuxedo. The cost of a tux can run anywhere from $200 to $2,000. So if you attend three or four formal events a year, it's worth it to buy. And as long as it's a classic style, you'll be able to wear it for quite a few years.

But even the most expensive tux on the rack will look and feel awful if it doesn't fit you right. Since you're pretty much at the mercy of your salesperson, it's nice to know your way around the tux shop. Here's what to keep in mind when you formalwear shop—share these tips with your groomsmen, too.

Comfort Is Key: Sure, looks mean a lot. But comfort, especially in a wedding tux, is a really close second—you'll be wearing it for four to eight emotional, fun-filled hours, after all. You should be able to move around easily—do lots of twists, turns, and arm raises when you're trying one on.

Try 'em on for Size: It's a good idea for everyone to pick up and try on their formalwear at least two days before the wedding. Sounds like a no-brainer, right? You'd be surprised. Many mismatched bridal parties or ill-fitting jackets are the result of guys skipping this simple step. Procrastinate at your own risk.

The Fit

When you're sizing up a tux, here's what to look for:

The Jacket: Should fit comfortably at the neck and shoulders and fasten easily. Try standing and sitting with it buttoned.

The Shirt: Should fit comfortably at the neck, shoulders, and waist. About one-quarter to one-half inch of cuff should show below the jacket sleeve.

The Vest: Should fit comfortably across your chest with the buttons lining up to the

Formalwear Contract Points

- ☐ Designer, style, and style number(s)
- ☐ Color of each
- ☐ Number of suits rented
- ☐ Accessories covered in rental fee (ties, shoes, vests, etc.)
- ☐ Date everything can be picked up
- ☐ Total cost
- ☐ Deposit paid and date balance is due
- ☐ Additional fees (fitting, cleaning, late return)
- ☐ How store will fix last-minute problems like poor fit, wrong style, etc.
- ☐ Refund and cancellation policy
- ☐ Date everything must be returned to store

Stand-Out Grooms

There are lots of fresh ways for the groom to contrast yet complement his groomsmen. You want people to know which one of you is the lucky guy, right?

Wear a white dinner jacket; best man and groomsmen wear black jackets. Or vice versa.
Wear a solid or patterned vest instead of a cummerbund.
Wear a long silk tie instead of a bow tie.
Wear different ties (e.g., groom in gold, groomsmen in silver).
Wear a different style or color shirt than the other men.
Wear different flowers in your boutonniere or be the only man to wear one.

front of your jacket. The bottom should fall slightly over your trouser waistband. Usually you can adjust the waist with a slide strap for a good fit. Or consider a vest with a full back, so when you take your jacket off during the evening you're not flashing a strap and the back of your shirt.

The Trousers: Should button comfortably and feel good when you sit down. Many styles have adjustable waistbands, or you can opt for suspenders. The hem should break just over shoe tops.

More Rental Tips

Choose a formalwear store that has updated their inventory regularly since 1976. (If you see powder blue and ruffles, run.)

A good formalwear dealer will know how to measure you properly (inseam, waist, jacket size) and give you a fitting in advance of the wedding.

The store also can supply you with all the accessories you'll need: bow tie, cummerbund, cuff links, suspenders, even shoes.

Finally, all the groomsmen should get their clothing at the same shop, to ensure color and style coordination. If you've got faraway groomsmen, get them to go for a fitting at a store near them (they can try on the tux you've chosen to check out how it fits them) and then send their measurements to you.

Dressing the Bridesmaids

First of all, we've got to tell you—bridesmaid dresses these days are nothing like the teal taffeta confections of weddings past. In fact, we think you'll be hard-pressed to find a dress your bridesmaids truly hate. That doesn't mean, however, that we're going to tell you to choose "something they can wear again." Why? Because, unless you pick a black velvet or satin sheath dress that hits at the knee, they probably won't. Even if they adore the dress you choose (or let them choose), it's still a bridesmaid dress. They'll associate it with your wedding. This is not a bad thing. It's a souvenir. The point is, don't get obsessed with the wear-again concept of every bridesmaid dress you see. Okay?

ODINE & DAVID

March 6, New York City

HOW DID THE BRIDE, from New York, feel about her English groom wearing a kilt to their wedding? "That's how I met him," Odine says, "that's how I was going to marry him." Odine and David met in New York—David had come from Australia, where he was living, to attend the wedding of a friend, who happened also to be a friend of Odine's. The wedding was formal, and David was thus in his standard formalwear—a kilt.

That gave Odine an easy way to introduce herself. "I asked him to dance by saying 'I've never danced with a man in a skirt before.' " She laughs. The couple carried on a "9,948-mile-apart" romance until David, once again in a kilt, proposed.

David's kilt has been in his family for generations—it's a McCleod tartan, meaning the pattern represents the McCleod clan, which is his Scottish ancestry on his mother's side. For the wedding, David wanted his father, brothers, and male cousins in their clans' kilts, as well. Almost none of them owned a family kilt, but, luckily, kilt shops in Scotland rent them, and David managed to locate the appropriate tartan for each man, which his dad then brought across the ocean.

Odine's mother is French, and Odine and David's friends are scattered around the globe, so the couple wanted to hold the wedding somewhere that would be a treat for guests coming from several continents. They found the perfect spot—a restaurant directly across the East River from Manhattan, so that the event's backdrop was the famous twinkling skyline of the Big Apple.

The Many Options

The choices for bridesmaid dresses these days are practically endless—and that's a good thing! And no longer do your maids all have to wear the same exact thing if you (and/or they) don't want to. Here's what to think about before you even start shopping.

Styles and Colors: You may be shocked at just how many styles of bridesmaid dresses you find out there. You'll see fitted sheaths, A-line styles, empire looks (with high waists), two-piece skirt-and-top sets, overskirts, stoles and chiffon scarves, and matching jackets with jeweled buttons. Most are in solid colors, but you'll also see two-tone dresses and floral prints (especially in spring). Especially great news: The options for bridesmaid dresses have expanded upward from the floor. That's right, it is now acceptable to show a little bridesmaid ankle. Naughty! Tea length and knee length are more common, but we are steering you clear of the thigh-baring mini-dress. Please. We're begging.

Identical Maids: Traditionally, all the bride's attendants have worn the same dress. This works best when all the women have similar body types—which doesn't happen all that often! Most of your attendants are tall and thin, and one is shorter and rounder? Keep in mind that she may need a lot of alterations done to her gown to make it fit her well and comfortably; you might want to let her wear a slightly different, more flattering style.

Stand-Out Honor Attendants: Some brides choose to put their best friend or sister (whoever serves as honor attendant) in a dress that's slightly different from the rest of the bridesmaids', to emphasize her place of honor in the wedding party.

Same Style, Different Colors: You might decide to ask your maids to all wear the same style dress, but each in a different color—of your choosing or the shade each woman feels she looks best in. You can create a rainbow of jewel tones or pastels this way, or put the attendants in different shades of the same color (purple, lavender, lilac, etc.).

Same Color, Different Style: One designer may have several dresses you like that flatter different body types, all available in the same color. If you go this route, your maids will match in shade, but each woman can choose the style that looks best on her.

They Gotta Be Them

Your maids don't have to be identical. Even if they all wear the same dress, let them each choose how to wear their hair or select their own jewelry. They're not going to upstage you—they're just going to be more comfortable, which will make you look even better (and the pictures, too.)

Bridesmaid Lore

Did you know that the bridesmaids' dresses all used to be *identical* to the bride's? They dressed just like her to confuse and stave off evil spirits on her wedding day.

ASK CARLEY

Pregnant Bridesmaid?

Q: My best friend, who's also my maid of honor, just told me she's pregnant—her due date is about a month after my wedding! Can she still be in the wedding party?

A: Just because your friend will be pregnant at the time of the wedding doesn't mean she can't be in the wedding! Let her wear an empire-style dress (the "waistline" is just below the bust), leaving lots of room for her tummy. You can have extra material added to the dress if need be. And make sure there's a chair for her to sit down in during the ceremony so she won't be on her feet the whole time.

Free Form: If you have no control-freak genes whatsoever, consider putting this decision into your bridesmaids' hands completely. Maybe you want everyone to wear a sheath, or something in a shade of pink or black, but beyond that you're comfortable with leaving it up to your maids to choose. They'll probably be grateful (this way they can control how much they'll spend, too), as long as they are all pretty confident about dress buying and/or have firm ideas of what looks good on them. Some attendants get thrown for a loop if they don't get *any* guidance from the bride, so be sure to give them *something* to go on.

Go to Chapter 11 for info on dress silhouettes and necklines.

Going Shopping

Once you've got the big wedding-dress search out of the way, it's high time to start looking for your bridesmaids' dresses. Ideally you want to start looking about six months before the wedding; it'll take a few months for the dresses to come in if you custom-order them, and you want to be sure you'll have time for alterations and to deal with any problems (wrong color, wrong style) when they arrive.

It's a lucky—and rare—bride who has all her attendants in the same town where she lives. That doesn't mean that your gals can't get in on the dress-hunt action.

Searching: Go to, you guessed it, theknot.com and search through thousands of dresses. You can send these gowns via e-mail to all your maids so they can offer up an opinion (if that's what you want, of course). You should always see the dress in person before making a decision. If they can find it locally, send them to a salon to check it out.

Measuring: If possible, your maids should have themselves measured by a professional seamstress or a good-natured tailor at a favorite department store. As silly as it sounds, you actually need a pro's expertise to measure the right spot. Warn your maids that, like gown sizes, bridesmaids dress sizes run a little small, so they shouldn't stress out if they end up having to order a gown a size or two larger. Don't be swayed by "I'm going to lose fifteen pounds by then so order me a size smaller." Just say no. Add that it's much easier to "take in" than "let out," and she looks fabulous just as she is.

Ordering: It's best to order all gowns at the same time so that they come from the same dye lot. You might be the one ordering the dresses yourself and collecting all the info and money for the salon to place the order, or your maid of honor might offer to take care of it. In any case, make sure the dresses are shipped to your bridesmaids as soon as they arrive. Chances are they will need a little altering.

Where to Look: Bridal salons almost always carry bridesmaid dresses as well. Some have separate rooms or even stores solely devoted to bridesmaids. You also can find maids' dresses at bridal warehouses, eveningwear stores (so many are identical to cocktail dresses these days), and in special-occasion dress departments at big department stores.

Whom to Shop With: You might want to go alone first to see what's out there or take along your honor attendant so she can test-drive dresses you like. If possible, try to take all your bridesmaids along on at least one shopping trip, so they'll feel like they have a say in what they'll wear.

Group Discounts

If the bride and bridesmaids' dresses are ordered at the same store, you (and/or they) may receive a discount, or free alterations. Some formalwear stores will rent the groom his tuxedo free if all the groomsmen rent at the same store. Ask before you order.

Dress Contract Points

- ☐ Designer, style, and style number(s)
- ☐ Color of each dress
- ☐ Delivery date
- ☐ Total cost
- ☐ Deposit paid and date balance is due
- ☐ Additional fees (alterations, ironing, etc.)
- ☐ Refund and cancellation policy

Go to Appendix B for contact numbers for bridesmaid dress and shoe manufacturers.

Alterations: Once the gowns arrive in the shop, every bridesmaid needs to go in for a fitting; as with the bride's gown, the shop probably can take care of any alterations—taking in the waist, bringing in the shoulders, hemming the skirt. The shop will call the bridesmaid when the altered dress is ready, so she can go in to try it on again and make sure it fits.

Shoes: Many brides ask their maids to buy dyeable shoes to match the color of the dress. Many national chain shoe stores carry these, in styles from pumps to strappy sandals. You (or the maid) simply brings in a swatch from the dress, and the store matches the dye of the shoes to the color of the gown. Or you may be able to find ready-made shoes in the right color (or in black or silver). Or, if you want to make your maids *really* happy, you can just ask them to wear a certain color like black, silver, gold, or taupe and let them wear their own shoes, or buy a style they actually like and can—oops, we're gonna say it—wear again someday.

Clothing Your Wedding Kids

When it comes to kid attendants' clothes, keep in mind that for little boys and girls who want to run around and play at the reception, comfort and practicality are key.

Junior Attendants

Preteen maids and groomsmen can wear the same dress or formalwear as their older counterparts. If your bridesmaids are wearing something a little less than appropriate for a twelve-year-old girl (a seriously plunging neckline, for example), put her in a more age-appropriate style in the same color or in a complementary shade.

Little Girls

Check Appendix B for contact websites for top child attendant clothing manufacturers. For more on child attendant roles, go to Chapter 4.

A general rule of thumb: A flower girl's dress should echo the styling of the rest of the bridal party or the bride's dress, whether with color, style, or length. Shop with your flower girl and her mom (who probably will buy the dress, unless it's a gift from you). She'll look adorable in any pretty party dress. White is the most common color choice, but it can be any shade you—and she—like.

Sweet dress styles for little girls include short or long sleeves with full skirts and satin sashes; white organza pinafores over velvet dresses; all-over lace confections in white or colors

ASK CARLEY

His Mom in White??

Q: His mom wants to wear a white dress! I feel like she's trying to show me up. What should I do?

A: First of all, it's just not *possible* to show up a glowing, gorgeous bride, so don't stress out too much over the situation. Your best bet here is to resort to some good old-fashioned etiquette: Let your fiancé talk to his mom and gently let her know that it's not appropriate for anyone but the bride to wear white. She may simply not be aware of this, or maybe she just didn't consider that it would upset you. Then you might ask your mother to give his a call to let her in on what she's planning to wear, since moms often discuss how they each are dressing for the wedding. If all else fails and you have a good relationship with her, don't be afraid to talk to her yourself.

with satin ribbons; or simple straight dresses, perhaps to match simply styled bride's and bridesmaid gowns. These darling little outfits, especially those made expressly as "flower girl dresses," can be pricey—be sure to check out the little girls' department at your favorite department store, and shop in local children's shops, too. Don't forget shoes—pretty ballet slippers or black or white patent-leather Mary Janes will match any choice you make. Floral hair accessories like headbands, wreaths, and combs are fun, too.

Little Boys

Traditional choices for ring bearers or pages are satin and velvet suits with short pants, often in dark colors, such as navy or hunter green. Or how about dark-blue jackets, white shorts, and blue or white knee socks? In England, little boys wear white in weddings. For summer, a seersucker or linen suit might be cute—or put the tiny guy in a little sailor suit, which you'll find in just about every children's clothing store. There's the "please, no mini tuxes" school, but you might find little boys in grown-up formalwear endearing (hey, if the flower girl gets to wear a bridal-gown replica . . .). Check to see what local department stores, children's specialty shops, and even men's formalwear stores have to offer.

Fashion Tips for Mom and Pop

Parents get gazed at quite a bit on wedding day—they should love what they're wearing.

Moms

It's a big day for your moms, too—they're concerned about wanting to look great. The best way to help them do this? Don't instruct them about what to wear or forbid them from wearing something. Moms should wear what they feel most beautiful and comfortable in. Since your mothers are two women with different personalities, the best look on each may be quite different, and that's okay. What you can do is help them with their decision by offering guidelines—suggest colors and styles that will go well with the overall look of your wedding. Each mom should wear a shade that suits her.

Log on to The Knot (www.theknot.com) to browse through thousands of bridesmaid and mother-of-the-bride dresses.

Moms usually dress with similar formality. This guideline simply ensures that one mom doesn't feel uncomfortable or embarrassed. Generally, if the bride's mom wears a floor-length gown, the groom's mom should, too—a pantsuit in a formal fabric like satin or velvet with wide pant legs will also do. If they seem paralyzed by indecision, this old etiquette rule might help: The bride's mother selects her dress first and fills the groom's mother in on what it looks like, so she'll have an idea of what *she* should look for. But we've been to plenty of weddings where the moms weren't dressed a bit alike—and each looked out of this world.

Dads

Dads have wedding dressing pretty easy. Here's the drill: If the groom and groomsmen are wearing tuxedoes, cutaway coats, or tail coats, the dads should, too—especially if you're also asking guests to dress way up. Even if the boys aren't going black tie, dads can feel free to don a tux for the big day. That said, formal suits in appropriate colors (black, navy, charcoal for evening or winter; navy, brown, beige for summer or daytime) are great. Just remember to give each dad a boutonniere—that's what'll tip guests off as to his special status.

Guest Dressing

Wedding guests basically dress as they would for any other social event held at the same hour and in the same season as the wedding. Most guests are comfortable using that guideline, but if anyone asks you, give them some suggestions.

For example, if it's a spring brunch or luncheon, a pretty suit or floral dress would be appropriate for women; a light-colored suit and/or shirt and tie for men. For evening, depending on how formal the wedding is (guests often take their cue from the formality of the invitation and/or where the wedding is being held), the dress code is cocktail dresses for women and dark suits for men. If you want your guests to dress to the nines, have "White tie" or "Black tie" printed at the bottom of the reception invitation. If you want to let guests know they *can* don tuxes and cocktail dresses but don't *have* to, make it "Black tie optional" or "Black tie invited." If the place where you are marrying requires that men wear jackets, add "jackets requested (insert uptight reception site here)" so that it doesn't appear that you are demanding this.

Black used to be taboo for women at weddings, but these days a black dress is perfect for evening—for female guests *or* bridesmaids—just as it is for a night at the opera. However, female guests should still stay away from white—the bride's color—and should try to avoid off-white and ivory, too. Brides, if a guest slips up on this one, try not to let it bug you. The person may just not know. And if she *is* trying to show you up (the witch!), don't let her get to you (or see that she got to you, at least). Trust us, you'll look *way* more fabulous.

NOTES

CHAPTER THIRTEEN

flower power

Who can resist the perfection of flowers, a pleasure-fest for the eyes, nose, and heart? Flowers are 100 percent romance—it's no big surprise that they have always gone hand in hand with weddings. Blooms can be an awe-inspiring backdrop for the ceremony, the perfect accessories for your big-day clothes, and gorgeous centerpieces (and conversation pieces) for the reception. But where to begin with all the amazing options? Choose your all-time favorite flowers, incorporate blooms based on color, or bank it all on their special meanings. Flowers have so much power that they even can *be* a wedding theme. (A daisy wedding sounds darling, no?) You really can't go wrong in this department, so find a great florist and have fun with it!

Which Blooms to Use?

You already may have definite ideas of your own regarding your wedding flowers. Maybe you're thinking tons and tons of orchids everywhere. Or you're more of a minimalist, and you just want simple pots of tulips on the reception tables or the wedding party carrying single lilies. No matter what you choose, of course, it'll be beautiful—that's the nature of flowers, right?

Floral Info: How to Decide

Consider these factors when choosing your wedding blooms.

Durability: If you're getting married during the hot summer months or need your flowers to last a long, long time (perhaps for the duration of your weekend celebration), steer clear of blooms that wilt easily. These include gardenias, lily of the valley, tulips, and wildflowers; ask your florist for other no-nos.

Originality: Roses, carnations, baby's breath, and gladiolus are quintessential wedding blooms. We're not saying don't get 'em, but think about incorporating some other, less-common flowers, too, for a super-unique look.

Color: Flowers that match your wedding colors or play off them in an interesting way are gorgeous.

Scent: In case you haven't noticed, many flowers have strong fragrances. Of course, that's one of the reasons everyone loves them, but consider how appropriate the scent will be for your wedding. (Take into account ventilation, the preferences of favorite family and guests, allergies.) Go with mostly gentle smells. Scents imprint a strong impression on the memory—which you want—but sometimes they can be overwhelming—which you *don't* want. Fragrant blooms include freesia, lilies, lilacs, tube roses, and gardenias.

Availability: Local, in-season flowers should be your mainstay. For starters, you're assured freshness—which means extra beauty. In addition, these are the blooms that will be the most affordable, which means more flowers for less money. Consult local florists or connoisseur friends about what's blossoming in your wedding region around the time you'll be tying the knot. Try to make those flowers the crux of your bouquets and decorative arrangements; use them as party favors placed in slender ceramic vases; incorporate them as the main elements of large structures such as huppahs, arches, and oversize wreaths.

Floral Lore

Brides in ancient Rome carried bunches of herbs to symbolize fidelity and fertility. The Greeks used ivy to symbolize indissoluble love. Brides today carry floral bouquets as a symbol of fertility and bounty.

Exotica: We're not going to tell you to give up on your favorite exotic flower. Keep in mind that imported blooms can be expensive, but if you adore birds-of-paradise, include several stems in your bouquet and centerpieces. If you *must* have lilies in December (your honey brought you a cluster on your first date), we understand. All we're saying is that by using seasonal fare as your base, you'll be able to maximize your flower-buying power and indulge your wildest floral fantasies.

Location: Your wedding locale will have a lot to do with your floral decisions. If, for example, you're marrying at a park, botanical garden, or vineyard, the flowers can be kept to a minimum (meaning, you can make a big impression wih fewer flowers). If your space is a blank loft or a simple ballroom, you may have to up the floral decor factor (take that into consideration when setting a budget, too).

The Root of It All: Flower Meanings

If you're sentimental, you might choose your blooms by what they symbolize. Here's the lowdown on some popular wedding flowers (as well as when they're in season):

- Anemone (fall to spring): Expectation
- Baby's breath (year round): Innocence
- Calla lily (spring/summer): Magnificent beauty
- Camellia (spring): Perfect loveliness
- Carnation (year round): boldness (pink), love (red), talent (white)
- Chrysanthemum (year round): Wealth, abundance, truth
- Daisy (year round): Share your feelings
- Freesia (spring/summer): Innocence
- Gardenia (year round): Purity, joy
- Gerbera daisy (year round): Beauty
- Holly (winter): Foresight
- Iris (spring): Faith, wisdom

- Lilac (spring): First love
- Lily (summer): Truth, honor
- Lily of the valley (spring/summer): Happiness
- Magnolia (spring/summer): Love of nature
- Orange blossoms (fall): Purity
- Orchid (year round; imported): Love, beauty
- Rose (year round): love; red—"I love you"; white—"I am worthy of you"
- Stephanotis (year round): Marital happiness
- Sunflower (fall): Adoration
- Tulip (spring): Love, passion

How to Huppah

Jewish couples say their vows under a huppah, a canopy that symbolizes shelter and the couple's new home together. The canopy can be decorated with (or wholly constructed of) flowers. In Israel, huppahs are usually a swatch of cloth hung between four poles and held up by close friends or relatives. Build your own with your fave quilt or a gorgeous piece of satin or organza: wrap ivy, ribbons, and flowers around the poles.

Ceremony Flowers

Traditionally, the entire wedding party—and other special guests—carry or wear flowers on wedding day. The traditional arrangements include the following:

The Bridal Bouquet

The bridal bouquet, of course, is the most in-the-spotlight flower arrangement, carried by the bride during the ceremony—and sometimes tossed skyward to the single women at the reception. On average, you'll spend $100 to $250 on this bouquet, depending on the size, the flowers, and the style.

Bouquet Styles

For the bride, maids, and flower girls:

Beidermeier: A nosegay made up of concentric circles of different flowers for a somewhat striped effect.

Cascade: A waterfall-like "spill" of blooms and greenery that's anchored in a handheld base. Looks like a miniature floral train.

Composite: A handmade creation in which different petals or buds are wired together on a single stem, creating the illusion of one giant flower.

Hand-tied: A dense bunch of "just picked" blooms tied together with wire that is covered with a ribbon.

Nosegay: A small, round cluster of flowers, all cut to a uniform length, which was all the rage in Victorian times and is enjoying a renaissance today. Usually made with one dominant flower or color, nosegays are wrapped tightly with ribbon or lace for a delicate effect. Or you can go all-out Victorian, inserting the nosegay into a silver carrying cone.

Pageant: This bunch of long-stemmed flowers is cradled in the bride's arms—think beauty-pageant winner. The best flower choices for this bouquet have long stems or branches, such as calla lily, lisianthus, delphinium, French tulip, tuberose, and rose.

Keeping Flowers Fresh

Have your flowers delivered boxed with cellophane and well misted—that way they'll look fresh through your ceremony and reception.

Bouquet Styles

Beidermeier

Cascade

Composite

Hand-tied

Nosegay

Pageant

Pomander

Posy

Round

Pomander: A bloom-covered ball suspended from a ribbon, perfect for child attendants. (Flower girls may carry a basket of petals instead.)

Posy: Smaller than a nosegay but similar in design, the posy is perfect for small hands, small weddings, petite brides, or for a bridesmaid's bouquet. Smaller blooms such as spray roses or grape hyacinths are ideal varieties. A few large-headed flowers, such as gardenias or peonies, can also make an impact.

Round: Similar in style to a nosegay but generally larger, a round bouquet usually consists of large flowers that are loosely arranged. A round bouquet is a good option for the bride in a formal wedding who wants something bolder than a nosegay but less conspicuous than a cascading bouquet.

Understated Blooms

Bridesmaids can walk down the aisle carrying a single, stunning stem—such as an orchid, sunflower, or calla lily—instead of bouquets.

Bridesmaids' Bouquets

Usually smaller than the bride's cluster, bridesmaids' bouquets play off of—and showcase—her bouquet by complementing its color, shape, or type of flowers. The average cost of these arrangements will be about $50 to $150 per attendant.

To keep things visually interesting, you may choose to have each bridesmaid carry a slightly different bouquet—variations on a theme that you've set. Switch up their flowers with ribbons, varying shapes, multiple shades, or with completely different colors all together (relating back to your wedding color scheme).

Groom and Groomsmen's Boutonnieres

Boutonnieres consist of a single bloom or bud (or several small ones) attached at the left lapel of the jacket, worn by the groom, his attendants, ushers, and the bride and groom's fathers. If you like, the groom's can stand out from those worn by the other men. (You might echo the dominant flower in the bride's bouquet.) Boutonnieres cost about $7 to $12 each.

Don't feel restricted by the formal rose or stephanotis—or even a flower, for that matter. Florists are breaking out of the mold and using everything from berries to herbs to small branches for lapel decoration, which can turn a line of ordinary groomsmen into a group of very stylish ones.

Flowers for Moms and Honored Guests

Wrist and pin-on corsages are the most popular choices for mom, grandma, and that special aunt who helped fold all the programs, to wear during the ceremony. If you're going to take the corsage route, ask ahead of time which kind each woman would prefer—mom might not want to put a hole in the lapel of her brand-new silk suit. Cost: $15 to $50.

As with everything else, corsages have evolved as well. Brides are choosing to have mom and other relatives carry a small nosegay down the aisle, $30 to $75. For other guests who deserve special recognition, a simple single rose has become a nice alternative, costing about $5 per stem.

Blossoms for the Flower Girls

Nothing makes an entire congregation go "Awww" than an adorable flower girl. A basket filled with rose petals is their standard accessory. Don't limit yourself to the basket, however. Have her carry a beach bucket for a seaside ceremony, a small silk purse for a more formal event, or even a wheeled wagon filled with flowers for a laid-back party. On average, the cost for a flower-girl arrangement is $30 to $75.

Other Ceremony Floral Arrangements

You may want to add some flower power to your ceremony site itself. Depending on where you'll wed and your budget, this can range from lavish to simple. Popular floral decorations include:

- A central altar/stage arrangement or two large vases on either side of where you two will stand
- Flowering huppah (Jewish bridal canopy)
- Blooms fastened onto pews or chairs (every two or three rows for cost-effectiveness)
- Flower or ivy chains draped between seats
- A lush wreath on the entrance door
- Large potted plants or flower arrangements to delineate the ceremony area (when it's the same as the reception site or outside)
- A blooming arch for the wedding party to walk through

Think Color, Size, and Shape

Don't choose the bridal and attendants' bouquets without regard to style of dress or body shape. A delicate nosegay will get lost against an elaborate, ruffled dress, for example, and a small bride will be overshadowed by a massive cascading arrangement.

Think like an interior designer when you're deciding on ceremony flowers. Is the ceremony site large or small? Ornate or plain? If you're getting married in an exquisite mosque, the architects have done you a good turn by providing you with a magnificent backdrop; pare down the flowers so as not to distract from the building's beauty. If you're marrying in a church around a major holiday such as Easter or Christmas, the sanctuary already may be fully decorated for the season—lucky you! Likewise, if you're marrying outside, especially in a garden setting, you'll likely save a bundle on blooms and greenery.

On the other hand, if you're having a nondenominational ceremony in a banquet hall or are sprucing up your uncle's living room, you may need some extra help from Mother Nature; think about a stunning floral construction, such as a rose petal-strewn aisle or a sunflower-entwined arch under which to say your vows.

ASTRID & CHRISTIAN

November 2, New York City

ON THE MORNING OF Astrid and Christian's wedding, the bride wasn't relaxing in a bathtub preparing for her big day. Instead, she and Christian were struggling with the roof of the floral huppah he had designed and built.

"I was complaining the whole time," Astrid says. "Everything was happening at the last minute."

Christian, an architect, had designed an elaborate floral runner and huppah for their wedding. The huppah design had a similar structure to a project they had worked on together in architecture school. The runner was made primarily of rose petals. Although the couple hired a professional florist for things such as table arrangements and reception decorations, Astrid and Christian—with the help of his sister—built the huppah and runner themselves.

"The most incredible thing about the flowers was their fragrance. As we walked down the runner it got more and more intense," Astrid says.

Although at several moments throughout the process Astrid wished they had let a professional florist take over, in the end she was happy with the way it was done.

"In retrospect, I was glad we did it. Constructing the huppah together that morning became symbolic to us. It was the beginning of building our life together."

Reception Flowers

Guests may not spend enough time at your ceremony site to fully appreciate the flowers there, but they'll spend the entire reception checking out the blooms. Centerpieces will be in closest range, but there are tons of other ways to dress up your reception room florally.

Arrangement Themes

Flower arrangements aren't just about pretty blooms; they're also about *style*. When you're choosing your ceremony bouquets and your reception centerpieces, keep in mind some of our favorite "themes":

A Whiter Shade of Pale: All-white bouquets have long been a popular wedding style, but the modern take plays with variations of off-white blooms for a deeper, richer look.

Serene Simplicity: A small nosegay created with one type of bloom is elegant and understated.

Victorian: Choose dense arrangements of such flowers as roses, Queen Anne's lace, delphinium, sweet peas, and peonies. Bouquets or vases decorated with organza or lace recall the Victorian era.

English Garden: Duplicate a garden with loose clusters of wildflowers, heather, ivy, lilacs, and lavender.

Herbal Accents: Fragrant herbs such as rosemary, thyme, and mint make a splash in wedding arrangements.

Brash and Bold: Colorful arrangements of unexpected, clashing blooms look modern and uncontrived.

Singular Sensations: Cluster small bud vases—either glass or silver—and fill each with one single yet strong bloom, like a rose or a gerbera daisy. Grouped together, the look is unified and full.

Ravishing Red: Arrangements made solely of red blossoms—like roses, amaryllis, anemones, and even hypericum berries—look bold and beautiful especially when the rest of the room stays in shades of white.

The Centerpieces

You can create pretty bouquets of mixed flowers, whimsical topiaries, or clusters of small vases with single stems inside. When designing your centerpieces, take into consideration:

Your Room: High ceilings are best complemented with tall floral centerpieces, such as angular glass vases holding sprays of long-stemmed roses or lush bouquets placed on raised silver platforms (so guests can see each other). Small spaces need tight, bright arrangements that liven up the room without distracting.

Your Theme: If you're having an Asian-inspired event, arrange small clusters of orchids and other exotic flowers in architectural lacquered boxes; for decor with a vintage flair, mix all shapes and sizes of porcelain vases (or even silver ones with a great patina) with pale shades of roses.

Your Taste: Are you sticklers for coordinated decor? If so, use the same centerpiece at every table, with a slightly more lavish arrangement for the head table (wherever you're sitting). Do you like a cozy, more cluttered look? Give your florist a variety of different vases that you picked up at flea markets; ask him/her to play with three or four different arrangement types that will create a mismatched but arty feel.

Your Budget: Tight on cash? No problem. Go for maximum effect by doing the unexpected. Use little hot-pepper plants—in shades of red, orange, and yellow—as take-home centerpieces. Or place one or two gorgeous sunflowers on each table, surrounded by a cluster of gold candles.

A Rose at Any Other Time . . .

Timing is everything, especially when it comes to buying red roses.

- Near Valentine's Day (not ordered in advance): $10 per stem
- Near Valentine's Day (ordered well in advance): $7 per stem
- Any other time: $5 per stem

Other Decorative Floral Touches

You also may accent key reception areas—the entrance, the cake table, buffet stations—with floral bouquets, wreaths, or blooming boas. Visit the reception site with your florist so s/he can get a feel for how you might want to decorate. But don't feel confined by *conventional* uses of flowers. Some of our favorite wacky-but-wonderful flower uses:

- Real flower petals as cake decorations
- Sprinkling edible flowers, such as nasturtiums, hibiscus, roses, orange blossoms, pansies, marigolds, geraniums, squash blossoms, mimosas, and chamomile, in salads and drinks—lemonade, iced tea, and rum punch—or using them as garnishes on entrees and desserts
- The bride sporting tiny blooms in loose hair, wearing a splendid head wreath, or tucking a stem behind her ear
- Wearing dramatic floral boas or leis (both of you!)
- Giving a dethorned rose to each guest upon arrival—and having a mass tango-fest!
- Topiaries instead of vases of blooms
- Giving bulbs tied in tulle with a bow or small potted plants like African violets as favors
- Placing pressed flowers (or autumn leaves) beneath sheer tablecloths
- Using large candles with dried flowers in the wax as centerpieces
- Draping ivy interlaced with flowers from the ceilings

They Work Hard for the Money

Labor costs make florist bills bloom. Trim them by opting for less labor-intensive arrangements—simple vases of seasonal flowers as centerpieces rather than elaborate wreaths. Also nix any elaborate blooming structures—gateways, window frames—that will take a long time to set up.

Finding a Fabulous Florist

Make a good florist your wedding gift to yourselves. As with all vendors, it's important to find one who is reliable, capable—and within your price range. But you also want a florist who is open to your ideas and who has an overall taste you respect. Your gown and tux are going to turn heads, that's a given, but you want the overall "look" of your wedding to make an impression, too—and your florist is a key player.

An important issue to hammer out before you hire someone is your budget. There is no limit to what you can spend on lavish blooms—$200 bouquets all around, a lush tea-rose huppah, vases of cut tulips as favors, wreaths of dried wildflowers in every bathroom, a floor-length floral boa to wear at your 1920s-inspired reception—you get the picture. But most people have a limited flower budget. A visionary florist should be able to come up with a magnificent concept that won't bust your piggy bank. It may mean scaling back here and there, but look on the bright side: Minimalism in design is *in!* So check out the phone book, ask your friends, and call floral associations for names of florists near you. Put together a list of people and make those appointments.

Setting Up

Don't assume your florist will have access to your ceremony and reception site early on the big day. (S/he may need several hours to set up.) Make necessary arrangements—get written permission and a key, if need be—to ensure that everything is coming up roses before you hit the aisle.

Floral Contract Points

Don't even think of signing on the dotted line unless all these items are included in your flower contract:

- ☐ The date, times, and locations of your ceremony and reception.
- ☐ An itemized list of all the flower arrangements you're buying, from bouquets to centerpieces, with exact names, amounts, and colors of flowers being used.
- ☐ Acceptable flower alternatives (in your price range) should a specific bloom be unavailable on your wedding day; also include unacceptable substitutions, if any.
- ☐ Arrival times for setup at the ceremony *and* reception sites.
- ☐ Addresses where bouquets and boutonnieres should be delivered, if not to your ceremony site (home, for example).
- ☐ The name of the florist who will be on hand during the wedding (should be the person you're working with); the name of an acceptable substitute.
- ☐ The cost and payment schedule; when the final balance is due.
- ☐ Any sales taxes, gratuities, overtime charges, or delivery fees.
- ☐ The cancellation/refund policy.

The First Meeting

- Describe your attire and the wedding party's, or show the florist pictures or fabric swatches of what you'll be wearing, so s/he'll be able to suggest flowers that match your style.
- Show photos of your ceremony and reception sites.
- Map out any other salient details, such as theme, color scheme, floral allergies, and flowers that have special significance to you. Also, show any adored flower images you've found in magazines or your cousin's wedding album.
- Have the florist go into the nitty-gritty of the options available given your budget. Cover everything from the bridal bouquet to reception centerpieces; name specific flowers.

The Second Meeting

- Your florist presents an exact proposal, itemizing the number and types of arrangements, the exact kinds of flowers to be used, and the cost for materials, as well as setup and breakdown.
- S/he shows you sketches or small models of complex orders, such as a flowering gateway for your outdoor ceremony, the perfect nosegay bouquet, table topiaries (little flower trees or other ornamental arrangements), or the special "medieval" arrangements you discussed.
- You should now make adjustments to both your floral budget and plan, making sure the two meet. For example, you may choose to throw in another $300 so your arrangements will be more lush, or decide to ax that floral hula hoop that you thought would make a splash at your Hawaiian-themed reception but is upping costs greatly.

- You'll sign a written contract that outlines the agreed-upon plan. (See "Floral Contract Points," earlier.)

Blooming Questions

Things to ask about a potential florist:

- Has s/he done many weddings?
- Can you see photographs or live examples of past work? (If no, cut to the door.)
- Will s/he supply you with references?
- Does the florist's style—and the overall look of the shop—make you gag or drool?
- Does s/he listen intently to your floral reveries, chiming in with useful suggestions, or does s/he brush you off and tell you what you *really* want?
- How big is the shop, and ultimately who will be carrying out your wedding-day flower plan? (In big shops, it's *not* a given that the owner will take care of you; make sure you get to know—and trust—the person who will.)
- How many weddings is the florist handling on the same day or weekend as yours? If s/he is handling multiple accounts, is there enough staff and time to go around?

Trim Your Floral Budget

- Focus on one eye-catching, strategically placed ceremony arrangement rather than multiple, smaller floral clusters.
- Transport ceremony blooms to the reception, where they can work a second shift. Ask your florist or a trusted attendant or friend to oversee the move.
- Use large clusters of simple, inexpensive flowers to make a lasting impression. (Dense bunches of Queen Anne's lace with variegated ivy can be stunning. Potted flowering plants are another great option that people also can take home.)

Other Decorations

Flowers are just one—albeit hugely important—part of your wedding decorating toolbox. According to your taste and overall wedding theme and style, you can also incorporate a variety of other decorations.

Candles

The perfect romantic lighting option: Place candles on each table and throughout the room. There are so many stunning and affordable variations out there today that you can color-coordinate candles with flowers, your dress, even the main course. You also can play with the fragrances of scented candles or opt for floating candles that look gorgeous reflecting dim light. Majestic candelabras will add drama to a room; traditional lanterns holding candles will transform any site into a cozy, old-fashioned inn.

German Candle Custom

In traditional German wedding ceremonies, both the bride and groom hold candles decorated with flowers and ribbon.

Tulle

This light-as-air fabric can be draped artfully over tablecloths or chair backs or hung from the ceiling in clusters for cloudlike columns. Glue-gun dried flowers or ivy to the material for a pretty accent. Other fabrics, such as organza, gauze, and satin, are also beautiful reception-decorating choices. They can be used for a huppah or archway for the wedding party to enter through or spread elegantly on the ground to create a magical aisle. Be careful with the amount of tulle you decide to drape around the location—you want the look to be soft, not like the place has been hosed down with marshmallow fluff.

Italian Ribbon Custom

Italian families tie a large ribbon across the front of the church door to symbolize the wedding bond.

Ribbons and Bows

What's a wedding without ribbons and bows, after all? They can be attached to chair backs, wrapped around vases, mounted on the walls at regular intervals (large ones), and otherwise used to wrap up the general "look." Use a variety of colors around cloth napkins for a spontaneous, festive look.

Balloons

Sure, some people consider them childish, but balloons are lots of fun. Steer away from balloons in tight indoor spaces (too claustrophobic) but go nuts in high-ceilinged rooms or outdoors, with metallic or pastel-colored helium balloons attached to chairs or arranged in clusters.

What a Resource

You may be able to get decorations like balloons, streamers—even decorative arches and pillars—from your florist.

Fruits

Flowers aren't the only thing Mother Nature intended for the center of the table. Fruits, either naturally or sugared (dusted with sugar crystals to give them a glassine effect), make a stunning and low-cost centerpiece. Apples, lemons, limes, grapes, and cherries all work well—and the options don't end there. The look is perfect if you're having an outdoor wedding (grapes at a vineyard wedding is an obvious pairing).

Don't Overdecorate!

Remember that the wedding's about you two getting married, not how elaborately you can spruce up a room.

Work It: Overall Design Ideas

Coming up with a decorating scheme for your reception can be hard as nails. If you're having trouble, begin with a central idea and expand your plan from there. Here are some starters.

A Personal Touch: Decorate personally with beautifully framed pictures of the two of you—together and apart, childhood and current—on each table; guests will get a kick out of making the rounds to see you at all your cute (and not-so-cute) stages. Another great idea is to incorporate favorite objects in the decorations. Throughout your engagement, pick up vintage vases, place settings, and candlesticks that appeal to you. So what if they're mismatched? If you have enough diversity, it will look like an intentional—and thoroughly hip—design choice. And be sure to play off your favorite colors and flowers.

Period Decor: If you adore a certain era, go with it. For example:

- Medieval: Candelabras; lush arrangements on iron stands; dried flower wreaths as centerpieces; parchment place cards with calligraphy; feather quills mixed into floral bouquets; bowls of gold chocolate coins placed about the room.
- Victorian: Lace tablecloths with mauve or blue place settings; lush centerpiece bou-

quets accented with antique ribbon; large dried-flower topiaries at the corners of the dance floor.

- '20s/Flapperesque: Potted palms and ferns; tall, tapered candles; incense burning for that smoky atmosphere; single-tone floral arrangements; a black-and-white color scheme; floor-to-ceiling sheer draperies.

Patterns: Don't think that everything wedding has to be solids and prissy florals. With the array of gorgeous patterns on the fabric front, you can carry a theme from the table linens to the bridesmaids dresses to the ribbon wrapped around your bouquet. Here are some patterns to consider:

Go to Chapter 8 for ideas on how to spotlight the season with your wedding decorations.

- Plaid
- Gingham
- Polka dots
- Stripes
- Hawaiian floral

CHAPTER FOURTEEN

eat, drink, and be married

Your choice of chow not only fills the tummies of friends and family who have come to see you wed; it also helps give your party personality and taste (pun intended). Guests probably won't remember the flowers the next week, but trust us, they'll recall the food. So, how to make your wedding meal worth the memories? First off, don't think your only choice is between chicken and beef. In this chapter we'll let you in on a few of our favorite feasts and give you some tips and tricks to keep them tasty.

Deciding Which Meal to Serve

Before you choose the menu, you need to know which meal you're serving, right? This depends mostly on when your reception will be: breakfast (9:00-11:00 a.m.); brunch (11:00 a.m.-2:00 p.m.); lunch (12:30-3:30 p.m.); tea (3:00-5:00 p.m.), cocktails (5:00-7:00 p.m.); dinner (6:00-9:30 p.m.); dessert (9:00-10:30 p.m.)—or even a cruise ship–style midnight snack (11:00 p.m.-1:00 a.m.).

Budget also influences what you serve, of course, and the price of your spread is set by a variety of factors. Generally, breakfast or brunch will cost less than dinner (because the foods involved take less effort to prepare). But other issues affect your bill, too—namely the day of the week your party is held, how much food you actually serve, how formal the service, how expensive (read: talented/popular) the caterer, and how costly your chosen ingredients. Be sure to get prices for each element of your ideal meal—you'll be discussing prices in a "per head" language and costs for a dinner can range anywhere from $20 to $200 per head. You can help lower the cost with a little creative substitution—using tri-tip instead of filet mignon, serving foods at room temperature instead of steaming, or changing the time or day or service style.

Buffet

Whether for breakfast, brunch, lunch, or dinner, a buffet offers your guests a full meal *and* the chance to choose exactly which foods and how much of them they want. Your buffet can be hotel-style formal or all-you-can-eat-smorgasbord casual. You might choose to have staff creating crêpes or pasta dishes while guests watch or just have food set up in large serving dishes. You decide whether or not to assign tables.

Pros: You save money on waitstaff since guests do their own legwork. Guests can tailor the meal to suit their taste buds. Food stays hot (or cold) longer because it waits in heated containers (or on ice) until it's time to eat. Food preparation can double as entertainment.

Cons: You may have to rent all the buffet equipment yourselves. Elderly or physically challenged guests may have trouble maneuvering. Long lines may force your guests to wait awhile.

Food Stations

This is like a job fair for wedding food. Guests are invited, in a buffetlike manner, to sample foods from a wide array of stations. Each station offers its own theme and a moderate assortment of cuisine. The food practically becomes the entertainment. For the most part, guests are not assigned seats or even tables, so they're free to move around and it will work for any size wedding, as long as there are enough stops (and seating) for all. Servers should be positioned at each station to help out.

Pros: The only limit to your food options is your imagination. Some favorite stations include a Mexican fiesta, a high-class caviar-and-blini stop, and a Delancy Street deli booth (à la New York City's famously delicious Lower East Side). There's also major mingling at a party like this—people who love to shmooze will love the idea of floating around the room. It's even better for you—the bride and groom get to visit with everyone!

Cons: There's a mob mentality here. Don't expect to have everyone seated and listening attentively when it's time for the best man's speech. It'll be difficult to get guests' eyes up and mouths closed all at once.

Delicious Discounts

Ways to save some dough on your dinner:

- Stationary appetizers (crudités, cheese and crackers, olives, bread with spinach dip) cost less than passed hors d'oeuvres, which also require waitstaff.
- Choose chicken instead of beef, or pasta instead of scallops. Simpler vegetables—broccoli instead of asparagus—cut costs, too.
- Cut down on courses. Do you really need soup *and* salad?
- Think ethnic! Mexican, Indian, Italian, or Chinese food is fun and much cheaper per person than traditional wedding fare.
- Consider a breakfast, brunch, or tea to save money on food and labor. Serving bloody marys and mimosas will save on alcohol. People also drink less liquor at these times of day.

Tea

Afternoon tea encompasses aspects of both a buffet and a seated meal. You can serve food on tiered stands on reception tables, where fancy scones, pots of jam, finger sandwiches, and fussy pastries will double as edible centerpieces. Or set up your spread buffet style. Offer three or four kinds of tea, ice water, coffee, and other favorite beverages. Hire waiters to pour, or make it self-serve.

Pros: Your guests will be floored by your taste and class. Older guests will adore your mellow sophistication—so much so that no one will realize that tea is far less expensive than a full meal. The reception will be shorter, which means you two get the entire evening alone together!

Cons: If you want hours of boogying to a rockin' band, a tea is not the party to do it at. It may be a little too "precious" for some crowds. Anyone expecting a full meal may walk away hungry (or start nibbling the doilies); be sure to note "tea reception" on your invites. It may feel rushed or insufficiently monumental for the scope of the event.

Cocktails

At a cocktail reception, you offer a slew of hors d'oeuvres instead of a full meal, and guests stand and chat while holding small, snack-laden plates and trying to balance their wineglasses. The variety of snacks depends on the length of the party. A good rule of thumb: For a two-hour party, serve at least six different kinds of hors d'oeuvres; for a four-hour affair, at least nine. Hors d'oeuvres are either arranged on tables or passed by waiters.

Pros: A classy, low-cost, low-stress option. You don't have to spring for silverware (other than those frilly-topped toothpicks). You don't have to pay for dozens of tables complete with centerpieces, chairs, favors, and place cards (though you do need a few serving platforms and a smattering of small tables and chairs for guests who want to take a load off). You can skip the extensive breakdown crew. Cocktails tend to take less time than a full reception, meaning you're out the door and on your way to Tahiti sooner.

Cons: Without all the dancing, talking, bouquet-tossing, and so on, your wedding may feel like less of a big deal (but then, that may be exactly what you're after). The standing-and-chatting approach may be less comfortable for older guests than a sink-into-a-chair soiree. Guests may drink more than they would at a full meal, so liquor costs may be higher.

Seated Meal

At a seated breakfast, brunch, lunch, or dinner, guests are served by waiters. All other things being equal (food cost, time of day), this is the priciest option. But for some, it's seated dinner or starve. There are four approaches; as you'd expect, the more formal the service, the more frightening the price.

- American service: Plates are prepared in the kitchen and servers bring them out to the tables.
- French service: Waiters prepare food on stands set up next to the tables, and then serve individual plates.
- Russian service: White-gloved waiters carry each course on a large tray and serve guests directly from it.
- Family-style: Multiple dishes are delivered to strategic spots along what are usually long tables; guests pass them politely (or grab and hoard, depending on your family).

Pros: Guests feel pampered. They can relax and sit comfortably, without having to lug plates, stand in line, or fret that the roast beef will be gone before they get their turn at the carving station. Less work for guests means more time to talk (particularly about how gracious and *classy* you are for serving a seated meal). You can keep better tabs on how the party flows.

Cons: Guests may never leave their chairs or talk to anyone other than their seated neighbors. The party may feel too stiff or formal for your taste. It may take a long time for the meal to be served and finished. Food might get cold because of such meticulous (and time-consuming) service. You may spend some *big* bucks.

Name Your Tables

Numbers are just sooo boring. Add a little fun to your meal by having guests find their dinner table by picking up an escort card with an idea rather than a digit. Here are some table name ideas to consider:

- Places you've traveled to together
- Flowers or herbs
- Historic buildings in the town
- Landmarks in the city
- Wines
- Famous works of art
- Romantic movies from the 1950s
- Chinese symbols
- Constellations
- Famous poets or authors

Dessert Only/Postnup Snack

The dessert-only party and the late-night snack have their origins in the church-hall cake and punch soiree. Even if you serve only a mint-chocolate-chip ice-cream cake and champagne in a box, you're still officially wed!

Pros: Saves you money! The dessert-only reception is the most economical, easiest, and fastest option (unless you decide to import all the chocolate for your 200-pound wedding cake from Belgium). Appropriate any hour of the day. (When is it ever the *wrong* time to eat cake? Or drink champagne, for that matter?)

Cons: Guests won't linger for long; you'll be disappointed if you want everyone to make a fuss over you for hours. You and your guests may wind up bouncing off the walls like the Energizer bunny on speed from too much sugar or leave the party still hungry. (Again, make sure your reception invite says "dessert.")

Choosing a Caterer

Now that you've decided what type of meal you want, you're ready to find the right person or company to execute your culinary plan. There are a number of ways to go.

An On-Site Chef

If your venue comes with its own caterer, your choice may be limited—to *him/her.* This isn't necessarily a bad thing—some of the most beautiful sites come with the region's best chefs. If you'd prefer having a bit more say over what your guests eat, ask if you can augment the meal by bringing some of your own dishes. Or see if the chef will prepare a special family recipe (or just something you both adore) along with the customary spread. You may be able to adapt the regular meal a bit, or choose only the chef's best dishes.

A Catering Company

If you don't have to use the on-site caterer (or there isn't one), call in a pro—a professional caterer who has done hundreds of weddings and already has worked out all the kinks. To find a caterer, ask everyone you know for recommendations. Ask your venue. Consult other recently married couples. Make a list of potential caterers, and then give each a call. Narrow down your appointment list to include those caterers who: (1) you like over the phone; (2) are available on your date; and (3) are willing to prepare the kind of meal you're craving.

Then it's on to the fun part: free food! You'd never buy new shoes without trying them on—why should you hire a caterer before sampling his/her wares? Ask to taste the offerings of every caterer you're considering. It's standard practice for caterers to prepare a meal just for you two or invite you to a group tasting (during which time you might meet other soon-to-be-weds and possibly learn of better or more-appropriate-for-your-reception caterers). Never say no to a caterer's meal—you're about to embark on one of the most expensive ventures of your lives, so accept all the free food you're offered! Besides, you're far too busy to cook—and every meal you sample may give you more reception food ideas, whether you work with that caterer or not.

The Restaurant Route

You met at a charming French bistro on the corner. Your eyes locked over your matching plates of foie gras and you were hooked. Obviously, you must have French food at your wedding—ideally that first dish you shared together. Is it possible? *Mais oui!* Ask your special place if they cater weddings. Many restaurants have catering departments or are willing to handle large affairs straight from their kitchens. The bistro may even be the perfect sentimental site for your soiree!

CHRISTINE & MARK

February 16, New York City

WITH STUNNING VIEWS of Central Park and a location just a few blocks from Carnegie Hall, Lincoln Center, and the chic shops of Madison Avenue, Essex House is considered the pinnacle of Manhattan sophistication and style. But on February 16, something rather unusual took place in the hotel's Petite Salon, where guests at the wedding of Christine and Mark had gathered for a cocktail hour. Delicious foods were arranged at a raw bar, stir-fry station, and Tuscan table. But heads turned when the waitstaff carried out trays filled with the evening's specially delivered delicacy—hamburgers, cheeseburgers, and chicken McNuggets from McDonald's!

"The staff could not bring the burgers out fast enough," says Christine, whose father and uncle own and operate several of the fast-food eateries. "As soon as they filled the serving tray, the guests cleared them out. One of our guests stuffed his pockets, and every once in a while, during the reception, you'd find him munching on a hamburger! It is still one of the things our friends talk about the most."

The hamburgers were a quirky addition, but Christine and Mark have always been game to try new things. "Make the wedding what you want it to be," says Christine. "We wanted McDonald's and plain chocolate cake and that's what we got!"

A word of caution: Even if dinner for two is divine, the same meal for 200 may not be. Clearly, it's easier for a kitchen to turn out small portions than huge ones. Ask how the restaurant handles big events—how many cooks are there? How many waiters will serve? What's the lag time between preparation and presentation? How will your favorite dishes be affected? Can you have a buffet? What recommendations does the chef have?

Getting a Head Count

Once you've found your caterer (or restaurant, or cook), let him/her know the size of your guest list. You'll need to hand your caterer an exact head count (based on invitation responses) about two weeks before the wedding. Likely your caterer will plan to prepare 10 percent more food than it looks like you'll need, just in case there are late additions (unless your budget is too tight to do this).

Don't forget to include your wedding vendors in the final dining tally—the DJ, bartenders, and photographer need to eat, too. Don't worry about feeding them if it's a short, informal affair (under three hours). Otherwise, plan *something* for these people to eat, even if it's deli sandwiches. (Some hungry vendors may put mandatory meals in the contracts you sign with them.)

Talking to Your Caterer

After you've chosen the caterer right for you, it's time to talk business (unless it's your mom, of course). Not all food providers work the same way, so pay close attention.

Lotsa Leftovers

Don't waste food. Donate extras to a soup kitchen. Make arrangements ahead of time.

Questions for Your Cook

- Does your caterer have a license? This is really important—having one means the caterer has met local health department standards and carries liability insurance.
- Does the meal come full service or no-frills? Will the caterer provide tables, chairs, plates, even napkins, silverware, and salt-and-pepper shakers? Or do you have to rent place settings and/or other equipment yourselves?

The Catering Contract

Your contract with your caterer or restaurant should include:

- ☐ The date and time of your party, including the *exact* location and room. (You don't want someone else's 400 guests noshing on your canapés!)
- ☐ The type of service (cocktails, buffet, tea, dessert, seated meal—French service, etc.) and the staff-to-guest ratio.
- ☐ The exact menu.
- ☐ What liquor is being served (if the caterer is handling it).
- ☐ The cost and payment schedule; when the final balance is due.
- ☐ The date the caterer needs a final head count.
- ☐ The name of the catering-company representative who will be on hand during the wedding (this should be the person you're working with); the name of an acceptable substitute should an emergency arise.
- ☐ Contact information for morning of wedding (cell phone number, for example).
- ☐ Any sales taxes, gratuities, overtime charges, bar, or extra-waiter fees.
- ☐ The cancellation/refund policy.
- ☐ Proof of license (liability insurance)

- Will the caterer provide waitstaff? How many people will each waiter serve? (Or how many people will work the buffet?) Will the caterer set out those cute little place cards and centerpieces you created, or do you need to do it?
- Who will oversee the event on your wedding day?
- Will the caterer arrange the food attractively on the buffet or on plates? Can you see photos of previous presentations?
- Are there extra charges, such as a security deposit, sales tax, gratuities, bar fees?
- Will the cook be willing to include a recipe you provide, like a special family dish or some sentimental appetizer? Can s/he prepare vegetarian or kosher meals for just a few of your guests?
- Will the caterer provide alcohol, or can you handle the bar separately?

Making the Menu Memorable

As a kid, you may have believed that green beans grew in a can, all meat was hamburger, and macaroni and cheese was a square meal (the square box = square meal philosophy). But these days, you know better (as do your guests). Fine dining is a national pastime. Whether you're planning a simple cocktail reception or an elaborate seated meal, your wedding is one more chance for your food-crazed family and friends to eat. Here are five great ways to make your menu terrific. Even if your caterer is doing all the work, being in the know will help you make better choices.

Think Seasonal

Great cooks plan their menus around seasonal food—whatever's freshest that month or season. Your favorite summer tomato salad, for example, just won't be as juicy in January; pasta with a rich tomato sauce would be a better winter bet for tomato lovers. Save the fresh salad for a summer party, when you might make it a produce feast—tomatoes with mozzarella and basil, grilled zucchini, prosciutto-wrapped figs and melon, huge mixed-lettuce salads, chicken with fresh raspberries, and drippingly ripe peaches. Ask your caterer and culinary pals what's fresh when; see if you can incorporate those foods into your wedding-meal vision.

Go Regional

Another great way to guarantee freshness (and authenticity, too) is to choose regionally grown or raised food. You've got a better shot at finding ocean-fresh lobster in Maine than in Minnesota, for example. Hometown food is also a great way to personalize your party and introduce your guests to the local cuisine, especially if you're having a lot of out-of-towners. Give them a taste of authentic Southern barbecue, Chicago deep-dish pizza, New England clam bake, or a total Tex Mex menu.

Consider Temperature

One of the biggest problems with party food is the lag time between preparation and presentation. That creamy seafood in puff pastry looks great in the kitchen, but by the time it gets to table 23 the cream may have soaked through, creating a gooey, chewy mess. For a large reception, choose food with a long shelf life. And think seriously about going with a buffet rather than a seated dinner. Buffet food can be kept hot over chafing dishes or cold over ice, reducing the oven-to-table time and helping preserve flavor.

Liven It Up

If you are having food stations, why not have the chef or servers prepare the meals right in front of your guests rather than simply serve them from a big platter. It adds a little entertainment and just feels, well, fresher.

- Raw bar: Oysters are shucked and kept on ice.
- Pasta station: Guests choose their sauce and watch as their pasta is tossed.
- Omelette or waffle stand: Dishes are made to order, with self-serve toppings.
- Sushi station: Chefs slice and roll fresh hand-rolls.
- Crêpe table: Cooks flip and fill sweet or savory crêpes.

International Eats

Where is it written that you must have filet mignon, salmon mousse, and chocolate-dipped strawberries? Yes, those are amazing eats, but you also can decide to make your meal a global adventure by serving ethnic cuisine. Ethnic foods often are prepared in large quantities, meaning your price per head may go *way* down—and your guests will have a ball getting a taste of another culture.

Chinese: A traditional Chinese wedding banquet has ten courses! Any restaurant will provide you menu options, but here are some musts: Start with prepared meats, soup, and small stir-fried dishes. Exotic entrees can include lobster with ginger and garlic, abalone, sizzling beef, and sesame chicken. Make sure to end with a noodle, as it ensures long life. A bowl of fortune cookies on each table is always a welcome touch.

Eastern European: If you're Polish, Czech, or Russian, serve caviar and chilled vodka shots for hors d'oeuvres, followed by hearty, beat-the-cold, meat and potatoes—potato knishes, pierogies, and pastries.

Ethiopian: To take this less-traveled culinary road, serve a huge spread of spicy vegetables, eggs, meats, along with spongy bread to scoop it all up.

Indian: Serve vegetable and banana samosas as hors d'oeuvres, followed by vegetarian, chicken, and beef curries. Put generous platters of rice and a variety of breads on each table. Make sure to offer plenty of mild dishes for the less intrepid diners!

Mexican: Start with "seven-layer" dip—layers of beans, guacamole, sour cream, and cheese, topped off with olives. Fajitas and tacos are always crowd pleasers. Serve rice and beans buffet style, and put baskets of chips and bowls of salsa on every table. Toast your good taste with margaritas.

Spanish: Serve tapas (small appetizer-size dishes) for a dinner-by-the-bite buffet. Also offer heaping bowls of paella (a mixture of rice, sausage, vegetables, and seafood) and arroz con pollo (chicken and rice flavored with saffron). Wash it down with sangria.

Thai: Serve chicken and pork satay (skewers of grilled meat dipped in a peanut sauce), followed by heaping dishes of pad thai, chicken and beef curry, vegetable dishes spiced with ginger and lemongrass, and sticky rice.

- Burrito bar: Guests choose their tortillas and fresh fillings (chicken, beef, scallops, spinach, or rice and beans).
- Grill: Barbecued chicken, pork, ribs, and vegetables are prepared on request.
- Tepanyaki station (a.k.a. Japanese barbecue): Guests choose raw meats, shrimp, veggies, noodles, and sauces and watch it get stir-fried.

Hot Menus from Cool Chefs

The Seated Dinner

Executive Chef Paul Wade, The Little Nell, Vail

First Course

Wild Mushroom Consommé
Porcini and Sunchoke Raviolis with Swiss Chard and Ricotta Salata

Blue Lump Crab Cake
Strawberry-Mint Salsa, Tamarind Syrup

Sautéed Maine Diver Scallops
Summer Truffle and Celery Root Rémoulade
Pea Shoot Salad and Mustard Oil

Second Course

Artichoke and Heirloom Tomato Salad
Fine Herbs and Truffle Vinaigrette

Summer Vine-Ripe Tomatoes and Mozzarella
Red Onion Jam, Cold Pressed Olive Oil, and 18-Year-Old Balsamic

Entrée Selections

Crispy Soft-Shell Crabs
Sweet Pea and Fava Bean Mash, Golden Tomato Relish
Roasted Garlic-Lemon Butter

Grilled Nebraska Rib-Eye Steak
Haricot Verts, Stilton Bleu Mashed Potatoes
Buttermilk Onion Rings and Triple Garlic Jus

Free-Range Chicken Breast
Sage Roasted Tomatoes, Herb Gnocchi, and Corn Succotash

The Station Reception

Executive Chef Dean Fearing, The Mansion on Turtle Creek, Dallas

Passed Hors d'Oeuvres

Sevruga Caviar on Quail Egg Salad with Potato Cake
Duo of Asparagus: Brie Tart and Chicory Mustard Salad
Pan-Fried Texas Crabcake with Smoked Tomato Rémoulade

Seafood Station

Chilled Gulf Shrimp with Tangy Red Sauce
Oysters on the Half Shell with Assorted Mignonettes
Thin-Sliced House-Smoked Salmon with Traditional Condiments and Toast Points
Bacon-Wrapped Scallops on Barbecued Duck with Sweet Corn Sauce

Carving Station

Elegant Tenderloin of Beef and Mustard Roasted Rack of Lamb
with Cognac–Green Peppercorn Sauce
Truffled Scalloped Potatoes, Petite Green Beans,
Wild Mushroom Sauté, Artichoke-Leek Gratin, and Petite Rolls

Asian Station

Sushi Bar Selections with Soy Sauce, Pickled Ginger, and Wasabi
Hoisin Barbecued Ribs with Iced Peppercress Salad
Barbecued Duck Potstickers
Velvet Chicken with Ginger Stir-Fry Vegetables and Fragrant Jasmine Rice
Sesame Seed Cucumber Salad

Table Settings 101

When you're chatting with your caterer or reasoning with the party-rental people, you need to know how to talk table settings. Here are all the pieces you could possibly need, what they're called, and where they're supposed to go.

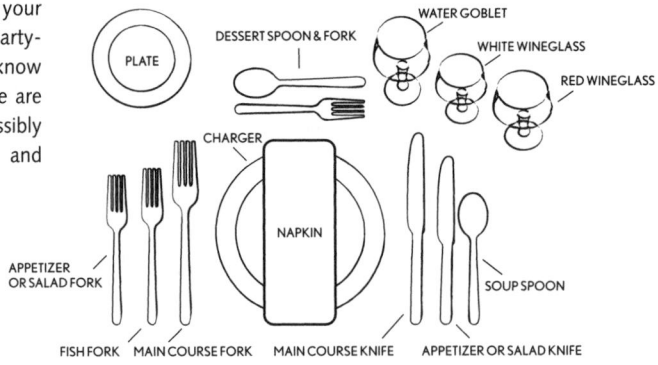

The Themed Buffet Reception: Carnivale

Chef Abigail Kirsch, New York

Hors d'Oeuvres

Shrimp Brochettes with Garlic
Miniature Lamb Empanadas, Golden Raisins, Cinnamon, and Tomato
Fried Green Olives Filled with Sun-Dried Tomato Basil Cheese
Scallop Seviche

Dinner

Carne Enrolada (Roulade of Beef Filled with Pimentos, Chopped Onions, and Cilantro)
Pollo con Frutas (Almond Crusted Boneless Breast of Capon Sliced with a Citrus Fruit Sauce)
Arroz y Fijoada a Brasileira (Brazilian Rice and Black Beans)

Camarones con Salsa de Tomate (Fire-Roasted Gulf Shrimp in a Piquant Tomato Salsa)
Corn Cheese Pudding

Pimentao Recheado (Stuffed Peppers Filled with Roasted Summer Vegetables)
Ensalada de Jicama y Naranja (Jicama and Orange Salad Tossed with Red Papaya, Chayote, Savoy Cabbage)

Dessert

Carnivale Bananas (Bananas Sautéed in Caramelized Butter Curaçao and Rum, Flambéed Tableside, Served with Coconut Ice Cream and Hazlenut Poundcake, Warm Butterscotch Sauce)
Torta de Chocolate
Chocolate Grand Marnier Mousse Layered on Bittersweet Ganache, Crust Striped with White and Dark Chocolate, Minted Berry Sauce

Signature Cocktail

Caipirinha (Fresh Squeezed Lime Juice, Sugar, and White Rum Served over Crushed Ice)

Drink Up

How much liquor will you need for a hundred guests? Talk to your bartender, but here are some averages:

- Beer: 2 cases
- Whiskey: 1–2 liters
- Bourbon: 1–2 liters
- Gin: 2 liters
- Scotch: 3 liters
- Light rum: 2 liters
- Vodka: 6 liters
- Tequila: 1 liter
- Champagne: 1 1/2 cases
- Red wine: 8 bottles
- White wine: 1 1/2 cases
- Dry vermouth: 2 bottles
- Sweet vermouth: 2 bottles

Keep Booze at Bay

Have someone watch over the bartender's bottle-counting process. You don't want any mistakes—unintentional or otherwise.

Serving Drinks

Weddings mean raising a glass, making a toast, imbibing the bubbly. For most couples (and guests, too), they mean enjoying a few drinks along with the rest of the festivities. Setting up the bar takes a bit of planning on your part. As always, you've got options.

Serving It Safely

If you plan to serve alcohol in a park, private home, or anyplace else without a liquor license, check your homeowner's insurance policy to make sure you're covered against liability.

The Open Bar

An open bar is the most gracious approach—no guest should have to pay for *anything* at the wedding—but it's also the most expensive. Guests can order any drink on the planet, and you (or your parents) pick up the often-hefty tab at the end of the party. Your bartender will count all the used and partially used bottles and charge you accordingly.

The downside of an open bar is pretty obvious. Because there's no limit, people may drink like guppies—and you may be concerned about a friend or uncle famous for imbibing. If the idea of confronting the issue is just too excruciating, point out any problem people to the bartender; s/he should be experienced enough at monitoring people's intake to able to smoothly offer soda when the time is right.

The Limited Bar

With a limited bar—probably the most popular option—you offer a selection of drinks (beer, wine, and mixed vodka drinks, for example) and/or set specific consumption times (say, cocktail hour, the toasts, and an hour after dinner). Consider having waiters pass drinks on trays rather than having guests go up to the bar. You'll have to *pay* for those waiters, of course, but you'll probably save money on alcohol, and fewer guests will go overboard—the fewer waiters, the longer it will take everyone to get served. If you decide to limit the amount of time the bar is open, make sure to have waiters circulate during dinner to refill glasses of water and soda.

Another sneaky way to limit alcohol is to serve a special drink that fits your party. If you're doing the *Great Gatsby* 1920s thing, serve Manhattans. If it's a brunch party, go with mimosas (champagne and o.j.). For a late-night, black-tie affair, think champagne punch. Mixed specialty drinks let you make a style statement, use less expensive brands of alcohol, tie into a theme—and limit consumption.

The Cash Bar

Don't have a cash bar unless you have a really good reason. (There really isn't one.) You don't invite people to your house for dinner and then charge them for butter, right? Trust us on this one. It's not a good cost-cutting solution—way too controversial.

A Dry House

If you, your families, and most of your guests don't drink alcohol, it's fine to skip it. Your bar can serve sparkling water, sodas, and nonalcoholic mixed drinks instead. If you want some bubbly to toast with, just serve glasses of champagne when it's time, or go for sparkling cider or grape juice.

Signature Cocktails

Pick a cool name, a color scheme, and a favorite liquor, and with the help of a friendly bartender you can have your own one-of-a-kind wedding cocktail. Here are a few ideas to help inspire you.

Coordinated Concoctions: Who says the bridesmaid dresses should be the only things radiating lavender? Let your drinks add flair to your wedding theme. For a lavender or purple motif, serve guests Flirtinis, a mixture of chilled vodka, pineapple juice, Chambord, and champagne. (Courtesy of Goodnite Gracie Jazz and Martini Bar, Michigan)

Seasonal Flavor: More and more brides are opting for fall and winter weddings, so offer drinks reminiscent of crisp fall evenings or cozy winters by the fireplace. Apple- or pear-infused drinks might do the trick. Treat guests to the Pear Martini—Ketel One vodka and Belle de Brillet pear liqueur shaken together until foamy, poured into a cold martini glass, and garnished with pickled ginger. (Courtesy of Fred McKibbin from Grace, New York City)

Kiddie Coolers: Of course, a signature cocktail doesn't have to be alcoholic. If you plan on having quite a few nondrinkers or young ones at your wedding, make sure to include them in your cocktail hour by offering a tasty, unique, eye-catching alcohol-free beverage creation or "mocktail." Ask your bartender about fun nonalcoholic options for your cocktail hour.

CHAPTER FIFTEEN

cut to the cake

Of all the wedding food you choose, cake just takes the . . . er, prize. Why have a wedding cake? The tradition dates back to ancient Greece, where newlywed couples would share crushed sesame cakes to ensure fertility. In the Middle Ages, guests crumbled wheat cakes over the couple's heads, again to wish them good fortune and children. The wheat cake concept slowly evolved into a sweet, edible dessert cake in sixteenth-century England. The French then one-upped the English, introducing the tiered, sugar-covered, cake as art that we know and love today.

Confection Reflections

Today, the wedding cake has become a centerpiece for the whole reception. You want your cake to represent your wedding, from the inside (the fillings) to the outside (icing and topper). It should taste as good as it looks, and, well, look as good as it tastes. Here are some of the things you have to think about when choosing yours.

Style: Don't decide on your cake until you've decided on your gown style and reception decor, as these elements can serve as a blueprint for the design and structure of your wedding cake. But the style of your cake can be drawn from a wide variety of inspirations, from the embroidery on your wedding gown to your mother's china pattern. Choose a detail that reflects your personality, the season, or a recurring theme throughout your wedding. Whether it's a simple cake that mimics the clean, classic design of your silk A-line gown or an Asian-inspired cake with octagon-shaped tiers and sugarpaste water lilies to celebrate your Asian garden ceremony location, tie in the design of your cake. If you're a "less is more" kind of couple who still wants to make an impression, try an understated yet whimsical design, such as a cake covered in blush-colored frosting and festooned with tiny, silver-dusted polka dots or monograms. Almost anything goes: Unusual designs, such as brilliantly colored Wedgwood motifs and *Alice in Wonderland*–like inspirations are also fun.

Got a Sweet Tooth?

You don't *have* to serve a dessert in addition to the wedding cake. These days cakes are so yummy and alluring that they're dessert in themselves. But if you're dessert lovers and want a sweet table—go for it!

Shape: Though round tiers are a classic, oval-, square-, octagon-, and hexagon-shaped confections are fun, too. Your options are as limited as your baker's imagination—and your budget of course.

Color: White is always alright. But why not cover your cake in hues of light blush, ice blue, pale pistachio, rum pink, lavender, or shades of butterscotch and cafe au lait to match your flowers or the bridesmaid's dresses? Rich chocolate-covered confections in all their cocoa-colored glory are also drool-inducing.

Temperamental Taste

When choosing a filling, taste your wedding-cake-to-be at room temperature—not just out of the fridge—so you can make sure it will hold up after it's been sitting out for a while. Canoli cream is a fantastic filling, but it's not tasty after five hours on a counter.

The Taste Counts

Though you may believe appearance is most crucial, don't underestimate the value of the cake's tastebud appeal. Try exotic flavors such as passion fruit buttercream or Grand Marnier Bavarian cream. If you have your heart set on an unusual flavor that your baker doesn't offer, ask whether he would be willing to find a recipe. Moist chocolate cake is always a favorite, especially when the rich layers are spread with fillings like mocha espresso mousse or Amaretto. Lemon, a strong summer choice, can be filled with tart lemon curd, and white chocolate or light lemon mousse. Other fabulous, fruity cake flavors to try (and try again if they'll let you): pineapple, marionberries, and wild cherries, along with passion fruit, mango, and blood orange mousses. Note that mousses such as mango, white chocolate, pistachio, and ricotta provide a lighter consistency without sacrificing richness of flavor.

Flirting with Flavors

Can't decide on a flavor? Each layer can hold a different combination of cake and filling—from cheesecake to carrot cake, from chocolate mousse to key-lime cream. It's a great way to give guests a chance to sample many fabulous flavors in one delicious wedding cake—and one less decision for you to make.

Feeling the Frosting

Because of its smooth consistency and delicate flavor, buttercream is a can't-miss choice for icing a tasty cake. But of course there is a compromise. Buttercream requires refrigeration and doesn't hold up well in hot weather. Fondant, smooth rolled sugar dough, yields a perfectly pristine surface and even helps preserve the cake. While not everyone loves the flavor, fondant does allow for some of the most gorgeous decorating options. Chocolate ganache, a chocolate cream glaze, provides a lustrous, rich appearance—definitely a chocoholic's dream. Looking for something different? Try rolled marzipan. Made from almond paste, marzipan has a smooth surface and light golden hue that create a perfect canvas for sculpted fruits, leaves, and nuts.

Our Take on Cake Toppers

You don't have to do this, but you can. Many designers will crown a cake with wide clusters of ribbon made of sugarpaste, fondant, or sheer organza. Sugarpaste flowers are always an option, and for many brides, fresh flowers are a no-brainer. Using vintage pieces like a cake topper that belongs to a parent or grandparent is always a lovely gesture, but one of our favorite ideas is custom-made marzipan figurines that resemble the couple. Pricey? Yes. Adorable? Of course. Worth it? You decide.

ASK CARLEY

Saving Cake

Q. What is the best way to save the top tier of our wedding cake so that it's actually edible on our one-year anniversary?

A. Before your wedding, buy a reusable, freeze-safe plastic container that will fit the top tier (you may have to cut it in two). Give the container to your caterer or reception hall manager before the reception so they can put the cake in immediately after it's cut. Then ask a parent or friend who lives in your area to be in charge of placing the container in her/your fridge as soon as possible. To freeze the top tier for the long haul, wrap your container in tin foil and place it in the freezer. One year later, you're ready to thaw, serve, stare at it, decide if you should *really* eat it, tentatively taste it, and find out it's not so bad after all.

The Final Cut

A symbol of your shared life together, the cake-cutting ceremony traditionally takes place about an hour before the end of the reception. Enlist the DJ or emcee to make a casual announcement to prepare everyone for the picture-perfect moment. Whether the cake-cutting event is ceremonial or silly, the choice is yours. In the conventional manner, the bride picks up

Savor the Flavors

Every cake has its flavor, and some are better than others. Here's what works well—and not so well.

Chocolate Cake

- Fruits like: raspberry, cherry, orange (Grand Marnier), banana, strawberry
- Nuts like: almond (including marzipan), pistachio, hazelnut, peanut butter, praline
- Mousses and creams like: mocha, coffee (Kahlua, espresso, cappuccino), chocolate, white chocolate, vanilla, mint, Bavarian cream
- Other flavors: cannoli or coconut cream, mascarpone cheese, chocolate ganache
- *No-nos:* Lemon curd, mousses such as passion fruit, apricot, key lime, mango, pineapple

Yellow/White Chocolate/Vanilla Cake:

- Fruits like: raspberry, cherry, orange, strawberry, lemon curd, passion fruit, apricot, key lime, mango, pineapple
- Nuts like: almond (including marzipan), pistachio, hazelnut, praline
- Mousses and creams like: Amaretto, mocha, cappuccino, chocolate, white chocolate, vanilla, Bavarian cream
- *No-nos:* Mint, mascarpone cheese, cream cheese

Lemon/Carrot/Poppyseed Cake

- Fruits like: lemon curd, raspberry
- Nuts like: almond (including marzipan), hazelnut
- Mousses and creams like: lemon, white chocolate, vanilla
- Other flavors: cannoli or Bavarian cream, cream cheese, mascarpone
- *No-nos:* Chocolate or coffee-based fillings, mint, coconut, key lime, passion fruit, mango

the knife, the groom places his hand over hers, and together they cut a piece from the bottom layer. The newlyweds then feed each other a bite, which is said to symbolize their commitment to providing for each other. In most cases, it's best to cut from the bottom tier, but be sure to ask your baker if there is anything you need to know before you start cutting—you'd hate to see your masterpiece collapse in a fit of frosting! And if we can, we'd like to request that you not smash the cake into each other's face while feeding it to each other. It's not as cute as you think. In fact, it's not cute at all. Okay? Thanks.

The Cake Contract

Before you sign anything, make sure your cake contract includes:

- Name and contact information for you and the vendor
- Wedding date, time, and location
- When, how, where (complete address of site), and by whom the cake will be delivered (or picked up)
- A detailed description of the cake ordered
- A list of anything you're renting (plastic cake tiers, cake stand, etc.)
- Delivery and setup fees
- Total price
- Deposit amount due
- Balance and date due
- Cancellation and refund policy
- Cake designer's signature

Finding a Baker

Ideally, you should start shopping for a cake designer at least four to six months before the wedding, but take note: Some of the country's best designers can be booked a year in advance. Before starting your search, inquire whether your wedding venue has certain regulations regarding wedding cakes; some require you to use particular bakers, while others may charge a fee for using your own.

Saving Dough

The price of your wedding cake is usually calculated according to how labor-intensive the design is and by the slice, with prices ranging from a few dollars to $15 per slice. Gum paste flowers are the most expensive embellishment. Formed meticulously by hand, these buds are beautiful but are also known to break the bank. For an affordable alternative, use fresh flowers or a combination of the two. That smoothly rolled fondant, which creates a perfectly flat, clean surface is also costly. One way to save is by purchasing a smaller-size wedding cake, plus several sheet cakes of the same flavor. If you have a dessert table in addition to the cake, consider a cake that's enough for half of your guests—servings will be smaller, but the cost will shrink, too. Bottom line: All add-ons, including marzipan fruits, chocolate-molded flowers, and lace points, will raise the rate. If you don't use an in-house baker, some venues charge a cutting fee (from $1.50 to $3.00 a slice) to divvy up the cake. Be sure to check with your reception manager or caterer before finalizing your cake budget.

Questions to Ask

It's important to ask whether you must choose a cake from a fixed selection or if the baker will work with you to create a design all your own. You should also ask how the baker establishes the price: Are cakes priced by the slice? Do all of the flavors and fillings cost the same? Before you make a decision, do a little investigative work. First and foremost, find out if the cake designer meets the requirements of the local health department. *This is very important.* (Most reception sites will not allow a baker without a license to serve cake on the premises.) Also find out if they supply a cake knife and server sets, and if so, the fee. Finally, will the baker deliver the cake and set it up himself? Occasionally, there is last-minute detailing to do, such as applying the fresh flowers or touching up slightly mussed icing.

The Groom's Cake

That other, smaller confection you may have noticed sitting quietly off to the side at wedding receptions in the past (especially in the South) is taking center stage these days. Grooms are getting creative, ordering their cakes in the shapes of soccer balls, golf clubs, or briefcases (those lawyers). And while the groom's cake used to be darker and heavier (chocolate or, traditionally, fruitcake) than the main wedding cake, today it can come in any flavor. Some couples decide to slice and serve it at the reception, along with the wedding cake, while others slice and box it for guests to take home. (Legend has it that a single woman who sleeps with a slice of groom's cake under her pillow will dream of her future husband.)

CHAPTER SIXTEEN

picture this

Your wedding is going to be gorgeous, scrumptious, and fabulously one of a kind. It would be mean, mean, mean of you not to leave a piece of it for future generations to ogle and coo over. And it would be cruel to yourselves not to ensure you have timeless mementos of this spectacular affair. Did we forget to mention that your parents might never speak to you again if you don't present them with some keepsakes of the big day? Unlike the work of your other wedding vendors (music, flower arrangements, dress, cake), photographs and videos are not things you can hear, smell, taste, or even see at first–you don't really know what you're getting until after the fact. That means careful research and pickiness regarding professional skills, artistic style, and personal demeanor are extra important. Luckily, we're here to help you out.

PHOTOGRAPHY

Photographs are quintessential wedding keepsakes. They speak volumes about the atmosphere and style of the big day and your and your guests' emotions. Arranged artfully in an album, photos narrate the story of your wedding, from your dress-up sessions—including your honey's contortions while trying to knot a tie—to the last revelers getting cozy on the dance floor.

In order to get photos that will best reflect your personal style—and make you feel warm and fuzzy for years to come—arm yourself with some basic information about what different photographic styles are available, where to find a talented pro, and when (and how) to get perfect shots.

Focusing on a Style

More and more photgraphers are hopping on the wedding bandwagon. The cream of the crop are those who are truly excited about the idea of shooting weddings and who bring some personal flair to their work. In order for their style to work for you, however, you two need to figure out what you want. Below, the basic style options.

Photojournalism

Instead of posing for a series of pictures in which the photographer directs you, photojournalists quietly buzz around you and your guests, getting pictures of people *and* the action. Their mission is to be a proverbial fly on the wall, seemingly everywhere at once. Typical shots might include the lavish raw bar before guests start digging in, your motley crew of cousins dancing, and you and your bridesmaids laughing, champagne in hand.

Pros: Many photojournalists use a combination of fast, light 35mms along with more cumbersome medium-format cameras. They create a collection of photos that tells the story of your whole day, from different angles and perspectives without manipulation of subjects. It's a fluid compilation that is fun, surprising, romantic, and true to life.

Cons: Sometimes the shots can be a little *too* real. If you've ever had a perfect picture marred by smudged mascara or bad hair, you know how that goes. Another drawback is that flexibility is key. The photographer might be across the room capturing your brother twirling grandma across the dance floor when you want a photo with your college roommate.

Traditional

If photojournalism is synonymous with an informal style, then traditional photography is assosicated with a classic style. Most often using a medium-format camera, which allows for a sharper portrait at larger print sizes, a traditional photographer will arrange you in different poses, with different mixes of people, in front of different backdrops.

Photo Lingo

Some technical terms you should know:

Small-format camera: The standard, uses 35-mm film. Most of your wedding photos will be snapped with a small camera. Make sure your photographer has one or two extra loaded cameras so s/he won't miss any shots to reload or because of a technical problem.

Medium-format camera: This one uses slightly bigger film, which means prints tend to be a little clearer. It's essential that your photographer have a medium camera on hand for formal portraits; you'll probably want to blow them up, which means you need an extra-crisp image.

100–200 ASA: Standard-sensitivity film. 100–200 film is perfect for snapping shots in sunlight, well-lit indoor spaces, or with a flash. Bring along some extra rolls in case your photographer runs out.

400 ASA and up: Light-sensitive film, ideal for shooting in darker interiors, such as a church or a candlelit ballroom. Make sure one of your photographer's cameras is loaded with this stuff.

Digital: No film required, digital cameras record the visual information of a picture in an entirely electronic form. The advantages are cost (no film development costs), archiving (all of your "negatives" can be kept on CDs), and ease of sharing (e-mailing your wedding photos without having to scan the prints). Ask your photographer if s/he offers this option.

LISA & MICHAEL

June 4, West Chester, Pennsylvania

AS A LITTLE GIRL, Lisa loved looking at the sepia-tint pictures of her parents' formal wedding. To document their own wedding day in such a way that their children would be able to picture it, Lisa and Michael wanted to find a photographer who would do something special.

Lisa contacted photographer Rob Fraser, who is known for his photojournalistic approach. "I just loved his photos. He doesn't do any formal, stilted poses. Almost everything is spontaneous, candid," Lisa says. Fraser shot both color and black-and-white film, the color capturing the vibrancy of the day, the black-and-white adding a nostalgic feel. Because Fraser does not take posed shots of each table of wedding guests, he suggested an alternative to Lisa and Michael. In the mansion where they held the event, Fraser set up one room with a white backdrop, where guests could go and pose—or cut up—while he shot photos. "Some people were really goofy," Lisa says, "and those are the fun ones. Also, people could group themselves however they wanted—for instance, all the college friends could be in a shot together." Afterward, Fraser hand-developed the black-and-white film, adding a sepia tint, which provided Lisa with a wedding album much like her mother's.

Pros: It's a sure way to get the family portrait (all forty-two of you!) and a flawless shot of the two of you. This doesn't mean that the photos will be bland, it means that the composition and the subjects will be as close to "perfect" as possible.

Cons: If you're leaning toward traditional photography, keep in mind that posing for pictures is time consuming, especially if you want to get every last combination of you, your families, wedding party, and friends. Also, depending on whether the photographer does a lot of candids, he might not capture the kind of mid-party hijinks you'll want to remember forever.

Stylistic Separations

Black-and-white film is often associated with photojournalism, but it cerrtainly doesn't mean your whole wedding will be shot without color. Black and white is more emotional and dramatic, making it a natural addition, but you'll also want to capture the vibrant colors of the flowers you painstakingly selected and the brilliant sunset during the ceremony. Most photojournalists use several cameras so they can switch back and forth and produce both black-and-white and color photos. Likewise, traditional photographers can also shoot with both color and black-and-white film. State your preferences up front so your photographer will favor whichever you like best.

Cost Considerations: Photojournalism is often more expensive for the simple reason that you will probably get more images and more time with your shutterbug. For example, a traditional photographer might take between 100 and 250 pictures of you, your families, and friends in different poses, whereas a photojournalist takes upward of 700 to capture the entire celebration. A common photojournalistic package includes six to eight hours, while a traditional photograher might take three or four. As with everything else—and we can't stress this enough—it all depends on your photographer.

Knowing Who's Who: Just because the pictures are black and white doesn't mean it's photojournalism. Many photographers are aware of the trend toward photojournalism and will try to sell themselves as photojournalists even though they're traditional. One way to tell the difference is to look at the subjects in the photos and where they are looking. In traditional wedding photography, subjects are almost always looking at the camera. With true candids, people are usually oblivious to the fact that their pictures are being taken. Many photographers will be able to mix styles, offering you the shot of your uncles hamming it up on the dance floor, as well as the family portrait in front of the lush evergreen trees; the emotional black-and-white shot of the father/daughter dance, and the classic full-color portrait of the bride and groom.

Hiring a Hot Shot

Once you have an idea of what style you're looking for, it's time to seek out a photographer who can deliver. As with all wedding vendors, your best bet is word-of-mouth. Ask relatives, friends, and newlywed couples for referrals to talented pros. The Internet might be the best thing that ever happened to wedding photographers—and to you, as well. Once you get recommendations, many photographers post samples of their work on their website. A few clicks can prompt you to set up a visit ASAP, or spare you a trip to visit him or her in person. Don't base your decision solely on what you see online, however—remember that the photographer will only post the very best shots, so you won't get a well-rounded idea of his or her work. You can check out hundreds of photographers' work at theknot.com/photography.

You should also turn to local wedding magazines in your area, many of which, like *The Knot Weddingpages,* offer real weddings and a variety of pictures from many local photographers. These magazines can prove to be an indispensable resource when you're looking for a visual pro. Other places to look to if you're still not turning up any leads: bridal salons, wedding consultants, even catering-hall managers—they've worked with countless photographers.

While your best bet is going with an experienced *wedding* photographer, there's no rule against hiring hot shots with other specialties (a fashion photographer whose work you admire, a local newspaper photographer), an amateur photographer fresh out of school, or even a friend. In each of these cases, take extra care checking that the individual knows what's involved in this assignment and has the necessary skills. Look at pictures from similar projects that required similar skills (journalistic reportage on a society function or a fashion shoot that took place in a crowded restaurant), including dealing with people doing unexpected things and working with naturally occurring light (lamps, candles, sunlight) as opposed to spotlights. Also check that the person owns (or can rent) several backup cameras; like the pros, a nonwedding photographer should be prepared in case of camera meltdown.

Finding Your Pro

Looking for a photographer? Check out www.theknot.com/photography for fantastic photographers in your area.

The Big Picture: What to Look For

Things to ask yourselves before you say "I do" to a photographer.

Do We Like Her Book? Check whether the person has mastered the basic photographic skills by looking at her "book," a collection of greatest

Picture-Perfect Contract Points

A glitch-proof photographer's contract should include:

- ☐ All locations where photographer will be expected to shoot, with exact addresses and starting times.
- ☐ Estimated number of hours to be worked.
- ☐ The name of photographer who'll be working for you and any assistants.
- ☐ The name of an acceptable substitute in case of emergency.
- ☐ Number of cameras that will be used, and which formats.
- ☐ Number of rolls to be shot (numbers for color and black and white).
- ☐ Number of proofs you'll receive.
- ☐ Other package details: number of completed albums, special-request shots.
- ☐ Schedule for delivering proofs and final package, as well as length of time negatives will be kept.
- ☐ Total cost.
- ☐ Overtime fee.
- ☐ Cancellation/refund policy.

hits. (If a "professional" photographer doesn't have a book, that means she's either severely unorganized or full of it, neither of which is a good trait for a wedding photographer.) While you're flipping through, look for crispness of images, thoughtful compositions (does a shot look good the way it was framed, are heads chopped off, is there too much clutter in the frame?), and good lighting (beware of washed-out pictures where small details are blurred). It's also very important that you detect sensitivity in capturing people's emotions; make sure the photographer's subjects look relaxed, not like deer caught in headlights.

Do We Like a Wedding Album He Created? Examine a real-life wedding album the photographer created. You should be able to get a feel for the couple's wedding from their pictures: the style, the overall mood, the main players. If all you see are formal shots and you've decided you want the bulk of your photos to be candid, feel out whether the photographer is open to that. Ask him to explain his philosophy in putting together an album and see if it meshes with yours.

Do We Get Good Vibes? This may be the most important question. Is the person excited by your vision when you describe it? When she makes suggestions, does she present them in a clear and respectful way? Is she rude? Is she timid? Does she laugh like a hyena? In order to get the best photos, go with a hot shot who has a firm grasp of social graces but is assertive enough to go out hunting for great images and who puts you at ease. (She will be shadowing your every move, remember.)

Your Friend, Your Photographer

Planning to hand the camera to a friend in addition to a professional—or in lieu of one? Offer friend photogs these suggestions from Rob Fraser, a New York photographer who specializes in creative camerawork. (Keep them in mind when choosing a pro, too.)

Shoot Between the Moments: You may want a traditional group shot of the wedding party, but why stop there? Fraser's found that great times to shoot are when people are getting ready for and breaking up after a formal photograph.

Go with a Wide Shot: Why make every shot a closeup? By varying the distance of your shots, you'll be able to capture both the intimate moments and the overall feeling of the event.

Shoot with Selective Focus: By using a shallow depth of field, a photographer can focus sharply on a face while making the background fuzzy; alternately, s/he could focus on a distant object. Isolating subjects in their environment can create great shots. Flip through some fashion magazines and pay close attention to the photography style, which often incorporates this technique.

Use Natural Light: Traditional wedding photography blasts everything with a hot flash. But reality isn't always quite that bright. Ask your photographer to re-create real changes in brightness by using available light instead of a strong flash for every shot.

Use Juxtaposition: Predictable shots can be jazzed up simply by adding some human involvement. Fraser once shot a bride and groom kissing by the cake while a little girl was stealing a piece.

Flash These Questions

If you determine that a photographer's skill set, style, vision, and personality are A-OK, it's time to get some specific information.

Will You Do a Switcheroo? Make sure that the photographer whose work you've seen and loved is the one who will show up to your wedding. Larger studios have several photographers on their roster.

How Do You Determine Price? You won't be able to nail down an exact dollar amount until you're sure of what you want and how many albums you need. However, get a general range based on the number of prints you think you'll want (usually a hundred or so). If the photographer is way out of your price range, try to whittle away extras (the album itself, enlarged portraits) or cut down on hours to find the price that's right. It's a good idea to shop around, but we don't recommend skimping on your wedding photos—they're the most durable thing you'll spend your money on; unlike a cupid-shaped cake or cream satin stilettos, you'll have them forever.

Do You Develop the Film? This is the norm with black-and-white pics, but many vendors now farm out their color processing to megalabs. While this will mean less ouch to your wedding budget, it also means that the quality of your photos may not be as stellar. If you can swing it, pay for someone who takes the do-it-yourself approach across the board.

What's Our Plan of Action? Schedule a follow-up meeting where you'll talk about specifics. Together you'll decide how many hours your photographer will spend at your wedding and discuss which specific shots you want (your entire wedding party and you, the garter toss, your honeymoon limo driving off into the sunset) and don't want (the cake shot, the schmaltzy posed kiss).

What Are Our Numbers? Hammer out how many rolls of film your photographer will shoot, how many proofs (sample developed pictures) you'll have to choose from, and how many prints will be in your final package.

What's Your Negative Policy? Most photographers save negatives for a year or two, during which time you can order extras. If you're moving (or live) far away or think you'll be needing more copies for years to come—it's going to be the Wedding of the Century, after all—consider buying the negatives at some point.

Photo Types and Twists

You two look dashing. Your guests look delightful. The flowers look fantastic, the food, scrumptious. Wouldn't it be a disaster if you didn't get this stuff on film? Pull up a chair and study our list of traditional wedding shots and the rundown of some of the best images to snag. (All of these go for wedding video must-haves, too.) A professional photographer probably will suggest many of these on her/his own; if a friend or family member is doing the photographic honors, this should be their guide. Of course, your wedding is going to be delightfully different, therefore, we're sure that you'll add a few of your own essential pics to the master list.

Chapter 1 walks you through the process of composing and submitting newspaper announcements with photos.

Bridal Portrait

Traditionally, the bride would go to a photographer's studio one to three months before the big day to be photographed in her wedding gown (perhaps even holding a replica of her big-day bouquet). While this practice is becoming less and less common—except down South, where the bride's portrait often is displayed at the reception—some women still choose to pose for this formal shot so they can include it with their wedding announcement. Our modern spin on this idea is to have a professional picture of the two of you (with or without wedding clothes) taken about two months before the wedding; you can use the photo for newspaper or sent announcements, wedding invitations, even thank-you notes.

"Day-Of" Portraits

Happy Couple: A posed picture of the two of you on your big day is a must-have. If you're not superstitious, take this shot before the ceremony, when you're all dressed up and ready to go. It's a nice together moment before you venture into the spotlight and means you'll have less to worry about once the festivities begin. More often, though, people pose for this shot in the moments right after the ceremony. That's fine, too, because you'll have that newlywed glow and be thankful for a moment apart from the crowd. Your photographer should take a number of shots in different positions; you two relax and smile. Add a personal flair to your big-day portraits by having them printed in a special technique that gives them a brownish, antique sheen (called sepia-toned) for a romantic memento, or by posing in a special locale, such as your favorite park or on your car. Be playful—sometimes the best couple pictures are those where you're acting goofy, lovey-dovey, or downright nutty.

Shoot for a Mix

Don't feel pressured to take tons of formal portraits just because your parents are urging you to. Compromise. Have your photographer shoot the basic formals—you two, you and your families—and spend the rest of the time doing candids.

Wedding Party: Take some shots with your wedding party, girls and boys separately and then everyone together, either before or directly after the ceremony. (Or you can step out for a bit during the reception if you'd rather.) You'll also want shots of you two and your two honor attendants and shots of each of you with your attendant (bride/maid of honor, groom/best man). Remember: There's no rule that you have to be stiff and still; hug each other, tell jokes, do the chicken dance.

Family: Photos of each of you with your parents and siblings—taken before or after the ceremony—are a must. Both of you together should be in a portrait with each of your immediate family members, and there should be one big picture of both families together (with you two smiling smack in the center).

Guests: It's becoming increasingly popular to ask all your guests to pose for a formal-yet-somewhat-informal portrait. Basically, a camera is set up in an out-of-the-way spot where guests can go to pose for a picture—either alone or with a group. It's a great way to get a visual memoir of everyone who attended your wedding, not just the people who walked down the aisle. Some couples go so far as to rent a photo booth—the kind you'd find at a carnival—which is another fun way to get everyone in a hilarious shot or two.

Must-Have Shot Sheet

Some wedding moments you don't want to miss on photo and/or video. (If you're more comfortable, enlist a trusted friend for behind-the-scenes shots.)

Getting Ready (before the ceremony)

- Your clothes, hanging in the closet or over a chair
- Bridesmaids doing bride's hair and makeup
- Full-length shot of bride with gown checking herself out in mirror
- Groom getting ready with Dad and pals (tying the tie is a classic)
- You two chatting with/crying with/hugging your parents and siblings preceremony
- Mom helping bride with one last detail, such as veil
- Dad whispering last-minute advice to groom
- Each of you ready to go—at the door
- Making your way to the ceremony (in backseat of limo, hailing cab, walking down the street)

The Ceremony

- Guests streaming into the site
- Ushers escorting guests to their seats (you get to see if they did it right)
- Closeup of the groom's adorably nervous mug waiting for his other half
- Flower girl and/or ring bearer walking in (how cute!)
- Gorgeous bridesmaids going down the aisle
- Closeup of bride just before making her entrance
- Bride and her escort(s) going down the aisle
- Wide shot of altar or canopy
- Wide shot of audience during ceremony, from bride and groom's point of view
- Closeup of your hands as you exchange the rings
- The kiss: zoom in!
- You two coming up the aisle, guests' smiling faces at your sides
- Congrats shots: you two hugging, laughing, crying with good friends

The Reception

- Bride and groom arriving (make it dramatic—your faces through the dark glass of limo, you two at top of staircase, pushing through a curtain)
- Receiving-line moments
- You two knocking back some champagne with your best friends
- Your parents whispering to each other during dinner
- Kids playing with balloons and streamers or sneaking a nap
- You two dancing (maybe with a slow shutter speed so the movement blurs the image a little)
- The musicians or DJ doing their thing
- Bride laughing with her bridesmaids
- Groom dancing with maid of honor
- The dance floor going nuts (again, slow-shutter speed could be effective)
- Bride and groom feeding each other cake (no smashing allowed)
- Closeup of your uncle making a toast
- The bouquet toss (perhaps a shot of just the flowers and outstretched arms)
- You two leaving, waving from the backseat

ASK CARLEY

Don't Make 'Em Wait!

Q: We want our photographer to shoot quite a few formal portraits and the ceremony, but we hate the thought of making our guests wait for us to show up at the reception. What to do?

A: Having your cake and eating it too is a snap in this situation. You definitely don't want to make people entertain themselves for hours while you pose for photos. It's perfectly acceptable to shoot some portraits *before* the ceremony; in fact, it's when everyone will be looking sharpest. (It also may help soothe your nerves to snuggle up with your honey preceremony.) Or have your photographer pull you and fellow posers away from the reception for ten or fifteen minutes to shoot your must-have portraits. It will be a breath of fresh air, figuratively if not literally, and you'll all be at peak excitement level.

Photography Trends

- Fast-speed film (good for shooting in dim light)
- Black-and-white pictures
- Candids over posed pics
- Behind-the-scenes shots
- Images of guests reacting
- Different-size photos in an album (quarter page, full page, etc.)
- "Storyboard" album (an overall narrative concept)
- Detail shots
- Library-bound albums in soft leather or quality fabrics

Ceremony Action Shots

Shots of your ceremony—beginning with your arrival and ending when you leave—are the meat of your wedding album. Classic pics include the groom waiting at the altar, the wedding party and then the bride and her escort going down the aisle, and ceremonial highlights (jumping the broom, exchanging rings, signing a marriage contract). Also get a shot of the entire crowd from where the two of you stand during your vows and several reaction shots of special guests crying/laughing/gasping/fanning themselves/sleeping—they tell the real story of the moment.

Reception Candids

Pictures of you and your guests mingling, munching, and moshing will bring you the most joy and laughter. Apart from totally spontaneous shots (give your photographer lots of freedom to roam and snap precious moments), reception highlights like the cutting of the cake and dances with your moms and pops also should be memorialized. It's also a great idea to encourage guests to shoot their own candids—which you can mix with pro pics in your album—by placing disposable cameras on their tables and asking them to leave them for you later.

VIDEOGRAPHY

Whether a wedding video is a must-have is still open for debate. It really depends on what you and your honey like and want and the budget you're working with. There are *many* compelling reasons to have your wedding videotaped: You'll get to see a lot of live action that you may have missed because you were off greeting guests/tending to those butterflies in your stomach/polka-ing with Gramps. You'll also have a vivid record of the sounds of your wedding—your processional music, your best man's hilarious toast, the cacophony of guests chatting and laughing—as well as key moving images, such as your dance with your mother, your honey's goofy line dance with her bridesmaids, the bouquet-toss pileup.

But before you plop down the $2,000-plus that it will cost you to hire a professional videographer, ask yourselves whether: you want to accommodate—and listen to—yet another camera person at the event; it's really important to you to have a real-time recording of your wedding (say, for someone who can't make it); if you're gonna watch the thing more than once. If you can afford a video without having to cut back on your photography package—or you've got an offer from a video-savvy friend—go for it! Don't feel badly, however, about only doing the photo thing; pictures are more durable and evocative anyway.

Zooming In on a Genre

As the stars of your own made-for-TV movie, you have a few options in the style department. Before you begin shopping around for a videographer, figure out which directorial approach most appeals to you.

Documentary Style

Your wedding is covered like a major news event (which it is, of course), blending real-time footage; voice-over commentary from you two, friends, and family; and on-screen interviews with key guests.

Pros: Very entertaining to watch, this style plays up the highlights of the big day.

Cons: You'll typically need two cameras to create a good, newsy tape, which will be more expensive and more intrusive. If done right, the editing process is quite elaborate, as well—using lots of audio editing and montages (multiple-scene sequences)—which again means more money.

Oscar-Winning Ideas: Get your videographer to shoot talking-head interviews with people near and dear to your heart; their comments will be moving and funny, no doubt. Go chronological: Record the proceedings from when you're getting dressed until "The End," perhaps even giving your videographer some honeymoon footage to edit into the mix.

Memory Lane

This format incorporates past home videos, shots of childhood/college/courtship photos, and commentary from close friends and relatives to create a holistic vision of your relationship—with your wedding as the main event.

Pros: Finally you'll do something with those dusty homemade reels your father keeps in the garage. Plus you'll have a quirky, sentimental synopsis of your life to view on anniversaries, birthdays, even during together time with your future kids.

Cons: If done wrong, this could smell worse than Roquefort cheese. Again, this approach requires lots of postproduction work (editing, captions, voice-overs), so it's going to cost you.

Freedom to Film?

Don't assume your videographer will have total artistic freedom at your ceremony. Some places of worship do not allow bright lights and may place restrictions on your vendor's movement. (S/he may not have access to a behind-the-altar audience shot, for example.) Check with your officiant about rules.

Oscar-Winning Ideas: Divide the first part of the video into two separate, titled sections, one about each of you. Then start the couple section with a montage of pictures of you together while your fave song plays. Have your parents, friends, and siblings talk about what they thought of your honey when they first met, memories they have of your early days, sweet things you've said in confidence about each other.

Rough Cut

This is unedited footage of your wedding: live, raw, uncensored. And it's probably the route you'll be taking if you're having a friend or relative shoot the event, unless they have access to editing facilities.

Pros: Cheap, cheap, cheap. You'll get spontaneous outbreaks and raunchy hilarity à la *The Osbournes* and lots of other images you probably would have never seen in a shorter, edited format.

Cons: Your hands are going to be sore from doing all that fast-forwarding. It's not that your wedding wasn't exciting; it's just that you really did need to *be* there to get the full sense of splendor.

Oscar-Winning Ideas: Have a ready-made script for the videographer of certain shots and interviews s/he must get so that the video has some rhyme and reason.

Hiring a Video Pro

Finding a good videographer is not as difficult as finding a contact lens in a haystack, but it still requires some effort on your part. Since your videographer is someone you really need to trust

Straight-to-Video Contract Points

When you're signing a contract with your videographer, make sure it includes:

- ☐ The wedding date and arrival time.
- ☐ Names and addresses of all locations where videographer will be shooting.
- ☐ The videographer's name.
- ☐ The name of an acceptable substitute in case of emergency.
- ☐ The hours they'll work.
- ☐ Number of cameras and assistant videographers (put in writing that they will bring at least one backup camera).
- ☐ The hours of raw footage they will shoot.
- ☐ The total edited time of your finished tape (get about five minutes of live footage for each edited minute, or two-and-a-half hours of footage for a half-hour video).
- ☐ Any editing features or special effects you've agreed upon.
- ☐ Total cost.
- ☐ Fees including overtime rates and cost of additional tapes if you want them.
- ☐ Date the final video will be ready.

Looking Supermodel-Slick

The wedding paparazzi want a piece of you two! And *you* want to look like stalkable celebs, if just for one day. To say "cheese" in the best possible way, follow our gouda ideas and brie-liant suggestions—you'll look like runway pros.

Smile: Baring your pearly whites definitely increases your odds of taking a good picture. Besides, the act of smiling alone has a calming effect that will translate into cool-looking pics. Don't force it; think of a funny joke your sister just told you or steal a peek at your jokester father.

Pick a Side: Don't sit on the fence; find your "good" side. Stick a pencil in your mouth, holding the center of it between your lips so it's parallel to the floor. Look in the mirror at the distance between the pencil and your eyes. You'll notice that one of your eyes is actually closer to the pencil—this indicates the shorter side of your face. In this case, shorter is *better.* Try to point that side toward the camera as much as possible.

Strike a Pose: Take a look at any fashion magazine. The models usually position their bodies toward the camera at a forty-five-degree angle, then turn their heads to face the lens directly. Notice that their hips are pushed slightly forward and their shoulders are pulled back. The foot closest to the camera points toward it while the other remains parallel to it. This all makes them look fab—practice in the mirror for your trip into the limelight.

Do Something: Pictures can look funny if the subjects are stiff, awkward, and unnatural. The best way to avoid looking like a dweeb is to grab hold of the person next to you (especially if it's your sweetie!) and show some affection. Throw an arm around a friend, plant a kiss on your uncle's cheek, laugh and hold up your champagne flutes.

Eye It: We know you're scared of blinking, but don't widen your eyes—it'll give you a creased-up forehead. To look naturally alert, shut your eyes quickly before a shot and then open them.

Hold Your Chin High: The best way to beat the dreaded double chin is to stand up straight and pull your head up.

Hair Dos: Keep your hair away from your face, so you don't look messy. Brush bangs aside with your fingers before a shot and tuck stray pieces behind your ears.

Sun Block: Stay out of direct sunlight. The sun shadows your face in pictures, making your nose look bigger and your eyes smaller. Head for a bright, not blazing, spot.

Chapter 11 briefs you on super hair and makeup.

and like, it's extra important to check the person out carefully. As always, ask around for glowing referrals or consult your wedding photographer (if you've already hired one) for some hot prospects. Find a pro who's in your price range, comfortable with the genre of your choice, and an all-around nice person.

Making the Cut: Questions to Ask

Even though we all watch lots of TV, it still can be hard to judge what makes a video good or bad. Ask prospective videographers if you may see a few tapes of their wedding work and ask yourselves some questions.

Does This Person Have Basic Technical Skills Down? Images should be bright and crisp, not dark and grainy. Faces should be natural-looking, not shiny or washed out by too much light. Edits—cuts from one shot to another—should be seamless. Don't forget to

Photo and Video Storage Tips

Keep photos and videotapes somewhere that maintains a moderate temperature and humidity level, away from direct light.

Videos should be stored upright (on end) in their cases and away from electronic equipment such as stereo speakers, which have magnetic coils at their centers.

Remove the clip at the back of your video so you don't record over it by mistake.

Keep a second copy of your video and the negatives of your photos in a fireproof box made especially for photographs and negatives.

listen for good, clear sound quality (no hissing or buzzing; sound level should be steady from scene to scene).

Does S/he Have Good Storytelling Instincts? Scenes should be put together in a coherent, logical fashion. Selected clips should be "best of" material (ergo, not boring). You also want your videographer to be a good interviewer who gets great quotes from friends and family. Make sure the people being interviewed on the tapes you're watching seem happy and comfortable, not besieged or annoyed. (That probably means the videographer is inappropriately pushy or familiar.)

Do We Like His/Her Personality? You want to hire someone with super people skills who will make your wedding day better, not bleaker. Avoid pushy types whom you just know are going to be elbowing your grandparents aside to get a "money" (exceptionally good) shot. Also steer clear of videographers intent on convincing you that you need a crew the size of that employed on the set of *Moulin Rouge* to get a decent wedding video; they probably are more concerned about their bank account than your needs and desires.

Getting your hands on a good wedding photographer and videographer will enhance the beauty of your big day, because you'll be able to enjoy those precious moments with friends and family—and all the fleeting wedding-day emotions—for years to come. Doing thorough groundwork about your options and prospective hires is somewhat time-consuming, but it's the best wedding present you can give yourselves. Who doesn't want to be immortalized looking model-gorgeous and being the center of attention? Those wedding images will be lifelong pick-me-ups, reminding the two of you how luminous, lucky, and loved you really are.

NOTES

CHAPTER SEVENTEEN

face the music

Like your favorite flick, your relationship has a soundtrack. During your time as a twosome, you've adopted certain songs as your own and shared your favorites with each other in the shower. Your musical repertoire is one of a kind, reminding you of all the wonderful times you've had together. Unveil this fantastic compilation to the world at your wedding.

Wedding music is an art. Incorporated into your ceremony and reception, it punctuates dramatic entrances and exits, augments the overall mood of your celebration, adds to the romanticism of the affair, and, of course, gets you and your guests shaking your booties! Whether you're classical music buffs or top-forty junkies (or one of each), the music you choose will personalize the festivities. It's time to add rhythm and soul to your wedding!

CEREMONY MUSIC

Start your wedding off on the right foot by including music in your ceremony. Ambient sound—whether generated by a klezmer (traditional Jewish) band, a bagpiper, a string quartet, or a group of African percussionists—can create a mood of breathless anticipation, entertain guests as they wait for your smash entrance, up the romanticism and spirituality quotient, and soothe frayed nerves. While in the past, many a couple's ceremony score was solely a classical composition, we also love the idea of allowing your ethnic heritage, personal taste, wedding theme, and level of romanticism, playfulness, and unconventionality to play a role in your ceremony-music selection.

Music-Deserving Moments

Music can be used throughout this monumental event, from the time your early-bird guests arrive to the moment you're outta there. Get hip to the traditional components of ceremony music so you can decide what's for you and when you actually prefer the sound of silence.

The Prelude

The music that's played first—the prelude—is there to distract and entertain guests until the ceremony officially begins. Prelude music should start when the doors to your site open, no later than twenty minutes before the start time on your invites. (There are many early birds out there, and a lot of them are your relatives.) Depending on how many guests you've invited, how long it takes you to tie a tie, or how many times your honey has to reapply her lipstick before facing the world, you may have to plan for as much as forty-five minutes of music here. That said, keeping people waiting much more than thirty minutes is downright rude.

Many musical choices are appropriate, from distinguished concerto excerpts by Bach, Chopin, or Handel to mellow jazz standards to covers of sweet R&B hits. You want to choose music that will mask awkward silences—as guests settle in their seats next to total strangers—but won't overshadow the energy of anticipation.

Establish a mood or theme with your prelude; remember, it's your invitees' first sensory impression of your wedding (along with the aroma of the flowers and the look of the site). For a fairy-tale affair, have a harpist make some heavenly music; for a casual beach ceremony, have a band play acoustic versions of Beach Boys' and reggae tunes; for a candlelit evening wedding, choose something mystical, such as Gregorian chants or Enya's haunting New Age songs. Even if you're not incorporating music anywhere else in your ceremony, do it here—a solo flutist, violinist, or pianist is a low-key choice.

Greatest Hits: Handel's "Water Music"; Saint-Saëns' "Benediction Nuptiale"; Bach's "Suite in D"; Haydn's "Violin Concerto in A."

The Processional

The pièce de résistance of your ceremonial concert, the processional is the music playing as you and your wedding party make your grand entrance, whether down the aisle, through your floral canopy, or parachuting down from the sky.

Think drama. Often a march is chosen—played by an organist or trumpeter—to keep you and your entourage movin' on forward like shiny, suave soldiers. However, any music (or instrument) will do as long as it's monumental and bold. Personalize your processional music by selecting an acoustic version of a song with sentimental value to you as a couple—your first dance, your parents' processional tune—or that shows off your ethnic heritage.

Greatest Hits: Purcell's "Trumpet Tune," Mozart's "Wedding March" from *The Marriage of Figaro;* Beethoven's "Ode to Joy"; Pachelbel's "Canon in D Minor."

Ceremonial Accents

Many couples choose to have music played to accent key moments during the ceremony (the exchange of rings, the breaking of the glass) or as actual elements of the ceremony itself, along with readings. Any tune is appropriate, from classic pieces such as Schubert's "Ave Maria" or Handel's immortal "Hallelujah Chorus" from *Messiah,* to folk songs such as "Amazing Grace" and the "Irish Wedding Song," to popular tunes such as "One Hand, One Heart" from *West Side Story* or Stevie Wonder's "You Are the Sunshine of My Life." Have pieces performed by a vocalist or an instrumental soloist/ensemble.

Since this is the most emotional stage of the entire affair, put some soul into it. Add some heritage, have a talented friend or relative sing an original tune, or have a particularly meaningful song performed. One of our favorite ideas is incorporating a group singalong; print the words of a hymn, folk song, or pop favorite in your ceremony program and have your guests double as performers for a true feeling of group harmony.

Greatest Hits: Thank heavens we're all so different—there is no top-forty countdown here. Be free.

The Recessional

The bride and groom should go out with a bang. The music that plays while you're walking back up the aisle together should reflect the giddiness of your just-marriedness and get guests revved up for the celebration to follow. Even if you're not technically leaving—say your ceremony and reception are in the same place—have your musicians play a show-stopping number once the rigmarole is over in honor of the big change that's just taken place. Again, classical music (like Widor's "Toccata" from Symphony No. 5 or Elgar's "Pomp and Circumstance") is a popular choice, as are upbeat contemporary songs.

Greatest Hits: High-energy pop hits—such as the Partridge Family's "C'mon, Get Happy," the Beatles' "Love Me Do," or Brancaccio & Aisher's "It's Gonna Be . . . (A Lovely Day)."

Postlude

Keep the good vibes going with more love-happy and spirited music playing as guests file out of the ceremony site, or—if your entire wedding is taking

The Familiar Wedding Tune . . .

The traditional "Here Comes the Bride" is actually the "Bridal Chorus" from Wagner's opera *Lohengrin*. Some Catholic churches will not allow it because it's a secular composition; many rabbis frown on it because of the composer's well-documented anti-Semitism. And if you're at all superstitious, you might want to steer clear—it was written about a union that goes super-sour.

Personalized Ceremony Tunes

Incorporate one or more of these elements into your ceremony music:

Ethnicity: Use traditional musical instruments, such as a sitar (India), mandolin (Greece), fiddle (Ireland), or a didgeridoo (Australia). Play national folk songs during the prelude.

Religion: Have a choir lead everyone in a hymn or religious tune; hire a gospel group or klezmer band; incorporate a Buddhist chant.

Wedding Theme: Match the musicians to the time period (fife and drums for a medieval affair; jazz trio for the 1920s). Select theme-appropriate songs, such as the Who's "My Generation" for a '60s wedding or Billy Ray Cyrus's "Achy Breaky Heart" for a country-western shindig.

Site Characteristics: Take musical cues from your site. Dramatic organ music goes well with a large Gothic church; a folk singer is perfect for your grandparents' living room; a string quartet goes hand in glove with a formal garden.

"Your" Songs: Choose tunes that have your honey's name in them (Elton John's "Daniel"; the Beatles' "Michelle") or bear special meaning for both of you (your first slow dance, something from the movie soundtrack you wore out on your first road trip together).

place at one location—as they make the transition into chow and cha-cha time. You could have your musicians stick around a little longer or play a CD. Figure on fifteen minutes' worth of fun, celebratory tunes.

Greatest Hits: You two singing a duet of "We're Off to See the Wizard"—just kidding. Think happy and you'll bring down the house.

Ceremony Music Options

Before you book that steel drum band or campy, drag-queen barbershop quintet, you need to assess your site and find out about any religious (or other) restrictions on music, discuss your personal taste, and find songs and instruments that are music to both of your ears.

Musical Restrictions

Your first step in determining what style of music in general, and which tunes specifically, you can include is to investigate whether there are any pertinent restrictions you should keep in mind.

Fast Forward

If you're using CDs or tapes for ceremony (or reception) music, create a playlist for the person in charge. Write down the names of the songs and the track numbers; make sure to provide extra backup songs in case things take longer than planned. If you're using tapes, make everyone's life easier—cue 'em.

- Check with your officiant about religious restrictions on *what* you can play. Some places of worship will not allow secular songs (many Catholic churches) or forbid music completely (Quaker and Orthodox Jewish wedding ceremonies).
- Check with the ceremony site's musical director, if there is one. These coordinators can clue you in to limitations regarding *who* can perform at your ceremony. Obviously, their preference is for you to hire in-house musicians; there may even be rules prohibiting outside performers. Be diplomatic if you want to farm out music duties; one smoothing-of-ruffled-feathers tactic is to consult the musical director about which pieces to choose. It's not only flattering, it's the smart thing to do—s/he probably has a better grasp of appropriate songs than you do.
- Consult the authorities in charge if you're tying the knot in a public place. When it comes to a city park or county beach, there may be time-of-day restrictions on playing music or limitations on noise levels. You may, for example, have to forgo that electric guitar riff you had planned in favor of an unplugged acoustic tune.

Sounding Out the Options

In terms of *who* you want making music at this important event, you have a wide variety of options, from a solo guitarist to a large choir. Before you track down referrals to specific musicians, decide what it is you want. This will depend on several things.

Site Acoustics: The sound of a delicate harp will get lost in a bombastic cathedral; a chorus of bagpipes could be deafening in a small space like your living room. If you're getting hitched at a conventional site, such as a house of worship or banquet hall, consult people there about what works in the space and what doesn't. If you've selected an unconventional site, such as a forest clearing, experiment with a battery-powered cassette player and imagine what type of volume level you're going to want once the space is teeming with gabbing guests.

Specific Tunes You Want Played: Classical compositions won't have the impact you want played on a fiddle, say, and Stevie Wonder on an organ just ain't funky. We're not saying you can't be creative, but if you have specific pieces you want played, envision in your mind's ear who's going to be able to play it successfully and who isn't.

Your Music Budget: The dollar amount you've allocated to wedding entertainment must cover both ceremony and reception music. If you're flush, anything goes, but if—like most of the free world—you have some limitations, keep the musicianship simple, with a solo performer or a small ensemble (or even prerecorded music). Since *you two* are the feature ceremony attraction, you can afford to scale back the backup help here. After all, the reception is where you really need a hand in keeping the guests happy and engaged.

Music to Your Ears

In general, ceremony music is best kept simple. After all, you don't want it to overshadow the intrinsic emotional intensity of the vows. Go for a focused sound rather than flashy bells and whistles. Some of our favorite options for ceremony music:

Keyboardist: A classical pianist or organist can do it all, from soothing prelude tunes to a dignified processional to jazzy, upbeat postlude music.

Trumpeter: A soloist or a horn combo can add either regal solemnity or peppy rhythm—or both—to your ceremony, depending on what music you ask them to play.

String Quartet: Strings are pitch perfect for classical compositions; they also add romantic elegance to contemporary selections.

Flutist: Usually paired with either a pianist or string instrument, the flute is a soothing way to start the festivities—think romance and springtime (two feelings that work year-round).

Harpist: The ideal choice for a small, romantic ceremony or springtime vows in the garden. Hire two harpists—to sit and strum at either side of the altar—for larger affairs or an accompanying flutist for a baroque tinge.

Blues Guitarist: The sound of a slide guitar is urban-romantic; it creates an all-American, down-to-earth, ultra-cool atmosphere. A mix of blues, jazz, and American classics can be played at different stages of your ceremony.

Vocalist/Choir: *Homo sapiens'* vocal chords are a beautiful instrument, say we. Hymns, gospels, pop hits, and classical compositions offer a wide array of feelings for the various stages of your ceremony.

Folk Singer: Like the troubadour of yore, a folk singer/guitarist has a unique, intimate, and sentimental aura. Scout local coffeeshops or performance spaces for a musician who touches you; perhaps even commission an original song for the occasion.

Musical Notes

- Don't book ceremony musicians before you check into the religious, cultural, and logistical restrictions at your site.
- For outdoor sites, look for a flat stage area and electrical outlets so that you and your musicians know what extra equipment (generator, stage, etc.) you need. This applies to your reception entertainers, too.
- If your ceremony will be outdoors and you've hired classical musicians, make sure they're sheltered. Violins, flutes, and harps are delicate; the slightest drizzle can put an end to the performance. If you want the music to go on, be sure to provide a tent or roof of some sort.

Jazz Combo: Have a trio, quintet, or singer/standing bass duet add some soul to your ceremony. Jazz standards create a sophisticated, glamorous atmosphere that's oh-so-romantic.

Hiring Your Music Makers

As with all wedding vendors, you want to make sure that you really, really know what you're getting for your music money. Hearing is believing. Once you've gotten the names of some good ceremony musicians (from friends, newlywed couples, your clergy, site coordinators, a wedding consultant), make sure you get a chance to listen to them play. Many performers today have recorded tapes of their craftsmanship, a good place to begin, but there is no substitute for seeing a live performance. Ask about sitting in on an event they're doing—whether a wedding or not—to find out if you like what you see and hear.

Pitch-Perfect Topics to Cover

Once you've zeroed in on some choice musicians, you'll need to talk about a number of issues.

Vision: Explain what you're thinking about in terms of musical selections. See if they respond openly and get excited. If there's a song you really want to incorporate and they don't know it, they should be willing to learn from sheet music you provide them. If they're resistant to the idea, find out if it's because they think it won't work with the instrument (they are, after all, more in the know than you; ask them to come up with some doable alternatives of a similar style) or just *because,* in which case: Keep looking.

Schedule: Is the performer available on the day of your wedding? Will he or she commit to an early-morning ceremony or a midnight one? Most important, make sure your musicians are hip to the idea of showing up at least an hour in advance on the big day; be wary of people who tell you there's no need because they just need "a few secs" to get ready. There are

Fine-Tuned Contracts

When it's time to seal the deal with your ceremony musicians, get it in writing (if you've been paying attention, you already knew this, star pupils). Be sure to include:

- ☐ Exact date, arrival time, location.
- ☐ Equipment needed—chairs, music stands, amplifiers. If the musicians are bringing their own, record any extra charges.
- ☐ Attire. You should have a say in what your performers wear, according to your overall ceremony vision.
- ☐ What they will play when. Write in a clause that ensures their flexibility should you need them to play longer (during the prelude, for example); talk to them about some B-list songs should they need to fill time.
- ☐ The names of the exact musicians who will play at your ceremony, plus the names of acceptable substitutes should there be an emergency.
- ☐ Fees and overtime rates.

always last-minute glitches, and you want your musicians to be good and ready long before the first guest arrives.

Price: Ceremony musicians can charge anywhere from $50 to $150 an hour, less if they're students. This typically is a per-performer fee, so the more elaborate you're going, the costlier. Make sure you're in the know about all extras; ask whether there's a two-hour minimum (not uncommon) and how much they'll charge you if you end up needing them to put in overtime. If you're having trouble finding what you want with what you have to spend, scale back your plans or enlist the help of musical friends and relatives in lieu of wedding gifts.

RECEPTION MUSIC

A party without music is like low-fat potato chips: decidedly unsatisfying and *no* fun. Good tunes help create a celebrational mood, get your guests loosened up, and even provide easy conversation fodder for awkward moments when people have nothing to say to each other. ("I just love Neil Diamond, don't you?" "Oh, yeah!")

Your reception is your opportunity to play *all* your fave songs that weren't appropriate for your ceremony, wow the crowd with any amazing dance moves you've patented, and generally let your hair down. Music is the fuel that keeps the party train chugging.

Band vs. DJ

There are two major parties in the reception entertainment scene: live ensembles playing original numbers, covers of popular tunes, and/or traditional standards and disc jockeys spinning records, usually in an eclectic mix of styles. Live music is seen by many as the traditional, dignified uncle with good taste; DJs as the younger, hipper, less-refined cousin. We can honestly say that both options can be spectacular or sorry; it all depends on the talent of the performer/s.

In a perfect world—where money is no object—to-be-weds probably would choose a little of both: a live band to please the more upright guests alternating sets with a DJ who'll excite the club kids. Heck, in an ideal universe you'd have your very own Weddingpalooza, with a variety of acts—a big band, a Latin house DJ, a folk singer, a punk band—in different rooms. But since you probably don't have unlimited funds to spend on your merrymaking, most likely you'll opt for either the band *or* the DJ, each of which has its pros and cons. Whichever route you go, remember that top talent will be booked up to a year in advance; the sooner you make reception music arrangements, the better.

Tune Time

Whether you hire a band or DJ, you may want to consider saving the dancing until after the meal (playing only ambient music while guests are eating). That allows for uninterrupted party time on the dance floor.

Bring on the Band

Many bands and orchestras specialize in wedding receptions, but your favorite local rockers also can be the entertainers at your wedding. The important thing is that the performers are fun, excited, sensitive to the crowd, and open to all of your suggestions.

CLAIRE & MATTHEW

May 4, Hempstead, Texas

CLAIRE AND MATTHEW wanted to have their wedding in a place that combined, as Claire describes it, "a down-home Texas feel and elegant Southern tradition," a mood that Liendo, an 1853 plantation house with a history of entertaining Texas high society, captured exactly. Not that the couple envisioned a stiff, formal affair: "We wanted our guests to kick off their shoes and dance—which they did," says Claire.

During the long, relaxed cocktail hour that followed the ceremony, a band played Cajun tunes while guests mingled on the lawn. But it was after dinner, when the Ronnie Renfrow Band took the stage, that the party began to really take off. The twenty-five-person band could play any request from country to Cajun to R&B, and the packed dance floor was testament to their skill. Says Claire, "They played the whole night and kept everyone out on the dance floor until the wee hours. It was definitely one of the best things about the night, because we both love to dance and really wanted everyone to have fun dancing at the wedding." When the party finally wound down, guests left with musical favors—CDs burned with favorite songs of the bride and groom—to remind them of the night they spent on the dance floor.

Cocktail Hour/Dinnertime Music

During the first hour or two of your reception, mingling, talking, sipping (of cocktails), and nibbling (of food) are going to be the greatest hits. You want the music playing to be:

Soft. The decibel level should be such that chatting is a breeze. The better your guests get to know each other at this stage, the more fun the rest of the party will be.
Romantic. Slide smoothly from your emotionally charged ceremony into your reception festivities by starting things off with lots of love songs.
Relaxing. Help everybody kick back.

If you can afford it, hire a string quartet, jazz combo, or harpist/flutist duo in addition to your main reception performers (perhaps the same people that played during your ceremony). A pianist/torch singer is another option—and very hip in today's cigar-happy, martini-worshipping world. If you don't want to spend the money (and energy) necessary to book an additional act, simply ask your band or DJ to think "mellow" for an hour or so. Request instrumental music, whether classical, easy listening, or jazz. Or ask your DJ to play "lounge" and "ambient" music, decidedly modern, laid-back, and oh-so-groovy club favorites.

Pros: There's something about the liveness of a band that's infectiously energetic. If they're good, they can get a crowd moving like nobody's business. A charismatic bandleader also can be a great master of ceremonies.

Cons: Generally more expensive than a DJ, a band also loses in the man vs. machine department—they'll peter out before a sound system ever does. (You'll have to pay extra for alternates to play during band breaks.) Also, even the most open-minded of music ensembles does not have the repertoire of a standard disc jockey, who can easily tote around stacks of different albums. And no matter how good they are, covers of songs never match the sound of the real things.

While this shouldn't make or break your decision, there's also the issue of people. See, you have to feed all of your entertainers, and an eight-person band costs more than a one-man DJ.

Disc Jockey in the House

DJs are becoming the increasingly popular option for weddings. They also are becoming more sophisticated, collecting a balanced and eclectic mix of musical styles conducive to all-ages affairs.

Pros: DJs are generally cheaper than bands. You also have more control over the sound of the songs—whatever your favorite recordings are, you can have 'em played—the variety of musical styles, and the length of the party. (Experienced DJs have enough tricks up their sleeve to last through a party that goes all night long; bands, understandably, can't play for much longer than five or six hours.) When DJs take breaks, they can play a great compilation record to keep the party going.

Cons: Disc jockeys do seem a little less personal than bands; for example, they can't time the song to match your dancing style during your first dance (and you worked so hard on that over-the-shoulder, through-the-legs move) or improvise to accommodate sweet surprises (your kids joining in the dance with you all excited, for example). The worst of them are also really cheesy, playing tired party songs (the macarena, the chicken dance, and anything with the words "Boogie, Oogie, Oogie" in it), wearing sequined vests, and making goofy comments.

Hiring Your Reception Entertainers

Good word-of-mouth is music to your ears. However, nothing compares to observing performers in action when it comes to finding a band or DJ that really can rock your (and your guests') world.

Get Your Hands on a Band

Bands that specialize in weddings can be tracked down by asking for referrals from newlyweds you know, your site coordinator, your wedding consultant, or another in-the-know vendor. As with every other wedding professional, the Internet has made this process infinitely easier, thanks to MPEGs and other music files. By listening to music samples online, you can literally weed out the good bands without leaving your desk. You could, of course, hire a bar band you've seen and loved; be extra-diligent about telling them what you want and need since they won't be as familiar with wedding protocol.

Let the Music Play

Some local branches of the American Federation of Musicians (212–869–1330) keep records of area musicians who play special events; call for referrals.

What to Look For: Go see the band in action, preferably at a similar function (although a club gig or videotape will do). Watch how the musicians interact with the audience: loud, gaudy, rude, and peacocklike strutting are bad; pleasantries, enthusiasm, and flexibility (playing audience requests, for example) are good. You also might want to look for an act that can play a wide variety of styles if it's important to you to get *everyone* up and hopping. When you see a band you like, schedule a meeting with the leader and discuss the type of music you'll want them to play as well as whether you want him/her to coordinate the reception "happenings," such as announcing the cutting of the cake and your major dances. Make sure s/he reacts with enthusiasm and openness.

What It'll Cost: A four-piece ensemble generally will charge between $1,000 and $4,000 for four hours of work, although prices can be significantly higher at peak times, in major cities, and for top talent. You generally will have to put down a 20 to 50 percent deposit. (Don't put down more than half of the total cost.)

Questions to Ask:

- What is their specialty? Needless to say, asking a really great swing band to play '70s jazz is simply asking for trouble.
- Does the band know your reception space and its acoustic and amplification requirements? If not, will they check it out beforehand?

- If you listen to/watch an audio- or videotape of the band, is it recorded live or studio produced? Is the sound technically enhanced? You want to hear how they *really* sound.
- How would they describe their style?
- No matter what their repertoire is, can they play other songs important to you, such as a horah or other ethnic classics and favorite pop hits?
- If you have an original or esoteric piece you want played, will they learn it and how much lead time do they need? What do they charge to arrange it?
- How many musicians are in the band? How many vocalists? Are there different options as far as how many musicians/instruments you can hire?
- Would you need to rent any instruments (a piano, for example)?
- Does the band use techno-tricks such as sampling? (You may or may not want these.)
- Will the band bring its own sound system? How large a room can it accommodate?
- Can the bandleader or another band member act as master of ceremonies?
- Who will do the setup and how early will they do it?
- Does the band have another gig before or after yours? Is the band prepared to play overtime?

The Way to a DJ

The best method for finding a good party DJ is, as usual, word of mouth. You also can call local dance clubs you like—and even radio stations—for references. Some of the best DJs work for professional entertainment companies that hire a fixed roster of spinmeisters. Check online or in local magazines for listings.

Band Contract Points

- ☐ Date, exact time, and location of the reception.
- ☐ Band's starting time and estimated total hours.
- ☐ During which stages of the reception they'll be playing (cocktail hour, after dinner).
- ☐ How many breaks they can take and whether taped music will play during that time.
- ☐ The names of the band members who will play and what instruments they're bringing.
- ☐ The names of acceptable substitute musicians in case of emergency.
- ☐ Emcee duties, if any.
- ☐ Commitment to play key songs.
- ☐ What equipment the band will bring and what you need to provide, including chairs, stage, amplifiers, speakers, etc.
- ☐ What they should wear.
- ☐ Whether you'll be serving them meals (some bands have this written into their contract).
- ☐ The negotiated rate, plus hourly overtime fees.
- ☐ Cancellation and refund policy.

ANNE & JASON

October 20, Canterbury, Connecticut

FOR EIGHT MONTHS before their wedding, Anne and Jason took swing dance lessons in preparation for their first dance to "More," by Bobby Darin, as played by their ten-piece wedding-day band. Their dance instructor choreographed a dance especially for the occasion, and the bride and groom practiced their moves until they had the routine perfected. On the wedding day, in preparation for all the lifts and throws, Anne changed out of her wedding gown and into a short, wedding-white swing dress and then changed back when the dance was over. She says, "Some of the moves were quite complicated, including lifts and throws, so it would have been impossible in a wedding gown." The couple's performance didn't reveal their predance nerves, and got the party off to a very spirited start. "It was a big hit with our guests, who had no idea that the lessons had progressed so far," Anne reports.

What to Look For: Attend one of the DJ's events, if possible, and see that s/he skillfully reads the crowd, is polite, and takes requests. At the very least, you should have a face-to-face interview where you explain which musical genres you like, specific songs that are on your must-have list, and information about the demographics of your guests (ages, ethnic groups, hipness factor). Make sure the DJ is attentive and sharp, asking questions that show s/he comprehends the situation. You may even want to ask to see the person's record collection; have him/her pull albums from the different genres you're into. It's a must to get phone numbers of other couples who have used the person's services; you want to make sure s/he is familiar with wedding protocol and etiquette and is sensitive to the sentimentality of the event.

What It'll Cost: Fees range from about $500 to $2,000 for a four-hour reception, with higher prices on the weekends, during heavy party months, and for big-name DJs, such as radio or club celebs. You also will pay more for more elaborate equipment (better speakers, for example) and a backup DJ.

Questions to Ask:

- Will the DJ or the agency check out the electrical requirements and acoustics at your venue, especially if s/he hasn't worked there before?
- What does the equipment look like? Does the DJ need a draped table for the CD player?
- What size are the speakers, and can they be camouflaged?
- Does the DJ plan to use any funky lighting?
- Is s/he comfortable with the emcee role as well as spinning tunes?
- Can s/he ensure a comfortable sound level for everyone in attendance, from the seventeen-year-olds to the eighty-seven-year-olds?

Toning Down the Entertainers

Don't forget to talk to your DJ or bandleader about how little or much you want *him/her* to talk. You may want him/her to give your guests cues at big moments ("Ladies and gents: It's cake time!"), but that's probably all. This is one of the important reasons to see the performer in action: You don't want to be stuck with a blabbermouth.

ASK CARLEY

Getting Your Tunes Played

Q: A lot of people have told us they had trouble getting their band or DJ to play the songs they wanted. How can we avoid this?

A: Our number-one tip: Talk to other couples who have used the performer to make sure that s/he's the play-what-*you*-want type. Then take a few extra precautions. Print out a list of your must-have songs and at what stage of the party you'd like them played, if you have a preference. Give your DJ/bandleader the list well in advance of the big day so s/he can get hold of sheet music or recordings. Then put one of your friends—someone who's assertive and knows music—in charge of monitoring things during the reception. Your delegate should have your must-have list and be willing and able to coax your vendor into playing your songs.

DJ Contract Points

- ☐ Date, exact time, and location of the reception.
- ☐ DJ's starting time and estimated total hours.
- ☐ During which stages of the reception s/he will perform.
- ☐ How many breaks they can take and whether taped music will play during that time.
- ☐ The name of the DJ(s).
- ☐ The name of an acceptable substitute in case of an emergency.
- ☐ Emcee duties, if any.
- ☐ Commitment to play key songs (and *not* play certain songs you hate).
- ☐ What equipment the DJ will bring and what you need to provide.
- ☐ What s/he should wear.
- ☐ Whether you'll be serving him/her a meal.
- ☐ The negotiated rate, plus hourly overtime fees.
- ☐ Cancellation and refund policy.

Home-Grown DJ

If you're really tight on cash, take the do-it-yourself approach. Burn a stack of great CDs, or borrow a 200-CD changer from a high-tech friend. You may also be able to rent one from your local rental center. Rent a high-quality sound system (your reception site might have one) and put a trusted friend or two in charge of the music. As long as you nab decent speakers, you're set.

Getting Everyone Groovin'

Any good band or DJ knows that there's an art to playing music. Like a well-constructed play, a party has a beginning, middle, and end. Your reception playlist should manipulate the audience skillfully, building up momentum and excitement with crowd-pleasing hits, providing an ample crescendo of the wildest and most party-friendly of tunes, and then winding things down with smooth, soulful, and sexy music. There are, as well, some super-important acts (your dances with each other and with your parents) that merit super songs.

Today's radio airwaves are awash with different types of music. For your reception, especially if most of your guests share your taste, you might choose one overall sound—hiring a reggae band or a country-western DJ, say. Most likely, however, you'll ask your musicians or DJ to play an eclectic

ASK CARLEY

Intergenerational Dancing

Q: We're inviting guests of all ages to our wedding, and we want there to be much dancing at the reception. Help!

A: No problem. What you need to focus on with your band or DJ is *variety.* Ask them to play songs that span a variety of decades, from 1930 Big Band standards to today's hits. Start the party off with songs so popular that everyone will know and enjoy them. Think Beatles, Elvis, Tina Turner—the major league. Disco classics, swing, and salsa are also intergenerational favorites. As the evening progresses—and presumably your less dance-happy relatives and friends of the family bid you adieu—feel free to shift into serious party mode, playing more dance, house, hip-hop, or alternative rock. With a healthy dose of sensitivity and open-mindedness, Frank Sinatra and Nirvana *can* coexist.

mishmash of tunes. That way you have more of a chance of making *everybody* happy (all right, almost everybody—as far as your Uncle Simon is concerned, Duran Duran is the only band worth its weight in solid gold) and ensuring that your dance floor is permanently crowded.

The best wedding bands and DJs know that genre-bending is the key to success. Even if you've enlisted the services of your favorite alternative-rock act, they should be open to going mainstream here and there, playing some Beatles or Aretha Franklin. Check that your DJ carries a potpourri of different records, so that even if you've asked for a predominantly hip-hop repertoire s/he'll be able to mix in some Kool & the Gang and Rolling Stones for variety's sake. Every genre has its charm and distinct way of moving people.

Dancers of the World Unite

Sure, organized dances are dorky, but with the right mix of good people, good champagne, good vibes, and good tunes, they also can be wildly entertaining. Depending on your musical tastes—and coordination—there are many different dances to do.

Country Western: Texas two-step ("Forever and Ever Amen" by Randy Travis); West Coast Swing; cha-cha; El Paso; Sweetheart Schottish; square dance ("Turkey in the Straw")

Ethnic Flair: horah (Jewish); depke (Greek); jig (Irish); tango (Latin America); tarantella (Italian); Highland fling (Scottish); polka (Polish)

Pure Goofiness: limbo; conga line (Cugat's "The Conga" or Barry Manilow's "Copacabana"); chicken dance; macarena

CHAPTER EIGHTEEN

something favorable

Favors have become a staple in the world of weddings, mostly because they're the most fun way to express your creativity (and the options are literally endless). Brides and grooms love them because they're a fun way to give something back and to say "Thank you for coming and sharing this day with us."

The Favor 411

Favors are now a required element—though it's likely that people won't miss or expect them. They're also a great way to carry out a reception theme, to give your friends and family something to remember the day by, and to give a little extra style to each and every table.

When and Where: Guests usually find favors waiting at each place setting when they take their seats. But favors might also be in fun party bags on chairs, piled in baskets by the door, or distributed at the end of the party. You might even use take-away centerpieces—piles of fruit and candy, plastic sand buckets filled with flowers, or individual bud vases with single stems.

The Cost: The great thing about your favors is that there is no set amount you should spend. A lovely favor can be as inexpensive as a small pack of flower seeds, and as extravagant as a bottle of Cristal. You can spend $1.50 to $15.00 per favor—and thankfully, there are plenty of great options out there that fall nicely into that range.

Who Gets What: Everyone at the wedding should get the same favor—or pretty much the same (maybe you're giving out white and red wines, or different travel games, etc.). That means you can't give "extra-special" favors to the wedding party or to your favorite aunt (give them gifts before or after the wedding); and you can't leave out favors for the groom's ex-girlfriend or that girl at work you didn't want to invite anyway.

Singles or Doubles: To cut costs, you can give favors out by couple—this way, folks don't end up with two of whatever it is you're sending them home with. This works best if you're planning on using place cards to designate where people are sitting (you don't want your single friends to leave empty-handed because they sat where a spouse was supposed to sit).

ASK CARLEY

Candy for Kids

Q: I am giving our wedding guests traditional tulle-wrapped candied almonds. We also have a lot of children attending the wedding. Should we give them favors, too?

A: Sure, why not? While their ears may perk up to anything involving the word "candy," they may not appreciate the taste of candied almonds. How about a handful of jellybeans wrapped in clear cellophane and tied with a bow to match your wedding colors? If you are really particular about minute details and consistency, give a cluster of colorful foil-wrapped chocolate eggs to mimic the shape of the tulle-wrapped almonds.

Ways to Give

Favor ideas span the globe—literally. Here's how you can show the love to all of your guests:

Go Familiar: Find favors that really relate to the two of you. If you met in Paris, wrap up a few croissants; if you're bookworms, cool bookmarks would be perfect. Get even more personal with a CD burned with some of your favorite songs—or songs that you plan to play at the wedding (so guests never forget the day).

Go Foodie: Give a regional specialty such as jalapeño jelly from Texas, hot sauce or Cajun spice rubs from Louisiana, Vermont cheddar or maple syrup, Atlantic City saltwater taffy, or Yankee cider from the Northeast. You could also incorporate favors in the reception flow—serve coffee in great imprinted cappuccino cups that guests can keep. You may be able to personalize your food favors—wrap microbrewed ale in specially printed labels for your wedding, or stamp jars of local honey with your names and wedding date. An easy and edible favor: Let guests take home tasty slices of that delicious wedding cake (just have pretty boxes printed with your wedding info set aside).

Go Functional: Favors don't have to just be aesthetically pleasing—they can be useful, too. Try giving friends and family favors they can take home and start using immediately. Give wine-stoppers or corkscrews, luggage tags, picture frames or photo albums, or even a Swiss Army knife (for the outdoorsy couple).

Go Fun: If you're the type of couple that just wants to have a good time, throw all the "rules" out the window and find favors that are totally irreverent. Give guests a pack of bouncing balls, a yo-yo, a book of crossword puzzles, or a heap of mind-teaser games (anything that would be considered formal or serious).

Go Floral: Symbolize the idea of marriage as a living, growing entity by giving seed packets, flowering plants, or individual flowering bulbs. Or use a dozen individual, potted herbs as centerpieces, and let guests choose their own. If you're really ambitious, you could grow your own favors. But if the idea of developing a green thumb for your wedding scares you, run with the floral theme and leave the sowing and reaping to someone else—give notepads adorned with flowers, satchels filled with lavender and other potpourri, or a floral-scented candle.

More Fantastic Favors

Want more ideas? Here are some of our favor-ites:

Travel-related

- Spanish-style multicolored paper fans folded at each place setting, with guests' names scripted on the handles, make a gorgeous display in any venue.
- For the bride with a few more bucks, Italian-style hand-blown glass ornaments are sure to be a crowd pleaser.
- For the couple that loves to travel, send guests (and their bags) home with personalized brass luggage tags boxed and tied with a "Thanks for Coming" ribbon.
- A set of four mint-chocolate shamrocks wrapped with a green organza ribbon will keep those Irish eyes smiling.
- Having a destination wedding? Send guests a travel guide (e.g., *Fodor's* or *City Smart*) of the city where you will wed prior to the wedding to help familiarize them with your chosen location. They can substitute for favors given at the reception.

Relaxation

- Send guests home in a state of relaxation with engraved meditative stones. Package them in boxes decorated with a meditative mantra (e.g., "Love conquers all") scripted on a scroll matching your wedding-day colors.
- Give a collection of small votive aromatherapy candles or one large aromatherapy pillar candle wrapped in tulle and tied with ribbon.
- For a meditative flare, place calm-inducing herbal incense like jasmine or lavender tied with a raffia ribbon at each table.
- Give your guests scrolled astrological readings tied with sheer ribbon (make sure you ask everyone to write their birth date on their RSVP card).

Seasonal

- Count down to the start of the New Year by placing little silver bedside clocks tied with white and silver ribbons at each place setting.
- Give guests attending your winter wedding a frosted snowflake cookie in a glassine bag tied with a white satin ribbon.
- A Valentine's Day wedding calls for miniature heart-shaped, hand-painted boxes with a single delectable truffle tucked inside.
- Send guests home with a scoop of kisses, Hershey's Kisses that is, wrapped in silver and red foil, resting in a silver ice cream scooper.
- Place handmade Easter eggs dipped in decorative colors in mini Easter baskets.
- Rest miniature watering cans filled with fresh spring blooms at each place setting.
- Supply small colorful umbrellas in case of April showers on your big day.
- Sand dollars might make a good memento for a summer beach wedding.
- Hand out sparklers for an outdoor Fourth of July celebration. Your guests can enjoy illuminating the skies once the sun goes down—and lighting your grand exit.
- Caramel apples are the perfect ending to a Halloween or autumn wedding.
- Marrying around the holidays? Give Christmas ornaments in ivory, silver, or gold tied with a deep burgundy or forest-green velvet ribbon with the bride's and groom's names and wedding date.

Sweet Charities

On a day when you are showered with so much love and affection (not to mention gifts!), think about giving a little something back. Instead of traditional wedding favors, put your money where your heart it. You can make a donation in each guest's name to a charity of your choice. Below are five of our favorites.

You can find more information on hundreds of charities at Justgive.org.

The American Red Cross. Over a hundred years old, this organization provides relief to victims of disaster. It's important that we support this cause both for our own lives and the lives of others. Make a donation: Red cross.org.

National Park Foundation. Founded in 1967, it works to preserve the beauty and life in our nation's parks. This is a smart and appropriate gift if you're having an outdoor affair. Make a donation: Nationalparks.org.

First Book. This recently founded literacy organization for kids provides low-income children in America with new books of their own. As clichéd as it sounds, the children are our future . . . let's encourage them to read. Make a donation: Firstbook.org.

Habitat for Humanity. Founded in 1976, the goal of this organization is to ameliorate poverty by asking volunteers to create and provide homes for the homeless. While you

Charity Favors

Beth and Alan planted trees in the name of each guest who attended their October wedding. They made arrangements through the National Arbor Day Foundation, which plants trees in national forests that have been destroyed by fire, insects, or disease. They also have a rain forest protection program. "We wanted to give something more meaningful and lasting than candy, matches, or wine," explains Beth. "We knew we wanted to do a charitable favor, but didn't want to just donate money. With the trees, each person knows there is a tree out there that has been planted just for them, which makes it very special and personal."

How They Did It: "I did it all online in about ten minutes!" exclaims Beth. Weeks before the wedding, she logged on to the National Arbor Day Foundation's website at arborday.com, visited the donate-a-tree section, and paid with a credit card.

The Cost: $130 ($1 per guest)

The Presentation: For each place setting, Beth and Alan designed small white cards that included an image of a tree and text that described the charitable donation. They included the following quote: "Enter the forest and the boundaries of nations are forgotten. It may be that some time an immortal pine will be the flag of a united and peaceful world."

and your sweetie are looking for your first pad together, you can help another couple find theirs. Make a donation: Habitat.org.

American Cancer Society. Nearing its one hundredth birthday, this organization provides a national consciousness of cancer prevention, education, and treatment. For those who have lost a loved one to the disease, it's the perfect way to acknowledge those who cannot (physically) be with you on your special day. Make a donation: Cancer.org.

CHAPTER NINETEEN

wheeling and dealing

Getting the show on the road means enlisting some top-notch transportation, and then mapping out the timing and the routes down to the last detail. Now is the time to grab an itinerary of your wedding day, a list of the main characters, and a map—and get ready to start your engines. Here's how to prepare for the ride of your life.

Setting the Budget

Traditionally, the bride's family pays for the bride's and bridesmaids' tranportation (to the ceremony, reception, and wherever the couple is going afterward), plus any parking expenses. The groom's family covers just the groom's and best man's ride to the ceremony. Depending on who's footing the bill for other wedding items, transportation and parking fees can and should

Getting Stretched

A limousine departure from your wedding reception is classic, classy, and, face it, more comfortable than the backseat of your uncle's Tercel. If you're going to rent—as opposed to buy, borrow, or steal—keep the following in mind:

Reserve at least six months in advance. A last-minute limo search is more likely to net you a car that says "Take us to the mortuary!" than something long and weddinglike.

Shop around. Call more than one service and compare prices. The national average is around $50 per hour plus a 15 percent tip.

Check the car out in person. One person's luxury is another's fuzzy dice. While you're there, also ask what the driver will be wearing. (For this event, appropriate means black jacket and tie, not a Winger T-shirt and jeans.)

Sign a contract. You'll want the full terms in writing, including total price, deposit, overtime, cancellation policies, and confirmation of all dates, times, and locations.

Haggle for extras. A TV's nice, but champagne's better. Work the charm and see what they'll throw in gratis.

Consider the color. If you're not a stickler for all things white, black and silver limos generally cost 10 per cent less.

Make sure the driver knows where he's going!

be easy to split between families. When renting cars, you're likely to be charged by the hour, and you will probably be required to contract the cars for a minimum amount of time. No matter what the wheels, a 15 to 20 percent gratiuity will almost always be added to your bill.

If you're on a tight budget and you're not a stickler for color, opt for a black or silver limo over a white one; the former generally cost 10 percent less. And leave out the TV, full bar, and sunroof. You might also plan to arrange for pickup and drop-off service only, so that drivers aren't waiting around (and getting paid) for the duration of the reception. Know this, though: The couple should be assured a ride home—or to the hotel or the airport—when the festivities are over. This is something an honor attendant (usually the best man) should provide or oversee.

Transportation Contract Points

We never tire of saying it: Don't even think about hiring your transportation vendor without getting everything in writing. You'll have peace of mind—and a piece of paper—to ensure it all goes smoothly. Points your contract should include:

- arrival time (pad an extra twenty minutes for safety's sake)
- reception departure time
- addresses of places where you'll need to be picked up and dropped off
- the size, color, and model of the car (with the license-plate number if you've chosen something specific)
- the name of the driver you want
- gratuity
- any special requests that you have, like champagne or a CD player

Making the Reservations

In general, it's best to reserve your ride about six months in advance. And if your wedding falls during prom time or graduation season (late March to late June) tack on another month or two just to be on the safe side. But be sure to call around and compare prices first.

Once you've found something in your price range, insist on checking out the actual car you'll be using. Then copy down the license plate number to make sure it's the same vehicle that shows up on your wedding day (have an attendant investigate this). You might also want to meet the driver and make sure you're both on the same page in terms of his or her duties and attire. Many limo drivers take on the additional responsibility of rolling out a red carpet for the bride, often at no additional cost, so be sure to ask about such flourishes if you're interested.

After you've hammered out the details, get it all in writing. A contract protects you and the limousine company. It should clearly state the date, correct locations, pickup times, specific vehicle, costs of any extras (such as champagne), hourly rate, estimated total cost, amount of deposit, overtime fees (if any), and cancellation policy.

The Preparation

We can't say it enough: Prepare a call sheet with names and all pickup/drop-off addresses and times, so that you (or preferably a maid or groomsman) can call to confirm these arrangements with the transportation company the day before, or the morning of, the wedding. The drivers should have this information well in advance, in addition to detailed directions to the ceremony and reception sites. Also make sure that everyone getting a ride has a copy of the directions stashed in their pockets or purses, with an emergency contact number in case the driver gets lost.

Getting to the Ceremony

Generally, the bridesmaids ride to the wedding ceremony with the bride. Meanwhile, the groom and groomsmen will require similar arrangements. If you have a large entourage, you're probably going to need a stretch limo or SUV. But many brides want to have private time with mom and dad on the way to the ceremony, and they may choose to hire one limo for the three of them and another for the bridesmaids (or they may simply have the wedding party drive themselves, or ask a friend to take them). The groom's parents like to arrive stylishly, too.

The solution? Take a head count and then calculate your needs. Be sure to allow space for the wedding gown—big petticoats, billowing skirts, and long trains need plenty of room. Here's a breakdown of average vehicle capacities: stretch limos, ten to twelve passengers; limos, six passengers; town cars, two to four passengers; personal cars, two to four passengers.

If you don't know exactly how long it will take to travel from prewedding hangouts to the ceremony site, drive the routes first yourself. Add in some time for possible traffic tangles and dealing with the chaos of getting a large group of nervous, gussied-up people into the car—figure you want to arrive at the site fifteen minutes before it's time to hit the aisle—and you have yourself a departure time. Schedule the limousine to arrive at least twenty minutes before your departure.

Including the Finer Things

In many cases, you can have your limo service provide you with a bottle of champagne and glasses free of charge. Some will even supply fresh flowers and a "Just Married" sign. Many even offer special wedding packages that include some or all of these little treats. If this isn't the case for you, put your honor attendant in charge of filling the car with goods. Things to include:

- The bubbly and glasses
- A plate or two of reception food
- A few pieces of wedding cake
- Utensils
- Napkins
- A cozy blanket
- A romantic mixed CD

Getting to the Party

In most cases, limousines that carry the wedding party to the ceremony will wait until the knot is tied and then take everyone to the reception. Postceremony, the bride and groom will leave together in their own car while the rest of the party and parents shuffle into the other limousines. Often the bride and

ASK CARLEY

Party on Wheels?

Q: We're looking for an inexpensive way to transport the bridal party. (We can just barely pay for a limo for ourselves!) Any suggestions?

A: Hey, getting there really *is* half the fun. It's up to you to make sure your attendants are where they're supposed to be, so now's the chance to flex your creative motoring skills. Ask around; maybe friends have vintage cars you can borrow for the day. For a rustic feeling, go for a tractor pulling a flatbed full of hay. We also love the thought of piling everyone into a camper for the ultimate portable party. With so many cool options, no one will be left behind.

groom choose to keep only one chauffeured car and let the additional limousines go after providing rides to the ceremony. This option will save money, but it can be a hassle. Do you really want your mom standing in the middle of the parking lot trying to hitch a ride?

If you do forgo a formalized ride, the wedding party can tag along with friends and relatives, but be sure that these rides are arranged at least one week before the wedding day. If you're taking pictures with the wedding party after the ceremony, make sure they know where to meet and at what time (just in case their rides want to take a detour on the way to the reception).

After the limos drop off the newlyweds and bridal party at the reception, one limo may wait for the duration of the party for the bride and groom's postreception getaway. The bridal party will usually have to make their own postparty transportation arrangements.

Extended Play

Have you thought about how you're getting home from the honeymoon? We love the idea of having a limo—or a specialty vehicle—pick you up at the airport to get that full we're-fabulous-newlyweds feeling. While you're at it, hang a banner that says "Just Honeymooned!" Consider it the last fun sign you'll get to show off before "Baby on Board."

Should You Include the Guests?

It does make some couples nervous to have their out-of-town wedding guests driving from place to place in an unfamiliar city or town, especially when they're on a schedule (not to mention drinking). In an effort to enable guests to relax and let their hair down at the party, more and more couples are choosing to provide transportation from the hotel to the ceremony, to the reception, and then back again to the hotel. In-town guests might even want to hitch a ride. It's not only safer, it's also fun—kind of like a school field trip, only your wedding is the planetarium. Let guests know you're giving them a ride by leaving copies of an itinerary with all the info at the hotel, and have the hotel staff hand it out as guests check in. If guest transportation is out of your budget, a small luxury bus for the wedding party and parents might be in order. Allow time if, for example, the bus will pick up the bridesmaids at the bride's home before the ceremony and then meet the groomsmen elsewhere before heading off to the big event.

Decorating Don't

If you think your friends might go berserk decorating your luxury getaway car with oodles of trailing cans and streamers, find out if the car company you are using allows it. Most don't, and it could end up costing a hefty clean-up fee. Instead, give a hint to your buds that they might want to check out some removable window stickers emblazoned with the "Just Married" slogan, which some car companies even provide.

Shooting the Getaway

Never underestimate the dramatic power of paparazzi pictures. If you really want to have a memorable ride to and from the wedding, make sure your photographer and videographer join you in the vehicle to capture all the giddy, nervous moments en route to the ceremony and the rosy, elated moments as you ride away. A stunning, ultra-glamorous shot of the bride and groom locking lips through the back window or waving good-bye in a convertible is a classic image.

ASK CARLEY

Parental Protocol

Q: After the ceremony, we are providing a limo to take our wedding party to the reception, but we're unsure if we should offer one to our parents. What is proper and polite?

A: If you are on a limited budget, most parents will understand that it may not be financially feasible for you to offer them a limo to the reception. Depending on how much they're helping out the day of the wedding, they may need to lag behind to tie up loose ends at the ceremony site as you make your way toward the party. Discuss your concern with your parents beforehand, and, above all, make certain they are taken care of and comfortable. Surely a relative or friend can give them a lift, if necessary.

CHAPTER TWENTY

giving and getting

Well, it looks like you've hit the jackpot with this wedding thing: Weddings equal gifts galore. From your engagement announcement to beyond your big day, you'll be showered with presents as loved ones celebrate your commitment. That means it's time to brush up on your knowledge of giving and getting.

Daydreaming about, registering for, and weathering the downpour of gadgets, trinkets, baubles, and cold, hard cash you'll get during the next year or so is one of the perkiest perks of engagement. What's really great, though, is the intense show of love and support these gifts represent. With their presents to you, your friends and family are blessing your union and contributing to your blissful future. Those thoughts are the best gifts of all—and a great motivator when it comes to penning those thank-you notes.

Signing Up for Stuff: Registering

Today's most popular present-related wedding tradition is, of course, the bridal registry. (Why it's called the bridal registry is beyond us—men use toasters, too!) This modern practice gets the happy couple prancing around a store (or a website), identifying objects that they would really, really like to own; having the retailer keep a record of these coveted items; passing on the word of where they've registered to family and close pals; giddily waiting as guests scout their choices and decide what to spring for; and receiving a bunch of packages containing their carefully selected treasures.

If registering sounds like winning the grand prize on a wacky game show, that's because it kind of is. You're big winners in the lottery of love, and registering is your reward.

Lest you think, however, that registering is a tacky fishing-for-presents tactic, remember that the most compelling reason for doing it is to help *your guests* in the daunting process of choosing gifts that you'll love and actually use. Sure, your closest friends and relatives probably have a good idea of the perfect wedding present for the two of you, something that will blow your socks off. But most people—those who aren't familiar with your board game fetish or your love of African art—need a hand. By registering (or at least making your gift preferences known to a select group of people who can discreetly spread the gospel), you're not dictating exactly what a guest should get you but rather offering a wide variety of suggestions guaranteed to make your day. Even if guests choose to be original and go out of registry, you've given them a good idea of the kinds of stuff you like, want, and need.

Register at Home

Exhausted from trolling the aisles in search of the perfect stuff to register for? Register online—it's super-convenient! At The Knot Wedding Gift Registry (www.theknot.com) you can sign up for everything from a tent to fine china, from Colombian coffee to bath towels. You'll make your guests' lives easier, too; they can shop from home. Call 1-888-WED-KNOT (888-933-5668) for information.

How to Do It: Registering Rx

Setting up a gift registry is not brain surgery, but there are some fundamental laws that will make the process go smoothly. With a little research, advance planning, and attention to detail, you two can quickly become bona fide gift gurus.

Time It Right: It's a good idea to set up a registry soon after your engagement, in time for all those prewedding bashes. In general, department stores suggest you firm up your present plans six to nine months before the big day. But since most gifts actually are purchased closer to your wedding, it makes sense to register even if you have only two months or less left—just get the word out lickety-split. On the other end, if you have more than one year to go before your big day, *don't* register right away; items you select now could go out of stock, even be discontinued, by wedding time.

Know Thyselves: Classic home accessories such as formal place settings, silverware, and fancy bed linens are customary registry items (and sweet things to have), but that may not be your bag. Maybe you've been playing house for a while and you already own all that stuff. Or perhaps you're into minimalist decor or eating out every single night of your lives. Luckily, today's couples have a huge range of options when it comes to registering, from contributions toward a dream honeymoon to handsome hardware tools. Whether you're going the major department store route or registering at a funky local boutique, sit down as a team and figure out what type of stuff you want to focus on. This will cut down on leg cramps caused by too much time spent wandering the aisles and paper cuts resulting from excessive catalog skimming. Having trouble finding a route that makes both of you smile?

We Can't Give It Back

Don't register at a shop that has unreasonable return deadlines. You don't want to get back from your honeymoon and find out you're stuck with four electric toothbrushes, useful as they are.

Don't Feel Restricted: It's become increasingly popular for couples to register at multiple places. For one, it helps when guests are scattered around the country—they may not have Store A near them, but they live down the street from Store B. Also, it will help give balance to your registries so that you both get things you enjoy. So, set up at least two registries—one for his gourmet cookware, one for your outdoorsy gear.

Get in the Know: Once you've narrowed down your options, get some important info on your dream store's registry policies (or how it can accommodate you if it doesn't have an established program). To figure out if what it's got is going to work for you, ask lots of questions:

- How do they keep track of the registry? You want the store to use a computer database, so gifts can be checked off your wish list as they're bought.
- Do they accept credit-card purchases by phone or fax? If you have lots of guests

coming from far away, you want them to be able to use your registry easily. The shop should be able to fax your guests your wish list and take their orders from a distance.

- Do they ship? Your best bet is a retailer that can arrange direct shipment of your gifts to an address you give them (yours, your honey's parents, etc.) so guests are spared a trip to the post office or the hassle (for them *and* you) of bringing gifts to the reception.
- Do they allow for easy refunds/exchanges? Even with the best technology in place, you may end up with duplicates and triplicates of some items. (You're also entitled to change your mind about those orange mohair drapes.) Make sure you're not stuck with them.
- How long will they keep your registry list? Make sure it stays in the store's system for at least a year after your wedding day, because that's how long guests have—etiquette-wise—to buy their gifts.
- Do they have any registering specials? Some stores offer a discount (between 10 percent and 20 percent off) after the wedding day for any items that remain on your registry. A sweet deal, if you have eight china settings left to buy.
- Will they remove gifts purchased elsewhere from your registry? That means, if Aunt June finds the toaster you want for a better price at a store near her, your store will gladly remove it from your registry so that Aunt Mae doesn't buy it also.

Get the Goods Now

When you register, make sure the items you're selecting are not way back-ordered and that the store has them readily in stock. You don't want to wait until your one-year anniversary for that leopard-print bed set (grrrrr!).

Sealing the Deal: After you've selected the gift-registry program/s for you, make sure that it's organized in a way that makes your—and your guests'—lives easier.

ASK CARLEY

No Gifts, Please!

Q: We want to put "please no gifts" on our invites because we disagree with the obligatory gift tradition. Are we tacky or rude for doing this? Are we the only ones who just want our guests to spend our special day with us?

A: Writing "your presence is your present" (or some such) on your invites is a nice way to let guests know that their attendance is the most special part for you—and that you don't want or expect gifts (which, by the way, are common but *not* mandatory). There are many good reasons for not wanting more stuff in your lives; you're not freaks. Perhaps you've been living together for a while and feel you have everything you need. Maybe you're getting married in an exotic location or are planning on a full week of wedding events and don't want your guests to have to spend yet more.

At the same time, recognize that most guests will *want* to get you a gift, something to help you begin your marriage with a bang. People derive joy from giving. While it's not tacky or rude specifically to ask for no gifts, it may make some guests feel awkward. One option is to spread the no-present-please word through close friends and relatives instead of jotting it on the invites. You also could indicate that you'd like guests to make a donation in your name to a favorite charity, so they still feel like they're doing something that makes you happy.

Grace Yourselves: The Traditional Registry

A classic registry includes essential items for a distinguished home, most important of which is the fine dinnerware that a freshly engaged couple (much like yourselves) probably doesn't have yet. We're talking about china, crystal, sterling silver, the works. Even if you think of yourselves as more Cap'n Crunch than caviar, there are some compelling reasons to consider registering for elegant tableware:

It looks great and adds instant pizzazz to any dinner party.
It's perfect for romantic, candlelit dinners for two. (Just remember to clear the table before you hop aboard for—umm—dessert.)
It makes you two bona fide adults.
It can be a beautiful decorative addition to your home—china hung on walls or crystal showcased in a glass cabinet is très elegant.
It's expensive! Might as well let someone else pick up the tab!

If you decide that you want to go the formal dinnerware route, here's what you're looking for:

China: Select a pattern that both of you like, in either procelain or bone. Don't be turned off by visions of your grandmother's cluttered birds-castles-hares-and-fierce-warriors china design; today's fine dishes come in a wide variety of styles, including many simple and chic options. Register for up to twelve five-piece place settings (dinner plate, salad plate, bread and butter plate, cup, and saucer) plus twelve rimmed soup/salad bowls. You also may want to sign up for some matching service pieces (large bowls, platters, a tea set, etc.).
Stemware: Today's crystal designers are keeping the young and hip in mind when doing their thing, carving out sleek and stylish designs. Or you can go the ultra-ornate, romantic crystal route. Register for up to twelve each of water goblets, white wineglasses, red wineglasses, and champagne flutes as well as other barware, such as double old-fashioned glasses, highballs, martini glasses, and a pitcher.
Flatware: The crème de la crème of cutlery is made of sterling silver, which is sparkling, elegant, gorgeous. Regular flatware, made of stainless steel, is slightly less expensive—and has the advantage of being dishwasher-friendly. Whatever you decide, you'll find a wide variety of cuts, ranging from classic curvaceous to modern flat; just find one that just makes you want to stick it in your mouth *now!* Register for up to twelve flatware settings (dinner knife, dinner fork, soup spoon, salad/dessert fork, and teaspoon). You also may register for serving utensils (large spoons and forks, a gravy ladle, a cake server, etc.) and butter spreaders.

- Ask for a registry form on which to indicate your desired objects. Either with the help of a store consultant (usually available at big retailers) or on your own, tour the store, website, or catalog, recording things you want. Include as much detail as possible for any given item, including color, stock number, pattern, size, and number of items where appropriate (these are usually part of the registry form).
- After you've done your picking and choosing, get a master list. Scan it carefully and correct any errors. Make sure the mailing address where you want your gifts to go is clearly indicated.
- Remember to get the name of a contact person when you are setting up your reg-

istry, possibly the registry consultant who guided you through the store. You want to deal with someone who'll know who you are when you call.

- Throughout your engagement, ask for periodic printouts of your registry list to keep tabs on the process, especially after each wave of gifts arrives (engagement party, shower, etc.). Cross off any purchased gifts the store didn't catch. It also should be possible for you to add more items to your list if you find that your generous loved ones are cleaning out your registry.
- If you're feeling particularly control-freaky about the registry, you may have the option of receiving e-mail updates about things that have been purchased from your gift list. This might not appeal to you, however, if you don't want to know when a slew of gifts are being bought right around your "surprise" shower.

Consider Guests' Budgets

Register for gifts in a variety of price ranges, with an emphasis on the $50 to $100 range. It's fine to choose some super-pricey pieces perfect for group gifts, but nice-but-reasonable choices like vases, kitchen appliances, pillowcases, and wineglasses will make you happy without turning your loved ones into paupers.

Gift-Getting Dos and Don'ts

As you can imagine, there's a lot of etiquette surrounding wedding gifts. There's the don't-include-registry-cards-in-invites cardinal rule, the write-thank-you-notes-or-else edict, and, of course, the be-tactful-about-returns law. We trust your healthy, sensible instincts, but we're sure you'll be happy to glean some more wisdom from our vast wedding experience. Here, then, is what we think about some sticky gift subjects.

Money, Money, Money: Cash Gifts

Let's say every single engaged couple in the country were to cram into a huge stadium and we were to ask them (over a high-power loudspeaker system) to raise their hands if they wanted to get cash, cool cash as their wedding gift. Our hunch is that there would be a whole lot of arms in the air. Obviously, there's a good reason for this enthusiasm—more and more young couples already have been living on their own (or together) for a while, and they may own all the plates, towels, sheets, and forks they could ever want. Engagement may be the first time they start thinking seriously about their long-term financial goals—financing a dream honeymoon, buying a house or a cool set of wheels, building up adequate savings for retirement—and some meaty checks would certainly help out.

If you've got dollar-sign gift aspirations, the first thing to remember is *not* to put your wish for moola on your invites. Instead, tell close friends and family that cash is your gift preference; they'll spread the news when guests ask them. Guests who give you checks will either mail them or bring the loot to your wedding, in a card. (Appoint a responsible friend to keep the money on his/her person.)

The most important things to remember about cash gifts are: (1) don't

Create a Registry

If a shop the two of you love doesn't have a registry program, approach the manager and see if you can work something out.

- Photocopy your wish list.
- Ask the manager to keep master list near the register and check off gifts as they're bought.
- Make sure the store can accept credit-card orders over the phone.
- Check in regularly to make sure list is being updated, see if you need to add items, and so on.

impulse-spend; (2) stash your money away in a joint bank account or, preferably, a high-interest mutual fund; (3) have specific goals in mind so you won't be tempted to fritter your bounty away on run-of-the-mill bills (*not* romantic). Decide together that you want any money you receive to go toward a down payment on a house, your annual vacation fund, the biggest stereo system you can get, or another major investment. You may want to enlist the help of a recommended financial planner after you come back from your honeymoon so s/he can tell you how best to put your money to work for you.

GAYLE & IRA

July 13, Benton Harbor, Michigan

WHEN GAYLE AND IRA were planning their wedding, they were looking for the right way to address an issue that was important to them—the fact that they could legalize their commitment when their lesbian and gay friends could not. "We were looking forward to this wonderful day," Gayle says, "and all the love and affirmation you get from everyone, and we found it painful that we would be gaining rights and privileges that our friends are denied."

The couple decided to address this through an unusual "registry": They included cards in their invitations requesting that gifts be in the form of donations to Lambda Legal Defense Fund's Marriage Project, a task force working toward legalization of gay marriage in the United States. "It's a very small step, but it felt important," Ira says. It also helped make their wedding a very personal expression of their values and their shared vision of the world.

Present Potholes: How to Deal

Not every gift you receive is going to be perfect, despite your loved ones' best intentions. Deal with these duds with grace, honesty (okay, white lies), sensitivity, and—most important—gratitude.

Broken Gifts: If the present was shipped by a store, you should be able to get a quick replacement by calling the customer service department. If the package was sent by givers directly, check for a postal insurance stamp. If there is one, simply mail the gift back, with a note of thanks and an explanation, and your friends will be reimbursed by the post office; then they'll rebuy and resend.

If the gift was neither sent by the store nor insured, it's your decision whether to inform the giver of the mishap or not. If you have a hunch the gift was bought using a credit card or carries some sort of insurance policy (i.e., the givers are wise/cautious/credit card-happy), do tell, because they can get an exchange easily and would be sorely disappointed if you didn't get to enjoy their present! However, if the piece looks like a one of a kind or you suspect the giver is creditless, you don't want to make your guest feel like she has to get you *another* gift; send a normal, gushing thank-you note. If you're asked later where the gift is, you always can blame your own personal clumsiness for its demise.

Duplicates: Sometimes—in the case of place settings, bath towels, and margarita glasses—doubles and triples aren't a bad thing. You can stash them away for when their kin break, tear, or wear. However, in the case of sterling silver tea tray, for example, one *is* enough. The great thing about exchanging duplicate gifts is that givers usually will never know you did it. Since you are keeping one of the thing, whatever it may be, you can conveniently attribute it to *all* of the givers (not at the same dinner party, though). If two close friends got you the same thing, however, honesty is the best policy. If asked about the gift, explain you received doubles and show your friend the fab replacement gift you got instead.

Unwanted Wares: It's not broken or duplicated, it's just ugly (not your style). When it comes to exchanging gifts like those Eskimo salt-and-pepper shakers and that Velvet Elvis, be sensitive. If the giver is a close friend or relative who probably will be visiting a lot, you may want to bite the bullet and keep the gift (bringing it out only on visitation days) for your communal happiness. It's fine, however, to exchange a gift from someone who is unlikely either to come over or to get his/her feelings hurt. In any case, do not mention exchanges in your thank-you notes.

Great Monetary Gift Traditions

- China: Guests give the couple money at reception in red envelopes.
- Italy: The reception ends with a receiving (or is it parting?) line, in which guests are given a box or satchel of candies in exchange for envelopes of money.
- Poland: Guests "buy" a dance with the bride to contribute to the couple's honeymoon fund.

Gift Receipts

We should give thanks to the genius who invented the "gift receipt," a slip of paper with the coded price (so you don't know how much they spent), the purchase date, and any other pertinent information that makes returning or exchanging a breeze. If your guests are smart, they'll include one, should you need to take back their gift for some reason. Don't thank them for the gift receipt in your thank-you note, though.

Expressing Your Gratitude

One of the wonderful things about getting married is witnessing your loved ones rallying for you and pulling out all the stops to make your big day huge.

ASK CARLEY

Cancel the Gifts!

Q: If the wedding is called off, do gifts already received have to be returned?

A: Yes. All engagement, shower, *and* wedding gifts, as well as any money, should be sent back to the givers in the case of a breakup. However, if it's been a long time since you got the gift, if you've used the thing, or if you know the giver really well and think s/he would want you to keep it, it's definitely your call whether to return or not to return.

Cashing In?

Make sending out thank-yous for cash gifts a priority. The envelopes and cards money comes in are easy to lose, and guests may fear you didn't receive their present if they don't hear from you promptly.

It's incredible the amount of love, generosity, kindness, support, and even out-and-out sacrifice they display during this period. It's of utmost importance, we're sure you'll agree, to show your gratitude for all this devotion. Here are some pointers on giving thanks where thanks is due.

Thank-You Notes

All right, then, brace yourselves. As fast and loose as we are about all this etiquette stuff, we are definitely *not* letting you off the hook in one department: thank-you notes. Simply put, you've got to thank every single gift-giver. No exceptions! Not optional! Engagement, shower, and wedding presents all apply. Limber up those wrists—it's thanksgiving time.

Who? We are only going to say this once—*both of you* are responsible for sending out thank-you notes. We don't care how bad your handwriting is or how much stress you're under at the office, the gifts you've received were intended for both of you and the karma police insist you both reciprocate. In order to establish equality on this front, divvy up your thank-you list. You send notes to *your* friends, family, and family friends; your honey does the same for his/her posse. Guests who "belong" to both of you get split down the middle.

Go to Chapter 9 for info on ordering your thank-you notes and other stationery.

Why? Because it's the nice thing to do, the right thing to do. Thanking people for their gifts reassures them that you got what they sent. And since most people have their gifts shipped (unless we're talking about engagement party or shower goodies), your thank-you cards are their only way of knowing you actually received the goods.

When? Some random idiot spread the rumor that up to a year after the wedding is an appropriate time frame for sending a thank-you note. Forget it. Etiquette says you should send out thank-yous within one month of receiving a gift (even less time than that when you receive something *before* the wedding). We'll give you a little more leeway; we're hip to how hard it is to juggle your jobs, your busy social life, and honeymoon recovery. Don't get your hopes up too high—we're giving you a few more weeks, not years. You have two months from the time you get back from your 'moon to send out those notes. If you each put aside fifteen minutes daily (or every other day) toward this end, you probably can bang them out at a rate of ten a day. Besides, it'll be fun together time for the two of you. (Play tunes, drink wine/hot chocolate.)

Organized Gratitude

Keep a copy of your invitation mailing list and record every gift you get, as you get it, next to the giver's name. That way you can be sure of writing thank-yous that are accurate, descriptive, and personal—and you'll have your guests' addresses at your fingertips.

How? Traditionally, thank-you notes are written in blue or black ink on simple ecru sheets or folded cards that match your invites. Consider having your stationer create cards with your married name/s or monograms, a pop-up ape holding a "thank-you" banana, colors that match your vibrant reception decorating scheme—or make them yourselves! Whatever you do, remember to purchase/create plenty of cards—you don't want to run out.

What Should They Say? Quite simply, a thank-you note expresses how grateful you are for a gift. The essential thing is to personalize each note by naming the present and addressing your unique relationship with the giver. It doesn't have to be a work of genius; a dash of humor and a sprinkle of loving sentiment are all you need.

Even if the gift wasn't (how shall we say) a "hit," and you're planning to exchange it or sock it away in the dark recesses of your junk closet, still allude to it in your note. You don't have to lie and say you're going to put that Godzilla rug smack in front of your fireplace, but you can say you're sure it will be all the rage at your next cocktail party. Make each guest feel like the effort in selecting your gift was duly noted.

You also should be specific when thanking someone for a gift of money; give as much detail as you possibly can about how you plan to put the generous gift to use (as part of a house down payment or second honeymoon, for example).

The Gifts You Give

Some people's roles in your wedding were, undoubtedly, much greater than just showing up and getting you a groovy gift. Whether their contribution was of money, time, or just old-fashioned running-around-doing-stuff energy, they deserve extra-special thanks for making your wedding the best that it could be. Buying gifts for these amazing individuals should be one of the most enjoyable parts of your wedding planning, a time to let your creative juices flow.

Family: Although it's easy to take them for granted, chances are your folks (and/or your siblings, grandparents, and other close relatives) were an indispensable part of your wedding brigade. Whether they contributed to your budget, scoped out vendors, or provided you a shoulder to cry on, let them know how grateful you are for their support by giving them a personalized gift at your rehearsal dinner or in a more private meeting just before your big day.

Many gifts are appropriate for your parents, from extravagant (a second honeymoon/weekend getaway) to sentimental (a blown-up wedding picture in a nice frame). For other family members, gifts of wedding mementos are great, from lockets with your portrait inside or framed reception snapshots to scarves in your wedding colors and CDs featured heavily during your reception party. If you're strapped for cash, sometimes the nicest thank-you for relatives is the honor of being the first people invited over to see honeymoon pics/slides. Cook up a tasty meal (served on your brand-new dinnerware) and make a festive evening out of it. If your parents and your honey's are friendly, invite them over together—and kill two birds with one lasagna and slide show.

Attendants' Gifts

- Boy toys: remote-control cars, etc.
- A certificate for an acclaimed restaurant
- Bouquet-of-the-Month club membership
- Spa certificates
- Champagne and caviar
- Picnic baskets
- Cufflinks, jewelry, and money clips
- Swiss Army knives
- Tickets to a game or play
- Silk or flannel pajamas
- Beer of the month club
- Cigars, flasks, lighters
- Journals, photo boxes, stationery
- Beauty basket, bath soaps, perfume

Attendants: They calmed your nerves, did your bidding, chatted up your parents' friends. Let's not forget those prewedding parties they helped organize. Give each attendant a gift of gratitude; go a little bigger for the honor attendant and best man. The rehearsal dinner is again a good time for giving, or you can throw a bridesmaids'/attendants' party shortly before the wedding. (We're highly in favor of a special fest exclusively for these hardworking troupers.)

You can go the traditional route and give your attendants something they can wear on the big day, such as cuff links, earrings, bracelets, or silk cravats. You can get everyone an identical item or (our preference) personalize the gifts; for example, your boating friend gets anchor cuff links, financial man gets dollar signs, actor boy gets masks. It's also cool to get your attendants something that has nothing to do with your wedding but everything to do with their enjoyment, such as ritzy bath product baskets or martini glasses. A set of earrings that only match your bridesmaids' dress is a lovely thought, but totally impractical after the big day is over.

Out-of-Town Guests: It's not compulsory, but we just love the idea of showing your devotion to friends and relatives who've made a long haul to come to your wedding. Place a goodie bag or basket in each hotel room before your guests show up. (Ask the hotel early on about distributing your gifts to your guests' rooms.) Our favorite out-of-towner gifts: small wine bottle and box of truffles; guide to the city and a disposable camera; gift bag of small bottles from a bath shop; certificate for a massage (or another amenity) at the hotel; a gourmet fruit basket.

Yourselves: Why not give yourselves a hand for all the hard work, the love, sweat, and tears you poured into making your relationship—and your wedding—such a rip-roaring success? On wedding day, exchange gifts that express your gratitude, devotion, and passion; a mushy card is a must. Getting a wrapped package on the morning of your wedding will help take your minds off the nerves and put an extra bounce in your step. Give your honey an outfit s/he's always wanted, a piece of jewelry, a book with an inscription, a spa certificate, expensive cigars, and the like. Have a private give-and-get session before you start getting ready.

Hosts with the Most

Don't forget to thank all your wedding party hosts (your honor attendant, your neighbors, or your coworkers) with a gift and grateful note. Flowers, wine, or a gourmet food basket are all good choices.

Anniversary Gifts

1st: Paper. Deluxe stationery set, hand-bound photo album, antique book of love poems, gift certificates.
2nd: Cotton. Luxurious bathrobe, chenille sweater, sexy undergarments, pajamas.
3rd: Leather. Cool pants or coat, nice bag or briefcase, fancy organizer, exquisite belt.
4th: Linen. Luxury bedding, nice summer outfit, a hammock.
5th: Wood. Hand-crafted bowl, antique chest, trip to the woods, rocking chair.
6th: Iron. Wrought bed frame, fancy candlesticks, gym membership (iron abs and buns).
7th: Wool. Cozy blanket or shawl, month's worth of warm socks, trip to Wales. (Lots of sheep there.)
8th: Bronze. Deluxe cookware (bronze, copper—close enough), sculpture, piece of jewelry.
9th: Pottery. An art class, certificates for mud mask (and other spa treatments).
10th: Aluminum: Set of fancy silverware, unique choker, durable hiking boots, fireplace tools.
Other important anniversaries: 15th—Crystal; 20th—China; 25th—Silver; 30th—Pearls; 40th—Rubies; 50th—Gold; 60th—Diamonds.

NOTES

CHAPTER TWENTY-ONE

the countdown

You've picked out outfits, pounced on bargains, pounded out vendor contracts, and pored over every detail of your wedding. It's two weeks and counting until the big day. While there are a few last-minute wedding details to attend to, this is the time to savor the moment. No matter how diligent you are, there are always going to be big-day glitches, curve balls, even boo-boos—and that's what will make your wedding unique and wonderful. No amount of obsessing will ensure against surprises, so you might as well just kick back. Trust yourselves—the groundwork you've done and the capable vendors and loved ones you've enlisted to help will ensure that your wedding is fabulous.

Unfinished Wedding Business

By this point, the bulk of your wedding planning has been taken care of. What's left for a couple to do? Mostly tweaking, finessing, and confirming plans with guests and vendors. These tasks can be dispensed with swiftly if you throw yourselves into them with gusto.

The Guest List and Seating

Now's the time to find out, once and for all, who's coming and who's not. The first thing to do just after the two-week mark is to call up people you've invited who haven't sent in their R.S.V.P.'s yet. Simply inquire whether they plan to attend. Divvy up the calls with your honey—each of you can phone the guests you're closest to—and you should be done in no time. (Try not to chit-chat or it *will* take forever.) Once you have your final head count, let your caterer or banquet manager know. For the most part, they'll need to have the details at least ten days in advance.

Depending on the kind of wedding you're having, you may or may not want to assign your guests reception seats. If you've invited under fifty to a lowbrow buffet, it's fine to let things fall into place spontaneously. You also don't need to worry about a seating chart if you're having cocktails or a casual brunch or lunch. On the other hand, if you're serving a seated dinner and your guest list tops a hundred, do yourselves a favor and make a plan. You'll cut down on the overall chaos, keep potential feuds at bay by separating dueling parties, spare your guests the discomfort of feeling like they want to "save" spots and shoo strangers away, and make everyone feel like you've thought of them (especially once they see those nifty place cards and out-of-this-world favors).

Once you have your final head count, nail down how many tables and chairs you're going to need. If you haven't already, ask your banquet manager or maitre d' how many guests each table will seat comfortably. Now you're ready to map out your seating chart.

Draw your reception floor plan on a large sheet of paper, using circles or squares to designate tables, and start penciling in names. Another alternative is to number the tables in your head—for example, deciding that the tables next to the entrance will be 1, 2, and 3, from right to left, and so forth—and use a separate index card to write down the names of guests assigned to each table. Count on the fact that some people might not show up that day (blame it on illness, travel isssues, whatever). Or consider that there may be a mishap that leaves someone without a chair. Don't fret. Assign a responsible bridesmaid the job of making sure that everyone has a seat, a place setting, and your sincerest apologies for the confusion.

Go to Chapter 7 for more reception-seating details.

Try to strike a balance between familiar faces and acquaintances. Every person at the table should know at least one or two of his/her neighbors, but consider adding some fresh faces, as well. After all, the essence of a wedding is bringing people together and taking a leap, neither of which is reflected in seating people who all know each other together. This is an excellent opportunity to get your relatives acquainted with your honey's, build bridges between your childhood and "adult" friends, and even play matchmaker.

Your Marriage License

One of your most important eleventh-hour missions is getting your marriage license. This state-issued permit to marry is proof that you two are fit to marry each other (i.e., officially single, divorced or widowed, and of legal age). You get it by going in person (*both* of you) to city hall, the city or town clerk's office, or the local marriage license bureau. Check online or call the appropriate office in advance to find out about operating hours and whether you need an appointment. See which documents you need to bring along; typical requirements include a birth certificate, photo ID, passport, and divorce papers or death certificate (if divorced or widowed). Our advice: Bring everything, as it's better to be prepared than sorry.

Have You Been Tested?

Some states require you to take a blood test in order to get a marriage license. Check online or call the marriage license bureau or county clerk in the town where you'll wed to see if you need one.

Timing is of the essence when it comes to getting your license; most states have both a waiting period between the time you get the license and the time you actually can say your vows as well as an expiration policy that dictates how long license is valid. In other words, a marriage license allows you a specific window of opportunity. (For many states, it's thirty days.) So it's crucial to find out the rules in the state where you're getting hitched. If you're getting married in a state other than the one where you live, you'll have to wait until you arrive in your wedding town/city to get your license. Be sure to leave time for this crucial task.

ASK CARLEY

Vows Abroad

Q: We're getting married out of the country. How do we find out about marriage license requirements there?

A: Call your wedding country's embassy, consulate, or tourist office. First off, make sure nonresidents can even get marriage licenses. (We're hoping that you've already got this covered.) Then get the low-down on specifics: which documents and medical tests you need, how long it will take to process the paperwork (so you can time your arrival accordingly), whether you need witnesses, and special requirements for a religious ceremony as opposed to a civil one. (Check Appendix B for requirements in some of the most popular foreign wedding destinations.) Get everything you need in order and pack it in a safe place. Bon voyage!

Changing Your Name

One of the most important logistical decisions you two need to make—*before* you get hitched, ideally—is what to do on the last-name front. Once wives had no choice but to adopt their husbands' names, but today's couples have many options.

Wife Takes Husband's Name: The traditional way, which will make your old-fashioned relatives happy and keep the question-asking to a minimum. Many couples also see this choice as a sign of real togetherness.

Husband Takes Wife's Name: A twist on the conventional decision, especially cool if the man dislikes his last name or the woman is the only child of her clan. A pretty rare choice, though. And his family might be miffed.

Wife Takes Husband's Name (sort of): Some women choose to adopt their sweetie's name socially but continue to use their given name for business purposes, even legally. This is a good option if you are a professional who relies on name recognition for your livelihood.

You Both Keep Your Own Names: You've spent your lives "building a name" for yourselves; changing what people call you may be painful. Bonus: You'll avoid the long lines at the DMV. Drawback: You may have to deal with in-laws who question your reluctance to take "their name."

Join Hearts and Names: Adopting a double or hyphenated surname is an ultra-modern option. A hyphen ensures that people use both names, although the bride might prefer using her given last name as a middle name. (Tina Brown becomes Tina Brown White.) Sometimes only the bride does the twin-tower last-name thing, but it's pretty cool if both of you do it.

Both Do the Switcharoo: You may decide to adopt a whole new name for yourselves. This is a good idea if your names don't go together (like Cherry Berry or Long-Dong) or if you want to revive an extinct family name. You could artfully combine both your last names (Warner and Yasser become Yasner, for example), or choose the name of a personal role model or one you just like.

Your final name decision probably will appear on your official marriage certificate. If you have changed your name/s, it's time to run a few errands to make your new identities official with the rest of the world:

- Contact the Social Security Administration (800-772-1213). Their automated system will talk you through the name-change steps; you'll get new cards for free. (Don't fall for companies that charge "a small fee" to do this; it's a scam.)
- Visit the Department of Motor Vehicles. This agency requires you to make a personal appearance when recording a name change. Bring a good book, every form of identification you can lay your hands on, and a bottle of water. *Don't* forget your original marriage certificate (with the official-looking raised seal).
- Tell the world. Once you have a social security card and driver's license in your married name, making the other changes should be fairly easy. Some institutions require only a phone call; others may ask for more (to see your marriage certificate, social security card, etc.). Here are the important people and places to notify:

  Friends and family (send name change cards or thank-you notes on married-name stationery)
  Banks and other financial institutions
  Credit-card companies
  Employers
  Schools and/or alumni associations
  Post office
  Phone company
  Registrar of voters
  Passport office
  Landlord

Playing Doctor

Choose a doctor together to be your family physician. That way s/he'll be able to take both of your symptoms and conditions into consideration when making a diagnosis—a healthy approach.

Last-Minute Vendor Questions

- Ingredients: Do they already have the specific blooms, liquor brands, fresh fruit you ordered? If your picks are unavailable, what replacements will be used?
- Legwork: Have labor-intensive, complicated tasks been completed?
- Access: Is your vendor all set to get into your site(s) ahead of time?
- Equipment: Does your vendor have everything s/he needs?
- Schedule: They know crucial arrival times, right?
- Assistance: Is there anything you can do to help?

Your Vendors

You and your wedding vendors already have hashed out all the specifics and signed a contract. Now let them do their thing without breathing down their necks. (You screened these pros carefully—trust your instincts.) That said, you definitely should check in with each vendor during the last two weeks to answer any last-minute questions, make sure preparations are on track, and get the reassurance you need.

We suggest one phone call at the two-week mark, a call (or visit) during the final week, and a final ring the day before the wedding to reconfirm arrival times and other important points. Have contracts on hand so you can go over what needs to be done in an organized fashion. Make sure, however, that your tone is friendly and helpful rather than suspicious and bossy. If you can, leave this final call to a trusted friend or family member who's capable and willing (Mom, you're a saint) so you don't have to tie yourselves in knots over any last-minute glitches.

Guest Hospitality

Now's the time to do the prep work that makes out-of-town guests feel welcome. Check with the hotel/s where they've booked rooms to make sure all is well. Make a round of phone calls to find out how and when your faraway guests are coming into town—if you can swing it, hire a car service to pick them up at the airport or train station, or arrange to have nearby family and friends fetch them in shifts. Make sure everyone has rental-car info, too.

On the day before the wedding, drop off gift baskets at your guests' hotel. They should include snacks, water, itineraries, maps, and some thoughtful items as well. Some ideas for your baskets:

- Beach wedding: A sand bucket filled with a beach pass, sunscreen, sunglasses, and an inexpensive beach towel.
- Vineyard wedding: A bottle of local wine, corkscrew, and a map of the area marked with any famous wineries.
- City wedding: A sight-seeing book, a mass-transit pass (like a subway or bus card), a restaurant guide, and a list of weekend events, including museum exhibits or show schedules.

Go to Chapter 20 for instructions for putting together guest welcome baskets.

Honeymoon Preparations

These final fourteen days are the perfect time to shore up your honeymoon plans. Get a print-out of your itinerary, if you haven't already. Reconfirm your flight and hotel reservations about five days before takeoff. Do any last-minute shopping. Pack several days before your wedding, so you'll have one less thing to fret about.

Don't Worry, Be Happy

Want to know the cardinal rule for looking and feeling your best on your big day? Three words: relax, rest, and rejoice. Honestly, happiness is the most effective beauty secret in the world, with sleep, wholesome food, and exercise close runners-up. During these two weeks, make time for the following.

Romps with Your Friends: Make the most of your bachelor/bachelorette bash, but also make other dates with those closest to you, like a trip to the mall to hunt for earrings followed by a scary movie, a Sunday afternoon chill-out in front of the television, a group work-out session topped off by a whirlpool and sauna powwow. Be silly, carefree, crazy.

Get-togethers with Out-of-Town Guests: All those great people are coming from afar to be with you on your wedding day. You'd be passing up a rare and special opportunity if you didn't spend some time with them. Greet them with a prewedding cocktail party, invite them over for a casual dinner, join them for a sightseeing tour, drop by their hotel rooms for some intimate conversation, have afternoon tea and snacks together. Chat, catch up, laugh, reminisce.

Intimate Moments with Your Honey: During the final stages of your engagement, you may have neglected each other, even had petty fights because of the mounting pressure. Now's the time to hang out, babble, and snuggle, so come wedding day you two will be a loving, winning team. Hit the gym together, book a table at your fave romantic restaurant, go to the movies.

CINDY & WAYNE

June 21, Livingston, New Jersey

"WE HAD A FOURTEEN-MONTH engagement—plenty of time to plan a wedding," Cindy says. "I had worked for a bridal magazine, and I'd hired a wedding consultant. With our experience, I figured we could practically guarantee that the day would come together smoothly. For the most part, it did—until the last ten days." The bridesmaids' dresses had arrived several weeks late—the wrong dresses—and the shop had to make a last-minute rush order. In the meantime, after a third round of alterations, Cindy's veil still did not look the way she wanted it. The seamstress assured her that she would fix the problem, but it wouldn't be ready until the day before the wedding! As if that wasn't enough, Cindy realized that one of her wedding shoes didn't fit: "The foot I had fractured when I was nine was swollen—probably from all the running around I was doing—and I couldn't put on my right shoe." Finding a new pair took her to ten different stores.

Everything went swimmingly on the big day, however. "I kept thinking that the mayhem that ensued before my wedding was due to the fact that we were getting married on a full moon and the summer solstice," Cindy says. "Little fairies somewhere were having a ball watching me go crazy! Even with all the knowledge and help that I had, I learned that things will go wrong, and you just have to find a way to deal with them."

'Twas the Night Before Wedding . . .

It's the eve of your wedding. The butterflies in your stomach are having a field day. These ten quick fixes will calm your stomach (a little) and help you sleep easier.

1. Be prepared. Lay out all your clothes and accessories so that they're ready to put on or be transported to your ceremony site.
2. Watch the Weather Channel so you know what Mother Nature has in store for you. If it looks like rain or snow, alert your wedding party and relatives and ask them to bring umbrellas, space heaters, whatever. You can't change the forecast, but you can work with it.
3. Get an at-home massage. If you're only going to get rubbed down by a pro once in your life, this is the time to do it.
4. Have a nutritious carbohydrate-heavy, low-salt dinner (pasta, gourmet sandwich). You need all the energy you can get.
5. Drink a cup of herbal tea. It soothes the stomach and will help you sleep.
6. Enjoy a laid-back rehearsal dinner with your attendants and family. Whatever you do, don't stay up too late; the idea is just to take your mind off the looming dawn.
7. Whisper sweet nothings in your honey's ear. They'll be much appreciated.
8. Meditate. Spend half an hour completely alone. Play soft music, light candles, stretch, hum, pray. Calm yourself with thoughts of how lucky you are.
9. Pamper yourself. Take a luxurious bath, soak your feet, slather your body with moisturizer.
10. Order a wake-up call—just in case your alarm clock lets you down.

It's All in the Timing

The sun's up. Your vendors are getting ready to do their thing. Your mother's having a cry. Your sister overslept (again), and your best man woke up with a hangover (again). It's all come down to this. The big day. Just a few more hours until all eyes are on you two. To make this time most manageable, sit down together a few days before the big day to write out a schedule of exactly what's going to go down when. This timetable will not only keep your whirling head in check; it also will be a useful tool for your wedding party and vendors, helping them plan and prepare for what they need to accomplish. (Don't go insane over sticking to this schedule—it's supposed to be helpful, not stress-inducing!)

Whether your vows are scheduled for when the rooster crows or when the stars come out, certain just-before-the-wedding preparations are universal. Each couple will add their own unique flavor, quirky rituals, and personal freakouts to the list. Here are some things you should *definitely* work into your schedule.

How to Be Punctual

Make sure you leave enough time for the big-day essentials:

Bride's dressing: 45 minutes

Bride's hair and makeup: 90 minutes

Bridesmaids' makeup: 30 minutes each

Groom's dressing: 30 minutes

Bride's arrival at ceremony site: 20 minutes early

Groom's arrival at ceremony site: 40 minutes early

Couple and wedding party shots with photographer: 1 hour

Early Preparations

Get alert, excited, and prepped—this period can last from two to eight hours, depending on your ceremony start time. It's time to:

- Wake up. Lie in bed gathering energy for a few minutes—you're gonna need it.
- Take a long shower or bath.
- Have breakfast. Eat your favorite things; you don't want to test your tummy with anything exotic today. Hold off on the coffee and tea refills, but hydrate yourself with lots of water. If your wedding is scheduled for late in the day, consider organizing a casual breakfast or brunch for your wedding party and immediate families—a team huddle before game time.
- Relax. If you're having a morning ceremony, take fifteen minutes or more to just chill. If your wedding isn't until the evening, fill your time with fairly routine day-off activities: jog, go for a drive with friends, get a pedicure (or barbershop shave) with an out-of-town pal. *Don't* obsess all day long!

Now You See Me . . .

Some say it's bad luck for the bride and groom to see each other before the ceremony. We say it's bad luck to do something just because it's tradition. Go with your gut—breakfast together might be just what you need.

Last-Minute Preparations

The two to four hours before showtime are spent getting ready, *really* ready:

- Get your hair styled. Brides: It's also makeup time for you and your bridesmaids.
- Dress with the help of your attendants. Hang out with your crew to calm nerves.
- Pose for formal portraits. Unless you're totally opposed to seeing each other prewedding, this is a great opportunity to get shots of you two with your wedding party and families out of the way. That way you can go straight to the party after your ceremony, or at least get there more quickly.

Chapters 6 and 7 give you info on what typically happens, and when, during the ceremony and reception.

It's Showtime!

Time to walk down the aisle, say your vows, kiss, greet guests, and, most important, have lots of fun. In your timetable, jot down your estimated ceremony start and end time and reception arrival time. The rest of the to-do will flow from there!

Last-Minute Craziness

Murphy's Law says there's always going to be a big-day glitch (or two). Problems will arise on your wedding day, some serious, some silly. Most will work themselves out; some you'll never even know about.

Emergency Remedies

Here are some common big-day problems and our favorite quick fixes:

Heat Wave: If your idea of a perfect wedding does *not* include a mass meltdown, beat the heat with huge water coolers (and cups!) on hand at your ceremony and reception, heavy-duty electric fan action, and paper fans as favors. (Ceremony programs will double in a pinch.) For outdoor affairs, make sure there's ample shade by hanging fabrics among trees, setting up an airy tent, or supplying sun umbrellas to guests. Make sure air conditioners are on early enough to get your sites cool before the crowds arrive. This is particularly important for early-morning events.

Rain/Snow: Monitor the weather forecast the week before your wedding. If things look like they could get wacky, prepare yourselves. In case of rain, bring as many oversized umbrellas for your guests as you can, and move festivities indoors. (That backup site we recommended comes in handy *now.*) For snow, hire a plow operator to clear access roads and parking lots (or make sure your sites do), rent four-wheel-drive vehicles to transport guests, and bring space heaters to your sites. In both cases, stock up guest bathrooms with grooming products so they can repair weather damage, and play appropriate songs, such as "Singing in the Rain," "It's Raining Men," and "White Christmas" during your reception.

Sick Relative: If a close family member falls ill and is unable to attend your wedding, the show should go on (unless, of course, things look really, really bad and you're too upset). Your loved one probably would want it that way. Find ways to include this person in the proceedings. Have him/her pen a piece you'll read during the ceremony; have your officiant lead a prayer for his/her recovery; play the absentee's favorite song during your reception and dedicate it to him/her; have a friend "broadcast" the ceremony to him/her by cell phone during your vows. Send flowers and a card on the morning of your big day and then make sure to visit your loved one at some point before you leave for your honeymoon.

Tight Ring: It fit perfectly in the store (and two days ago!), but between the heat and nerves your fingers have grown to monstrous proportions. This common ailment can be prevented easily by running your hands under cool water and coating your ring fingers with Vaseline just before the ceremony to ensure a smooth, easy glide.

Fainting Guest: This is a highly emotional event for you and yours, and depending on the season it can get hot in that church, so it's not uncommon for someone to pass out. Don't panic. Have someone attend to the fallen guest; once the person has revived, have him/her sit with head down until s/he feels better.

Drunken Guest: Every party has at least one guest who goes overboard. Have one of your assertive attendants on sober (okay, almost sober) duty to take care of disruptive behavior. If necessary, have a designated driver take beyond-drunk guests home or back to the hotel. In general, it's a good idea to close the bar an hour before your reception ends, so people won't be *able* to have one for the road.

Hangover: Drink lots of water from the moment you wake up. Amazingly enough, greasy foods will help calm your stomach (presumably they absorb the alcohol), as will a bottle of Coke. Take a long, cool shower and pop some aspirin if you need to.

Vendor Problems

Careful screening and contract-writing are important preventative measures against vendor mishaps. However, even the best of vendors can—and do—slip up.

The Big Picture: On your wedding day, it's too late for your vendor to undo the damage if s/he brings the wrong order, sends a less-qualified re-

Keep in Touch

Take a contact list with the numbers of all the critical people—vendors, attendants, family—along to the wedding. Go to Appendix A to get started.

placement, shows up late or never, or otherwise fouls up your agreement. In the short run, you need to:

- Take a deep breath.
- Point out to your vendor the items or services that are not satisfactory.
- Try to track down a vendor missing-in-action.
- Either return unsatisfactory orders or get a verbal commitment to be compensated financially.

If you have a clear and precise contract and have paid your deposit using a credit card—we can't emphasize the importance of this enough—you are fairly safe as far as getting your money back in the case of a no-show or a fouled-up job. Either your vendor will do the right thing by reimbursing you, or your credit card company will take up your case if you dispute a charge. Worst-case scenario: You take the out-of-line "pro" to small claims court.

Immediate Fixes: All is not lost if you don't get what you expected from your vendor. Even the worst screw-up can be covered up with a little help from your friends and a bit of initiative.

- Food: If the caterer brings food you don't want—or nothing at all—order in lots of pizzas, Chinese food, deli salads, or other goodies. Have friends and relatives run out for hors d'oeuvres platters as well as soft drinks, cakes, and anything else you need. Who knows? Your makeshift cuisine might be an even bigger hit than the catered fare would have been.
- Flowers: If your florist botches things up, raid the nearest farmer's market for the day's best blooms. Send some attendants to a local flower shop to buy as many bouquets as you can afford; ask relatives to bring vases by as soon as possible. Candles—all shapes and sizes—are quick-fixes and can turn an ordinary space into one that's moody and romantic.
- Photography/videography: If these crucial pros are no-shows, have someone run out to the drugstore for tons of film and get the word out for everyone with a camera (or camcorder) to go crazy. Ask a particularly talented photographer friend to do you the honor of shooting your formal pictures.
- Transportation: If your limo never arrives, it's time to hail a cab (they'll stop in a sec for a chick in a wedding dress) or hitch a ride with the bridesmaids or Mom and Dad. Know someone with a fancy set of wheels, like a sleek sportscar or a vintage vehicle? Now's the time to hit them up for a ride. Promise to take them out for lunch when you come back from the honeymoon.

Having a Ball

Your big day will come and go like a beautiful, blazing comet. If all you're doing is obsessing, worrying, and fretting, you'll miss its fleeting glory. In order to make your wedding a truly special event, you two need to revel in it, milk it, seize it by the horns. Focus on the excellent things—your honey's smile when you're pronounced husband and wife, your adoring guests, the scrumptious food, watching your friends dance—not the glitches or slip-ups. Not only will this make your big day better and put your attendants and guests at ease, it'll also be good practice for marriage—and life (i.e., always look on the bright side). Ways to really savor the day:

- Take a minute to write in your journal on wedding morning.
- Tell your parents you love them.
- Get in the middle of a group hug with your best friends before the festivities begin.
- After the ceremony, retreat with your honey to a quiet, private place. Kiss, gaze into each other's eyes, and tell each other how happy you are.
- Chat with friends and family you adore but hardly ever see.
- At some point during the reception, grab your honey's hand under the table and squeeze it tight.
- When you take a pit stop during the party, look at yourself in the mirror and smile.
- Eat something even if you're nauseous with nerves—it will keep your stamina up.
- Shake your bootie on the dance floor. Tango with your baby. Lead a silly line dance. Twirl your nephews and nieces around. Twist with Grandpa.
- Toast all your guests.
- When the reception's in full swing, stand back for a couple of minutes and just take in the sights and sounds.
- Keep a camera on you, so you can snap shots from your own point of view.

Forget the preparations, the decisions, the agonizing, the coordinating, the orchestrating, the finessing. Your most critical task at this point is having the time of your lives. *This* is what it's all about: love, happiness, fun, good friends, and family. Oh, yeah, and how simply amazing your sweetie is.

Where to Next?

Depending on what your honeymoon plans are, there are several options for where to spend your first night together as husband and wife.

The Honeymoon Suite

Without a doubt, the most common big-night destination is a nearby hoity-toity hotel. The night is earmarked as one of the most memorable of your life, and special, fancier-than-normal surroundings can set the perfect tone. As we all know, however, all hotels were not created equal—even the four-star kind—so it's important that you do a little prewedding reconnaissance and select your lodgings with care. Consider these points as you formulate your battle plan.

Is the Joint Actually Nice? Reputation is one thing; firsthand inspection is another. Just because a hotel is famous doesn't mean the rooms are habitable and the service is friendly—all-important components of a successful big-night environment. Take a look for yourself.

Is the Room Fully Stocked? Do a walk-through of the room and check for: (1) an inspiring view; (2) a squeak-free, king-size mattress; (3) a fully stocked minibar; (4) a clean tub (preferably with Jacuzzi jets) large enough for two; (5) a cable-equipped TV (with adult pay-per-view options); (6) room service.

What Can You Scam for Free? Most hotels worth their Bibles offer some sort of upgrade or thoughtful freebie for newlyweds, from a chilled bottle of bubbly to a better view or larger suite. If you don't feel comfortable asking, get one of your parents or friends to call and talk to the manager.

Gotta Fly Now

If you're one of those daring couples jetting straight to your honeymoon location, you won't be able to enjoy the comfort of a cushy hotel room immediately, but that doesn't mean you've got to suffer like any other anonymous airport slob. Au contraire!

The first step to a comfy newlywed flight is booking with a reputable airline. This is your honeymoon, after all—don't skimp and try a bargain-basement carrier. When you arrive at the airport, notify the ticket agent of your newlywed status—feel free to flash your marriage license, rings, the smear of wedding-cake frosting on your lapel, or any other convincingly authentic items—and ask if you can wait for the flight in their VIP lounge.

If you're flying coach, ask if a first-class upgrade is possible. The better the airline, the better your chances of flying up front with the genuine swells. If there's room, you're almost guaranteed to get first-class seats, and maybe even a bottle of champagne to boot. This trick works both ways if you're returning from a country that subscribes to a Westernized understanding of marriage (monogamous, licensed, free of sacrificial offerings), so feel free to push your luck.

PART THREE

STICKY SUBJECTS

CHAPTER TWENTY-TWO

love patrol

At first, getting engaged seemed like the perfect culmination of a passionate romance. It added a new sheen to your usual routine. Work passed more quickly. You walked around in a haze of just-engaged joy. Your copy of the *Kama Sutra* became downright dog-eared from use. But then . . . the details of wedding planning came slamming down like a meat cleaver, cutting right through your relationship.

Welcome to engagement. While getting married is the first step to an eternity of sublime togetherness, the actual planning process can be so tension-ridden that it threatens to tear you apart. Wedding planning brings life's five major flash points speeding toward you all at once—family, money, sex, religion, and change. And the resulting arguments and doubts can put a strain on your relationship. We're here to help steer you through the labyrinth of engagement-time tension and get your relationship back on the freeway of love. Read on.

Fending Off Your Family

Your mom wants the reception at her country club. Your honey's dad wants it at the restaurant he owns stock in. Your honey thought maybe you'd hold it at the bowling alley where you had your first date. And none of them understands why you're being driven nuts! Will the Number-One Wedding-Planning Stress Factor please stand up? Let's hear it for families. Weddings are rarely just about the couple getting married. If you're getting flak from your folks that's causing you two to tangle, try these solutions.

Present a United Front

Wedding planning has a way of pitting people against each other—even madly in love to-be-weds. Decide how you feel about various elements *together,* before discussing them with your family. Even if your parents are paying for the wedding, your honey's opinion should matter most to you (along with your own). Don't let your parents think they can get their way by cornering you alone. And don't promise your mom a full seated dinner in a hotel ballroom unless you check it out with your partner first (who, it turns out, had his heart set on hot dogs at the park).

Focus the Interference

The two of you should decide what you do and don't care about. (Big dress? Yes! Big band? Whatever.) Then talk with your parents about which elements they feel strongly about. Ask for their help with those things that are more important to them and less so to you.

If they're helping pay, you might ask them to foot the bill for specific items—such as the band, the bar, and the food—rather than underwriting the whole thing, allowing you to maintain some control. Or reconcile yourselves to planning the ceremony and letting them go wild with the reception. And comfort yourselves with the fact that you can live your lives exactly as you want to *after* the wedding.

Don't Betray Each Other

Trying to appease the parents—at the expense of your sweetie—can make your future spouse feel like a second-class citizen. Family loyalty should not mean dissing your honey. Don't let yourself be pressured to reveal a confidence, expose an insecurity, or make a plan that you know conflicts with your honey's belief system. If you find yourself fighting with your sweetie about something you don't actually care about, figure out who else is in the room (in your head, rather). Once you're married, "looking out for number one" means watching out for yourself *and* your partner. Start practicing now.

ASK CARLEY

Shy of the Spotlight?

Q: I love the idea of being married, but I hate the thought of being the complete focus of the party on wedding day. The anxiety is making me tense and mean. Is there a way to avoid being the center of attention during my wedding?

A: Not entirely—but if it really freaks you out, there are ways to minimize it. First, admit your discomfort to your honey (and apologize for being snappish!). Together you can figure out ways to handle your stress.

Some suggestions:

Have a couple's shower so he can share the limelight.
Skip the whole "dining-on-stage" head table thing. Sit at a regular, floor-level reception table.
Make your first dance a family or all-couples affair.
Let your family and friends know that you'd like to keep a relatively low profile, so they don't plan a surprise party, stage a two-hour toast-a-thon, or send a congratulatory strip-o-gram to work.
Share the spotlight with others. Include special people in the ceremony (as readers, performers, speakers, child attendants) and the reception (dance leaders, toasters, greeters). Make it a cast of dozens, rather than your star turn.

Managing Money Madness

First-place wedding flash point—money. Just because you love each other doesn't mean you like each other's fiscal policies. Your expectations and approaches to the green stuff (not to mention the amount your parents can contribute) may vary greatly, particularly if you come from different backgrounds. How can you avoid conflicts over cash?

Go to Chapter 24 for more help with family.

Agree on a Budget

Face it—there's *never* enough cash. But you can have an awesome wedding with whatever you've got in your coffers. Set an objective, *joint* budget and stick to it. Put your money into a shared pot, and forever after refer to it as *Our* Budget. No pointing fingers or subtly inflicting guilt. This is Your Budget, and you've both got to deal with it. There's no skipping this step, either. Without a budget, you will surely lose track of the dough (no matter how hard you try to calculate in your head), thus starting your married life in a sea of debt. Yuck.

Reconcile Family Fortunes

If your honey's family owns General Motors and your family owns . . . a car, you quite likely learned different ways of dealing with dough. When you find yourselves fighting over finances, stop. Back up. And look at the issue objectively. Are you really ready to kill each other over the relative merits of caviar versus chili? Or are you defending your family's honor ("They may not be well off, but they're honest!") while your honey is championing his clan ("They're not crooks, just smart!")? This isn't about which family is better or which of you is right. You had different experiences, and you need to devise a joint financial approach that works for you both. Talk about the ways your families dealt with money, what you liked and didn't like. Chances are you both learned some pretty valuable tactics that you can combine to create a new and improved fiscal policy.

Separate Money from Emotion

We've all done it—mistakenly judged one's commitment by his/her willingness to spend C-notes. If you're putting 20 percent of your income toward the wedding and your honey isn't, you might feel that her reluctance to pay means she's only lukewarm about the marriage. She, meanwhile, may think your willingness to drop a bundle on a heated buffet means you're not serious about planning for future needs.

Take a look at the offending person's financial past. If her behavior is consistent with her track record, that's a good sign that this is a question of loot, not love. Talk with the tightwad (sorry, financially responsible partner), or spendthrift (um, live-for-the-moment one) calmly about her approach. Really listen. And then try to explain that her spending policy is making you feel unloved. See if there are nonfinancial ways you each can express your commitment to the marriage. By separating money from emotion, you've got a better shot at dealing with both elements more sanely.

Go to Chapter 3 for help creating a wedding budget you both can live with.

CAROLYN & MATTHEW

September 7, New York City

"A PRENUPTIAL AGREEMENT is an uncomfortable thing to discuss, so I think it's important to see how your partner responds to the issue," Carolyn says. "I asked Matthew one night at dinner, and luckily we felt similarly about it." The couple knew they would have a prenup, but, says Carolyn, "When we finally did the agreement it was extremely stressful because we left it until a few days before the wedding, which is the *worst* time to do it. You're feeling so happy and romantic and a prenuptial agreement is cold and harsh."

Although it was sobering, Carolyn says she found the experience ultimately empowering. "Women often are not brought up to think about money. If you have a career, however, and you're going to have children, you need to think about issues such as 'What happens if I give up my career?' You're not just protecting yourself, you're protecting your children." Carolyn acknowledges that as a romantic, she finds the idea of a prenuptial agreement somewhat sad but that, in reality, it has helped her relationship with Matthew. "It opens communication about important issues and makes you talk about things like your will, which you might not talk about otherwise," she says. "It's not for everyone, but it is something the couple needs to agree on."

Passion Patrol

Sex is one of the most important intimacy builders in a relationship and, sad to say, one of the first things to go when people get overwhelmed. Desire is a complex mix of emotion, attraction, and straight-out libido—a delicate brew that can get out of balance when you're stressed out, exhausted, angry, frustrated, or scared. Not to mention busy. Juggling the many tasks of getting married can leave precious little time for gettin' biz-zay.

Your pending wedding adds some unique pressures to your bedroom life. You may wake up in a cold sweat, staring down those big questions: "Will our sex life grow bland once we're wed?" "Will we still find each other attractive?" and "Is our sex really good enough to be the only sex we have, as long as we both shall live?" Not to mention, "What if we don't do it well together?" for you first-timers.

Relax. Almost every engaged person we know went through the same deal. The good news? A lot of married couples we know say that their sex lives actually improved *after* the wedding. They grew more comfortable with each other and gained the confidence to spice things up with experimentation. As they say, practice makes perfect. Meanwhile, the planning process can take a big bite out of your love life. Here are some ways to bite back.

Procrastinate and Be Blissful

When it comes to putting the passion back in your love life, a little procrastination can go a long way. Here are our scientifically proven remedies for plummeting pleasure; they also can be used preventively.

Movie and Make-Out: Take the afternoon off work (tell your boss it's an emergency—not a lie, technically) and go see back-to-back screenings of two hot new flicks (or romantic oldies). Buy a jumbo popcorn-and-soda combo (hey, you'll save $1!) and a pack of Twizzlers. Before the previews, practice your synchronized licorice-eating skills (nibble from opposite sides). Sit in the back so you can sneak in plenty of smooching.

Healthy Healing: Save up and book full-day spa treatments for both of you on your next free Saturday. Wake up early, have a lavish breakfast, and surrender yourselves to hours of massages, facials, and wraps. See if the spa can seat you next to each other for treatments. (Strapped for cash? Opt for a do-it-yourself spa at home.)

Recycled Fun: Tool around the closest flea market, garage sale, or antique and collectibles store. Play the $5 game: You each have five bucks to buy a gift for the other, not a penny more. When you're done rummaging, go to a bistro or diner and exchange presents.

Play Games: Pull out your dusty board games (or go buy brand-new editions), stock up on soda, beer, and munchies, and spend an evening in hot competition. You'll work out any couple "issues" you may have and be reminded that two is better than one. (Solitaire sucks!) Ah, yes—any one of these venerable games can be adapted to the strip variety.

Afternoon Delight: Take a long lunch break and meet at your favorite secret spot—in the middle of a bridge, on a park bench, on the observation deck of the tallest building—for an afternoon rendezvous like in some steamy French film. Bag a lunch and a bottle of wine for your clandestine date. After a few long, passionate kisses, head back to work, truly refreshed.

Use Your Mouth

To talk, that is. Discuss your fears, concerns, and sexual preferences. Give each other guidance. Read a few good manuals. Be open about your issues. If you have different ideas (religious or otherwise) about the role of sex or different levels of desire, talk about those, too. The nitty-gritty of creating a killer sex life takes time and communication.

Make Time for Sex

Too busy to have sex? Take a break and *just do it.* If the stamps don't get stuck tonight, they'll stick tomorrow. Be flexible. If you're too tired at bedtime, make love in the morning. Or right before dinner, after *Friends,* or on your lunch break. There's no right time (or place) for sex. Make a standing sex date, if you have to, to ensure you fit it in. (Thursday, at seven. In the bedroom. Be there.) And when you get the urge to bring up a great centerpiece idea during foreplay, bite your tongue.

First-Time Fears

Waiting until after the wedding to do the deed? No wonder you're nervous. Discuss your fears with your sweetie. Plan to go very slowly on that first night, and remember that sex gets better as you grow more comfortable with each other. If you don't see fireworks on your wedding night, it doesn't mean you never will! You'll have to keep on trying. (Not a bad deal!) For you, the work of creating a compatible night life will come after the wedding.

Religious Rifts

Planning your ceremony can bring up all the major how-will-you-handle-religion questions—where you'll worship, how you'll raise your kids, where you'll spend holidays. If you have different religions, these issues can take on the complexity of an international summit. But even if you share the same religion or spiritual beliefs, you may not share the same level of intensity or involvement. Small differences may start seeming like chasms. How do you keep religion from ripping you apart?

Respect Each Other (and Yourself)

You go to church every Sunday; your sweetie refuses to step inside a chapel. You fear she'll ask you to stop going, while she's afraid you'll try to pressure her to join the church choir. What do you do? Make a pact to maintain your individual feelings about faith. You continue to go to church, alone or with family and friends. She'll worship as she sees fit. No pressuring each other to change. Don't turn your back on your beliefs—but don't expect her to do so for you, either. Appreciate each other's differences. Some of the most well-rounded relationships involve those who bring different ideas and ideals to the table.

Whose Beliefs Are These?

Your parents are worried you'll abandon the faith they taught you once you marry "that heathen," and you're letting their fears affect you? Stop, and take some time to figure out which beliefs are yours—and which are theirs. You don't have to live according to their practices, and neither does your sweetie. Let them know that your beliefs are *your* beliefs—not theirs or your partner's—and you can manage your own faith, thank you very much.

Make a Plan for the Future

You want your kids to go to Hebrew school (or weekly Marxist theory classes) and he says absolutely not? Now is the time to talk about how the two of you will deal. Map out a game plan. By figuring out where you stand as a couple, you'll be better able to field questions from others. Don't sweat it, however, if things don't fall into place immediately. These overwhelming subjects take time and patience to deal with.

The Challenge of Change

Even if you've been dating since high school, getting married is a major threshold to cross—your lives will be different forever after. It's normal to feel anxiety in the face of so much change—even when something better is about to come along. Change is pretty much the major life stress factor. (Right up there with divorce and moving, which you also may know something about.) If fear of change is giving you the jitters, read on.

Have That Last Fling

As you feel your single life slipping through your fingers, you may find yourself clinging desperately to old habits, suddenly aching for activities that grew boring years ago. (All-night club-hopping? A slumber party with the girls? Party on!) The good news is, that's your fear of change speaking, not some latent desire to regress. Go ahead and indulge yourself. (In moderation, of course—you can't handle hangovers the way you used to!) Fill your sweetie in on your plans, and ask him to be patient with your bout of temporary insanity. If your honey is the antsy one, encourage him to hit the town. Give each other space. Chances are, you'll both remember exactly why you put your past behind you in the first place. (Were clubs always this smoky? And loud? And expensive?)

Recognize That Change Equals Loss

Every time you make a major life change, you're going to feel some sense of loss; it's one of those quirks of human nature. And a wedding is a big bucket of change. Gaining a permanent partner also means losing your single status. Moving in together also means leaving your bachelor pad behind. Marrying Prince William also means kissing your summers backpacking across Europe with your three closest guy friends good-bye.

Acknowledge your feelings of loss, but don't confuse them with regret; they don't mean you're making the wrong decision. Feel sad about what you're giving up, and then focus on what you're gaining. You might even mark this rite of passage in some fun, silly way—turn your little black book over to your best pal with grand ceremony, or write a guide on the fine art of flirting (based on your years of experience) to present to your little sister. Whatever you need to do, try not to take these feelings out on each other.

How's Marriage Different from Living Together?

If you have been living together, you've already made a lot of the changes that can come with marriage. (He's learned to differentiate between potpourri and party mix, usually; she tolerates Howard Stern.) But if you think nothing more can change when you tie the knot, you may be surprised by some of these factors:

Your sense of stability: You always can move out of a live-in arrangement, and you've probably thought about it at least once. But lots of couples who lived together first say that marriage closed this escape hatch, really solidifying their sense of being a team.

The way your in-laws/parents treat you: Parents tend to see a live-in as a transitory fixture and avoid making an emotional commitment. Once you're married, however, they may come running over with that emotional Welcome Wagon.

The way acquaintances/strangers treat you: You may suddenly garner more respect among your conservative workmates/fishing buddies/shop clerks. Saying "I must go meet my wife" carries greater clout than "I've got to go get my girlfriend."

The way your honey's insurance policy treats you: Bring on those benefits!

Your legal status: Yep, it's time for the joint tax return, the merged bank account—physical factors that reiterate the seriousness of your union.

Your expectations of your spouse: You may discover an untapped marital routine lurking in the back of your brain. "Dinner is at six, damn it!" you find yourself saying. "Be at the table, napkin under chin!" Or "It's time for you to go get a *real* job now, Messenger Boy!" Try to use these last months of living together as a "practice marriage" to avoid being clobbered by your own unexpected expectations after the wedding.

Stay Single *and* Be Married

Fearing your individuality will dissolve into your couplehood? You're not alone. Keeping your own identity intact can be one of the toughest challenges of making the big hook-up. Create some boundaries for yourself. Set up a once-a-week gin game with the girls. Sign up for that pottery, cooking, or spin class you've been thinking about. By working to maintain your own interests and friends, you actually help make your marriage stronger.

Fighting Right

What happens when all these stress factors bear down on you at once? The big explosion. The showdown. The ultimate match. We're talking big-time fighting. It may seem like you disagree on absolutely everything about your wedding—from the ceremony site to the honeymoon—and your fighting tactics have reached new lows. (You've slammed the door so many times, the frame is wobbly.) And then there are all these decisions to make, enough cause for constant conflict even if you weren't feeling so much pressure. All this strife may even make you wonder if you'll actually get along for the long haul.

The good news? All of this potential fighting material provides a great test case for how you'll handle problems later on. While life may not be a dress rehearsal (according to the great bumper-sticker soothsayer), wedding planning is. We like to say that wedding planning magnifies everyone's annoying traits by about 100 percent. The important thing is not to avoid conflicts but to learn how to handle them—*now.* And if you can handle them at this stage of the game, you'll be good to go in the rest of your life.

ALISON & CRAIG

September 6, Rhinebeck, New York

"THE PROBLEMS IN OUR relationship didn't go away just because we got engaged," Alison says. "In fact, after the engagement they seemed all the more important. For example, Craig and I don't fight well. He'll just storm out and come back two hours later. I like to talk things over right then and there. Before we got engaged, it bothered me. But afterward, it became the biggest deal in the world. I'd think to myself, do I have to live with this man doing this to me for the rest of my life?"

How'd they resolve it? "We slowed down and remembered the reasons why we're getting married in the first place," Alison says. "That we love and complete each other, not to mention that we have a unique ability to crack each other up. All that put our problems in perspective. But we're working on them, too. I try to give him the space he needs, and he promises to resolve our fights as soon as possible. And I talked to some of my married friends—it turns out that each of them went through a similar period early in their engagement."

Communicate, Don't Sublimate

He's sulking in the corner, or she's flinging dishes across the room, and you don't know why? You're not mind-readers—the *only* way to understand each other's needs and neuroses is to talk about them. Voice your feelings clearly and not critically. Often the difference between a discussion and an argument is a matter of style. Follow these tips to keep your disagreements civil (and your makeups fast and steamy).

Skillful Problem Solving

"Pay less attention to what's wrong—to how many problems and disagreements you have—and more attention to how you resolve them. That's what will carry through into the marriage. If you work through problems by brainstorming and coming up with new solutions, that's a good sign."

—Jane Campbell, Ph.D., Houston-based therapist

- Chill out before you begin discussing a sensitive topic. No one is reasonable when ticked off.
- Adopt the same-side-of-the-table approach. Before you begin, say "This isn't you against me. If we're having a problem, it hurts us both. We're on the same side of the table here." Make the problem the enemy, not each other.
- Don't insist on solving a problem before you go to sleep. The later it gets, the more irrational you get. Go to sleep. (Try to kiss each other first.) There'll be plenty of time to fight in the morning (and, chances are, a lot less reason and inclination to do it).
- Write it down. Afraid you'll forget your points? Jot notes and then go through each item together. It'll help keep you from interrupting each other, which can cause even more hurt and anger.
- Take the "I feel . . ." rather than the "You did this . . ." approach: "I feel like you're not interested in my opinion when you turn on the TV while I'm talking," rather than "You always turn on the TV when I'm talking because you don't give a damn about what I'm saying." By attacking your honey, you force her to defend herself. By expressing how you feel, you give her an opportunity to comfort you.
- Paraphrase for clarity. To make sure you understand her, listen to your honey, then repeat what she said in your own words. This not only helps you both clarify your complaints, it also shows that you're paying attention.

Learn the Art of Compromise

You're not always going to get your way, during the wedding or after. Acknowledge that you have different priorities. To reach a compromise, try the XYZ method:

Your backgrounds—religious, cultural, social—will affect how you deal with the details of your wedding and your life after. For help dealing with conflicts of difference, go to Chapter 23.

- eXpress the other's side.
- Yet . . . (Give your feeling.)
- Zip it up. (Present a solution.)

For example:

X: I understand that you want a vegetarian buffet because you feel very strongly about animal rights.

Y: Yet my fear is that my meat-eating relatives will accuse me of being cheap.

Z: Maybe we could give my relatives the option to choose between a vegetarian *or* meat entree, and we can have all-vegetarian hors d'oeuvres.

Fight Fair

There's no way to avoid fighting completely. It happens, and it's far better to get something out in the open than to let resentment build. A little tiff can reduce stress, but only if you fight fairly. No low blows or permanent scarring. Here are our tips for fair fighting:

- No manipulative tricks like crying fits or stomping off. You're both adults—act like it.
- If your sweetie says something that hurts your feelings, don't lash out with the meanest thing you can think of to say. Take a breath. And tell him he's hurt your feelings, instead.
- Temper your honesty. Too much bluntness can cut deeper than sharp words. If you think her parents are stupid bigots, don't say so. Think of a way to address the problem their bigotry creates instead.
- Always attack the problem, not the person. "I'm worried that this invitation wording will confuse people" is an issue you can address together. "What are you, nuts?" is just an insult. No name-calling. *Ever.*
- Don't ask for proof of love. Yes, your sweetie may make a sacrifice or decision to do something because she knows it will please you. But she'll do it voluntarily. Love is *not* a bargaining point. Sentences like "If you really loved me, you'd agree on a swing band" are not about love but manipulation.
- Recognize that it takes two to fight. It's almost never *all* one person's fault.

Bridezilla vs. Couch Monster

It's possible (okay, probable) that you aren't experiencing wedding obsession to the same degree. We hate to stereotype, but the fact is, a lot of times women become just a *teensy* bit more interested in the details than men do. Unequal distribution of labor and concurrent bridal wackoness can build resentment on both sides. What to do?

Find Out Why He's Not Helping: Chances are, he is not just a big lazy lump. A lot of guys don't participate because they feel unsure about what to do or don't feel welcome. He may also think that he'll just get in the way, especially if you have a clear-cut vision already worked out in your head.

Find Out Why She's Obsessed: Likewise, she's probably not a *total* control freak. What's causing her mania? Is she trying to please anyone other than the two of you? Is her parents' recent divorce making her even more nervous? People often go crazy trying to control details as a way to address a feeling of powerlessness in some other area. There's also the issue of "keeping up with the Joneses." If a lot of her friends are getting hitched, chances are she's been bitten by the competition bug.

Divvy Up Duties: You, Great Planning One, might as well take the lead. Assign specific tasks to your less-than-enthusiastic planning partner. Be very clear about what he should do. We're not recommending you become a dictator—just give him tasks he'll be interested in, like picking the band or choosing the cake. But make sure he has all the info *and* your true support to do it.

Cures for Cold Feet

All this stress and fighting making you think about calling it quits? You're obsessing about all the things that annoy you about each other and wondering if s/he's really the one? If you're racked with doubts about the wisdom of this wedding, look at them seriously. There's a difference between healthy doubts, which everyone has, and real warning signs. Chances are your cold feet just mean your relationship needs some TLC. Here's how to tell.

What Are You Questioning?

Is it your honey, or the idea of marriage? If you love your honey as much as always but you're waffling about the whole wedding thing, your relationship isn't in jeopardy. You've good reason to question a wedding. We live in a country where half of all marriages end in divorce, a factor that can make anyone skeptical about the lifetime-commitment aspect (especially if your family is in the split-up camp). We're a generation of broken commitments. Who's to say that yours will be different?

You're to say. Your relationship is a private affair, completely under your control. It has nothing to do with failed marriages around you. You create your own shared vision of the

ASK CARLEY

Calling It Off

Q: I thought this was the guy for me—but now I know it's a bad idea to get married. What happens if I call off the engagement?

A: Unfortunately, not all love stories are meant to be. The planning period is a trying time for every couple—people chicken out, discover huge incompatibilities, and sometimes even drive each other away. What you don't want to do is lose yourself in a cloud of anguish and despair. There is, however, some difficult business to attend to. First off, the ring. We think you should return it. (Unless there was major foul play involved, in which case, think *Melrose Place* mean!) Why would you want such a reminder of the engagement? It's also respectful to return any family heirloom, ring or otherwise, given to you as gifts by your ex-fiancé/e's relatives as well as any other gifts you both received.

Depending on how far into the wedding preparations you are, you'll also have to cancel all vendor agreements and site reservations. We hope you signed contracts that will let you get at least 50 percent of any deposits back. (There's no etiquette about being reimbursed for your loss if your fiancé broke up with you, so don't hold your breath.) If invitations already have gone out, recall them by sending out rush notes ASAP. (You don't need to delve into the sordid details of your romantic meltdown, just let everyone know the wedding won't take place.)

Once you take care of all the unpleasant details, book a full-day session at the spa, take in a movie with some friends, or go paint the town red!

ideal marriage, and live within it. Talk about what you want from your marriage. Ask each other—and yourselves—the hard questions: What do you like most, and least, about each other? What factors make you think you'll be happy together? What is really important to you in life/love? Look to role models—other couples with relationships you admire—for inspiration. Or, for some outside input, consider going to a couple's counselor to talk out your doubts. As we said earlier, change always makes people feel uncomfortable.

Whose Doubts Are These?

Your parents think you need to be with someone more like you, while your friends keep subtly suggesting that you find someone funnier, smarter, prettier, richer, or more ambitious. Your job is to figure out what *you* want. There is no formula for a perfect relationship. Happy couples range from having nearly nothing in common to sharing essentially every aspect of their lives. Regardless of how much others try to impose their vision of a perfect union on you, all that matters is that the two of *you* agree on what works.

If you're doubting your choice for any reason—too poor, too rich, too young, too old, too lazy, too obsessed with work—figure out whose doubts these are. Are *you* worried about never having enough money for an annual Carnival cruise and a maid three days a week, or are your parents the ones with that concern? Try to comfort your parents, kiss your honey, and then carry on with your planning.

CHAPTER TWENTY-THREE

combining cultures

Maybe you two grew up next door to each other, or you're high-school sweethearts. Perhaps your beloved is from another generation or from a country on the other side of the world. You may have grown up in the same town or state but in different religious or cultural communities.

No matter how different or alike your backgrounds are, you're still coming to your marriage from two different places. The chasms some couples have to cross may be larger and wider than they are for others—your families or friends may be less than supportive of your decision to marry "outside the community." But for everyone, marriage should mean reveling in your differences, not letting them create conflict between you. It's important to come up with good problem-solving solutions now—both for your wedding and for your life after the party.

Differences and Your Relationship

You may be soul mates, but you're not the same person. It sounds obvious, right? But it's something couples in love don't always address. Even if you grew up next door to each other, your families probably used different brands of toothpaste, drove different cars—and related to one another in different ways. We know that you love each other deeply and that nothing could pull you apart. But we also know that the stress of wedding planning—with its focus on tradition, family, and endless financial minutiae—inevitably can bring differences to the surface, where they may simmer for weeks or escape in spurts of steaming insults, shouts, and tears.

If you come from different religions, races, countries, generations, or (it sometimes seems) galaxies—these disagreements may be more profound, looming over an otherwise serene horizon like a huge monster from one of those old black-and-white horror films. Every once in a while, you may even find yourself pondering the wisdom of this marriage.

Relax. Prewedding disagreements do not necessarily mean postwedding unhappiness. It's perfectly normal to have a few fights. After all, you're planning a profoundly private event that all your friends and family will watch (the ceremony), followed by a party that's supposed to express your personalities *and* double as the best bash your circle has ever seen, meanwhile juggling your disparate belief systems, religious values, and social styles. It's no wonder you're feeling some stress.

On the other hand, wedding-planning disagreements *can* indicate larger, underlying conflicts. Which makes now the perfect time to identify your primary areas of friction and to develop good problem-solving skills for the big day and all the days after. The truth is, everyone has conflicts, but that usually doesn't mean you should call the whole thing off.

In our experience, conflicts of difference tend to arise in three places: between the two of you, among your families, and with your pals. Learning to deal with them will help you live happily ever after (not to mention saving you thousands of dollars on therapy, late-night phone calls home to Mom, and dozens of boxes of chocolate doughnuts).

Different Worlds, One Address

You may be the Man from Atlantis, while your honey's the Daughter of Frankenstein, but once you're married, you both become the Atlantis-Frankensteins (metaphorically speaking). This isn't about my way or your way. It's got to be our way, or—sad to say—the highway. Marriage is all about compromise. How do you create your own new family, incorporating both your beliefs?

Knowing Me, Knowing You

Get to know your honey's culture better. Learn her native language, read books about her background, or take a class in her culture or religion. Cook foods from her home country or plan a vacation there. Embrace both cultures—you've got two great traditions in your lives.

Admit It: You're Different

Don't pretend you're exactly the same. Bring up those uncomfortable, maddening, frustrating differences now. For example, you want a Christmas tree, and he refuses. Whether you like it or not, come the end of December, Christmas is going to come again. Don't shy away from those types of problems or attempt to sweep them under the entertainment center and hope they go away. Issues confronting you now—which religion should permeate the ceremony, or how much wedding money to spend—will still be there when you return from your honeymoon—which religion to raise your kids, or how to spend your hard-earned cash.

Issues That Need Resolution—Soon

You want to raise your kids Catholic; your honey doesn't believe in organized religion.
You assume you'll both keep your jobs; your honey assumes women stop working once they're wed.
You plan to avoid your families if they give you grief; your honey values family above all else.
You plan to spend every dime you both make; your honey plans to scrimp and save until retirement.
You plan to keep all your friends, including those of the opposite sex; your honey thinks men and women can't be just friends.

We're not suggesting you spend all your time dwelling on your differences. You obviously share the most important thing—your love for each other, and the desire to spend your lives together. But accepting the fact that you have differences will allow you to move toward resolving them.

RACHEL & JEFFREY

October 6, Los Angeles

THE DAY BEFORE he was to propose to Raquel (known as Rachel), Jeffrey sat across the kitchen table from her father, making jittery small talk as he worked up the nerve to ask him for permission to marry Rachel. "Finally, I just asked," remembers Jeff. "With a slight smile, her father reached across the table and said 'yes.'" Next, Jeff asked Rachel's mother for her permission. "Only this time it was a little more difficult, because my mother-in-law doesn't speak much English and I had to ask in Spanish."

Rachel was a lucky bride indeed. Her brother (the "man of honor"), Mike, is an interior designer by trade. Says Rachel, "My brother coordinated our entire event. He brought magic to our wedding." Mike chose the color palette, he selected the flowers, and he designed the bride's and junior bridesmaid dresses. "He even went to all twelve gown fittings," marvels Rachel. The bride walked down the aisle of strewn rose petals on the lawn at the Hotel Bel-Air, on the arm of her father. The couple was wed by a former Catholic priest.

Following the newlyweds' jubilant first kiss, their sixty guests gathered on the lawn, where tuxedoed waiters served cocktails and hors d'oeuvres. Then, guests were invited indoors for a five-course meal and live Cuban jazz music. Rachel and Jeff view themselves in many ways as an unlikely couple. "He's from the East Coast. I'm from the West Coast. He's white. I'm Latin. He's twenty-six. I'm thirty-five," says Rachel, adding, "but he's not only my husband, he's also my best friend."

Clarify Your Expectations

A lot of people have one set of expectations for their lover and an entirely new slew of requirements for their spouse. It may be fine for your boyfriend to be a starving artist, but your *husband* better damn well bring home the bacon. Or maybe you love having a girlfriend who wears miniskirts and high heels, but you think a *wife* should dress "respectably." Different backgrounds tend to widen the expectation gap when it comes to planning your wedding and your future; the two of you may have different assumptions about the role your families should play, who will handle the social calendar, even whose job it is to take out the trash. Bring those assumptions into the open now.

How Not to Avoid Stuff

Make uncomfortable wedding-planning discussions as pleasant as possible by setting up "an appointment" to talk and then heading to your favorite place to do it. Take yourselves to dinner afterward.

Bang Out Your Beliefs

A lot of fights over nitty-gritty wedding details actually boil down to underlying beliefs. For instance, she doesn't want kids at the wedding, and you want your three-year-old nephew there—end of story. If you haven't already, talk about your views on religion, sex, money, kids, and family. Are there specific points of contention that make you want to gnaw your finger down to the knuckle? Bring them up now! All this talking isn't a way to exhaust each other into agreement. You don't have to agree on everything. But it will help you figure out which beliefs you share (money, religion, favorite houseplants), which issues you disagree on (children, family, which is smarter—cats or dogs), and what your individual opinions are on each of the disputed points. If each knows where the other stands, you can make informed, effective choices about both big and little things. Knowledge is power in the game of life—and blissful wedding planning, too.

Go to Chapter 22 for more on healthy communication skills.

Compromise 101

Ah, conflict resolution. No one said this was going to be easy—just very necessary. There are several different ways you two can come to a compromise on the various issues that are coming up right now. At least one of the following approaches should work for any conflict.

Talk This Way

Try this method of discussing differences—with your beloved, parents, friends, anyone:

1. Show empathy and understanding for the other person's position.
2. State what you feel yourself.
3. Indicate what you'd like to see happen.

Do Both

You want a Catholic wedding. Your honey wants a Jewish wedding. You decide to blend both traditions into one ceremony. Or you want to go to your parents' house for Thanksgiving. Your honey wants to go to her parents' house for Thanksgiving. You decide to take turns—your parents' one year, her parents' the next.

Do Something Else Entirely

You want a Catholic wedding. Your honey wants a Jewish one. You decide to go Unitarian; still religious, but not filled with emotional/familial landmines. Or you want to go to your parents' house for Thanksgiving. Your

LYNN & BEN

October 8, New York City

LYNN AND BEN planned their wedding to incorporate both of their faiths—he's Jewish, she's Episcopalian. "We wanted to celebrate both but also recognize the two different traditions," Lynn says. Because the couple did not want to choose one religion over the other, they decided to hold both their ceremony and reception at the Americas Society in Manhattan. "We liked it because it had no religious affiliation. We wanted an intimate place that would give us a close sense of family and friends," the bride says. "It was perfect."

While Lynn and Ben put aspects of each religion into their ceremony, they chose a nondenominational officiant. "We worked very closely with him on different elements of the ceremony," Lynn says. "The vows we wrote had universal themes that could be applied to both of our religions."

The couple hopes that the blending of faiths will carry into their marriage. "We plan on continuing to honor both religions," the bride says. "We want to celebrate our backgrounds as much as we can."

ASK CARLEY

The Parents Are Coming!

Q: Help! My honey's parents are coming from India for the wedding, and then they're staying with us for *three months.* They plan to stay in our bedroom, while we sleep on the couch. Haven't they ever heard of the Holiday Inn? My fiancé said, "You people in this country are so cold. You don't care about anyone beyond yourselves." So I said, "You're hopelessly enmeshed in your family. Why don't you grow up? And tell them not to be so inconsiderate." Now we're not speaking to each other. (Which is a big problem, since we're in the middle of choosing caterers.) We love each other, but what do we do?

A: First of all, stop making this personal! Your honey was obviously raised to value his family *very much,* and in a very hands-on way. You were clearly brought up on the more independent plan. Locate these difference within the broader context of your cultures—and normalize relations by understanding their cultural base. These are two different belief systems you're dealing with. Once you recognize that it's not mere personal stubbornness, you can begin to arrive at a compromise. Maybe they stay with you, but for a shorter length of time.

honey wants to go to her parents'. You decide to have Thanksgiving at *your* house, and invite both sets of parents.

Do Neither

You: Catholic. Your honey: Jewish. After talking about it, you realize that neither of you really wants all the rigmarole of a religious wedding. You decide to bag the whole debate and have a fabulous civil service on the beach. Or, You: Thanksgiving dinner at your parents' house. Your honey: Dinner at her parents' house. After some discussion, you discover that you both hate turkey and both of your families spend every Thanksgiving fighting. You decide to go out for Mexican food instead.

Family Friction

Of course, differences and conflicts don't always stop with you. If you're marrying outside your religion, race, socioeconomic background, or suburban subdivision, you may be getting plenty of unpleasant, unsupportive, downright negative feedback from your family about now. So how, exactly, should you respond to this kind of familial "support"?

Show Affection, Not Rejection

A lot of parents view their child's choice of a "different" partner as a direct hit, a rejection of them, a slap in the face to all that they've taught you. If your parents are feeling defensive, rejected, and rebuffed, there's *no way* they're going to listen to why your honey is so great. Tell them how much you love and value your own religion (or race or culture) first. Assure them you're *not* turning your back on what they taught you and that your children will learn it, too. Let them know that you want their support. If you convince them that you value their opinions and beliefs, you have a lot better chance of them laying off of yours.

Go to Chapter 24 for more help dealing with family.

Give Your Folks the Floor

Let your parents voice their opinions and give you their advice (even if only *they* consider it "advice"). Then ask them what conflicts arose during their own wedding planning. How did their families react to news of their engagement? If they had it to do over again, what would they handle differently? What "truths" have they learned about marriage? Find out their concerns. Really listen.

Talking to your parents accomplishes three things: (1) It lets you know what their issues are so you can address their real fears; (2) it gives you ammunition to diffuse future attacks effectively; and (3) it shows respect. Asking their opinion is a form of honoring them. It gives them the sense that you value them, which can go a long, long way toward helping them stop undervaluing *your* decisions.

Accept a Little Disapproval

If there are some points on which they just don't, or won't, agree with you—guess what? They don't have to. They can harbor different beliefs or a different view of how you should do things. And you still can go about your business as usual, aware of their disapproval but loving each other anyway.

Keep the Door Open

We believe (as do most therapists) that you should try to keep your family in your life as much as is humanly possible. If your parents are giving you flak, don't resort to the silent treatment. Alone in your living room, that disapproving comment can start to feel like an avalanche of rejection. By keeping in contact, you've got a better shot of maintaining your perspective and remembering that this dispute is only a part of your relationship with them. Accepting your family—foibles and all—is part of accepting yourself, really. Of course, that doesn't mean that you need to take abuse. If you get together to go over your guest list and the talk turns into a rousing round of "Criticize the Kids," get out of there (gracefully) and return later, when everyone has calmed down.

Healthy Mental Attitudes

Consider that differences can be good: Rather than viewing differences as monsters you must kill, adopt the attitude that they are challenging, invigorating, and stimulating.

Look at issues through your honey's eyes: When resolving issues, don't try to force your spouse to *prove* his love. Think of what you can do to show yours instead. Healthy couples go out of their way to do things that they know will make the other person happy.

Wear rose-colored glasses about your partner's uniqueness: In lasting relationships, couples see their partner's quirks as charming. You probably already see your honey's bizarre behavior in the best possible light (and adore him/her because of it). Make a habit of continuing to do so.

R-E-S-P-E-C-T: Don't go back on your agreement to respect each other's beliefs. If you're secretly hoping your beloved will give up his/her religion after a few years with you, you're going to be in for some heartache down the line. Get it out in the open. If you've agreed to maintain your differences, no fair going back on that.

If your parents are the ones shutting *you* out, we still advise keeping your door unlocked. Go ahead and send them a wedding invitation anyway. They very well may turn around and show up at your wedding.

Set Boundaries

Even if your parents' input feels too painful to endure, you should try to keep them in your life, *with limits.* If, every time you get together to discuss ways to include both families in the wedding, conflicts arise or pot shots are taken, try your best to keep them involved in your planning, but do it by telephone. Or control the discussion by asking for input on specific items *only* and then changing the subject. Let them know, if you have to, that you'll stick around until you hear *one word* against your beloved, and then you'll slip out the back. You're adults now. If you choose to keep your family in your life (which we hope you do), you can set the terms.

What Will the P's Think?

"Give up on the idea that everyone is going to be enthusiastic and positive about everything you do. Children think that they should receive 100 percent approval from their parents for everything, and that's a myth. Generally, people adjust, slowly. A lot of parents may not be excited about a marriage to begin with, but they get over it."

—Jane Campbell, Ph.D., Houston-based therapist

Fair-Weather Friends

If you're choosing an "unconventional" path, recognize now that at various times during your life together, you'll probably receive unpleasant, unsolicited feedback from the narrow-minded world out there. The following is some ammunition to help you through it.

Decide Whose Opinion Matters

It's important to distinguish between prejudices spouted by perfect (or rather, imperfect) strangers and acquaintances and genuine concerns raised by good friends and family members. The clerk at the Stop 'n' Go casts a sideways glance at you because you're black and she's white? Who cares? You don't owe that clerk any explanation for how you live your life.

If that store clerk is your best friend, though, his opinion will be harder to dismiss. You've heard it a million times but we'll say it again anyway: If

Questions to Answer Now

What religious or cultural traditions are you going to use in your wedding?
Are you going to address your differences in your vows or readings?
How are you going to get your families to mingle at the reception?
What religion are you going to raise your kids?
How can you turn your back on all we've taught you?
Aren't you afraid your kids will be teased because you're different races?
How are you going to handle random prejudice?
Isn't s/he old enough to be your mother/father?

someone is really your friend, she's not going to turn her back on you because she disagrees with your choice of a life partner. On the other hand, give your good friends a chance to say their piece. They may really be concerned about you and only trying to help. Hear them out and then make your own decisions.

Assess Your Commitment

If others' opinions really make or break your day, now is the time to realize that. The world isn't going to change during your ceremony. (Though it's true that peoples' opinions may change over longer periods of time.) It may help you to think of yourselves as pioneers. If you can't hack that role, admit it now. Be honest about who you are and how committed you are to this relationship.

Go to Chapter 24 for more help with friends.

There's no rule that says all happily married couples must share the same religion, background, skin color, or age group. What they do share, however, is respect for each other. View your differences as the assets they are; two great cultures to draw from, two backgrounds to tap, and plenty of zesty conversation fodder for the rest of your lives.

CHAPTER TWENTY-FOUR

in-laws & outlaws

As you embark upon this final frontier of togetherness, don't be surprised to find just about everyone in your lives crammed into the space capsule with you. You may have believed marriage was a private affair between the two of you, but unless you're secretly eloping (which may sound like a pretty good idea right about now), announcing your wedding likely will inspire everyone you've ever met to rev up their opinions and let them loose. Not everyone will be thrilled with the way your new status impacts them—nor will they all keep their feelings to themselves.

Fact is, your personal ceremony *does* affect others. It not only joins two families who may not have much in common (other than you two), but it also changes the relationships you've created as single people. If the behavior of relatives and friends seems bizarre, here's a little insight that may help you deal.

Dealing with Your Parents

At the head of the line of potential interference stand your parents—those people you love who, come wedding time, may take to making your life a living hell. They might be questioning all your decisions, insisting that you do things their way, or exploding into angry harangues with no apparent provocation. (They also may be the most helpful people around, but we're just looking at their less lovely traits, for now.) Why are they acting so strangely? They have good reason. Tying the knot is a huge rite of passage—for you and for them. Getting married is the final act dividing the adults from the kids, especially in your parents' eyes. And since their main role in your life, to date, has been to protect you—their precious cub—from the outside world, watching you take adulthood for a test drive can be pretty unsettling—more so than other transitions, because it's the one that makes their usefulness wane (and their mortality wax). But you can, and should, help make the transition smoother.

Look at the Subtext

Is this family feud *really* about the color of the napkins? Probably not. Although we will say that sometimes, napkins might actually just be the problem. Fights over frivolous details tend to mask some other struggle—they're the symptoms, not the cause. Rather than arguing endlessly about trivialities, get to the root of the problem. Here are a few common "hidden" conflicts that may be motivating your parents' bizarre behavior.

Go to Chapter 4 for ideas on how to include your dads in your wedding preparations.

A Slipping Sense of Control: As your parents feel their influence on you becoming less crucial, they may become obsessed with micromanaging every detail of your wedding, instead. If you respond by screaming "I don't need your dumb old ideas anymore!" you're adding fuel to the fire of their sense of lost significance. Instead, assure them that you love them and still value their opinions. As out-of-left-field as it may sound, acknowledging their importance in your life may help them ease up a bit. If not, tell them you'd like to handle some of your wedding tasks yourselves and see if they'll turn any over to you, or consider the joy of letting someone else do all the work while you just slip on your dress and tux and attend. You'll have plenty of details to deal with once you're married.

Whatever you do, *don't* get defensive. You don't have to prove that your decisions are sound or your choices sane. You're going to get married, regardless of who chooses the flowers. The ultimate power (of growing up and moving on) is in your hands.

An Uneasiness About Change: Remember what we said about change—about how it equals loss? Things are changing for them, too, and in a big way. You'll have someone new to depend on, to go to when you're sick, and so on. Empathize. As cheesy as it sounds, they're losing their little baby and the wedding is just the first of the major decisions in life that you're going to be making without them. Think of it as heading off to college multiplied by a thousand.

A Desire to Rewrite Their Past: Perhaps your mom didn't have her fantasy ballroom wedding, and she's decided that you damn well will. Never mind that you want a civil service and a backyard barbecue—this is her chance (in her mind) to right that earlier wrong.

This is pretty tough argument to win. Mom is not being logical; she's spewing emotion. *Of course* this is your wedding, not hers. *Of course* she's had a happy marriage, despite her "failed" wedding. But as anyone who has ever been in a fight knows, a logical rebuttal just skips right over the surface of a cauldron of seething feelings. Try to unravel her tirade, instead—figure out what part of her dream nuptials she's sorry she missed. Chances are there's a common thread you can work with.

Thanks for the Memories

Ask your parents about their wedding—what they wore, served, danced to. Take a look at their wedding photos. Not only will you help ease parental tension by showing your interest in and respect for them, but you also may get some great ideas for your own wedding.

Fear of How It Will Reflect on Them: Some parents are hyperaware of their place in society. If you get married in the back of your VW van, they know that Mrs. Snotface of the country club will lord it over them for years. Peer pressure among parents? It happens. If your parents are pushing you to have a Trump-style wedding when all your lives you've been strictly Simpsons (as in Homer), they may have status woes.

This is some pretty warped thinking, but you may not feel comfortable confronting them directly about it. Instead, see if you can figure out which status symbols are critical to them. This will give you an idea of what elements you should try to be flexible about. And question your own motives,

ASK CARLEY

Who Gets to Plan This Thing?

Q: My parents are paying for my wedding. Does this mean they have the final say on *everything*?

A: If your parents are doing the Lord of the Wedding dance, do your best to accept it. There's no rule about who has the final say—and we'd hope they'd give *you* the honor, since it is your wedding—but those with the cash can always take it back. (And you might consider being a bit indulgent toward a set of parents willing to foot the whole bill!) If you can't handle their incessant demands, try asking them to pay for specific items rather than underwriting the whole wedding.

too—make sure you're not opting for a down-market affair just because you know it will embarrass them. This is the time to try to heal old wounds, not gain the upper hand. If your parents have always been status-conscious, you already know what to expect from them. Try to let their "needs" figure into your planning. Two words: Humor them.

How to Cope

Even if you've figured out why your mom or dad is acting so strange, you still have months of planning ahead of you. Try these conflict-solving tactics to make the process more fun.

Apply the Five-Year Test: Whenever you feel yourself about to explode over some disputed detail, ask yourself how much you'll really care about this five years from now. "Your bridesmaids *must* wear the same dress or the whole wedding will be ruined!" your mom screams. "I refuse to dress my friends like Barbies. I'd rather kill myself!" you scream back. Stop. Breathe deeply. And ask yourself, "Will I really care about their dress five years down the road?" If you work in the fashion industry, you might. Otherwise, probably not. Is it worth the grief? You decide.

Give Each Time You Take: Every time you win a round, make sure Mom gets something she wants, too. Or offer up a tasty tidbit first to help you gain ground. For example, Mom wants the matching dresses. And you know she also wants the men to wear tails. Say something like "What if we dress the men in tails, to keep it formal, but put the bridesmaids in assorted styles?" Or: "How about tails for the guys, the same color and material for the girls, but each in a style that flatters her figure?"

Soften Them with Sweetness: Like the give-when-you-get approach, kindness can carry you far in the game of compromise. If you hurt someone's feelings, you're not only fighting an opposing opinion, you're also paying reparations for your slight. Keep everything cozy. Assure your parents that you think they have great ideas and want what's best for you. Actually listen to their points (which you actually may agree with sometimes, in spite of yourself). Then calmly state yours.

Stop When Things Get Heated: If the discussion becomes a diatribe, take a break. Good solutions rarely arise from mud-slinging contests. Excuse yourself. Take a walk. And then resume talks in a better mood.

ASK CARLEY

No Love Lost?

Q: My parents are ripping into my fiancée, and I don't know what to do about it. I love her, but I love them, too.

A: Your parents may be criticizing your choice for several reasons. Perhaps they feel dismissed, as if you prefer her over them (an immature stance, but a stance nonetheless). Perhaps they fear she's the wrong one for you. Perhaps they just like to criticize. The solution depends on their motivation, of course. But try these tactics:

Listen to their complaints, *alone.* There's no reason for your sweetie to sit through a character assassination. Hear them out and really think about the issues they raise. If you decide their points are sound, you've got some serious thinking to do.

Focus inward, not outward. Make sure you're not putting so much energy into defending yourself and your fiancée that you fail to look inward at your relationship to be sure it's really what's right for you.

Explain your side. If their complaints are invalid, explain why, *calmly.* They may genuinely not have noticed your sweetie's good points. Give them a chance to see her through your eyes. But if you've chosen someone unlike them for a good reason (such as they're bigots and your sweetie's not), steer clear of the flash-point issues and focus on the traits of hers that they'll appreciate.

Help them get to know her better. Take them out to dinner as a couple. Invite them to your honey's art opening/bowling league final match/handball championship. Start with light, brief activities that you know they will enjoy or that let them see your sweetie as you do.

Set boundaries. If your parents refuse to change their minds, it's time to create some rules. Your loyalty has to be to your new relationship. Tell them you love them but no longer want to hear complaints about your honey. Continue to include them as much as possible in your wedding planning, but only in ways that don't hurt you or her.

Divorced Dilemmas

If you've got two sets of parents, you also have twice as many people whose tender feelings you can hurt. If your plethora of parents is adding angst to your planning, try these tactics.

Make Them Feel Valued

Let's face it, if you grew up with your mom and stepdad, there were probably nights when your biological dad sat home alone in his living room thinking about how his children were being raised by another man. During a wedding, everyone's insecurities become more pronounced. And when you've got more than two parents vying for your affection, they can be hypersensitive about how you treat them, how you address them, and how you include them in your wedding.

Go out of your way to make everyone feel important and wanted. We know you're busy, but a little extra warmth now will save you a lot of unwanted grief later (like next week). It's worth the time to call your dad (or mom, if she's the more distant parent), or drop a note. Think about the good times you've had together, and bring them up. While you're at it, be extra-nice to the parent who raised you and stepparents, too.

Include Them All

Find specific ways to include *all* your parents. Ditch the traditional breakdowns and assign your own roles. Maybe you'll have a father/daughter dance, stepfather/daughter dance, *and* a stepmother/daughter disco number. Maybe you'll ask your biological dad to lead you down the aisle and your stepdad to lead the toasting. However you divide the tasks, focus on each person's job when you talk to him/her, stressing how important it is to you. Your goal is to make each parent feel honored.

Beyond the wedding details, you may need to assure your parents of their continued role in your new life, even if it takes a little adjusting of old roles. Make a date for lunch with Mom and Dad and talk about *them,* for a change. Or see if Mom is up for that weekly yoga class you want to join. Changing a relationship can be awkward—with parents or with friends. But stick with it; once you establish your new roles, you'll be back on smooth ground with your folks.

Where will all these steprelatives sit? Go to Chapter 6 for the skinny on ceremony seating, Chapter 7 for the essentials on reception seating charts.

Discuss Wedding Roles Early

Lay out the plan way ahead of time so everyone has a chance to adjust and to voice any objections. Go over the proposed ceremony structure, seating arrangements, toasting order, and the like. If someone opposes a specific element, ask for an alternative that would make him more comfortable. If you're afraid your ceremony plan (speech, seating, etc.) is going to make a parent squirm (or make a scene), talk to her about it *now.*

Go to Chapter 4 for new ways to include your assortment of parental types in your wedding.

Interacting with the In-Laws

Your honey is so unique—the way she folds socks instead of rolling them into balls, how she makes gallons of chicken soup and then instantly freezes them "for later." Where'd she ever get such charming quirks? From her parents, who apparently do things quite differently from yours. And while her family's unusual ways probably seemed charming while you were dating, those same quaint traits and differing tastes can drive you nuts during wedding planning.

Accept That Both Ways Can Be Right

Even if her parents do seem like extras from *One Flew Over the Cuckoo's Nest,* they did manage to produce that fabulous being known as your fiancée. Their ideas can't be *all* bad. Try to be open-minded about their views, and look for ways they might benefit you. They're tightwads compared to your free-and-easy folks? Let them help you sketch out a budget. Embracing them does not mean being disloyal to your own family. You have room to include them all in your heart (and wedding).

Don't make it into a me-against-them struggle. There's no need to compete. You already won; your fiancé obviously chose *you.* Pushing him to "side" with you on wedding stuff will create stress, not closeness.

Leaving a Parent Out?

If you don't want to include a parent in your planning—you don't have a good relationship or any relationship at all, say—that's okay. Just be aware that the person may approach you about it. Think about how you'll respond and whether there's any way to include him/her that won't make you uncomfortable.

Have Realistic Relationship Expectations

You don't have to love her parents. You love her—that's enough. But you *do* have to be considerate and pleasant. Unfortunately, there's no magical instant-friendship formula. You'll get to know them as time goes by and you spend more time together. If you want to speed things up, invite his mom out for lunch. Or see if her dad could go for a round on the golf course. Not up to the one-on-one thing? Grab the phone and say "hello" the next time he's chatting with his mom. Chances are good that you'll become close. You've already got one very important thing in common—your love for your sweetie.

Address Potential Conflicts Now

If they're homophobes, bigots, or rabidly antismoking, for example, and your family is, well . . . one-third gay and primary stockholders in RJR-Nabisco, things are bound to be tense. Have your honey tell her folks about your family's background long before the wedding, even if it makes you nervous (since you know how they feel). They probably had no idea they were offending you by voicing their opinions. A lot of people just repeat the same old stock prejudices without really listening to themselves or considering how their audience feels.

If they're strongly committed to their point of view, your honey should let them know that he expects them to curb their words around you and be on their best behavior during your wedding. Let your family in on your in-laws' beliefs, too. By letting everyone know what to expect in advance, you give them time to adjust their attitudes (or at least their behavior) now—not at your wedding.

Sibling Rivalry

Sibling rivalry doesn't automatically cease just because you're grown up. We know some very nice grandparents who have managed to keep their sibling struggles alive and well. If your siblings are less than loving, try to:

Be the adult: To change long-established behavior, one of you has to start acting differently—and we nominate you. While you can't change other people, you'd be amazed at how easily you can change someone's reaction by adjusting your own actions. Talk to your sibling. Explain that you're individuals and that what one of you does is not a reflection on the other. Focus on him. Be a friend to him. If he can't handle hearing about your love life, don't force it on him. Don't get dragged into juvenile shouting matches.

Include, don't exclude: On the flip side of the sibling rivalry issue is displaced sibling syndrome. If you and your sis have always been close, your gain may feel like her loss. And it just may be—you always turned to her for guidance, but you've just replaced her with your sweetie. It's up to you to go out of your way to include her and find a role for her in your new family. Talk to your spouse-to-be about this; she may have suggestions of ways to welcome your sister (like setting her up with her brother).

Recognize a pattern: If you've always been the one to get the girl, the grades, or the goods, your sibling might view your wedding as one more example of how you always come out on top. Old perceptions and resentments are hard to change. It's probably not your honey that's ticking her off, but you and your damn good fortune.

Confront Your Own Folks

If your parents seem to be competing for worst in-law-of-the-year award or have elevated meddling into an Olympic sport, your best bet is to separate and each confront your own. You have more experience with your folks, while he knows best how to handle his. Try to be as kind as possible while clearly expressing your loyalty to your soon-to-be and your plans.

MERI & STEPHEN

February 2, New York City

FOR MERI, who is Jewish, and Stephen, who is Catholic, a civil service just wasn't an option. "We—and our families—wanted our wedding ceremony be special, to have the importance and the gravity we felt it deserved," Meri says. "Stephen and I are not religious per se, but we are spiritual people."

Their families, as Meri is quick to point out, were fully supportive of the couple. "At every step of the way when we were planning our wedding, our parents truly just wanted us to be happy," she says. But they had their own small wishes: Stephen and his family wanted the wedding to be recognized by the Catholic church; Meri wanted to be sure her family would see the familiar elements of a Jewish wedding. And Stephen's mom had only one thing that she really, truly wanted at the ceremony: She wanted to hear "Ave Maria."

The couple found their answer in Reverend Gwen Gillespie, a family friend and a minister who regularly performs interfaith services. They had a cantor (Meri's cousin) ready and willing to participate, as well as a priest (who was recommended by a rabbi). "The minister did the bulk of our ceremony," says Meri, "but all of them took part."

Meri and Stephen spent a great deal of time, along with their minister, planning their service. They attended Catholic pre-cana (premarriage) classes. On the wedding day, the couple married beneath a birch huppah (a Jewish wedding canopy), signed a ketubah (a Jewish wedding contract), had readings (normally not included in the Jewish wedding ceremony), lit a unity candle, and Stephen broke a glass with his heel. A friend of the couple sang "Ave Maria," accompanied by a small orchestra.

Says Meri, "I know it sounds funny, but I still remember so much about the ceremony. We weren't just going through the motions, because we had thought about every detail." She adds that with a minister, a priest, and a rabbi present, just about every guest at the ceremony felt connected, too. "We figure we're blessed by everyone," she laughs.

ASK CARLEY

Top-Ten Family Q and A's

Most of the wedding "etiquette" dilemmas to-be-weds tell us about have to do with family conflicts. The following are some common problems and our best solutions. As always, use what you can, and otherwise rely on your common sense.

Q: Is it okay for my mother to give me away at my wedding? My father expects to, but he hasn't been a part of my life since I was two.

A: It's absolutely appropriate for Mom to give you away. The larger issue is breaking it to your dad. It's understandable to feel uncomfortable with having him as your aisle escort if he hasn't been a very big presence in your life. Tread carefully, and try to break it to him gently, even if you don't feel "gentle" about it—you don't need big blow-ups right now—and enjoy walking with your mom.

Q: My father recently remarried—but told me two weeks after the wedding. I now have a stepmother and a stepsister, neither of whom I'm very fond of. I would love for my father to attend my wedding, but do I have to invite his new wife and stepdaughter?

A: Since your dad didn't tell you he had remarried until two weeks *after* it happened, you probably don't feel like being super-gracious to him right now. But *not* inviting his new family to your wedding isn't the answer. That's only going to cause bad blood between you and your dad—and these other two people who, like it or not, are now family. You probably have enough to stress about, right? Why not be a bigger person and invite them all. If they come, great—it's not like you have to sit and talk to them all day. You'll be busy enough to just say a kind hello and go about your business.

Q: Should I invite my ex–parents-in-law? We became very close after my divorce and they are loving grandparents to my six-year-old son. However, their son, my ex, is a total jerk (they freely admit this), and I am afraid they may feel uncomfortable around my new family and old relatives who hate their son.

A: Especially if it will comfort your son to have his grandparents at the wedding, it's totally acceptable to invite them. The matter of whether they will be comfortable is something they need to consider. Talk to them about it before you send out the invites—say you'd really love to have them there for you and your son, and that your continued relationship with them means a lot to you, but you understand that they might feel awkward about it. Let them think about it and make their own decision.

Q: My oldest son is getting married next fall. I love his fiancée and I'm thrilled. The only problem is that my son, whom we adopted at birth, wants to invite his birth mother (whom we recently found) to the wedding. I have always been grateful to her for giving life to my son and making the decision to give him up for adoption, but I do not want to share this day with her. I want him to be happy, and this is his day, but she was not there for the zits, mumps, broken hearts, tears, etc. When he realized I was upset by the idea he immediately dropped it, but now I feel guilty!

A: You said it yourself: You want him to be happy, and this is his day. Your feelings are totally understandable and normal—you raised him, and you feel that it's your right to be the mother of the groom on his wedding day. What you need to remember is that you *will* be, whether his birth mother is present or not. Any relationship he builds with her is not going to compare to or replace his relationship with you. Talk to your son about your feelings—tell him you're feeling like his birth mom is going to take your place at the wedding, even though you know that's foolish. Let him reassure you. And then give him your blessing and let *him* make the decision about whether to invite his birth mom or not.

Q: My parents are divorced and both are happily remarried. Both couples regularly attend family gatherings, although my mom and dad amicably avoid each other as much as possible. My mom wants to walk down the aisle with my father and me. Is being given away by both parents okay from an etiquette standpoint? (I wouldn't mind.) They do make the effort to get along.

A: How great that your parents are willing to coexist, even if they really don't have much to say to each other these days! This alone is helping you to avoid wedding stress, trust us. There is absolutely nothing improper about having *both* your parents walk you down the aisle—in fact, it's the norm in Jewish weddings. (You even could consider having your fiancé's parents walk *him* in, as well—but they don't have to if you'd rather meet him at the altar!) Just make sure Dad is cool with walking with you and Mom, and you're in business.

Q: My parents can't stand my fiancé's parents (and vice versa). They also don't like my fiancé. They think I can find someone better. My parents (mostly my father) even went as far as saying that if we did get married, they would not come to the wedding or support it. I'm hurt, and I don't know what to do. We're not getting married until two years from now, but it's like a war when I want to talk about the wedding. It's putting a strain on our relationship, too, and I do not want to lose him.

A: The key here is your time frame. The wedding's not for a while, so maybe the actual marriage part doesn't have to be at the forefront right now, either, as far as your parents/families are concerned. Instead, concentrate on your relationship—and let your parents know that you love this person and you hope they will come around and be happy that he makes *you* happy. It's always tough when your parents don't support what you're doing or don't approve of the person you've decided is the *one*. But ultimately, you're the one who has to make the decision, with or without their approval. All you can do is let them know you hope they will change their minds and then quietly show them that you've made the right choice.

Q: I've already decided that my stepfather, who raised me, will walk me down the aisle. My real dad has not shown the slightest interest in my wedding. He even called my mom and questioned her about my fiancé and said he really didn't think he was the one for me. Anyhow, my dad's wife threatened my relationship with him if he didn't walk me down the aisle. Please help!

A: It's always difficult when you've got a stepdad whom you love and respect and a real father who—well, who's your father. But it sounds like you've made up your mind to walk with your stepdad, and rightly so—if he is the person who has really been a father to you, then he should be the one to escort you to the altar. As far as your real dad, our best advice as far as deciding how much (or if) he should be involved in the wedding is that you should make your decisions about that based on how *you* feel about *him,* not because someone else told you what to do. Perhaps it would help to sit down with your real dad and talk it out. Remember that it's *your* wedding day, and call upon all your family members to try to coexist for your sake.

Q: I had a huge falling out with my future brother-in-law. Okay, I hate his guts. I really don't want him in or at our wedding. My fiancé knows his brother is an idiot, but he's still his brother, after all. How do I approach him with the idea of his brother not being invited? And if I have no choice, how do I deal with that loser being there?

A: No one wants someone they detest at, much less in, their wedding. But you're right, no matter how much of a moron this guy is, he's your fiancé's brother, and you are going to be related to him soon. We'd advise against telling your honey you want to bar his bro from the wedding—it will only make things tense between the two of *you.* It's fine to let your fiancé know how you feel about what happened between you and his brother, and that you feel far from close to the guy and would prefer not to have any more contact with him than is absolutely necessary. But uninviting him will only make things worse for everyone. Instead of focusing on the problem, just dismiss it. There are going to be plenty of people at your wedding whom you are going to want to hug and kiss and pay attention to. Focus on them, and put the brother out of your mind.

Q: My fiancé's parents went through a messy divorce, and his sisters and mother hate his dad. His sisters say we should have two ceremonies, one for their mother's side and one for their father's side of the family. I think this is an unfair demand!

A: It's definitely an unfair demand, and you can only hope they were kidding! There's no reason you have to put on two ceremonies to placate everyone. As for what to say to them: "We're sorry you feel that way, but we really want everyone to put aside their differences and come to our wedding. We're inviting both sides of your family, and we hope everyone will attend and be happy for us." They may be upset, but hopefully they will be able to deal on your wedding day.

Q: My father is remarried, and my stepmother refuses to be in the same room with my mother. I find her attitude unreasonable. What do I do?

A: Sounds like your stepmother is acting freezing cold. You're right that she's being unreasonable. It's your wedding, and of *course* your mother is going to be there. Duh! Talk to your dad and see if he'll talk some sense into his wife, or talk to her yourself if you feel comfortable. Just tell her you're sorry she feels the way she does, and you hope she will reconsider and be there on your big day.

Why Friends Freak Out

Naturally, all of your pals are thrilled with the news of your engagement. They're calling you up with congratulations and sending fruit baskets. For your single friends, especially, the news of your union is like a shot of adrenaline: "It can happen!" they're all saying, popping the corks on the vintage champagne that they've been saving for just this kind of monumental occasion.

Um, right. Unfortunately, friends may get pretty bizarre around engagement time, too. Gaining a spouse shouldn't mean losing a friend, but sometimes even people you count among your closest buddies seem to turn on you the moment they hear your blissful news. What should you do?

Your Bliss, Their Bummer

Fact is, your good news might feel just a *teensy* bit negative for them. When you change from a bar-hopping, all-night-partying stud muffin into a happily married guy, it's a loss of lifestyle—and possibly bar companion—for your friends. People react to loss in different ways. For the most part, they don't call you up and say, "Hey, man, I love you. I really hope you'll still be my buddy now that you're getting a wife." Instead, they may withdraw or become combative or angry. They probably don't even realize they're doing it.

Accept that your gain might be a loss for others, and be sensitive to their feelings. Don't pretend everything is the same. You're *not* going to go out for all-night beer brawls any more (at least not every weekend). You probably *will* start making more couple friends. But that doesn't mean you're going to ditch your best pals. Assure your friends of your continued commitment to them *and* your to-be. And make sure to make time for them.

Redefining Your Relationships

Friendships change when situations do, and you can't always tell who will weather the transition, or in what way. But you *can* make the decision to keep a VIP (very important pal) in your life. Make a dinner date with your friend and talk about what your marriage means to each of you. Discuss ways you think it might affect your friendship, and come up with a plan. You might decide to sign up for that dance class/basketball league/croquet team you've been discussing, ensuring that you'll spend Wednesday nights together. Or agree to double date with any of her prospective beaux, rather than going out to the bars with her to find them. Getting all those fears out in the open (yours and hers) and addressing them can actually bring you closer.

Are You Wedding Obsessed?

All right, admit it. Somewhere way, way back in your mind, you fear that maybe you're contributing to your friends' abominable behavior by becoming an obsessed bride-to-be whose unending fascination with her own wedding overshadows all other issues and people in existence. How do you diagnose this sickness? And what do you do?

Survey Your Sensitivity: Your best friend has been trying to find Mr. Right for years. Now that you've found *your* dream guy, do you start every sentence with "Thor and I think . . ." or "Thor and I are going . . ." or "Thor says . . ."? You're acting a little self-absorbed. (Okay, a lot.) Be sensitive to your friend's insecurity and feelings of frustration/unfairness. She doesn't need to know everything Thor thinks. Whenever you feel yourself saying the "Th"-word, stop and ask about her life instead. We're not saying you should never talk about your sweetie again. But to break the habit, he's subject non grata for a while.

Even if your friend is happily married/partnered herself, a steady diet of wedding and nothing else can turn the best of buddies into zombies. It's just not that interesting to everyone else. Even we wedding-world enthusiasts can find the subject just a little bit unfascinating every once in a while. Don't lose your perspective.

Examine Your Expectations: We've all heard stories of horrible bridesmaid behavior. And yes, sometimes your wedding party, or a specific member, can turn on you. But we've also heard of brides who ask their ten best friends to spend $300 each on an unflattering dress they'll never wear again and then expect a shower as grand as the reception. Your bridesmaids don't have parents footing the bill. And they do have lives beyond your wedding. Are you making realistic requests? They're supposed to be your *friends.* How about a little friendly concern for their finances here?

And what about the dress itself? You know how picky you are about your clothes. How would you like to squeeze into the exact wrong cut and color—and then pay for it out of your vacation kitty? Are you choosing a dress that's going to make half the party look like sausage casing? Get their opinion on what they're going to wear.

We know it's hard to turn a critical eye on yourself when it seems like that's just what everyone else is doing. But take the time to look at the situation from others' points of view. If you find you've been acting a bit monstrous, it's not too late to change. Invite your attendants over for an apology and a pizza. And then talk about something else!

PART FOUR

THE GREAT ESCAPE

CHAPTER TWENTY-FIVE

honeymoon highway

How often in life is it encouraged—all right, *demanded*—that you drop everything and rush off to the most romantic spots on earth to while away the days in unabashed bliss? Once—right now, on your honeymoon. This is your chance to take the biggest trip of your lives (to date) and splurge to your hearts' content—with everyone's deep approval and warm good wishes.

There's only one rule: Take the trip of *your* dreams. Talk about what kind of vacation floats your boat (cruise?), makes your hearts soar (a B&B high in the hills?), or sends goose bumps down your spines (an Arctic adventure?). Or maybe you're just ready for a good old-fashioned beach honeymoon. Banish that six-letter "B" word from your mind; budget has no place in your honeymoon vision (yet). Just get your dream trip in sharp focus; we'll help you figure out how to foot the bill in Chapter 24.

Go to Chapter 26 for help planning your trip.

So what are the options? Here's a sampling of some of our favorite spots.

The Best Beaches

Calm breezes, sandy beaches—it's a classic honeymoon scenario. A beach vacation can be Ritz-Carlton chic or Ritz-cracker casual. It can be quiet and deserted—just a strip of sugar sand, swaying palms, and thee—or Baywatch–meets–Spring Break boisterous. You decide what type of sand scenario says "romance" to you. Whichever way you go, you'll find miles of excellent beach right here in our very own hemisphere—meaning you don't have to cross the globe to get good sand. The one drawback of the sun-and-surf approach is that it's weather-dependent. While we know you'll think of something to do if it rains, plan to hit your tropical isle of choice when hurricanes generally don't. Here are some of our top beach spots.

Honeymoon Love

Newlyweds used to drink mead, a honey-based wine, for their first married month, or "moon"—honey + moon = honeymoon. This fermented brew of honey, water, yeast, and spices, originally created by medieval monks, was used to ease any postwedding tension (and help the couple get busy in the bedroom!).

Kauai, Hawaii

The least developed of the Big Four Hawaiian islands (Hawaii, Kauai, Oahu, and Maui), Kauai lets you experience Hawaii's legendary lushness without tons of T-shirt shops, traffic, or tourists. After an easy five-hour flight to Honolulu from California, it's a quick hop on an interisland airline to this westerly wonderland.

Why You'll Love It: Possibly the most romantic island in the world, with green mountains, crashing waterfalls, and geyserlike water flumes shooting over rocks. About as exotic as you can go and still get the Sunday *Times.* Peaceful. Serene. Awe-inspiring.

When to Go: Year round (December and January are the rainiest months).

Must-Dos: Hike Waimea Canyon (called "the Grand Canyon of the Pacific") to see plants that grow nowhere else in the world. Take a helicopter tour around the island for an aerial view of the rivers, waterfalls, and the stunning cliffs of the Na Pali coastline. Snorkel at Ke'e Beach. Stroll through the town of Hanalei. Pig out at a Hawaiian luau. For info, call the Kauai Hotline at 800-262-1400.

Anguilla

This little-known, formerly British island has what many consider the best beaches in the Caribbean—and the most private. Chances are you'll see more goats than people on your trip.

Why You'll Love It: Dozens of beaches (thirty-three coves, to be exact) with white sand, aquamarine water, and no one but you and your beloved anywhere in sight. Charming, English-speaking locals. A totally quiet, private hideaway that feels like a deserted island—but with room service. A short ferry ride from the stores, restaurants, and bustle of St. Martin/Sint Maarten, the half-French/half-Dutch island visible on the horizon that's as bustling as Anguilla is calm.

When to Go: December-August.

Must-Dos: Take off your watch. Discover a different isolated cove every day. Explore the island by bike. (Ride on the left side of the road!) Have fresh snapper at Ernie's. Eat conch stew. Drink plenty of rum punch. Snorkel, swim, and snack at Shoal Bay. For info by mail, call the Anguilla Tourist Board at 800-553-4939, or log on to www.anguilla-vacation.com.

Puerto Vallarta, Mexico

Once a quiet fishing village on Mexico's Pacific coast, Puerto Vallarta hit the headlines after the Elizabeth Taylor/Richard Burton film *Night of the Iguana,* inspiring millions of star-struck lovers to follow their footsteps to this beachfront town—turning it into the bustling resort/quaint Mexican village you'll find today.

Why You'll Love It: Deluxe hotels, super-fresh food, and sizzling night life. Crooked cobblestone streets lined with funky, whitewashed adobe restaurants, indigenous crafts, and international boutiques. Genuine local color, despite the tourist comforts—look up from your cappuccino at a new, Seattle-style café to see fifty women in fuchsia feather headdresses parading down the street. Safe and friendly. Most people speak some English.

When to Go: February-May (November-January is a bit rainier; June and July are hot day *and* night).

Must-Dos: Visit the Playa de los Muertos (beach of the dead—but filled with very lively sunbathers). Eat fresh fish grilled over charcoal pits on the sand. Buy silver, wood carvings, rugs and serapes from strolling vendors. Get turtle cream (a great after-sun moisturizer) on the island in the Rio Cuale. Indulge in a Mexican version of fancy French food at the terraced garden of Café des Artistes. Snorkel, scuba dive, go deep-sea fishing. Walk hand in hand along the oceanfront *malecon* (boardwalk). Sip Corona with lime at the bars. Call Mexico tourism at 800-44-MEXICO, or check out www.mexico-travel.com.

St. John, U.S. Virgin Islands

The U.S. Virgin Islands are American territory—no passports required. The smallest of the three main U.S. Virgin Islands (St. John, St. Croix, and St. Thomas), it's also the most pristine.

Why You'll Love It: Two-thirds of the island is national park. Caribbean beauty with the comforts of home. Excellent snorkeling, hiking, biking, and swimming. Accommodations ranging from super-luxurious Caneel Bay (with its seven amazing beaches) to rustic-yet-romantic campgrounds at Cinnamon Bay and Maho Bay.

When to Go: December-August.

Must-Dos: Hike the Reef Bay Trail through forest and cacti, past an old sugar mill and pre-Columbian petroglyphs. Do the snorkel trail at Trunk Bay, an underwater "hike." Try "Snuba," a cross between snorkeling and scuba diving, at Cruz Bay. Shack up in an ecofriendly hillside tent overlooking the beach at Maho Bay or Cinnamon Bay for at least one night. Call the U.S. Virgin Islands at 800-372-8784, or see the site at www.stjohnusvi.com.

Less Can Be More

Lack the funds for your ultimate fantasy? Find a less-expensive alternative with the same great features. Great beach? Caribbean instead of the South Pacific. Big city? Chicago rather than New York. Big nature? Yellowstone rather than Africa. Save up for that dream trip on your first (or fifth, or tenth) anniversary.

South Beach, Florida

Located on the southern tip of Miami Beach—an island connected to the city of Miami by "causeways," or long bridges—South Beach was the hot spot in the 1930s and looks to be the hippest beach resort once again at least through the millennium.

Why You'll Love It: A huge, palm tree-lined beach and the hottest nightlife in the country. Great Cuban cooking (and Miami's own spicy "New World" cuisine). Tons of shopping, from Lincoln Road's eclectic boutiques to the super upscale shops in nearby Bal Harbor. A chance to use your Spanish. Glamorous, completely renovated, pastel-painted Art Deco hotels from the 1920s and '30s facing the beach. Easy and cheap to get to. American with an international feel.

When to Go: October-April (May and June are less crowded, cheaper, and hotter).

Must-Dos: Take an Art Deco walking tour. Observe octogenarian Cubans playing dominoes on a card table in the shade. Stroll the strip with model wannabes. Dance it off to a salsa band at night. Call the Greater Miami Convention & Visitors Bureau at 800-283-2707, or cruise over to www.miamiandbeaches.com.

Virgin Gorda, British Virgin Islands

At ten miles long and two miles wide, it's the third largest British Virgin Island and the second most populous, while still remaining quiet and exotic.

Why You'll Love It: Virgin Gorda is a water sports haven. Here you'll busy your days snorkeling, sailing, and swimming in the stunningly crystal-clear waters.

When to Go: Mid-April to mid-December

Must-Dos: There's one popular strip of beach that features caves, grottoes, and pools formed by huge boulders—for pivate baths with your sweetie, head out in the early morning or late afternoon; charter a sailboat for a tour of the island; hike Little Fort National Park, the site of a wildlife sanctuary. Buy the trademark line of rum products from Pusser's Company Store. For more information, call the BVI Tourist Board at 800-835-8530.

St. Croix, U.S. Virgin Islands

If you feel St. Thomas is too busy and St. John too quiet, St. Croix may be just what you're looking for: a great balance of culture, beaches, history, and heart-thumping outdoor—and underwater—activities.

Why You'll Love It: The spacious island, with rolling valleys, has terrain perfect for hiking, biking, and golf. And, of course, the beaches are to die for.

When to Go: Mid-April to mid-December

Must-Dos: Snorkeling. Sunset cruises on Buck Island; pedaling around the island via St. Croix Bike & Tours; kayaking with Caribbean Tours. Head to the Royal Poinciana, where they sell the island's seasonings, hot sauces, and herbal teas. Call USVI Division of Tourism 800-372-USVI.

Cancún, Mexico

It's as jam-packed with tourists as Las Vegas, but it boasts the aesthetics of any desired honeymoon spot—white sandy beaches and aquamarine blue waters.

Why You'll Love It: Seemingly carved out of the jungle, Cancún sits at the tip of Mexico's Yucatán peninsula, twinkling with big resorts and a boisterous nightlife.

When to Go: May to Mid-December

Must-Dos: See a bullfight (year-round), with mariachi bands and flamenco dancers to entertain you. Visit El Cejas in the bustling Mercado 28 (the pulse of the city) for seafood and a signature "Return to Life"—*Vuelva la Vida*—drink, or the garden restaurant La Habichuela for Yucatán-style food; bars are hopping with flamenco, jazz, blues, and Brazilian music; Isla Mujeres, just a few miles off Cancún, is a hot spot for relaxing at quieter beaches and swimming with dolphons. Mexico Tourism Board 800-44-MEXICO.

Perfect Stretches of Sand

The ten most romantic beaches in the United States, according to Dr. Stephen Leatherman, Ph.D., author of *America's Best Beaches* (published in conjunction with Florida International University, 1998):

1. Captiva Island, Florida
2. Hamoa Beach, Hana, Maui
3. Kiawah Island, South Carolina
4. Little St. Simons Island, Georgia
5. Kapalua, Maui
6. Santa Catalina Island, California
7. Keewaydin Island, Naples, Florida
8. East Hampton, Long Island, New York
9. South Nauset Beach, Chatham, Massachussetts
10. Bald Head Island, North Carolina

Adrenaline Adventures

Why not begin your marriage with heart-pounding excitement—on an action-packed honeymoon? For some, adrenaline is the ultimate aphrodisiac—making an adventure trip the perfect escape. Whether you go high-octane athletic or low-impact leisurely, find out the peak season for the sport you'll be doing, the safety record of your outfitter, and a list of supplies you must bring. If you're taking a group trip, be sure to ask how much privacy you'll have.

Biking in Ireland

Grab your hybrid cycle and hop on for a tour across southwestern Ireland. You'll pedal through County Cork and the small villages of Kenmare, Baltimore, Ballylicky, Inishannon, and Kinsale—a fishing town known as the "good food circle" for its numerous fine restaurants. This is a trip for experienced riders—we're talking hills, hills, hills.

VELA & JOHN

September 29, Hawaiian Islands

FOR VELA AND JOHN, honeymooning in Hawaii was like diving headfirst into paradise. They decided to spend twelve days island hopping, since they couldn't pick a favorite after weeks of research. The problem? That meant six flights in one vacation. "I hate flying," explains Vela. "And I cry every time during the takeoff and landing." Once over her fear, and the ten-hour flight there, Vela was able to enjoy her whirlwind island vacation.

First stop, the Big Island. "The landscape was all black lava. It was unreal," says Vela. With no television, clock, or telephone in their private cottage, the couple was able to fully escape from the stress of their busy city lives. They spent four days feasting, snorkeling, and treating themselves to late-night dips in their private Jacuzzi on the porch under a perfectly clear, star-studded sky.

Next, it was off to Kauai, where they tackled more adventurous activities. They went hiking in the famed Na Pali Coast State Park, with its trails that cross above towering sea cliffs and through 6,175 acres of lush valleys. "It's an eleven-mile trail that takes an entire day," says Vela. Their remaining days in Kauai were spent happily hanging out by the pool.

Finally, they ended their trip in Oahu. There they visited Oahu's prime snorkeling destination—Hanauma Bay, a sanctuary to hundreds of reef fish and gigantic sea turtles. On their last day, it started to rain—and despite a fabulous time, they knew it was time to go home.

Why You'll Love It: Steep mountains carved by glaciers. Medieval castles. Emerald-green fields. Sheep. Stone fences. Celtic ruins. Seaside towns with beautiful ocean vistas. Good riding on open spaces. Plenty of pub action at night.

When to Go: Late June-early August.

Must-Dos: Hit the pubs, even if you don't drink; locals in these quaint villages will see you bike in and want to chat (and buy you a beer). Drink Guinness on tap, Ireland's most popular stout. Dance an Irish jig to a live band. See tropical plants at Derreen Gardens on the Beara Peninsula. Call Tourism Ireland at 800-223-6470 or check out www.irelandvacations.com.

A Honeymoon You Can Handle

Make sure you're familiar with at least one element of your high-adventure honeymoon. If you've never been on a boat, never seen Latin America, and never learned to speak Spanish, that weeklong Galapagos cruise may be too much adventure at one time. Consider staying at a great, land-based hotel instead and day-trip to the islands.

Sea Kayaking in Vancouver

Dart among dozens of tiny islands and inlets along the coast of Vancouver in British Columbia, Canada's westernmost province. By day you'll paddle among whales, sea lions, and seals; by night you'll camp on sandy beaches or private islands in a tent for two or kick back before a roaring fire in a cedar-walled lodge.

Why You'll Love It: The two of you in your own slim boat, practicing teamwork as you paddle to remote inlets that a monster cruise liner could never reach. The thrill of crashing through wild waves in the icy blue water. Millions of spawning salmon streaming by your boat. Eagles overhead. Among the highest concentration of Orca whales anywhere in the world. (They're surprisingly gentle.) Dense forests. Pristine beaches.

When to Go: June-September.

Must-Dos: After your morning paddle, hike, play boccie ball, and watch the whales surface. Explore ancient Native American sites complete with totem poles and longhouses. Fish your own salmon for dinner and cook it over a fire. Dress in layers—days can be chilly. Call British Columbia Tourism at 800-663-6000 or check the Web at www.travel.bc.ca.

Roughing It Resources

Backroads Travel (800–462–2848) is the most expansive soft-adventure company (140 destinations in 35 countries). Call for info on bike trips around the world as well as walking, and multisport adventures. For an adventure afloat in your own sea kayak around Vancouver Island (or around the world), call Northern Lights (800–754–7402).

Skiing in Sun Valley

Swoosh to the "secret" ski escape of the rich and famous (Arnold Schwarzenegger, Jamie Lee Curtis, and Clint Eastwood have homes here). Idaho's Sun Valley has some of the best skiing in the West. You'll fly into the Sun Valley airport from Salt Lake City, Utah, and then head to one of the super-luxurious resorts.

Why You'll Love It: High-speed quad lifts and relatively short lines, meaning more time vertical. Spectacular views with awesomely clear, crisp mountain air. A remote location—secluded and romantic. Higher peaks than the East—Sun Valley's Bald Mountain ("Baldie" to locals) rises 9,150 feet. Some of the best-groomed slopes in the West. The chance to tan while you ski—more than 325 days of sun a year. Great food. The Sun Valley opera house. Outdoor ice-skating rink.

When to Go: February-March.

Must-Dos: Try cross-country skiing or snowshoeing. Snowmobile at the base of the Boulder Mountains. Lunch on the mountaintop at Seattle Ridge Day Lodge. Do a Friday night gallery walk. Tour the town of Ketchum, where the Hemingways lived (and live). Call the Sun Valley-Ketchum Chamber of Commerce at 800-634-3347 or check out www.visitsunvalley.com.

Diving in Cozumel

Dart with fish among the living reef in Cozumel, off the coast of Cancún on Mexico's Yucatán Peninsula, one of the Caribbean Sea's scuba meccas. (Its coral reefs were featured in Jacques Cousteau films.) You'll find beginner to advanced diving and a full certification course you can take during your trip.

Why You'll Love It: Mexico's best—easy drift diving in crystal-clear waters along tropical reefs with jewel-colored fish. Underwater visibility often exceeds 150 feet. An intact, living coral reef that's protected by the Mexican government. Lush tropical jungle by land; flora, fauna, and floating *thingees* by sea. Easy to get to and relatively cheap once you're there. Accommodations ranging from all-inclusives (with dive packages) to five-star resorts and small local inns. Dive boats pick you up and drop you off right at the hotel.

When to Go: December-August.

Must-Dos: Slip into your sleek new scuba gear and check out the Yucatán's ancient underground caverns, called *cenotes,* in nearby Akumal. Take the ferry to the mainland to tour the Maya ruins at Tulum. See six species of giant sea turtles at the sanctuary on Isla Mujeres, off Cancún. Tour Cozumel's tiny town to see the local fishing boats. Work it off in a disco. Call 800-44-MEXICO or log on to www.mexico-travel.com.

More Hot Scuba Spots

- Australia's Great Barrier Reef
- Belize
- Bonaire
- Borneo
- Costa Rica
- Fiji
- Grand Cayman
- Hawaii
- Honduras
- Maldive Islands (Indian Ocean)
- Micronesia's Palau
- Papua New Guinea
- The Red Sea

Disney World

Not your first thought when we say "adrenaline adventure"? What makes your heart beat faster than racing down a roller-coaster track at 40 mph, wind in your face, screams in your ears, cotton candy in your hair? Disney World remains one of the top honeymoon spots for those who like their action fast, shiny, and man-made. It's a natural vacation for honeymooners with kids—or with that kids-at-heart spirit.

Why You'll Love It: Forty-two square miles of activities—from raucous rides and wild animal safaris to super shows, cooking classes, and every sport imaginable. Surprisingly luxurious hotels with romantic themes (Polynesian, turn-of-the-century). Super spas. White-sand beaches. Beautiful manicured grounds. Complete cleanliness unlike anywhere else on the planet (except maybe Singapore). The chance to meet Mickey and Minnie. Escapism. Regression. Pure delight.

When to Go: Year-round.

Must-Dos: Ride everything. Get soaked at Splash Mountain. Grab a seat for the Jungle Cruise. Shiver through the Haunted House. Have a picnic lunch in the Wildlife Sanctuary. Ride the monorail to the elegant Grand Floridian hotel for a bodacious buffet. If you're taking kids, drop them off at one of the Children's Activities Centers at night so they (and you) can live it up in an age-appropriate style. See an over-the-top dinner show. Be prepared for lots of references to "Disney Magic." Plan ahead! Get a good guide, such as *Walt Disney World for Couples,* by Rick and Gayle Perlmutter (Prima Publishing, 2003), to help you navigate the World. Call Disney World's info line at 407-824-4500 or check out www.disney.go.com; for general info on all Orlando attractions, call the Orlando-Orange County Convention & Visitors Bureau at 407-363-5871 or see www.orlandoinfo.com.

Super Spa Honeymoons

Your idea of working out is a good rubdown after a mineral bath? Take a spa escape for two. Some of our favorites:

- Canyon Ranch, Tucson, Arizona
- The Doral Golf Resort and Spa, Miami, Florida
- The Four Season Resort and Club, Irving, Texas
- The Golden Door, Escondido, California
- Grand Wailea Resort and Spa, Hawaii

Urban Escapes

For some, nothing is more romantic than window shopping at Tiffany's, dressing to the nines for dinner at ten, and hitting the clubs around midnight. If you're set on an urban adventure, plan what to see before you go—so much to do, so little time! And see if you can get that friend of your cousin's former boss who lives there to give you some recommendations; nothing beats insider advice.

New York City

You want to be a part of it—the glamour, the excitement, the fast pace. This is the Capital of the World, after all. There are more things to do on a single day in New York than you could possibly fit in all year. And crime is way down, meaning things are looking up for the ultimate urban vacation. You still shouldn't hang your purse on a parking meter, but you can walk just about anywhere in Manhattan safely, use Central Park, and zip about on the subway with ease.

Why You'll Love It: The latest fashions, the best restaurants, the coolest stores, the top theaters, the hottest cabaret acts, the hippest nightclubs, the trendiest bars, the most amazing museum collections and galleries—basically, the chance to put your finger on the pulse of the country (and reach deep into your pocket to do it). That feeling of being alive that comes from ducking out of the way of thousands of harried New Yorkers.

When to Go: Fall. Runner-up seasons: *very* late spring, summer, Christmas.

Must-Dos: See a Broadway or off-Broadway play. Window-shop along Fifth Avenue. Visit the Empire State Building, the Statue of Liberty, and Ellis Island. Check out the antiquities wing in the Metropolitan Museum of Art and then head over to the Guggenheim—a winding, white spiral tower of a museum designed by Frank Lloyd Wright. Watch daredevil in-line skaters in the skate circle in Central Park. Have a drink at Rockefeller Center's Rainbow Room. Lose yourselves among the West Village's charming, tiny streets. Check out Chinatown for hot noodles on the street ($1) and fake Chanel handbags and Rolex watches ($15-$35). Stroll across the Brooklyn Bridge and share bagels, lox, and cream cheese on the Promenade in Brooklyn Heights. For info, call New York City's Official Visitor Information Center at 212-484-1222, or check out www.nycvisit.com.

San Francisco

Latte lovers, unite! San Fran is up there with Seattle when it comes to sheer numbers of people walking around with coffee-to-go cups. This moderately sized northern Californian city on the bay combines big-time sophistication with the laid-back, dressed-down attitude of the West Coast. It's urban without being overwhelming.

Why You'll Love It: Candy-colored Victorian houses. Intensely steep hills rolling down toward the brilliant blue San Francisco Bay. Romantic in that windswept-hair, fog-rolling-over-the-mountains, panoramic-view-of-the-ocean-every-ten-feet way. The chance to feel like cover models for a steamy romance novel. People are polite. There's tons to do. And it's always spring.

When to Go: Year-round.

Must-Dos: Order steaming clam chowder in a sourdough bowl at the touristy Fisherman's Wharf and carry it to Pier 26 to dine while watching the sea lions sunning on the docks (free). Wander through Chinatown. Take the ferry to Sausalito. Hang out at a café in Berkeley. See the Yerba Buena Gardens, the view from the Downtown Marriott. Shop on Union Square. Watch the sun set from Coit Tower. Ride a cable car at midnight. Choose a romantic old hilltop inn with a fireplace and a canopy bed. Dress in layers! Call the San Francisco Convention and Visitors Bureau Visitor Information Center at 415-391-2000 or check out www.sfvisitor.org.

For the most up-to-date info on great honeymoon destinations, plus tons of traveling tips, go to The Knot Online at www.theknot.com/travel.

Paris

Let's face it—Paris is synonymous with romance. Whether you adore the art, the food, the fashion, or the French (*mais no,* we're not rude!), a seven-hour flight from New York will land you in the quintessential city of love and lights.

Why You'll Love It: Beautiful old stone buildings with garreted windows. Flower-filled gardens with rows of perfect trees. Countless outdoor cafés. Street vendors selling books, postcards, and Picasso prints. Breakfasting on croissants and café au lait. Steaming sugared crêpes. Museums galore. The river Seine. That misty pink sky like an Impressionist painting. *La vie elegant.*

When to Go: Fall, spring, summer (except August, when the locals are on holiday and the city is empty).

Must-Dos: Stroll along the Champs-Elysées, the Seine, the Boulevard St. Michel, the Jardin du Luxembourg. Stop every hour at a sidewalk café for coffee and a chance to practice your French. Visit the Picasso Museum and the Louvre. (Don't even try to see it all in one day; you can spend hours merely admiring the architecture.) Head to Les Halles to see street performers. Check out the clubs at the Place Pigalle. Call France On-Call at 410-286-8310, or try www.franceguide.com.

Venice

This northeastern Italian city rises up out of the water like Atlantis, presubmerged. All that water reflects the sun against the Gothic-style architecture in the unique way Venice calls its own. Fly to the island airport and then take a water taxi to this amazing aquacity, small enough to cover by foot.

Why You'll Love It: No cars; you take boats—or feet—everywhere you go. Water, water everywhere. Gondoliers who really do sing. Super shops where you can buy Venetian glass. Brightly colored laundry fluttering over winding streets. Ornate, gilded churches with mosaic ceilings. A charming hotel room overlooking a canal. Great food.

When to Go: Spring, fall (winter for a romantic, misty ambience).

Must-Dos: Feed the pigeons at the Piazza San Marco (St. Mark's Square) and tour the Basilica di San Marco. Walk across the small Bridge of Sighs and the large Rialto Bridge crossing the Grand Canal. Wander down tiny, twisting streets. Take a gondola ride. Eat *pannini,* flat cheese-and-prosciutto sandwiches, at a sidewalk café. Tour the Accademia, the city's best museum, across the Grand Canal from Piazza San Marco. Duck down a little alley for some smooching *al fresco.* Hire a motorized water taxi to take you to other islands. See the glassmakers of Murano. Call the Italian Government Tourist Board at 212-245-5618, or visit www.italiantourism.com.

Québec City

The only walled city in this hemisphere north of Mexico, this terraced, nineteenth-century town carved into a cliff in southeastern Canada is like Paris, only hillier. And far cheaper to visit—with the dollar's current strength, all of Canada feels like it's on a 30-percent-off sale.

Why You'll Love It: Streets so drippingly romantic, you inevitably wind up making out in public. (The first French kiss on the continent is rumored to have taken place at Québec's Auberge du Trésor.) Perfectly preserved seventeenth- and eighteenth-century architecture lining cobblestone streets. The thrill of speaking French with the backup of everyone also speaking English. The feeling of living in a picture postcard.

When to Go: May-October (February for WinterFest if you're hardy as a polar bear).

Must-dos: Explore Old Town by foot. Take the glass-walled funicular down the 300-foot cliff to Lower Town. Buy an ink drawing of the city on the rue des Trésors. In February, March, and April, have a maple-sugar feast at a *cabane à sucre* (sugar shack). Rent a car to tour the surrounding tiny, French-style towns, eastern British villages, and Montreal. Call Québec Tourism at 800-363-7777 or check out www.bonjourquebec.com.

Head Trips

A walking tour of ancient ruins, open notebooks, glasses, furrowed brows—rev up your brain while you recharge with an educational/historic honeymoon. Learning can be exhilarating, and downright sexy, if you know where to do it. To get the most out of your head trip, do some reading first, and consider hiring an expert guide the first day for an overview of the area. Don't forget to plan education-free hours—you'll need recess between all that brainwork!

Scottish Castle Tour

This vast, open country north of England is home to hundreds of castles, each holding its own piece of British history. Fly to Edinburgh, rent a car, and drive north, deep into Castle Country. Overnight in castles turned hotels. (You also could do a castle tour in England, France, Spain, Portugal, or Eastern Europe.)

Why You'll Love It: Everything you ever wanted to know about being a prince and princess. Rooms full of armor, antiques, and charters from the king. Rugged cliffs and purple heather. Friendly people (outnumbered by sheep, two to one). Shaggy, orange Highland cattle that are possibly the cutest cows on the planet. European without feeling foreign.

When to Go: May-October.

Must-Dos: See Glamis Castle (Queen Elizabeth's childhood home), medieval Huntingtower (complete with window slits and gun loops), and the ultra-luxurious Crathes Castle and Gardens. Inquire about the ghost stories. Visit the town of Stirling (of *Braveheart* fame), site of Scotland's independence wars. Tour the creepy, narrow alley called Mary King's Close in Edinburgh—the site of some of the city's goriest chapters. Eat smoked salmon and cullen skink—a fish chowder that tastes better than it sounds. Call Visit Britain at 800-462-2748, or go to www.visitbritain.com.

Parlez-Vous What?

First time abroad? Consider a country where the natives speak English. It'll give you the thrill of an overseas vacation with the comfort of still having a bit of control. Good choices: England, Scotland, Ireland, Australia.

Wine Lover's United States: Napa Valley

Stimulate your brain *and* palate with a wine tour of California's great grape-growing regions. Called the Tuscany of the United States, Napa Valley (and neighboring Sonoma) has one vineyard after another (more than 200, actually), most offering educational lectures, extensive tours, and guided wine tastings. About an hour outside of San Francisco, Napa feels ten degrees warmer and ten times more relaxed than the city.

Why You'll Love It: Endless opportunities to sample wine and see how it's made. Golden hills covered with dark-green vines. Warm California sunshine. Small towns with pristine streets, perfect air, and subtle sophistication. Fabulous fresh food. Elegant small hotels and B&Bs.

When to Go: Year round (August-October is harvest and crushing time).

Must-Dos: Take the Napa Valley Wine Train through the valley for a narrated introduction to the region and a wine-cellar tour. Visit no more than three wineries a day—too much info (and wine) to take on more! Check out Sterling Vineyards, a touristy spot whose tram to the top of the hill and balcony overlooking the valley make it worth the crowds. Discern the difference between Chardonnay and Chablis. Take a mud bath for two in Calistoga, Napa's spa town. Call the Napa Valley Tourist Bureau at 707-944-1558 or log on to www.nvtouristbureau.com.

Explore Your Heritage

Travel to the town (or towns) where your family (or families) were born. Look in the town registry for names. Find family tombstones, streets, houses, stores. Interview your grandparents or other relatives before you go. Take photos, names, numbers, and other leads with you.

Mexican Colonial Towns

To learn about Mexican history and culture where it happened, head inland and upland to the Silver Cities—tiny towns founded by Spanish silver prospectors in the mid-1500s. Stay in San Miguel de Allende (150 miles north of Mexico City), the most Americanized of the colonial towns, and one of the prettiest.

Why You'll Love It: Beautiful, Spanish-style buildings with interior courtyards. Central squares, or *zocalos,* where townsfolk meet to chat, read the paper, sip coffee, and eat fried snacks coated with hot sauce. Funky museums. Genuine Mexican culture with little tourist activity. The sense of being very far from home.

When to Go: Year-round.

Must-Dos: Check into San Miguel's elegant Casa de Sierra Nevada, then check out the music, dance, or various art classes in the former courtyard convent Bellas Artes or at the Institute de Allende. Spice up your cooking skills at one of several different schools. Pick up *The Insider's Guide to San Miguel* for the lowdown on the leisure life. Visit the mummies in Guanajuato (an hour north) as well as the Don Quixote Iconographic Museum and the Diego Rivera Museum. Hear the Cervantinos—strolling musicians dressed like sixteenth-century Spaniards. Brave the bus ride to Zacatecas (five hours farther north) to see the Mask Museum—more than 3,000 indigenous masks in a crumbling ex-convent—and buy popcorn roasted over an open flame and eat homemade potato chips. Fly to Mexico City or León and take a Primera Plus bus to San Miguel. Call 800-44-MEXICO for info or see www.visitmexico.com.

Washington, D.C.

This swamp–turned–world capital on the Maryland side of the Potomac (bordering Virginia) is a world-class city and a surprisingly romantic destination.

Why You'll Love It: Awesome architecture, monuments, and statues. Great museums that, because they're federally funded, are free. The chance to learn about your country and reconnect to your childhood pride in the good ol' U.S. of A. Elegant hotels. Beautiful parks. Sophisticated nightlife. A short drive from pastoral countryside.

When to Go: Spring.

Must-Dos: See the cherry blossoms bloom (in April) along the central green, or "Mall," and visit the Capitol Building; the Lincoln, Washington, Jefferson, Vietnam, Korean, and FDR memorials (a lot of memorials, but they're all fantastic!); and the Smithsonian museums (all free!). Visit Kennedy's Tomb, the Tomb of the Unknown Soldier, and the Women Veterans Memorial in Arlington National Cemetery. Take a mule-drawn barge ride down the old canal in Georgetown. See the giant pandas at the National Zoo. Rent a canoe and paddle out on the Potomac. Try African food in the sophisticated Adams-Morgan area, and listen to the city's hottest jazz. Call the Washington D.C. Convention and Tourism Association at 202-789-7000 or try www.washington.org.

Exotica

Berlitz books in your backpacks, creative cuisine, places so exotic your friends have never heard of them—you've been everywhere and done everything. You're ready for the adventure of a lifetime before that lifetime adventure—marriage—officially kicks in. If you've got the time, the money, and the courage, make your honeymoon a voyage to the ends of the earth. And make sure to give yourselves time to look around once you get there!

Australia

This huge country, the size of the United States, is about as far away as you can go (fourteen-plus hours from the West Coast). Choose an area of reasonable size to cover on your trip—you couldn't "do" the entire United States in one week, so don't even think about it with Australia. You'll adore what you do get to see.

Why You'll Love It: Rugged landscapes and sparkling cities. Fresh air, beautiful people. Lush tropics merging with vast stretches of desert. Giant rocks rising in the Outback. British-style traditions mixed with a West Coast attitude. Plenty of places to hike, bike, dive, and drive. The chance to try a Vegamite sandwich.

When to Go: February-April, October and November (but it depends where you go).

Must-Dos: Check out Sydney, Australia's glamorous waterfront city with a healthy outdoorsiness, like a cross between L.A. and Seattle. Rent a boat at the Whitsunday Islands, on the southern edge of the Great Barrier Reef, to dive, snorkel, or just bob around. Explore the rugged northern territory, where you'll find aboriginal artists and the wild rock formations of Kakadu National Park. Climb to the top of the lighthouse at Byron Bay for a spectacular view of the ocean. Take high tea at your hotel. Call 800-DOWNUNDER. Also check out www.australia.com.

Eco-Honeymoon

You're "Love me, love my planet" types? Take an eco-trip—one of the hottest options on the vacation front. But know what you're getting into before you go. "Eco" can mean "extra-rough." Err on the over-cautious side, and find someone who's been before you buy your tickets. For ideas, head to the library for back issues of *National Geographic Traveler* and *Adventure Journal*. Or take ours:

Stateside Safari: Head to Yellowstone National Park, the largest intact ecosystem in the Lower 48. We're talking wall-to-wall (tree-to-tree) wolves, elk, moose, bison, bear, eagles, and deer.

Ecuador's Cuyabeno Wildlife Reserve: The world record-holder for biodiversity, Cuyabeno has more than 500 species of exotic tropical birds, 12 species of monkeys, freshwater dolphins, caiman, tapirs, peccaries, anteaters, and more than 277 species of plants.

The Galapagos Islands: The inspiration for Charles Darwin's *On the Origin of Species,* this UNESCO World Heritage Site 600 miles off Ecuador's west coast has some of the world's unique wildlife: flightless cormorants, marine iguanas, equatorial penguins, giant tortoises, and blue-footed boobies.

Eco-Vacation Organizers

Alaska Discovery (800–586–1911 or www.akdiscovery.com)

Colorado Trail Foundation—build and maintain mountain trails (303–384–3729)

Florida Oceanographic Society—explore Florida's coastline (772–225–0505 or www.floridaoceanographic.org)

Wildlife Expeditions in Jackson Hole, Wyoming (307-773-2623 or www.wildlifeexpeditions.org)

Audubon Nature Odysseys—natural history travel programs (800-967-7425 or www.audubon.org/market/no)

Smithsonian Journeys—educational travel (877-338-8687 or www.smithsonianjourneys.org)

World Wildlife Fund Travel—conservation tours (202-778-9683 and 888-993-8687 or www.worldwildlife.org/travel)

Bali

When you think of mystical palaces, aqua water crashing on jagged cliffs, natives wrapped in brilliant saris, and exotic food with names you can't pronounce, you're thinking Bali. This Indonesian island north of Australia is the original Enchanted Isle. While natives don't stroll around topless anymore, European tourists do.

Why You'll Love It: Pagodalike palaces rising from the water. Colorful Hindu festivals. Remote villages, each dedicated to a single handicraft. More things to buy for less money than you ever thought possible (jewelry, batik, puppets, paintings, baskets, carvings). Beautiful women carrying pyramids of fruit and flowers on their heads. Some of the planet's most luxurious new resorts (and rooms with their own personal plunge pools).

When to Go: Year-round (best weather May-October).

Must-Dos: In Ubud, the center of Bali's cultural tourism, take a walking tour of a working rice field, see a puppet show, and eat at one of the open-air cafés on the main drag, Jalan Raya. Visit the Puri Lakisan Museum to see all types of Balinese art. Head to the Bali Barat National Park for a sunrise hike/climb around the Gunung Batur volcano. Check out Penestanan, a quiet village twenty minutes by foot from Ubud. Tour super-commercialized Kuta (near the airport) to sample unique local cuisine at the food carts near the beach, get in some great surfing (or watch the pros do it), and stock up on batik paintings and jewelry to take home.

Tahiti

The 115 islands of the South Pacific nation of French Polynesia cover an area of ocean larger than Europe. Your seven-hour-plus flight from California lands in bustling Papeete, on the island called Tahiti. From there you can set out for your more remote piece of paradise. Locals speak French and Tahitian.

Why You'll Love It: French style on a tropical isle. Foliage-covered volcanic peaks. Deep mountain jungles. Brilliant blue lagoons with rainbows of fish and coral. Fresh roadside baguettes. Ripe-from-the-tree pineapples, papayas, and coconuts.

When to Go: Year-round (best weather May-October).

Must-Dos: Buy vanilla sticks, woven bracelets, and straw hats at the market in Papeete. Eat steak frites, followed by ice cream made from fresh vanilla beans, at a roadside *roulette.* Visit the Gauguin Museum. (He fled France for Tahiti, determining never to return, twice.) Climb among the ruins in Huahine. Learn the *tamure,* the island's provocative dance. Catch the ferry to Moorea and take a jeep safari into the hills. Hole up in a thatched-roof bungalow on stilts over a clear lagoon in Bora Bora. Call Tahiti Tourisme at 310-414-8484 or check out www.tahiti-tourisme.com.

Rio de Janeiro

This Brazilian city is synonymous with sultry, sexy romance. An eight-hour flight from Miami puts you in another world—it's like Portugal with the heat turned *way* up.

Why You'll Love It: Huge humpbacked mountains. Miles of cream-colored beaches. Sunny days. Nights like silk—soft, sensual, alluring. Gorgeous, gregarious locals called *cariocas,* or "exuberant people." Fabulous spicy food. Shopping. Music. All-night excitement.

When to Go: April-November (February for Carnival).

Must-Dos: Hit the beach at Ipanema, a local hangout where you'll see perfect bods in "dental floss" bikinis. Take the funicular to Corcovado, topped with the gigantic 125-foot-high statue of Christ the Redeemer. Ride a cable car to Sugar Loaf, Rio's postcard peak. Sip *Caipirinha* (a knock-your-socks-off concoction of sugar-cane liquor, crushed lime, and sugar) at an open-air café along Avenue Atlantica. Have an all-you-can-eat *churrascaria rodizio*—twenty kinds of meat served tableside by waiters wielding long skewers. Samba 'til you sweat at one of a hundred nightclubs. Call the Brazilian Vacation Center at 800-342-5746 (in New York State, 800-848-2746).

Thailand

The Kingdom of Thailand, covering an area of 514,000 square kilometers, lies in the heart of Southeast Asia, roughly equidistant between India and China.

Why You'll Love It: Thailand is an exotic experience for the senses—the tropical terrain, ornate guided palaces, mouthwatering Asian cuisine, and Buddhist mantras will help anyone reach nirvana.

When to Go: October through April

Must-Dos: See the 150-foot-long reclining Buddha at Wat Pho. Hike to rapids and waterfalls among protected wildlife and through rain forests of Khao Yai National Park, just 110 miles from Bangkok; floating markets where fruits, veggies, and spices are bought and sold as peddlers paddle along in their narrow skiffs. For more info, call the Tourism Authority of Thailand at 212-432-0433.

Bora Bora

Truly majestic, tranquil, and exotic, Bora Bora is French Polynesia's most exclusive island and is considered one of most beautiful in the world.

Why You'll Love It: A forty-five minute flight from Tahiti, it's a nature-lovers dream, with three verdant volcanic peaks and offshore islets inside a protective necklace of coral.

When to go: May to October

Must-Dos: Tandem parasailing with Bora Bora Parasail. Swim with the dolphins and exotic sea creatures at the Lagoonarium, feed the shark, learn to surf, and lounge around to your heart's content; tour one of the numerous pearl farms and see authentic black pearl oysters. Call Tahiti Tourisme at 800-365-4949 for more info.

Canadian Rockies

Cuddle up amid eight thousand square miles of wilderness. This honeymoon spot is definitely for the laid-back ski bunnies.

Why You'll Love It: From Banff to Vancouver, this stretch of majestic land boasts some of the most beautiful views on the planet.

When to go: Year-round

Must-Dos: Cozy horse-drawn sleigh rides on Lake Louise. Relax at Banff Upper Hot Springs; ski or hike at Banff National Park; embark on an ice climbing or cross-country skiing excursion or a guided snowshoeing tour. Get in touch with Alberta Tourism at 800-661-8888.

Classic Cruises

If you spent your childhood glued to the tube during *The Love Boat,* we know where you'll be heading for your honeymoon. Just the two of you, the open sea, and 500 other passengers. (A martini, Isaac!) A cruise is like a floating all-inclusive resort with everything on deck—except all those great ports of call. Wherever you go, make the most of your time at sea. Order breakfast in bed. Stay up for the midnight buffet. Lounge at every pool, try every dance floor, and watch the stars in the sky from the deck late at night. Read up on your ports before you go—a little planning will let you make the most of your time on land.

Alaska

Get up close and personal with some of the country's most spectacular scenery and wildlife. Then tour northwestern cities like Seattle, Vancouver, Victoria, Ketchikan, Petersburg, and Juneau. Alaska is an ideal summer cruise destination.

Why You'll Love It: Glistening icebergs and glaciers. Land of the Midnight Sun phenomenon—almost constant daylight during the summer months. That last-great-place feeling—undisturbed nature at its most awesome. Glacier Bay National Park. Easy to get to from the West Coast.

When to Go: Mid-May to mid-September.

Must-Dos: Take the Inside Passage tour—the route between Alaska's western coast and a string of offshore islands—to see humpback whales and sea lions. Listen for glaciers cracking off jewel-blue icebergs into deep-green fjords. Eat salmon and tour the totems in Ketchikan. Relive the Gold Rush days along the boardwalks of Juneau and Skagway. See Czarist Russia-style architecture in Sitka. Check out slopes and cliffs of Valdez, called the "Switzerland of Alaska." Buy smoked salmon, carved wood totems and animals, Native American crafts, and masks. Don wet suits for a whitewater rafting trip.

Who Goes There: Carnival Cruise Lines, Celebrity Cruises, Crystal Cruises, Holland America Line, Norwegian Cruise Line, Princess Cruises, Radisson Seven Seas, Royal Caribbean. Call Alaska Travel Industry Association Visitor Information Center at 907-929-2200 or try www.travelalaska.com.

Greek Islands

Cut through the crystal waters of the Aegean Sea to the Greek Islands—the world's most popular place to cruise. You'll fly to Athens and board your ship from the port city of Piraeus, for island-hopping, ship style.

Why You'll Love It: Whitewashed buildings covering steep hillsides. Unbelievable vistas. The history of Western civilization at your fingertips. Great Mediterranean food. The chance to wear next to nothing. English-speaking (often) locals.

When to Go: April-October.

Must-Dos: Wander among the ruins of the Temple of Zeus in Katakolon. Bronze on the beach in Mykonos. Sip a Greek coffee at an outdoor café and watch the sun play across the water. Eat *mezedes* (traditional appetizers) and drink licoricelike *ouzo* on Patmos, a strikingly rugged island that's home to shepherds and fishermen. Visit the birthplace of mighty

Joy Rides

Just the two of you on the open road, Dylan on the radio, and the late-afternoon sun in your eyes—a road-trip honeymoon is the ultimate joy ride. If you're planning to put the pedal to the metal for some serious postwedding togetherness, make sure to map out some must-see stops and leave plenty of time for wandering those old back roads. Plan where to stay for the first few nights, at least; this is a great opportunity to check out the charming inns across the country. Take along your Polaroid camera, your favorite tapes, maps, guidebooks, and two weeks' worth of conversation. Our top road-trip picks:

The Florida Keys: This string of islands is connected to mainland Florida (and to each other) by one smooth, two-lane highway. From Key Largo to Key West, you spin along the perfect strip of blacktop, watching the land falling away on either side. It's the open sky, the endless sea, and a feeling of freedom unlike anywhere else in the United States.

New England: Plymouth Rock, Salem witch trials, Ivy League schools, the Headless Horseman, Hester Prynne, the Boston Tea Party—they're here, in Connecticut, Rhode Island, Massachusetts, New Hampshire, Vermont, and Maine. Stay at some charming inns along the way.

Southwest: From New Mexico to Arizona and Nevada, this wide-open country is great if you *love* to drive. You'll see the southern edge of the Rockies and some of the most unusual land on Earth, including red rocks as tall as skyscrapers (but shaped more like some extraterrestrial habitation). See Native American culture, awesome natural monuments, the Grand Canyon, and Las Vegas. Experience the feeling of being part of the free-wheelin', fast-dealin' Wild West.

The California Coast: From south of San Diego to north of San Francisco, California's Pacific Coast Highway is the most spectacular stretch of road in the country. Wander slowly through flower-filled towns so beautiful you'll swear they're movie sets. Brilliant bougainvilleas the size of small cars bloom in the medians, the Pacific Ocean is right out your window, the weather is flawless, the towns are charming and historic, and the resorts are deeply luxurious.

Aphrodite—the Love Goddess—in Kithera. Climb the Acropolis in Athens. Explore the Palace of Grand Masters in Rhodes, set among olive and cypress trees. Climb to the top of Santorini for a view over the lost city of Atlantis. Learn at least one Greek word—we suggest *Opa!* meaning bravo, wonderful, hooray!

Who Goes There: Costa Cruise Line, Crystal Cruises, Cunard Cruise Lines, Holland America Line, MSC Cruises Orient Lines, Princess Cruises, Radisson Seven Seas, Royal Caribbean, Royal Olympic Cruises, Windstar Cruises. Call the Greek National Tourist Organization at 212-421-5777 or check out www.greektourism.com.

The Caribbean

Can't decide which Caribbean island is for you? Choose a cruise and check out a handful. Most Caribbean excursions leave from south Florida (though there are other ports) and cover a collection of Caribbean countries, often including a stop at a private island.

Why You'll Love It: The bluest seas, the whitest sands, the greenest palms. Bubbling waterfalls. Exotic markets. Fresh fruit. The smell of cocoa butter. A very pared-down wardrobe (swimsuit, shorts, sunglasses, one fancy getup). Warm days, warm nights, warm people.

When to Go: December-August.

Honeymooning at Home

Can't leave town just now? Even if you're planning your *real* honeymoon for next May, take a long weekend after your wedding for a whirlwind of intimacy and indulgence. For the perfect forty-eight-hour honeymoon at home, try these tips:

Make the weekend as romantic as possible, even if it means being downright extravagant.
Hire a maid to do a complete overhaul before you begin.
Fill the house with huge bouquets of fresh flowers.
Stock up your fireplace with wood, your bed with pillows, your pantry with snacks.
Put new sheets on your bed.
Put a sexy CD like Maxwell or India Arie on repeat on your CD player.
Turn off the ringer on your phone. (Don't check your messages!)
Take a bubble bath together. (Turn off the overhead light and use fifteen candles, instead.)
Give each other a hand massage and manicure.
Pack a gourmet picnic for lunch at a local park or lake.
Book a half day at the local spa.
Dress up for a super-fancy dinner out (or order in and eat on your best new china and crystal). Have a limo pick you up.
Wear your sexiest lingerie and boxers to bed.
Rent a steamy video for super-late-night viewing.
Have chilled shrimp cocktail and champagne waiting for midnight snacks. (Or ingredients for gooey nachos, if that's more your style.)
Treat each other to breakfast in bed.
Do something only the tourists do. Visit the pretzel factory; ice-skate in the park; ride a horse-drawn buggy.
Plan a surprise for each other—a professional masseuse after dinner, a new martini shaker for cocktails; something battery-operated for the bedroom.
Take pictures! This *is* a vacation.

Must-Dos: Climb the Dunn's River waterfall in Jamaica. Bargain at the straw market in Nassau, the Bahamas. Learn to beat the bongo drums. Have an espresso at a harborfront café in French St. Martin. Take high tea in British Barbados. Bronze your bods on black sand in Grenada.

Who Goes There: Carnival Cruise Lines, Celebrity Cruises, Costa Cruise Line, Crystal Cruises, Cunard Cruise Lines, Holland America Line, MSC Cruises, Norwegian Cruise Line, Premier Cruises, Princess Cruises, Radisson Seven Seas, Regal Cruises, Royal Caribbean, Royal Olympic Cruises, Windstar Cruises. Call for a Caribbean Vacation Planner at 800-356-9999.

Western Mediterranean

Board a cruise in the western Mediterranean and wake up every morning in a different country—from France to Italy, Spain to Tunisia. You'll fly to your departure city (the port depends on the cruise line you choose); airfare to Europe may be included in the overall price. Book a water/land package to spend a few days tooling around town before you hit the seas.

Why You'll Love It: A chance to see a handful of Europe's most beautiful cities and practice your Italian, Spanish, or French. A small circuit, meaning more ports of call, less time at sea. Maximum culture, minimum effort.

When to Go: Mid-May to late October.

Must-Dos: Eat pizza in Naples, birthplace of the pie. Tour the ruins of Pompeii. Light a candle in a Gothic church. Wander through the fourteenth-century maze of the Barrio Gotico (Old Quarter) in Barcelona or take a tour of Gaudí's famous drippy architecture. Drink café con leche while watching Sardana dancers. Eat bouillabaisse (fresh seafood stew) in Marseille, France's oldest city. Bargain in Tunisian street markets. Peer at the illuminated manuscripts of the Koran. See the ornate Palace of Dar Ben Abdullah. Leave plenty of room in your luggage for souvenirs.

Who Goes There: Costa Cruise Lines, Crystal Cruises, Cunard Cruise Lines, Holland America Line, MSC Cruises, Norwegian Cruise Line, Orient Lines, Princess Cruises, Radisson Seven Seas, Royal Caribbean, Royal Olympic Cruises, Windstar Cruises.

Norwegian Fjords

Whether you chug along in a huge ship or poke among the fjords in a private boat, cruising Norway puts you on top of the world—literally. If you take the big-ship route, you'll probably leave from Amsterdam or Copenhagen, stop in Oslo, and then head up Norway's west coast toward the Arctic Circle.

Why You'll Love It: Towering cliffs, shooting geysers, and ice-fringed fjords. Pure white glaciers topped with packs of penguins. Fairy-tale towns with red, yellow, and orange steep-roofed buildings lining the waterfront. Great gray mountains rising up behind wooden churches. Strange, desolate capes over which the sun never sets. Polar bears, reindeer, white whales, arctic foxes, and seals.

When to Go: June-August.

Must-Dos: Sail up the Oslofjord to Norway's capital city, Oslo—just like the Vikings. Tour the Viking Ship Museum. Buy Norwegian crafts in the town of Stavanger, the oil capital of Norway. Wander among the old Hanseatic Wharf in Bergen—a medieval shipping port. Drive up the wiggly *Trollstigen* (troll's ladder) to see crashing waterfalls and sheer mountains. Have a coffee in a hip café in Tromso—a city way above the Arctic Circle. Visit Hammerfest, the most northerly town in Europe, on Norway's northern coast.

Who Goes There: Bergen Line, Costa Cruise Line, Crystal Cruises, Cunard Cruise Lines, Holland America Line, Norwegian Cruise Line, Princess Cruises, Radisson Seven Seas, Royal Caribbean, Royal Olympic Cruises. Call the Scandinavian Tourist Board at 212-885-9700 or try www.goscandinavia.com.

CHAPTER TWENTY-SIX

honeymoon helper

You've agreed on the perfect honeymoon place, bought the books, registered for that Louis Vuitton luggage you *had* to have. Now all that's left between you and euphoria are the details—booking the trip, packing your bags, and finding someone to feed Fido while you're gone. Here to help you with the nitty-gritty of honeymooning are our foolproof, fabulous trip-planning tips. Whether you're experienced globetrotters or novice travelers, you need a good grip on the rules and language of the travel world before you set out. We'll give you the inside scoop on everything you need to know to make your honeymoon great. So put on that calypso CD, make some rum punch (for inspiration!), and get ready to plan.

Making Some Decisions

By now you've done your destination research—you've read Chapter 25, talked to friends, checked out your newspaper's travel section, and surfed the Web for possible packages. But before you stroll into your travel agent's office and whip out your Gold Card, there's some additional information you need to have—namely how much honeymoon money you've got and how you want to spend it.

Getting the Most from Your Budget

So just how much will the trip of the century cost you? An average eight-day honeymoon costs between $6,000 and $8,000. That includes airfare, hotel, taxis, meals, alcohol, snacks, and souvenirs. Plane tickets and hotel costs suck up more than half of the total. But you're not the average couple. You're you. Use those figures as a ballpark range, then plan to spend less if you're driving rather than flying or staying for a shorter amount of time; more if you're planning to cross the globe and/or check into a five-star resort. Always overestimate honeymoon costs and leave padding for an unexpected splurge. Plan to take along a few hundred "safety" dollars and a credit card for emergencies—you never know when you'll blow the engine in your car or *feel compelled* to upgrade to the Cleopatra Honeymoon Suite.

If your budget doesn't live up to your dream trip, talk about your priorities and decide where to scrimp and when to splurge. Some couples don't care where they go as long as they can stay in the most luxurious room; others will sleep in a tent as long as they can go far, far away to pitch it. Talk about how you'll spend your time, what makes you feel pampered (expensive meals? in-room massage? a beautiful view?), and what you care less about. Since we're fully aware that you never have enough money for all your honeymoon dreams, here are our top tips for saving dollars:

Get Married, Get Miles

Pay for your wedding on a credit card that gets frequent-flier miles. Then cash in those air awards for that flight to Fiji. If you don't have a mileage-generating card, call your current credit card company and ask to enroll in its frequent-flier program. Need lots of miles? Switch your long-distance service to the miles-for-minutes program with the same airline.

- Go during "shoulder season"—the week or two before and after a destination's peak season. You'll save up to 40 percent on your room, avoid the crowds, and still get great weather. Ask your hotel or travel agent for specifics on your honeymoon spot.
- Get a second opinion. And a third. Prices vary widely.
- Start your research early. (Travel pros recommend nine to twelve months.)
- Check airfare from nearby cities: Newark rather than New York, Milwaukee rather than Chicago, Indianapolis rather than Cincinnati, Baltimore instead of D.C., Oakland or San Jose instead of San Francisco.
- Stay over a Saturday night for lowest fares.
- Beach bums? West Coasters, head to Mexico. East Coasters, think Caribbean. Midwesterners: either!
- See if you can use your employer's, AAA, or alumni association discount.
- Avoid hotel restaurants. Food tends to be cheaper (and better) at local joints.
- Tell everyone you're honeymooners and ask about specials. You may at least get an upgrade.
- Buy a package trip including air, hotel, and transfers. (See "Choosing Your Trip," below.)
- Use a credit card that has automatic trip insurance rather than buying separate insurance.
- Compromise. Stay an extra day by choosing a cheaper room. Or go high luxury for less time.
- Ask your parents to give you the gift of their frequent-flier miles.

Choosing Your Trip

Now that you've got your budget in order, it's time to decide what type of trip to spend it on. Decide now how you feel about each of these options, and whether they figure in your honeymoon vision.

Package Possibilities: Packagers are companies that buy hotel rooms, airline seats, and other trip elements at a low bulk price and then combine them into one "package" deal. A package does not mean a guided trip in a tour bus. It just means you're buying all of your pieces of paradise together—air, room, hotel transfers to and from the airport, theater tickets, a boat tour, and so on. You'll see packages advertised in the travel section of your Sunday paper, or your travel agent might suggest some.

On the plus side, a package is easy to book and can mean big savings. But it also may mean a tiny hotel room. Some packagers cut costs by squeezing travelers into the hotel's lowest-end accommodations. If you see a package you like, call the hotel directly to find out

ASK CARLEY

Who Pays Your Way?

Q: Is the groom's family responsible for the honeymoon? We want to go to Thailand, but his parents don't have that kind of cash. Do we settle for Cincinnati?

A: Not unless you *love* the Reds, the Ohio River, and Skyline Chili. Traditionally, the groom's parents paid for the honeymoon (and the bride's parents funded just about everything else). But today the entire budget is up for grabs. If you have the cash, pay for your dream trip yourselves. If his parents feel the honeymoon is in their hat, ask them to contribute toward your Thai trip—by picking up the hotel tab, covering the airfare, or springing for new luggage (depending on their budget and interest) while you cover the rest. If they don't have the dough, and you don't, either, then it's time to think about a less exotic location, a shorter trip, or less luxe accommodations.

just what category room you're reserving. Then call the package company to see if you can upgrade.

Tour Trips: A tour is a package that generally includes a guide and other travelers. It may be a huge trip with hundreds of people or a small, specialized group. You may *have* to take a tour if you're going somewhere remote, like a trek through the Himalayas. But think seriously before signing on. Not only can traveling en masse make it hard to get to know a place, but it also means forced togetherness with people other than your sweetie. This is your *honeymoon,* after all—do you really want to spend it with thirty members of the Akron Super Strikers bowling league? Of course, an organized tour does mean less planning—and you may want the security of that big group in a country where you don't speak the language. Some companies offer private tour guides for challenging terrain—at an equally challenging price. A private tour eliminates the presence of others, but it also nixes the substantial savings. We aren't saying tours are always a bad idea—just be careful.

The All-Inclusive Option: You've seen the ads for all-inclusives—a love-struck couple sprawled on the sand, clad in bathing suits and wedding bands. Same couple, laughing over cocktails, snorkeling in chartreuse or fuchsia flippers, springing across the tennis courts in new Nikes. "What is this?" you've asked. "Camp for adults?"

Sort of. At an all-inclusive resort, you pay one price for your room, meals, entertainment, activities, and (sometimes) alcohol. Everything is within the resort's compound. These resorts vary in price, size, ambience, and degree of luxury—an all-inclusive can be a private, 60-room hideaway where you'll eat meals alone, albeit in a dining room with other vacationers. Or it may mean 300 other couples, a social director urging you to join in on games all day, and group meals. Some all-inclusives are "couples only," meaning it's just you two and a gazillion other lovers. You'll find all-inclusives throughout the Caribbean, in the Poconos, and, increasingly, in Mexico, Europe, and the South Pacific.

On the glass-is-half-full side, an all-inclusive is easy, easy, easy. You roll out of bed and start playing. It's impossible to get bored or lonely, and there are plenty of other people to swap

Register and Escape

All you want for your wedding is a fabulous trip? For a landlocked honeymoon, try HoneyLuna (800–809–5862 or www.honeyluna.com), a service that lets your guests choose which part of the trip to give—part of the airfare, room costs, even that welcoming champagne.

wedding stories with. Because you pay one price, you can try every activity—from swimming, boating, parasailing and water-skiing to dining and dancing till dawn, without ever thinking about cost while you're there.

On the half-empty hand, staying at a self-contained resort may prevent you from getting to know the local culture. You *can* explore the island outside your resort, of course, but since you've already paid for all your meals and activities, you may not be motivated to. If you're not joiner types, a huge all-inclusive with "manufactured fun" (volleyball around the pool, couples-only Ping Pong contests) may be more annoying than entertaining.

Call for brochures and look at the photos; you should be able to tell what kind of vibes a place has from its promotional materials. Consider the activities, the rooms, the amount of privacy you'd have, and the cost. And try to talk to someone who has been there.

Good Tour Operators

- Abercrombie & Kent: 800–324–7308 or www.abercrombiekent.com, private guides to exotic places. Big trips. BIG price tags.
- Amelia Tours: 800–742–4591 or www.ameliainternational.com, upscale (read: expensive) group or independent tours.
- Contiki Tours: 800–CONTIKI or www.contiki.com., for people eighteen to thirty-five years old.

Booking Your Trip

Unfortunately, you can't beam from the ballroom to the beach as in *Star Trek*. (If you can, call and tell us how.) You have to buy tickets (air, rail, or ship), and book a room for when you arrive. Whatever trip you take, there are a variety of ways to book it—and different prices depending on how you do it.

Using a Travel Agent

A travel agent can do everything from making your airline reservations to reserving theater tickets—saving you time and frustration. S/he also may save you big bucks by finding cheap fares, recommending less-expensive alternatives, or selling you seats on a flight his/her company has chartered (a service offered by some agencies). This service is free—agents get a commission from the hotel or airline, not from you.

Finding a Travel Agent

- Get a referral from a friend.
- Call the American Society of Travel Agents (703–739–2782) for a referral.
- Log on to www.astanet.com.

What to Look For: Find an agency that specializes in your dream trip—luxury travel, cruising, the Caribbean, adventure—and an agent who's flexible and willing to work with you. But beware—travel agents vary in terms of experience and talent. Some have been everywhere and know next to everything. Others sit in their office and book trips to places they've never been, meaning you're getting tourist brochure advice, not firsthand experience. In general, don't go anywhere *solely* on the recommendation of a travel agent, unless s/he's actually been there. Be wary if s/he's really pushing a particular place. Since s/he does get a kickback, s/he may be thinking of other things besides your good time.

What to Ask: When you call your travel agent, state your destination, dates, budget, desired room type, and any other preferences you have (an ocean view, kosher food, nonstop flights). The agent's working for you; tell him/her your needs. And get answers to any questions you may have, such as:

Destination Questions

- Is it safe? Are there areas to avoid?
- Can we drink the water and/or eat fresh foods?
- Do we need shots, our passports, special visas, or other papers?
- Is there a good taxi or bus system, or will we need a car to get around?
- What's the weather like during the time we plan to go?
- Do we need a converter for our hair dryer/curling iron/handheld massager?
- Have you been there yourself?

Service Questions

- Can we request special in-flight meals?
- How do we get from the airport to the hotel? (Are transfers included?)
- Will you reserve us a room with a view?
- Is there a special honeymoon package?
- Can we change hotel rooms if we're not satisfied? How much will it cost?
- Do you have any suggestions to save us money?
- What's your policy if we have to cancel?

Touring Tips

The United States Tour Operators Association (800–GO–USTOA) will send info about all its member companies and advice for selecting a tour or package. Check 'em out at www.ustoa.com.

Travel Agent Talk

Talking to a travel agent makes you feel like you've already entered a foreign land. What the heck do all those terms mean? Here's our Glossary of Professional Travel Gibberish.

Hotel

EP (European Plan): Price covers room only
CP (Continental Plan): Continental breakfast comes with room
AP (American Plan): Three meals come with room
MAP (Modified American Plan): Breakfast and dinner come with room
Double occupancy: The price of a package if two people stay in one room
Rack rate: Retail rate for a room (what you get if you call the hotel)

Air

Bulkhead: The first seat in coach (the one with the tray table in the arm)
Exit row: The seat over the wing (more leg room, but the seat back doesn't recline)

General

Tariff: A tax, generally an added travel or border tax
Departure tax: A tax you pay at the airport to leave the country, usually about $10 to $15 (included in the price of some packages)

How It Works: Your agent will do some research and call you back with the possibilities. You'll probably have to decide whether to take a morning or evening flight, which airline to use, if you want to stay an extra day to get a better rate, and the like. You may also want to set up an e-mail system, where your agent can send you revised itineraries until you're satisfied with the plan. Once you agree on the details, the agent will book the tickets and let you know when to pay (either by credit card over the phone or in person in the office).

Go to The Knot Aloha Travel Auction at www.theknot.com.

Before you leave, your agent should give you the plane tickets, hotel confirmation numbers, a complete itinerary with phone numbers and addresses of all the places you're staying, his/her phone number in case you have a problem (an 800-number or a number to call collect), vouchers, directions, maps, and anything else you'll need.

If you've asked an agent for help, you are not obliged to book with him/her. If you find a better deal by calling the airline or hotel on your own, book it yourself (or ask the agent to do it for you, but make sure s/he gets the same rate you were quoted).

Doing It Yourselves

If you have the time and inclination, you may be able to find better rates by booking your trip yourself—but only if you can stomach the prospect of spending hours on hold listening to the Muzak version of "Send in the Clowns." Booking on your own can be very time-consuming and frustrating, but it may be a good option if you're relatively experienced travelers who've read about a place (or talked to a friend who went) and have all the info you need. Stay organized: Keep track of phone numbers, rates, flight times, and pay-by dates in one notebook. There are several approaches for do-it-yourselfers.

Surf the Web: You may have noticed a few thousand advertisements boast the best online travel deals. Internet travel sites are popping up all over the place, meaning you can do much of your destination research and booking at home. Whether an online agent (like Expedia.com) or an online auction site (like Priceline.com), these sites can offer deep discounts but little traveling flexibility (their flights are so cheap because no one else wants them).

Most major hotel chains have websites, too, letting you reserve rooms, pay for them, and maybe even take a virtual tour of the grounds without ever leaving your desk. But make sure you know exactly what you want before typing in your credit card number!

Dial Direct: Call each airline directly and ask about dates, rates, and upcoming specials. For a list of hotels in your honeymoon hot spot, call the country's U.S. tourist board; then call the hotels directly, too. (Remember, if you're calling a charming little country inn deep in the Tuscan hillside, be prepared for a hotel operator who doesn't speak English.) If you dial direct, you're being your own travel agent; make sure to get all the information you'd expect from a pro.

Getting Ready to Go

You've got your tickets, reserved your room, and stocked up on all the sunblock, cool shades, and trashy novels you'll need. But if you're heading abroad, you may have a few extra pretravel steps to take.

Glossary of Rooms

You'll probably spend a lot of time in your hotel during your honeymoon. Make it a room you love. Here's the rundown on rooms for rent.

B&B: While a bed and breakfast sounds romantic, it often literally means a bed in someone's guest room and breakfast. This is either incredibly charming or not private enough (walls too thin for you-know-what, an overly talkative owner). Check it out first or talk to someone who has stayed there.

Cottage: Usually an independent structure.

Inn: A small hotel, often privately owned. More privacy than a B&B; more romantic than a huge hotel.

Motel: Stands for "motor hotel"—usually means a roadside, low-rise building where you park your car near your room.

Suite: Officially two rooms—a bedroom and living room—separated by a full wall. A "junior suite" may have a comfortable sitting area rather than a complete second room. A "housekeeping suite" usually includes a kitchen.

Villa: An upscale take on the cottage—usually with a kitchen, maid service, balconies, and elegance. (You may have to stay at least a week.)

Identify Yourselves

Whenever you travel out of the country, you have to pass through immigration and customs. You'll need to show your passport to get through. Check online or call your local passport agency (check for yours under government listings in the phone book) or ask at your post office for info on how and where to get it. You also may need a tourist card, which the airline gives you on the plane.

Exceptions to the passport rule include Canada, Mexico, and parts of the Caribbean. While a passport is easiest, you can get in with a photo ID (driver's license or other ID) and proof of citizenship (an original birth certificate with raised seal or U.S. naturalization papers for Mexico and the Caribbean; the same items or a voter's registration card for Canada). The Dominican Republic also requires a $10 tourist card, which you buy at the airport.

If you're driving to Mexico, it is recommended that you travel with your passport, which may be needed to prove citizenship for readmission into the United States, according to travel.state.gov. Some countries, in addition to the Dominican Republic, may require a tourist card.

As for driving in Mexico, there is a "Sonora Only" permit. Tourists wishing to travel beyond the border zone with their car must obtain a temporary import permit or risk having their car confiscated by Mexican customs. To acquire such a permit, one must submit evidence of citizenship, title for the car, a car registration certificate, and a driver's license to a Banjercito branch located at a Mexican Customs office and pay a processing fee of about $25. Mexican customs law also requires the posting of a bond at a Banjercito office to guarantee the departure of the car from Mexico within a time period deter-

Just Charge It

If you're buying in a foreign currency, put everything on a credit card. You'll get the bank's official exchange rate, which is almost always better than that of a store, hotel, or restaurant. And you'll get an itemized record of exactly what you spend.

mined at the time of the application. For this purpose, American Express, Visa, or MasterCard credit card holders will be asked to provide credit card information; others will need to make a cash deposit of between $200 and $400, depending on the age of the car. In order to recover this bond or avoid credit card charges, travelers must return to the same Mexican Customs office immediately prior to departing Mexico. For further information, U.S. citizens should inquire with Mexican Customs offices about appropriate permits for their vehicle.

Some countries require you to have a tourist visa in addition to your passport. You get one from your vacation destination's consulate before you go. Countries requiring visas change all the time, as does the length of time it takes to get one. Ask your airline or travel agent about visa requirements as soon as you make your travel plans. Then call the country's consulate to double-check.

How to Stay Flush

Take your cash card with you! You'll find ATMs all across Europe, where you can get local currency as you need it and pay the same great bank rate. Withdraw in bulk to save on the sometimes *big* transaction fees. And make sure you have cash in your checking account—some machines don't offer the option of taking from savings.

Immunization Alert

The more exotic the country, the greater your chance of contracting some equally exotic disease. If you're traveling to Africa, Asia, Latin America, or India, ask if your doctor does travelers' immunizations or can point you toward a local hospital or clinic that does. To check the status of your destination, check out the Centers for Disease Control and Prevention website—www.cdc.gov.—or call their Travelers' Health hotline (877-394-8747).

Safety First

Safety is priority number one when traveling to uncharted territory (uncharted to you, that is). For the most current information on travel warnings and related updates, call the U.S. Department of State's Bureau of Consular Affairs (888-407-4747), call the U.S. State Department Travel Advisory (202-647-5225) for an update on global hot spots. Or check out their website at travel.state.gov/travel_warnings.html. State Department advisories tend to be even more cautious than your overprotective mother. If an advisory says "Don't go," we say "Don't go." But if there's a slew of warnings for things such as pickpockets and theft in your ideal city, think about them in terms of your personal experience. If you're traveling to Rome from New York City, for example, chances are you've already got your urban defenses in place.

Get Insured

Your honeymoon can cost as much as a new car. But before buying travel insurance to protect your investment, see if your credit card and/or homeowner's policy covers you if your luggage gets lifted, your trip is delayed, or you have to cancel. If not, you can buy a separate, trip-only policy. Call your insurer, or ask your travel agent for details.

Packing Like a Pro

What you bring depends on where you're going—from a fancy frock for dinner at the captain's table to hiking boots and a sun visor for a Galapagos trek. If you're unsure what wardrobe you'll need, call your hotel, cruise ship, or tour company. Or look in a guidebook to the area for advice.

Choose luggage that fits your trip—a garment bag for evening attire, a backpack for a European hike. Bring an extra duffel (or expandable suitcase) for all your loot.
Take clothes in colors easy to coordinate—navy, black, and white, for example, or beige, white, and tan.
Dump everything you might want on the bed, then take half of that. Or envision your trip day by day and plan an outfit for each day, repeating shorts, pants, and sweaters.
Slip shoes in plastic bags.
Wrap your white silk blouse or other easy-to-wreck items in the cleaner's bag to protect them.
Put things that spill in resealable baggies.
Put heavy things on the bottom of your bag, or over the wheels; delicate items go on top.
Label your luggage clearly with sturdy luggage tags.
Lock up your zippers and put the key somewhere you'll remember.
Pack important items in your carry-on, including *anything* valuable—tickets, passports, itinerary, jewelry, cash, medicine, ID, and phone numbers—as well as an outfit for the first day and essential toiletries. Airlines *do* lose luggage.
Make sure your traveling outfit is comfortable enough for hours on the plane.
Plan to wear bulky things, such as hiking boots, on board.

Tips from Experienced Travelers

However you get there, you can take steps to make the traveling part more fun. Each mode of transportation has its own unique requirements. Here are our top tips for making getting there almost as good as being there.

Air Advice

While that plane is an essential part of your dream trip (you gotta get there), the actual flight can be pretty damn boring. Not to mention so dehydrating your skin may feel like a sun-dried tomato by the time you land. So what can you do to improve your in-flight experience?

- Try to book nonstop flights. Changing planes, while sometimes cheaper, makes for a loooong trip.
- Reserve special meals (vegetarian, kosher) ahead of time. Usually they're fresher than the standard fare and bear a closer resemblance to real food.
- Take moisturizing lotion for your hands and face.
- Drink a glass of water every hour you're aboard to keep from dehydrating.

And Your Name Is . . .

Even if one (or both) of you is changing your name, make all international reservations in your given names. You can't apply for a passport using your married name until after the wedding; keeping everything consistent will save you big-time headaches. And if you need a passport, make sure to apply at least six weeks before your trip.

- Dress in layers. Air on? Sweater on. Air on the blink? Sweater off.
- Have a sip of celebratory champagne, not the whole bottle. Alcohol contributes to dehydration.
- Save the coffee for the end of the flight. (More dehydration!)
- Contacts drying up? Take 'em out. Or make sure to bring saline.
- Bring a deck of cards, which makes a flight fun (pun intended).

On Board that Boat

Whether you're taking a 2,000-passenger cruise ship or a private yacht, rocky water can make landlubbers feel like deflated rubber duckies. Big cruises have some special factors to consider:

- In huge–cruise ship land, bigger does not mean calmer; just longer lines at the midnight buffet.
- Don't trust listed prices. Check the website or call the 800 number and pay less.
- Find out *exactly* what's included. (Food? Yes. Drinks, port charges, taxes? Yikes!)
- Consider an outside room—that little porthole of light can save a claustrophobic.
- Ask about the dress code. There's usually at least one formal night on board.
- Take a sweater and windbreaker for that chilly night air.
- Take along Dramamine and antiseasickness, acupressure "bracelets," just in case.
- Read up on the ports of call and plan what to see to maximize your land time.
- If you hate your room, tell the purser. You may be able to change it.
- Buy shipboard gifts at the end of the trip; cruise line gift shops often mark everything way down on the way back.

Don't Leave Home Without . . .

- Birth control
- Bug spray, sunblock, antiseptic, antibacterial ointment (for an outdoor trip)
- Extra pair of glasses or contacts
- Film
- List of important phone numbers
- Money, one credit card, a cash card
- Notebook or travel journal
- Prescription medicine (in original bottle), aspirin, allergy pills
- Toothbrush
- Voltage converter (if needed in a foreign country)
- Batteries

Road Rules

Good news, speed lovers—highway speed limits are back up to 70 mph in some states. But more speed means even more need for safety precautions. And while nothing beats a road trip for hours of alone time, too many days of staring at that white dividing line can make even the loviest couples feel like slapping each other. Road-trip tactics:

- Join your local branch of AAA (800-AAA-HELP) for free maps, guidebooks, roadside help (just in case), and a personalized Triptik with your ideal route highlighted on an easy-to-hold, flip-style map.
- Check the air in your tires, gas in your tank, and fluids in all those other, enigmatic under-the-hood vessels.
- Stock up on your favorite music, books, books on tape, and an Itty Bitty Booklight.

- Take sunglasses (and sunscreen!) for late-afternoon glare.
- Take snacks, but not a cooler of meals. Stopping for lunch is an important part of seeing the country.
- Forget your health regime. It's a scientific fact that nothing beats behind-the-wheel boredom like curly fries and a Dairy Queen Blizzard.
- Get enough sleep before heading out.
- If you get tired, pull over! This is not the time for a who-can-drive-the-longest-without-stopping or who-has-better-hand-eye-coordination-while-asleep contest.
- If you're renting, specify automatic or stick shift when reserving your car (especially in Europe, where stick shifts are standard).
- If you're headed abroad, ask AAA about an International Driving Permit or other needs.

Making Tracks

Whether you're taking an Amtrak across the United States, zipping through the Canadian Rockies, or riding the rails through Europe, going by train lets you see the sights without having to keep your hands on the wheel. Here're our tips for a terrific train trip:

- If you're taking a sleeper car to a faraway destination, pack a separate carry-on; you can't get to your checked baggage en route.
- Trains are far noisier than you'd expect—but your ears adjust and you forget about it.
- If you're training across Europe, hang on to your hat (and bag, purse, wallet, etc.).
- Pack snacks. Unless your train has a high-class dining car with a real chef, you'll be eating microwave meals from here to eternity (or wherever you're going).

Advice for a Harmonious Honeymoon

And now a word from our sponsor—romance. It's the ultimate reason to take a honeymoon, regardless of where you go. But romance isn't guaranteed to happen (though things like a hot tub under a moonlit sky, the sound of the ocean, and a big bottle of bubbly do help). Your attitude and actions really dictate how much fun you have. Here's our best advice.

Pack a Positive Attitude

There are always rough spots when traveling. How you handle them determines the quality of your trip. Constant complaining exaggerates the downsides, while ignoring imperfections and focusing on the positive will leave you both feeling like you planned the vacation of the century. Your goal—make sure your sweetie has a fabulous time. You not only guarantee that she'll love the trip madly (and you, of course), but you also protect yourself from getting into the traveler's rut of obsessing about the inevitable little glitches that can be so annoying. And keep your sense of humor intact! If your car's engine is overheating, and you have to run the heat to keep it cool, and it's August, and it's raining (meaning you have to roll the windows up), it could be a tragedy. Or it could be pretty damn funny.

Honeymoon Tipping Table

Here's how much to tip the people who make your honeymoon amazing:

Dining

- United States and Caribbean: 15 percent of total, pretax bill.
- Mexico: 20 percent of total, pretax bill.
- Europe and Canada: 10 percent of total bill unless it says "service included."
- South Pacific: No tip expected.

Travel

- Airport porter: $1 per bag.
- Train porter: At least $1 each night in a sleeper car.

Hotel

- Bellman: $1 per bag.
- Maid service: Leave about $1 on the nightstand each morning in the United States and the Caribbean. In Europe, it varies; ask at the front desk.
- Doorman: $1 for each service rendered (taxi hailing, door, bag carrying, etc.).
- Room service: About 15 percent of the bill in the United States, 10 percent in the Caribbean, nothing extra in Europe.
- Special service: If someone from the housekeeping staff brings you an iron or a bottle of champagne, give $1 or $2.
- All-inclusives: Check the info in your confirmation package for tipping suggestions.

Cruises

- At least $16 for each day aboard (management divvies it up for you).

Cabs

- United States: About 15 percent of the fare.
- Caribbean: About 10 percent, generally; no tipping in the Dominican Republic or the British Virgin Islands.
- Europe: Generally, just round the bill up to the nearest dollar; in Italy, Portugal, and Britain, go with the 15 percent rule.

Tour Bus Driver

- At least $4 per day for the two of you.

Tour Guide

- At least $5 per day for the two of you; if there's a group of you going in together, have everyone contribute about $2 per person, per day.

Instructors/Activity Organizers

- About 15 percent of the cost for water-skiing, scuba, boat ride, horseback riding, tennis lessons.

Take Realistic Expectations

First time traveling together? Expect to learn a lot about each other. Even if you like to do all the same things at home, you may discover that you have very different travel styles. If he wants to hole up in the room and you discover you need to disco till dawn with all the new friends you've made, it doesn't mean you're headed for divorce court when you get home. Be indulgent and supportive of each other. A rocky first vacation just means you need to plan another one soon.

Honeymoon blues? Believe it or not, a lot of couples spend the first days of their trip in the doldrums, depressed by so much calm after all the commotion. It's normal to feel in limbo—you just planned the biggest event of your shared lives and then left before basking in the afterglow. Spend your first day "debriefing" about your wedding—who wore what, who came, how it felt compared to your expectations. Then, when you've gone over every single detail, you'll be ready to start focusing on the fun in front of you.

Take a Little Time Alone

Don't feel obliged to spend every moment together. Even the most passionate, sex-crazed newlyweds need some time apart. Lie on the beach while she does yoga; have a cappuccino while he watches TV. A lot of long-married couples say they had more fun on a "second honeymoon" because they were able to relax and pursue their own interests occasionally.

Talk to Strangers

Yes, this is the opposite of what you learned in kindergarten. We're not suggesting that you hitchhike your way across Mexico. But the best way to get to know a place is to talk to those who live there. Ask the waiter for disco recommendations. Talk to that nice-looking couple

Honeymoon Snapshots

"Souvenir" does not mean "tacky mermaid made entirely of sea shells." It's French for "remember." Here are some great ways to remember your terrific trip:

Take photos. Enlarge your best shot and frame it for your office.
Write it down. There's nothing like a daily journal to keep your experiences alive.
Collect matchbooks. Every time you light a candle you'll think of that bistro on the Left Bank.
Buy a local-cuisine cookbook. Learn to make your favorite dishes.
Take a taste. Buy edible souvenirs—rum from the islands, chocolate from France, flavored honey or spice rub from Louisiana.
Breathe deeply. Focus on a scent during your trip—the lilac tree growing off your balcony, coconut-scented sunscreen, the incense burned in the Buddhist altars—and then re-create that aroma back home for instant sensual memories.
Name that tune. Buy the nightly steel drum band's CD.
Practical makes perfect. Buy crafts you'll use—pottery from Mexico, a wool sweater from Scotland, even a new bedroom set from North Carolina.

on the beach. Ask the Scottish bank teller if she has a ghost in her house (guaranteed conversation-starter *anywhere* in Scotland). If you're at an all-inclusive, meet a few of your co-honeymooners. It not only enhances your experience of the place, but sharing a *little* time with others also gives you more conversation fodder and inevitably makes the trip more fun.

Plan a Surprise

Even if you're making all the arrangements together, you still can spring a romantic surprise on your sweetie. Call the restaurant ahead of time and ask for a bottle of champagne to be waiting at your table. Plan to get up early one morning and bring him breakfast in bed. Or return from your walk across the resort with a bouquet of flowers (just don't get caught picking them!). Think of anything romantic that you know she'll love.

Linger Over the Last Night

Plan something special for your last night—a moonlit cruise, a romantic dinner. Then talk about your favorite part of your vacation and ways to incorporate it into your home life. Love the hotel's predinner cocktail-on-the-balcony hour? Vow to make it part of your daily grind. (So what if your balcony at home overlooks the neighbor's garage, not the ocean?) Maybe you want to continue eating more fruits and vegetables, or sipping cinnamon-spiced coffee together in bed on weekends. Take a little bit of the luxury back with you.

Honeymoon Planning Calendar

12–6 months before: Talk about your dream destinations. Start looking for a travel agent, reading up on your favorite spots, and investigating costs. If you're taking a time-specific trip (Mardi Gras in New Orleans, Carnival in Brazil), book your room and flight *now*.

5 months before: Get your passport, visa, and immunization info if you're going abroad.

4 months before: Nail down your budget. Look for deals in the paper and online.

3 months before: Book your tickets, rooms, rental car, and so on. Pay necessary deposits.

2 months before: Find out about the weather and any dress-code or special attire requirements. Start shopping for your trip.

1 month before: Line up someone to feed your plants or watch your pets while you're gone.

2 weeks before: Pick up traveler's checks. Write down your airline, hotel, and rental car confirmation numbers, as well as traveler's check numbers.

1 week before: Give a copy of your itinerary to your folks or honor attendants. (They may want to surprise you with flowers in your room.) Change about $50 (if you're going abroad) to get you started.

A few days before: Pack your bags. Double-confirm international flights.

Day before: Confirm domestic flights.

Day of: Enjoy!

NOTES

Appendix A: Checklists and Worksheets

YOUR TO-DO LIST

We've put together a twelve-month planning calendar because a year is the length of the average engagement, but you can start planning even earlier, or make it all happen in under six weeks. If you've got more time, you can linger over your initial decisions a little longer and you'll likely get first dibs on the best vendors (florists, photographers, sites, etc.). If you've got less time, start at the top of the list, get busy, and don't be as picky. Most important, don't panic. Your wedding will be fantastic regardless of your time constraints.

Twelve-plus Months Before

- ☐ Begin envisioning your wedding—formal hotel or friend's loft? Backyard barbecue or exotic beach? (Chapter 2)
- ☐ Pick preferences for wedding date and time and finalize after okaying with important guests, location, or officiant. (Chapter 2)
- ☐ Decide on budget and hash out who's contributing. (Chapter 3)
- ☐ Hire wedding consultant and/or ask for vendor recommendations from family and friends. (Chapter 2)
- ☐ Start a notebook/file folder to house all your wedding planning paperwork in one place.
- ☐ Begin working on guest list—decide on approximate size, get request lists from parents, create your own wish list (more realistic version to come later). (Chapter 2)
- ☐ Register in a few places.
- ☐ Brides: It's never too early to start shopping for the dress. (Chapter 11)

- ☐ Begin looking for main vendors (caterer, photographer, musicians) and set appointments to review their work.
- ☐ Start looking for the officiant who suits your style and spirit. (Chapter 6)

Nine to Eleven Months Before

- ☐ Scout out ceremony and reception sites and book as soon as you see something you love that's available on your date. (Chapter 10)
- ☐ Choose attendants and ask them to do the honor. (Chapter 4)
- ☐ Contact newspapers to announce your engagement. (Chapter 1)
- ☐ Brides: Start thinking about finalizing your dress decision.
- ☐ Contact out-of-towners so they can start making travel plans.
- ☐ Decide on and meet with your officiant to discuss ceremony structure and any marriage requirements (counseling, etc.). (Chapter 6)
- ☐ Choose caterer, begin working on menu, send deposit and/or execute a contract. (Chapter 14)
- ☐ Reserve photographer and/or videographer, decide on package. (Chapter 16)
- ☐ Set up appointments with florists to discuss options. (Chapter 13)
- ☐ Book reception band or DJ, execute contract. (Chapter 17)
- ☐ Start planning your honeymoon. (Chapter 25)
- ☐ Consult with stationer or graphic artist about invitations and other stationery needs. (Chapter 9)

Six to Eight Months Before

- ☐ Brides: Order your gown. (Chapter 11)
- ☐ Brides: Shop for and decide on bridesmaid dresses; collect necessary measurements from attendants. (Chapter 12)
- ☐ Reserve tent, chairs, or other equipment with rental company (unless caterer or site is taking care of it). (Chapter 10)
- ☐ Order your invitations and announcements. (Chapter 9)
- ☐ Send out save the dates.
- ☐ Start planning the rehearsal dinner. (Chapter 5)
- ☐ Book your florist. (Chapter 13)
- ☐ Book a baker for wedding cake. (Chapter 15)
- ☐ Choose ceremony music/musicians. (Chapter 17)
- ☐ Register for your wedding gifts. (Chapter 20)

- ☐ Set aside blocks of hotel rooms for out-of-town guests.
- ☐ Start planning honeymoon.

Three to Four Months Before

- ☐ Finalize guest list and start addressing invitations. (Chapter 9)
- ☐ Finalize order with florist and execute contract. (Chapter 13)
- ☐ Finalize menu and service details with caterer. (Chapter 14)
- ☐ Brides: Confirm delivery date for gown and bridesmaids' dresses, and schedule fittings. (Chapter 11, Chapter 12)
- ☐ Talk to people you'd like to do performances or readings as part of the ceremony. (Chapter 7)
- ☐ Compile packages for out-of-town guests with hotel and city information. (Chapter 5)
- ☐ Shop for and purchase wedding bands.
- ☐ Research local marriage-license requirements. (Chapter 21)
- ☐ Consider specific ceremony and reception decoration needs, such as a huppah, aisle runner, etc.
- ☐ Pick out or design a Ketubah or other marriage contract required by your religion.
- ☐ Grooms: Start looking to buy or rent tux or other formal attire. (Chapter 12)
- ☐ Coordinate the groomsmen's outfits. (Chapter 12)
- ☐ Make or buy favors. (Chapter 18)
- ☐ Schedule portrait session if you need one for a newspaper announcement.
- ☐ Book rehearsal-dinner site and finalize guest list.
- ☐ Get passports and visas if you're traveling abroad for your honeymoon. (Chapter 26)
- ☐ Start taking better care of yourself (eat right, exercise) so you look/feel great come wedding day.
- ☐ Talk to your honor attendant and best man about shower and other party plans. (Chapter 6)

Two Months Before

- ☐ Send out invitations.
- ☐ Brides: Have final wedding-dress fittings (probably several).
- ☐ Order or make ceremony programs. (Chapter 9)
- ☐ Choose menus.
- ☐ See a mock-up of your centerpieces.
- ☐ Begin working on vows, particularly if you're writing your own. (Chapter 6)

- ☐ Arrange wedding-day transportation for you, your wedding party, and guests (as needed). (Chapter 19)
- ☐ Have fun at showers and bachelor/ette parties. (Chapter 5)

Six Weeks Before

- ☐ Brides: Decide on and purchase all accessories (veil, shoes, lingerie, etc.) prior to final fittings.
- ☐ Brides: Make sure your attendants have dealt with dresses and shoes.
- ☐ Brides: Take the veil to your hairstylist and make sure your current 'do and veil work together.
- ☐ Buy gifts for the wedding party.
- ☐ Submit your announcement to newspapers (if you so desire).

Three to Four Weeks Before

- ☐ Work out wedding day timing and details—who will get the bride there, will the wedding party dress before arriving at the site, etc.
- ☐ Get marriage license and make appointments for blood tests (if necessary).
- ☐ Pick up wedding rings.
- ☐ Have final meeting with officiant.
- ☐ Finalize vows, readings, and other special ceremony details.
- ☐ Confirm wedding-night and honeymoon reservations. (Chapter 26)
- ☐ Send rehearsal-dinner invitations.
- ☐ Start putting together the seating plan if there's a seated reception meal. (Chapter 7)
- ☐ Work on a list of "must-play" (and must-not-play) songs for your DJ or band. (Chapter 17)
- ☐ Brides: Get final prewedding haircut if necessary. (Chapter 21)
- ☐ Do trial runs of hair and makeup and schedule wedding-day appointments. (Chapter 21)
- ☐ Send out thank-you notes for gifts you've received prewedding

One to Two Weeks Before

- ☐ Start calling guests who haven't R.S.V.P.'d for the wedding and rehearsal dinner. (It's okay to do this, you need a final head count!)
- ☐ Finalize seating chart and make placecards.
- ☐ Confirm date, location, time, and playlist with band/DJ and ceremony musicians.
- ☐ Touch base with officiant.
- ☐ Work out schedule and transportation for greeting guests and attendants.

- ☐ Confirm location, date, and time with photographer and forward a "must-take" photo list.
- ☐ Confirm location, date, and time with videographer.
- ☐ Confirm final headcount with caterer.
- ☐ Confirm head count, delivery time, and location with cake maker.
- ☐ Confirm delivery locations, times, and final arrangement count with florist.
- ☐ Call location manager and make sure your vendors all have access at the time they need it.
- ☐ Grooms: Get your final haircut.
- ☐ Fax transportation providers' schedule and addresses for pickups on wedding day.
- ☐ Call entire wedding party to make sure everyone has the date, time, and directions.
- ☐ Brides: Pick up the dress and veil.
- ☐ Brides: Practice walking in your wedding shoes.
- ☐ Grooms: Pick up your tux and try it on. (Don't wait till the day of to do this.)
- ☐ Prepare your toasts. (Chapter 7)
- ☐ Confirm all final payments with your vendors.
- ☐ Plan any additional night-before activities for friends and/or attendants.
- ☐ Shop and pack for honeymoon.

Day Before

- ☐ Cut checks or make arrangements for vendors' final payments.
- ☐ Calculate tips and give necessary cash to appointed person(s).
- ☐ Put final payments and tips in carefully marked envelopes and give to responsible person to distribute on wedding day.
- ☐ Brides: Pull together wedding gown, all accessories, and a last-minute emergency kit.
- ☐ Distribute wedding-day directions, schedule, and contact list to all parents, attendants, and vendors.
- ☐ Confirm all travel plans (including transportation to airport, etc.).
- ☐ Prepare announcements to be mailed on wedding day.
- ☐ Brides: Get manicure and pedicure and confirm big-day beauty appointments.
- ☐ Rehearse the ceremony.
- ☐ Have fun and relax at your rehearsal dinner.

There is a fully interactive to-do list on The Knot Online at www.theknot.com/checklist.

YOUR BIG-DAY BUDGET

Before you make any financial commitments, decide where your dollars are going to be spent. We've created this worksheet with approximate percentage breakdowns to give you some general guidelines—but don't be restricted by it. Every couple's priorities are different, and you may decide to allot more money to the things that are important to you.

Budget Category		Estimate	Actual
Ceremony	**3% of budget =**	**$_____**	
Ceremony Location Fee		$_____	$_____
Officiant fee/Donation		$_____	$_____
Ceremony Accessories (chuppah, candles, etc.)		$_____	$_____
Ceremony Sub-Total		**$_____**	**$_____**

Budget Category	Estimate	Actual
Reception **48% of budget = $_____**		
Reception Location Fee	$_____	$_____
Rentals (tent, tables, toilets, etc.)	$_____	$_____
Food/Service	$_____	$_____
Champagne/Wine	$_____	$_____
Bar/Bartenders	$_____	$_____
Cake(s)/Cutting Fee	$_____	$_____
Reception Sub-Total	**$_____**	**$_____**
Attire **10% of budget = $_____**		
The Dress	$_____	$_____
Alterations	$_____	$_____
Headpiece/Veil	$_____	$_____
Bride's Accessories (gloves, bag, jewelry, etc.)	$_____	$_____
Shoes	$_____	$_____
Lingerie	$_____	$_____
Hair & Makeup	$_____	$_____
Manicure & Pedicure	$_____	$_____
Groom's Tux/Suit	$_____	$_____
Groom's Accessories (shoes, tie, cufflinks, etc.)	$_____	$_____
Attire Sub-Total	**$_____**	**$_____**

Budget Category	Estimate	Actual
Flowers & Decorations	**8% of budget = $_____**	
Ceremony Site Decorations	$_____	$_____
Bride's Bouquet	$_____	$_____
Bridesmaids' Bouquets	$_____	$_____
Boutonnieres	$_____	$_____
Corsages	$_____	$_____
Centerpieces	$_____	$_____
Other Reception Decorations	$_____	$_____
Flowers Sub-Total	**$_____**	**$_____**
Music	**8% of budget = $_____**	
Ceremony Musicians	$_____	$_____
Cocktail Hour Musicians	$_____	$_____
Reception Band/Disc Jockey	$_____	$_____
Music Sub-Total	**$_____**	**$_____**

Budget Category	Estimate	Actual
Reportage **12% of budget = $_____**		
Photographer's Fee/Package	$_____	$_____
Videographer's Fee	$_____	$_____
Additional Prints/Videos	$_____	$_____
Wedding Cameras	$_____	$_____
Reportage Sub-Total	**$_____**	**$_____**
Stationery **3% of budget = $_____**		
Invitations & Reply Cards	$_____	$_____
Announcements	$_____	$_____
Postage	$_____	$_____
Thank You Notes/Stationery	$_____	$_____
Ceremony Programs	$_____	$_____
Stationery Sub-Total	**$_____**	**$_____**
Wedding Rings **3% of budget = $_____**		
Bride	$_____	$_____
Groom	$_____	$_____
Rings Sub-Total	**$_____**	**$_____**

Budget Category		Estimate	Actual
Transportation	**2% of budget = $_____**		
Limo/Car Rental		$_____	$_____
Guest Shuttle/Parking		$_____	$_____
Transportation Sub-Total		$_____	$_____
Gifts	**3% of budget = $_____**		
Attendant Gifts		$_____	$_____
Favors		$_____	$_____
Gifts Sub-Total		$_____	$_____
SUB-TOTAL		$_____	$_____
Tips, Taxes, Overages 5% of Sub-Total		$_____	$_____
Wedding Consultant Fee (optional) Up tp 10% of budget		$_____	$_____
GRAND TOTAL		$_____	$_____

There is a fully interactive budgeter on The Knot Online at www.theknot.com/budgeter.

YOUR PHONE BOOK

Bridal Shop/Seamstress

Name: _____

Address: _____

_____

Contact: _____

Phone: _____

Fax: _____

Hours of Operation: _____

Amount Budgeted: _____

Estimate Provided: _____

Date of Contract: _____

Payment Method: _____

Date/Time of Final Confirmation: _____

Bridesmaids' Dress Shop/Seamstress

Name: _____

Address: _____

_____

Contact: _____

Phone: _____

Fax: _____

Hours of Operation: _____

Amount Budgeted: _____

Estimate Provided: _____

Date of Contract: _____

Payment Method: _____

Date/Time of Final Confirmation: _____

Formalwear Shop

Name: _____

Address: _____

_____

Contact: _____

Phone: _____

Fax: _____

Hours of Operation: _____

Amount Budgeted: _____

Estimate Provided: _____

Date of Contract: _____

Payment Method: _____

Date/Time of Final Confirmation: _____

Ceremony Location

Name: _____

Address: _____

_____

Contact: _____

Phone: _____

Fax: _____

Hours of Operation: _____

Amount Budgeted: _____

Estimate Provided: _____

Date of Contract: _____

Payment Method: _____

Date/Time of Final Confirmation: _____

Officiant

Name: _____

Address: _____

_____

Contact: _____

Phone: _____

Fax: _____

Hours of Operation: _____

Amount Budgeted: _____

Estimate Provided: _____

Date of Contract: _____

Payment Method: _____

Date/Time of Final Confirmation: _____

Reception Location

Name: _____

Address: _____

_____

Contact: _____

Phone: _____

Fax: _____

Hours of Operation: _____

Amount Budgeted: _____

Estimate Provided: _____

Date of Contract: _____

Payment Method: _____

Date/Time of Final Confirmation: _____

Caterer

Name: _____

Address: _____

_____

Contact: _____

Phone: _____

Fax: _____

Hours of Operation: _____

Amount Budgeted: _____

Estimate Provided: _____

Date of Contract: _____

Payment Method: _____

Date/Time of Final Confirmation: _____

Baker

Name: _____

Address: _____

_____

Contact: _____

Phone: _____

Fax: _____

Hours of Operation: _____

Amount Budgeted: _____

Estimate Provided: _____

Date of Contract: _____

Payment Method: _____

Date/Time of Final Confirmation: _____

Florist

Name: _____

Address: _____

_____

Contact: _____

Phone: _____

Fax: _____

Hours of Operation: _____

Amount Budgeted: _____

Estimate Provided: _____

Date of Contract: _____

Payment Method: _____

Date/Time of Final Confirmation: _____

Musicians (Ceremony)

Name: _____

Address: _____

_____

Contact: _____

Phone: _____

Fax: _____

Hours of Operation: _____

Amount Budgeted: _____

Estimate Provided: _____

Date of Contract: _____

Payment Method: _____

Date/Time of Final Confirmation: _____

Musicians/DJ (Reception)

Name: _____

Address: _____

_____

Contact: _____

Phone: _____

Fax: _____

Hours of Operation: _____

Amount Budgeted: _____

Estimate Provided: _____

Date of Contract: _____

Payment Method: _____

Date/Time of Final Confirmation: _____

Photographer

Name: _____

Address: _____

_____

Contact: _____

Phone: _____

Fax: _____

Hours of Operation: _____

Amount Budgeted: _____

Estimate Provided: _____

Date of Contract: _____

Payment Method: _____

Date/Time of Final Confirmation: _____

Videographer

Name: _____

Address: _____

_____

Contact: _____

Phone: _____

Fax: _____

Hours of Operation: _____

Amount Budgeted: _____

Estimate Provided: _____

Date of Contract: _____

Payment Method: _____

Date/Time of Final Confirmation: _____

Transportation

Name: _____

Address: _____

_____

Contact: _____

Phone: _____

Fax: _____

Hours of Operation: _____

Amount Budgeted: _____

Estimate Provided: _____

Date of Contract: _____

Payment Method: _____

Date/Time of Final Confirmation: _____

YOUR WEDDING-DAY CONTACT LIST

ROLE	NAME	CONTACT NUMBER	ARRIVAL TIME
Bride:			
Groom:			
Bride's Parents:			
Groom's Parents:			
Maid of Honor:			
Best Man:			

ROLE	NAME	CONTACT NUMBER	ARRIVAL TIME
Bridesmaids:			
Groomsmen:			
Ushers:			
Officiant(s):			
Photographer:			
Videographer:			
Bridal Shop:			
Formalwear Shop:			

ROLE	NAME	CONTACT NUMBER	ARRIVAL TIME
Hair & Makeup:			
Reception Hall Manager:			
Rentals:			
Caterer:			
Baker:			
Car Service/Limo:			
Ceremony Location Contact:			
Ceremony Musicians:			
Reception Musicians:			

BRIDESMAIDS' MEASUREMENTS

Name: _____

Address: _____

_____

Phone Number: _____

Fax Number: _____

Bust: _____

Waist: _____

Hips: _____

Height: _____

Shoe Size: _____

☐ Send style order form

☐ Call in measurements

☐ Have fitting

☐ Buy shoes

Name: _____

Address: _____

_____

Phone Number: _____

Fax Number: _____

Bust: _____ ☐ Send style order form

Waist: _____ ☐ Call in measurements

Hips: _____ ☐ Have fitting

Height: _____ ☐ Buy shoes

Shoe Size: _____

Name: _____

Address: _____

_____

Phone Number: _____

Fax Number: _____

Bust: _____ ☐ Send style order form

Waist: _____ ☐ Call in measurements

Hips: _____ ☐ Have fitting

Height: _____ ☐ Buy shoes

Shoe Size: _____

Name: _____

Address: _____

_____

Phone Number: _____

Fax Number: _____

Bust: _____ ☐ Send style order form

Waist: _____ ☐ Call in measurements

Hips: _____ ☐ Have fitting

Height: _____ ☐ Buy shoes

Shoe Size: _____

Name: _____

Address: _____

_____

Phone Number: _____

Fax Number: _____

Bust: _____ ☐ Send style order form

Waist: _____ ☐ Call in measurements

Hips: _____ ☐ Have fitting

Height: _____ ☐ Buy shoes

Shoe Size: _____

Name: _____

Address: _____

_____

Phone Number: _____

Fax Number: _____

Bust: _____

Waist: _____

Hips: _____

Height: _____

Shoe Size: _____

☐ Send style order form

☐ Call in measurements

☐ Have fitting

☐ Buy shoes

Appendix B: Resources

YOUR WEDDING CLOTHES

Bridal Gown Designers

Alvina Valenta: www.alvinavalenta.com
Amsale: www.amsale.com
Amy Michelson: www.amymichelson.com
Angel Sanchez: www.angelsanchez.com
Anne Barge: www.annebarge.com
Atelier Aimée: www.aimeeusa.com
Bonny Bridal: www.bonny.com
Bridal Originals: www.bridaloriginals.com
Carmela Sutera: www.carmelasutera.com
Casablanca Bridal: www.casablancabridal.com
Christina Wu: www.christinawu.net
Christos: www.christosbridal.com
Clea Colet: www.cleacolet.com
Demetrios: www.demetriosbride.com
Eden Bridals: www.edenbridals.com
Edgardo Bonilla: www.edgardobonilla.com
Eugenia: www.eugeniacouture.com
Ines Di Santo: www.inesdisanto.com
Janell Berté: www.berte.com
Janet Nelson Kumar: www.janetnelsonkumar.com
Jasmine: www.jasminebridal.com
Jenny Lee: www.jennyleebridal.com
Jessica McClintock: www.jessicamcclintock.com
Jim Hjelm: www.jimhjelm.com
John Russell: www.johnrussellapparel.com
Judd Waddell: www.juddwaddell.com
Justina McCaffrey: www.justinamccaffrey.com
Kirstie Kelly: www.kirstiekelly.com
Lazaro: www.lazarobridal.com
LEBON: www.lebonbridal.com
L'ezu Atelier: www.lezu.com
Liancarlo: www.liancarlo.com
Lynne Carter Bride: www.lynnecarter.com
Maggie Sottero Couture Bridal: www.maggie sotterobridal.com
Manalé: www.manale.com
Mary's: www.marysbridal.com
Matthew Christopher: www.matthewchristopher.com
Melissa Sweet: www.melissasweet.com
Michael of Boston: www.michaelofboston.com
Michelle Roth: www.michelleroth.com
Mon Cheri Bridals: www.moncheribridals.com
Mona Lisa Designs: www.monalisadesigns.com

Monique Lhuillier: www.moniquelhuillier.com
Moonlight: www.moonlightbridal.com
Mori Lee: www.morilee.com
Oscar de la Renta: www.oscardelarenta.com
Palazzo: www.palazzobridal.com
Paloma Blanca: www.palomablanca.com
Paula Varsalona: www.paulavarsalona.com
Peter Langner: www.peterlangner.com
Priscilla of Boston: www.priscillaofboston.com
Pronovias: www.pronovias.com
Reem Acra: www.reemacra.com
Reva Mivasagar: www.revadesigns.com
Rivini: www.rivini.com
Romona Keveza: www.romonakeveza.com
St. Pucchi: www.stpucchi.com
Vera Wang: www.verawang.com
Wearkstatt: www.wearkstattbridal.com
Watters & Watters: www.watters.com
Yolanda Couture: www.yolandacouture.com
Youlin: www.youlinnewyork.com
Zurc for Impression Bridal: www.impressionbridal.com

Traditional African Wedding Wear/Accents

Cassandra Bromfield: 212-502-5277
Jonathan Adewami (Nigerian Fabrics and Fashions): 718-260-9416
Laurie A. Sanders: 718-217-2899
Therez Fleetwood: 212-714-8058

Veils and Headpieces

Affordable-Bride.com: www.affordable-bride.com
Che Bella: www.chebella.com
Elen Henderson Designs for Malis-Henderson: www.mhtiara.com
Elizabeth Caroline: www.elizabethcaroline.com
EvesCircle: www.evescircle.com
Fenaroli for Regalia: www.fenaroli.com
JL Johnson Bridals: www.jljohnsonbridals.com
Mirabella: www.mirabellabridal.com
Naugi.com: www.naugi.com
Nelson D'Leon: www.nelsondleon.com
Paris: www.paristiaras.com
Parker Designs: www.parkerdesigns.com
PrincessBrideTiaras.com: www.princessbridetiaras.com
Reem Acra: www.reemacra.com
Regina B.: www.reginab.com
Stephanie's Bridal Millinery: www.stephaniesbridalmillinery.com.au
TS Tiara: www.tstiara.com
Winters & Rain: www.wintersandrain.com

Bridesmaid Dresses

Anakha: www.anakha.com
Aria Bridesmaids: www.ariadress.com
B2: www.jasminebridal.com
Bari Jay: www.barijay.com
Belsoie: www.jasminebridal.com
Bill Levkoff: www.billlevkoff.com
Bridalane: www.bridalane.com
Charsa: www.charsa.com
Currie Bonner for Bridesmaids: www.melissasweet.com
Dress Fancy by Jane Hamill: www.dressfancy.com
Eden Maids: www.edenbridals.com
Jenny Yoo Collection: www.jennyyoo.com
Jessica McClintock: www.jessicamcclintock.com
Jim Hjelm: www.jimhjelm.com
Jordan: www.jordanfashions.com

Kathlin Argiro: www.kathlinargiro.com
Lazaro Bridesmaids: www.lazarobridal.com
Mary's Modern Maids: www.marysbridal.com
Miracle on Saint Mark's: www.miracleon stmarks.com
Mori Lee by Madeline Gardner Bridesmaids: www.morilee.com
Priscilla of Boston Bridesmaids: www.priscillaof boston.com
Saeyoung Vu Couture: www.vucouture.com
Serafina Bridesmaids: www.serafina.net
Silhouettes Bridesmaids by Bridal Originals: www.bridaloriginals.com
Simple Silhouettes: www.simpledress.com
Siri: www.siriinc.com
Thread: www.threaddesign.com
Vanessa Fox: www.vanessafox.com
Vera Wang Maids: www.verawang.com
Watters & Watters: www.watters.com
Zure for Impression Bridesmaid: www.impression bridal.com

Women's Shoes

Coloriffics: www.coloriffics.com
Dyeables: www.dyeables.com
Fenaroli for Regalia: www.fenaroli.com
Peter Fox Shoes: www.peterfox.com
Shelley George Design: www.shelleygeorge.com
Special Occasions By Saugus Shoe: www.saugus shoes.com
Stuart Weitzman: www.stuartweitzman.com
Vanessa Noel: www.vanno.com

Bridal Bags/Purses

Gioia Handbags: www.gioiahandbags.com
Isabella V: www.isabellav.com
Che Bella: www.chebella.com
Fenaroli for Regalia: www.fenaroli.com

Gloves

Carolina Amato: www.carolinaamato.com
LaCrasia: www.lacrasia.com

Flower Girl Dresses

Belle of the Ball: www.belloftheball.com
Christian D'Gray Couture: www.flowergirl dress.net
Katina Katoo: www.katinakatoo.com
Kaya Collection: www.kayacollection.com
Little Flowers by Odyssey: www.little-flowers.com
Mary's Cupids: www.marysbridal.com
PEGEEN: www.pegeen.com
Storybook Heirlooms: www.storybook.com

Ring Bearer Outfits

PEGEEN: www.pegeen.com
Oscar de la Renta, After Six, Raffinati: 800-351-6767
The Wooden Soldier: 800-375-6002

Tuxedos

Oscar de la Renta, After Six, Raffinati: www.tuxedos4u.com
Ralph Lauren Chaps, Claiborne, Perry Ellis: www.tuxedos.com

Men's Accessories

Brooks Brothers: 800-274-1816
Joseph Abboud: 800-999-0600
Raffinati: 800-554-8212
Ralph Lauren: 800-775-7656
XMI (ties and vests): 800-745-0010

Men's Shoes

Allen-Edmonds: www.allenedmonds.com
Bally: www.bally.com
Brooks Brothers: www.brooksbrothers.com
Cole Haan: www.colehaan.com
Johnston & Murphy: www.johnstonmurphy.com
Kenneth Cole: www.kennethcole.com
Paul Fredrick: www.paulfredrick.com

Cleaners

Imperial Gown Restoration Company: 800-WED-GOWN or www.gown.com

FOR YOUR WEDDING

Online Resources

The Knot, the number one wedding resource; www.theknot.com and AOL keyword: weddings.

Organizations

Association of Bridal Consultants www.bridalassn.com
American Rental Association www.ararental.org
International Special Events Society www.ises.com
National Limousine Association www.limo.org
R.V. Nuccio and Associates (wedding insurance) ww.rvnuccio.com

Personalizing

The Essential Guide to Lesbian and Gay Weddings, by Jess Ayers and Paul Brown (HarperCollins, 1994).

Going to the Chapel: From Traditional to African Inspired and Everything in Between the Ultimate Wedding Guide for Today's Black Couple, by Signature Bride Magazine (Berkley Public Group, 2001).

Jewish Weddings: A Beautiful Guide to Creating the Wedding of Your Dreams, by Rita Brownstein (Simon & Schuster, 2002).

Joining Hands and Hearts: Interfaith, Intercultural Wedding Celebrations—A Practical Guide for Couples, by Susanna Stefanachi Macomb (Fireside, 2002).

Wild Geese and Tea: An Asian-American Wedding Planner, by Shu Shu Costa (Riverhead Books, 1997).

Locations

America's Best Bed & Breakfasts: Over 1,600 Delightful Places to Stay in All 50 States, 3rd edition, by Caroline V. Haberfeld (Fodors Travel Publishing, 1999).

America's Historic Places: An Illustrated Guide to Our Country's Best (Reader's Digest, 1988).

Dinner and Spirits: A Guide to America's Most Haunted Restaurants, Taverns, and Inns, by Anne Powell Wlodarski, Robert James Wlodarski (iUniverse.com, 2001).

Gene Kilgore's Ranch Vacations: The Complete Guide to Guest and Resort, Fly-Fishing, and Cross-Country Skiing Ranches in the United States and Canada, 6th edition, by Gene Kilgore, Jeff Cahill, George Gaines, Barnaby Conrad (Avalon Travel Publishing, 2001).

The National Trust Guide to Historic Bed & Breakfasts, Inns and Small Hotels, 4th edition, by Suzanne G. Dane (John Wiley & Sons, 1996).

Nights to Imagine: Magical Places to Stay in America, by Peter Guttman (Fodors, 1996).

The Outrageous Atlas: A Guide to North America's Strangest Places, by Richard A. Rogers and Laurine Rogers (Citadel Press, 1993).

Places: A Directory of Public Places for Private Events and Private Places for Public Functions (Tenth House Enterprises, updated annually; call 212-737-7536 to order).

Sacred Places North America: 108 Destinations, by Brad Olsen (CCC Publishing, 2003).

Invitation Catalogs

The American Wedding Album www.american-wedding-album.com
Ann's Wedding Stationery www.annswedding.com
Crane's www.crane.com
Creations by Elaine www.creationsbyelaine.com
Invitations by Dawn www.us.invitationsbydawn.com
The Knot www.theknot.com/weddingsupplies
Now & Forever www.now-and-forever.com
The Precious Collection www.preciouscollection.com
Rexcraft www.rexcraft.com

FOR YOUR HONEYMOON

Great Escape Resources

Tourism Offices Worldwide Directory www.towd.com
Australian Tourist Commission www.australia.com
Bahamas Ministry of Tourism www.bahamas.com
Caribbean Tourism Organisation www.doitcaribbean.com
Costa Rica Tourism Board www.visitcostarica.com
Disney World www.disney.com/disneyworld
Fiji Visitors Bureau www.bulafiji.com
Hawaii Visitors & Convention Bureau www.gohawaii.com
Jamaica Tourist Board www.jamaicatravel.com
Las Vegas Chamber of Commerce www.vegasfreedom.com
Mexico Tourism Board www.visitmexico.com
Niagara Falls Convention & Visitors Bureau www.nfcvb.com
Puerto Rico Tourism Company www.gotopuertorico.com
U.S. Virgin Islands Department of Tourism www.usvi.org

Tour Operators

The United States Tour Operators Association www.ustoa.com
Backroads Travel (biking, walking, and multisport getaways) www.backroads.com
Contiki Vacations (18–35 years old) www.contiki.com
Amelia International (specializing in travel to Sicily and its Mediterranean neighbors) www.ameliainternational.com
Abercrombie & Kent (tailor-made private travel or escorted small groups) www.abercrombiekent.com

Discount Travel Brokers

Cheap Tickets www.cheaptickets.com
GoCheap.com www.gocheap.com
Quikbook www.quikbook.com
Hotel Reservations Network www.hotelreservationsnetwork.com
Pleasant Holidays www.pleasantholidays.com

Hotels

All-Hotels Directory (77,000 luxury, chain and discount hotels worldwide) www.allhotels.com
Bed and Breakfasts, Country Inns, Small Hotels & Vacation Rentals (throughout the U.S., Canada, Mexico, Australia, Caribbean & Europe) www.virtualcities.com/ons/0onsadex.htm

Popular All-Inclusive Resorts

Almond All-Inclusive Resorts, Barbados www.almondresorts.com
Club Med www.clubmed.com
Couples Resorts www.couples.com
Palace Resorts www.palaceresorts.com
Sandals www.sandals.com
Super Clubs www.superclubs.com

Miscellaneous

American Society of Travel Agents www.astanet.com
Travel Facts www.travelfacts.com
Best Beaches in the USA www.ptrix.com/beaches.index.html
National Park Service Parks Guide www.nps.gov/parks.html
American Zoo and Aquarium Association www.aza.org
Las Vegas Wedding Chapel Listings www.vegas.com/weddings/hotelchapels.html

Index

Page numbers of illustrations appear in italics.

African-American traditions, 81, 113
  bridal gown alternative, 170
American Federation of Musicians, 266
American Formalwear Assn., 196
American Gem Corporation, 8
American Rental Assn., 151
American Society of Travel Agents, 372
Asian themes
  Adela & Nathan, Japanese traditions, Denver, CO, 98
  Akari & Seth, Japanese traditions, Brooklyn, NY, 90
  bridal gown alternative, 170
  Chinese red, 113–14
  Chinese tea ceremony, 114
  Japanese saki ritual, 115
  Sallie & Jason, Korean customs, Cliffside Park, NJ, 102, *102*
Assn. of Bridal Consultants, 22
attendants
  best man, 41
  bridesmaids, 41–43
  candle lighters, 46
  children, roles for, 45
  gifts, 44, 293, 294
  groomsmen, 43, 45
  huppah holders, 46
  maid/matron of honor, 39–41
  parties, 64–65
  pets, participation of, 46
  positions at altar or huppah, Christian, *74,* 75
  procession, 72, *73*
  readers and class acts, 46
  recession, 77
  rehearsal, 78
  rehearsal dinner, 62–64
  toast of the table, 46–47
  transportation, 281–82
  transportation captain, 46
  two maids of honor, 40
  uneven number, 40
  usher, 46
  who pays for what, 44
  See also groom's and male attendant's clothing
bachelor and bachelorette parties, 60–62, 301
  alternative ideas, 62
  rules of the game, 61–62
  who plans it, 60
beauty. *See* hair and makeup
best man
  duties, 41, 43
  getting couple to the airport, 280
  gift, 44, 293, 294
  position at altar or huppah, *74,* 75
  procession, 72, *73*
  recession, 77
  toasting, 41
Book of Common Prayer, 68, 87
breakfast parties
  morning-after, 65
  prewedding, 65
  wedding day, with fiancé/e, 304
bridal accessories, 180
  gloves, 185
  headpieces, 180, 182–83
  hosiery, 184–85

jewelry, 183–84
lingerie, 184
shoes, 185–86
"something old . . . ," 183
veils, 180, *181,* 182
bridal bouquet
color, size, shape, and style of dress, 212
cost, 209
preserving, 101
single flower, 211
styles, 209, *210,* 211
toss, 101
bridal dressing checklist, 178
bridal gown, 161
alterations, 178–79
authorized dealers, 175
Bridal Building, NYC, 171
bustling the train, 169
cleaning advice, 177
colors and shades of white, 168–69
contract points, 177
cost, 170, 171, 172, 176
cost-cutting tips, 36, 171
embellishments, 167–68
ethnic options, 170
fabrics, 167
fabrics, hot vs. cold weather, 167
formality, 163
getting a dress made, 172–73
Knot's Bridal Search, 171
neckline, 163, *164–65,* 165–66
ordering tips, 177
period costumes, 170
preserving your dress, 179–80
renting, 171
shopping, when, with whom, and what to wear or take with you, 173–76
shopping tips, 176
silhouettes, 161–63, *162*
size, 178
sleeves, 166
Timberly & Robert, NYC, 172
trains, 169
vintage or heirloom gown, 173
where to buy, 169–71
white and Queen Victoria, 168
working with salespeople, 174–75
bridesmaids
choosing, 41
contract for gown, 202
duties, 41–43
gifts, 44, 293, 294
gowns, 198, 200–2
gowns, alterations, 202
group discounts, 201
limiting number and offering alternative roles, 43
lore, 200
positions at altar or huppah, *74,* 75
pregnant, 200
procession, 72, *73*
recession, 77
retaining individuality, 200
shoes, 202
Buddhist ceremony, 84–85
interfaith, 89
budget, 25–31
average, 25
breakdown by items, 30–31
bridal gown, 170, 171, 172, 176
calculating online, 25, 31
deposits, credit cards for, 35
drinks, 232
factors affecting cost, 25–26
flowers, 216, 217
food, 221
Heather & Greg, North Caldwell, NJ, budget breakdown, 31, *31*
honeymoon, 369–72
how to ask parents for money, 28
invitations, 123
Jessa & Jeff, Deep Creek Lake, MD, do-it-yourself, 34, *34*
music, 261, 263, 266, 269
one-third budget model, 26–27
parents footing the bill, 29, 30
paying for it yourselves, 27–29
prioritizing, 26
savings potential, 29
site, 156
transportation, 279–80
twenty-five cost-cutting tips, 35–36
ways to fund your wedding, 28–29
who pays for what, 27, 28

cancellation of wedding
cold feet, 322–23
decision, 322
written mailer, 141
ceremony, 66–93
Adela & Nathan, interfaith wedding, Denver, CO, 98
African-American traditions, 81
aisle runner, 72
Akari & Seth, interfaith wedding, Brooklyn, NY, 90
attendants, 39–45
basic elements in, 70
breaking the glass, Jewish, 81, 82, 86
bride's accompaniment down the aisle, 76
Buddhist, 84–85
charge to the couple (saying "I do"), 73
Church of Latter-Day Saints (Mormon), 86–87
civil, 68
civil ceremony wording, 68
closing remarks, 76
commitment (same sex couples), 92–93
ethnic ideas, 87, 98, 113–16
exchange of vows, 76
honoring the deceased, 84
interfaith weddings, 88–90, *90*
Islamic, 85
Jewish, 85–86
kiss, 76
music, 83, 257–62
officiant, do-it-yourself, 70

officiant, fee, 71
officiant, finding your, 69–70
officiant, opening remarks, 72
pew cards, 138
positions at altar or huppah, *74*
procession, 71–72, *73*
Protestant, 87
Quaker, 87–88
readings to remember, 83
recession, Christian, 77
rehearsal, 78
religious, 67–68
religious, prewedding counseling, 71, 341
ring ceremony, 76
roles for other important people, 45–47
Roman Catholic, 88
Sallie & Jason, Korean customs, Cliffside Park, NJ, 102, *102*
seating of guests, 75
second wedding, 91–92
separate guest list, 20
site, 19–20
spiritual but not religious, 68
Suzanne & Tripp, Lake Glenville, NC, 82
unity symbols, 81, 84
wedding announcement, 140–41
wedding program, 81–82, 138
children
announcing engagement to (yours), 4
avoid giving them critical duties, 45
candle kids, 45
clothing, 202–3
flower children, 44, 45
as guests or not, 18
junior groomsmen/ushers, 44
Mexican piñata for, 115
page/train bearers, 45
positions at altar or huppah, *74,* 75
procession, 72, *73*
recession, 77
ring bearers, 44–45
roles in second weddings, 92
Chicago, IL, 153
Church of Latter-Day Saints (Mormon), 86–87
before the ceremony, 86
nontemple wedding, 86–87
temple ceremony, 86
contracts or written agreements. *See* vendors
counseling, prewedding, 71, 341

date and time
arrival time for reception, 16
blackout periods for clergy, 16
budget considerations, 25
cost-cutting tip, 35
days in demand, 16
florists' busiest days, 15
Melani & Herb, wedding date, Oracle, AZ, 15, *15*
monster months, 16
power hours, 16
priorities and, 15
variables to consider, 14
destination wedding, 116, 117
Lee & Jeff, destination wedding, Orcas Island, WA, 117, *117*
marriage license and documents, 116, 299
doctor, choosing, 300

elopement, 119–20
website info for, 119
emcee, 96, 100
emergency kit, 188
engagement, 3–11
announcements (samples), 5–7
fielding questions, 7
friends, negative, 7–8, 344–45
length, 3
photo, 6
telling children (yours), 4
telling ex-spouse, 5
telling friends and relatives, 7
telling parents, 4
who to tell first, 4
engagement party, 7
gifts, 55
host your own, 56
parent parties, 55–56
thank-you notes, 55
English wedding walk, 114
Essential Guide to Gay and Lesbian Weddings, The (Ayers et al.), 92

father of the bride, 49
attire, 204
duties, 49
position at altar or huppah, *74,* 75
father of the groom, 49
attire, 204
duties, 50
position at altar or huppah, *74,* 75
favors, 272–77
charity donation, 276–77
for children, 274
costs, 273
ideas for, 274–75
Victorian wedding, 109
Fearing, Dean, 230
flowers, 207–19
Astrid & Christian, NYC, 213
bridal bouquet, 209–11, *210,* 212
bridesmaids' bouquets, 211, 212
ceremony arrangements, 212
cost-cutting tips, 35, 217
costs, 209, 211, 212, 215
emergency remedies, 306
finding a florist, 215–17
flower girls' blossoms, 212
flower meanings, 208–9
groom and groomsmen's boutonnieres, 211
how to decide, 207–8
huppah, 209
keeping fresh, 209
lore, 208

for moms and honored guests, 211
reception, 213–15
reception flowers, themes, 214
red roses, ordering, 214
set-up, arranging, 215
written contract, 216
See also bridal bouquet; wedding decorations
food and drinks, 221–39
afternoon tea, 222
budget considerations, 25
buffet, 221–22, 231
choosing a caterer, 224–27
Christine & Mark, alternative foods, NYC, 225
cocktails, 223
contract, 226
cost-cutting tips, 35, 222
deciding which meal, 221
dessert only, 224
drinks, average for 100 guests, 231
drinks, cost-cutting tips, 35
drinks, open, limited, or cash bar, 232
drinks, signature cocktails, 35, 232, 233
emergency remedies, 306
food stations, 222, 230
getting a head count, 226
leftovers, 226
menu, international, 228
menu, memorable, 227–29
menu, samples, 229–31
price per head, 221
questions for cook, 226–27
restaurant route, 225
seated meal, 223, 229
table name ideas, 223
table settings, *230*
Victorian wedding, 109
See also wedding cake
Francesco, Rev. Richard G., 71
Fraser, Rob, 243, 246
friends
attendants, limiting number and alternative roles, 43
fair-weather, 332–33
negative, 7–8, 344–45
gay and lesbian weddings, 92–93
books on, 92
commitment ceremony, 92–93
finding an officiant, 92–93
gay-friendly religions, 93
gift receipts, 291
gifts, anniversary (chart), 294
gifts you are given, 285–94
cash, 289–90, 291, 292
classic registry, 288
consider guests' budgets, 289
creating a registry, 289
dealing with exchanges, 291
donations to charity, 290
Gayle & Ira, personal values, Benton Harbor, MI, 290, *290*
honeymoon registry, 371
no-gift request, 287
recording gifts, 292
registering, 285–89
thank-you notes, 291–92
gifts you give, 293–94
attendants', 293, 294
family, 293
out-of-town guests, 294
yourselves, 294
Gillespie, Gwen, 341
groom dressing checklist, 178
groom's and male attendants' clothing
accessories, 195–96
collars, 195, *195*
fit, 197–98
formalwear, 193, *194*
formalwear contract, 197
guide, 196
Odine & David, cultural garb, NYC, 199
rental costs, 196
rental tips, 198
shopping, 197
stand-out grooms, 198
tuxes, 196
what to wear when, 196–97
groomsmen, 43
gifts, 44, 293, 294
positions at altar or huppah, *74*, 75
procession, 72, *73*
recession, 77
refusing bride's request for, 45
guest book, 142
guests
attire, 204
buddy system for out-of-town guests, 52
ceremony seating, 75
coordinator for, 50
emergency remedies, 305
family of bride and groom, 47–50
get-togethers with, 301
hospitality, 301
keep them entertained, 51–52
keep them informed, 50
lists and seating, 297–98
map-hotel info cards, 137–38
pew cards, 138
photos, 248
reserving rooms, 51
seating at reception, 98–99
show your love, 52
tips for talkative tables, 99
transportation, 50, 282
welcome cocktail party or brunch, 62

hair and makeup
all-in-one pro, 188
beauty and hair questions, 187
beauty countdown, 189
beauty emergencies, 190
big day makeup bag, 186
choosing a stylist, 186, 187
consultation, 187
costs, 187
hair stylists, how many, 188
headpiece and veil, 187–88
makeup artist, 186–87
photos, 188
tips for a perfect face, 186
Herrera, Carolina, 173
honeymoon, 348–82
adrenaline adventures, 352–56
airline advice, 377–78

airline reservation and upgrade, 308
ATM and cash cards, 376
best beaches, 349–52, 374
booking: travel agents, tour operators, do-it-yourself, 372–74
credit card use, 375
cruises, 364–67, 378
destination questions, 373
eco-honeymoon, 361
exotic trips, 360–63
48 hour at-home, 366
getting ready to go, 374–77
on gift registry, 371
glossary of rooms, 375
immunization alert, 376
insurance, 376
intellectual, historical, or literary trips, 358–60
last-minute chores, 301
packing, 377, 378
passports, 375, 377
photography, 381
planning calendar, 382
rail trip, 379
relationship advice, 379, 381–82
road trip, 365, 378–79
roughing it resources, 354
safety, 376
service questions, 373
super spa honeymoons, 356
tipping, 380
urban honeymoons, 356–58
Vela & John, Hawaiian Islands, 353, *353*
wedding night, 307–8
who pays, 371
hope chest, 5
huppah, 85
Astrid & Christian, designing of, NYC, 213
flowers for, 209
holders, 46
positions at, *74*, 75

Indian traditions
bridal gown alternative, 170
henna, 114
insurance
honeymoon, 376
wedding and event, 32
interfaith or intercultural weddings, 325–33
Adela & Nathan, Japanese traditions, Denver, CO, 98, *98*
Akari & Seth, Jewish and Japanese, Brooklyn, NY, 90, *90*
compromise, 328
dual-officiant, 88
fair-weather friends, 332–33
healthy mental attitude, 331
Lynn & Ben, combining religions, NYC, 329, *329*
Meri & Stephen, family obligations, 341, *341*
officiant for, 88–89, 329
parents, 327, 330–32
planning, 89–90
questions to answer now, 332
Rachel & Jeffrey, Los Angeles, 327, *327*
relationships and, 325–30
religions which accept, 88
religions which somewhat accept, 88
religious rifts, 316–17
two separate ceremonies, 89
International Gemological Institute, 10
Internet
finding photographers, 244, 245
finding reception sites, 145
finding stationers, 133
road trips, 365
The Knot Big-Day Budgeter, 25, 31
The Knot Bridal Search, 171
The Knot Checklist, 14
The Knot photography, 245
The Knot Wedding Gift Registry, 286
wedding Web page, 50, 118–19
invitations
addressing, 130–31
addressing, early, 132
assembling the invites, 130
common titles, 131
cost-cutting tips, 36
do-it-yourself, 134
earth-friendly, 139
envelopes, 126
glossary for paper and printing, 125
how many, 126
inner envelope, 131–32
Margaret & Richard, sugar invitations, NYC, 135, *135*
order in advance, 126
order in bulk, 132
paper prices, 123
postage, 126
printing techniques, 123–25
reception or ceremony cards, 135–36
response cards, 136–37
R.S.V.P. deadline, 138
selecting a stationer, 132–34, 137
thermography vs. engraving, 124
Victorian wedding, 109
what style, 126
when to send, 126
wording, 127–29
Irish traditions
Adela & Nathan, Irish elements, Denver, CO, 98
Claddagh ring, 114
toasts, 114–15
Islamic ceremony, 85
meher, 85

Jewish ceremony, 85–86
Akari & Seth, interfaith wedding, Brooklyn, NY, 90
breaking the glass, Jewish, 81, 82, 86
huppah, 85
interfaith, 89
Ketubah, 85–86
minhag, 85
position at huppah, *74*, 75
procession, 72, *73*
recession, 77

seven blessings, 86
tangible goods, 85
wine, 85
Yichud, 86
See also ceremony
Jumping the Broom: The African-American Wedding Planner (Cole), 113

Kirsch, Abigail, 231

Latin American traditions, 115
Mexican piñata, 115
Legal Guide for Gay and Lesbian Couples, The (Curry et al.), 92

maid or matron of honor
at bridal shower, 56
bustling the train, 169
choosing, 39
duties, 39–41
gift, 44, 293, 294
position at altar or huppah, *74,* 75
procession, 72, *73*
recession, 77
marriage license, 298
blood test, 298
destination wedding, 116, 299
out-of-state, 298
Morley, Helen, 175
mother of the bride, 47
dress, 203–4
duties, 47–48
mom and stepmom, 48
position at altar or huppah, *74,* 75
procession, 72, *73*
seating during ceremony, 75
mother of the groom, 48
dress, 203–4
duties, 48–49
position at altar or huppah, *74,* 75
seating during ceremony, 75
music, 257–71
Anne & Jason, dance performance, Canterbury, CT, 268, *268*
band, 266–67
band vs. DJ, 263, 265–66
Cara & Chris, theme wedding, Belle Isle, MI, 110, *110*
CD or tapes, 260
ceremony, 83, 257–62
Claire & Matthew, Hempstead, TX, 264, *264*
cocktail hour/dinnertime, 265
contracts, 262, 267, 270
cost, 261, 263, 266, 269
cost-cutting tips, 35–36
dancing and, 270–71
DJ, 267, 269–70
do-it-yourself, 270
"Here Comes the Bride," 259
hiring musicians, 262–63
Jeannette & DeMarco, Atlanta, GA, 147
outdoors, cautions, 261
personalizing, 259
reception, 263, 265–67, 269–71
theme wedding, 109, 111

name change, 299–300
Native American traditions, 115
New Jewish Wedding, The (Diamant), 85
Norwegian traditions, 116

officiant
clergy teams, 89
do-it-yourself, 70
fee, 71
finding, 69–70
for gay or lesbian ceremony, 92–93
interfaith, 88–89
online planning
finding photographers, 244, 245
finding reception sites, 145
finding stationers, 133

parents, 335–45
announcing engagement to, 4
bride's accompaniment down the aisle, 76
dealing with, 335–37
disapproving of fiancé/e, 338
divorced dilemmas, 338–39
engagement party hosts, 55–56
father of the bride, 49, *74,* 75, 99–100, 102, 204
father of the groom, 49–50, *74,* 75, 204
footing the bill, 26–27, 29, 30
how to ask them for money, 28
in-laws, 339–41
interfaith/intercultural, 327, 330–32
leaving a parent out of the wedding, 339
mother of the bride, 47–48, *74,* 75, 203–4
mother of the groom, 48–49, *74,* 75, 203–4
photos, 248
positions at altar, Christian, *74*
positions at huppah, Jewish, *74*
procession, Christian, 72, *73*
procession, Jewish, 72, *73*
receiving line, 97
seating during ceremony, 75
stepparents, 48, 97, 102, 342–44
top ten family Q and A's, 342–44
transportation, 283
who pays for what, 27, 28
wording, invitations, 127–29
wording, wedding announcement, 140–41
parties
attendants' parties, 64–65
bachelor and bachelorette bashes, 60–62, 301

engagement, 55–56
Erron & Scott, wedding weekend, Moraga, CA, 64, *64*
morning-after breakfast, 65
prewedding breakfasts or brunches, 65
rehearsal dinner, 62–64
showers, 56–59
welcome cocktail party or brunch for guests, 62
working parties, 65
photography, 240–54
best images, 247–50
contract, 245
cost-cutting tips, 36
emergency remedies, 306
finding online, 244, 245
hiring a photographer, 244–47
ideas for taking your best picture, 253
Lisa & Michael, photojournalistic shots, Westchester, PA, 243
must-have shot list, 249
photo terms, 242
storage tips, 254
style, 241–42, 244
trends, 250
when to take portraits, 250
See also wedding video
prenuptial agreement, 314
proposal, Bill & Emily, 5, *5*
Protestant ceremony, 87
interfaith, 89

Quaker ceremony, 87–88
letter of intent, 87
wedding committee, 87

receiving line, 96–98
stepparents in line, 97
what you do, 97–98
when and where, 97
who stands in it, 97
reception, 94–104
announcing the couple, 99
blessing, 96
bouquet and garter toss, 101, 103
choosing a vendor, 32
cutting the cake, 103
dance, first, 99–100
dance starters, 100
dancing, 263, 270–71
dancing, organized, 271
donating leftover food, 226
emcee, 96, 100
escort and place cards, 139
ethnic ideas, 113–16
favors, 272–77
getaway, 103–4
guest book, 142
Heidi & Aaron, personalizing, Miami Beach, FL, 51, *51*
Jeannette & DeMarco, Atlanta, GA, 149
Jewish, 95
blessing, 96
menu cards, 139–40
music, 263, 265–67, 269–71
order of events, 95–96
receiving line, 96–98
rentals, 151, 158
R.S.V.P., 297–98
Sallie & Jason, Cliffside Park, NJ, 102, *102*
seating of guests, 98-99, 298
timetable, 97
tipping, 33
toasting, 41, 42, 100–1, 103
toast of the table, 46–47
written contract, 33–34
See also flowers; food; site
rehearsal, 78
rehearsal dinner, 62–64
relationship with your fiancé/e
Alison & Craig, engagement tensions, Rhinebeck, NY, 319, *319*
calling off the wedding, 322
Carolyn & Matthew, prenuptial agreement, NYC, 314, *314*
challenge of change, 317–18
cold feet, 322–23
communication, 320–21, 328
compromise, XYZ method, 320
engagement-time tension, handling, 311–12
fighting, 318–19, 321, 325–26
honeymoon advice, 379, 381–82
interfaith or intercultural, 325–30
issues that need resolution, 326
managing money, 313
marriage vs. living together, 318
passion, keeping and putting it back in your life, 315–16
pre-wedding, final stages, intimate moments, 302
religious rifts, 316–17
unequal distribution of labor, 321–22
rentals, 151
check the contract, 158
choose your crew, 158
know your needs, 158
ring (engagement)
appraisal of the diamond, 10
band, 10
basic diamond facts, 8–9, *9*
conflict diamonds, 10
cost considerations, 8
gems other than diamond, 8, 10–11
how to examine the stone, 9
jeweler, reputable, 8
settings, 10
sneaky ways to get her ring size, 8
ring (wedding)
ceremony, 76
choice of bands, 77
Claddagh ring, 114
lore, 78
Roman Catholic ceremony, 88
banns, 88
interfaith, 89
nuptial mass, 88
Ruskin, Myrna, 4
Russian road trip, 116

Schindler, Rabbi Judy, 71
Scottish traditions
bridal gown, 170
Highland Fling, 116
second weddings, 90–92
children in the ceremony, 91
ex-spouse and ex-family, 91
footing the bill, 90–91
major religions on, 91
roles for children, 92
skipping the veil, 91
showers
activities and games, 57, 58
gifts, keeping track of, 56
helpers, 57
his 'n' hers, 57–58
history of ritual, 57
inventive gifts, 59
maid of honor at, 56
themes, 58–59
when and where, 57
who hosts, 56
who's invited, 56
women-only affair, 56–57
siblings, 340
site, 19–20, 145–58
active or adventure wedding, 119
A to Z suggestions, 146, 147
backup, 112
boats, trains, trolleys, 152, 155
cancellation, 157
ceremony, 20
check the place out, 155
color, 148
cost, 156–57
cost-cutting tips, 35, 156
destination wedding, 116, 117
eating, drinking, and partying areas, 148
electrical outlets, 148
Emily & Sean, The Trois Estate, Austin, TX, 151
finding online, 145
good vibrations, 148
great party rooms in unusual places, 155
great view, 148
inside or out, 20
Jeannette & DeMarco, Block Candy Company Bldg., Atlanta, GA, 149
Lee & Jeff, Orcas Island, WA, 117, *117*
lighting, 147–48
location budget, 25
long-distance planning, out-of-town wedding, 19–20
mansions, castles, and other great buildings, 152
marrying at home, 150–53
meeting with managers, 155–58
Melani & Herb, Oracle, AZ, 15, *15*
outdoor considerations, 21, 112, 152
parking, 147
privacy, 147
reception budget, 25
size, 147
starting your search, 145–46
style and choice, 20–21
Suzanne & Tripp, Lake Glenville, NC, 82
Tarika & Michael, Old Stony Hill, Jamaica, 21
ten great cities, ten great locations, 153–54
theme weddings, 107–10
traditional sites, 150
Victorian wedding, 109
wedding consultant for out-of-town wedding, 20
when to walk away, 156
written contract, content, 150
size, 17–19
budget considerations, 25
children invited or not, 18
cutting the list, 17–19
figure out before choosing location, 19
guest list, what to consider, 17
separate list for ceremony, 20
who invites how many, 17
Southern California, 154
Spanish bridal accessories, 170
style
budget black-tie, 20
budget considerations, 25
date and time and, 14, 16
four types, 20
site and deciding on, 20, 22
staff dress code and, 34
Victorian wedding, 109

thank-you notes
engagement gifts, 55
how they look, 293
stationery for, 142
wedding gifts, 291–92
wedding party hosts, 294
what they say, 142, 293
who sends them, 292
The Knot
Aloha Travel Auction, 374
Big-Day Budgeter, 25, 31
Bridal Search, 171
Checklist, 14
"Destination Wedding Requirements," 117
photography, 245
Wedding Gift Registry, 286
The Knot Weddingpages, 245
themes
bibliophile or literary, 108
Cara & Chris, fun theme, Belle Isle, MI, 110, *110*
career couple, 109
colors, 107
destination wedding, 116, 117
environmental, 107–8
ethnic, 113–16
extreme, 119
movie set or theater, 108
music, 111
period or old-fashioned, 109
seasonal, 111–13
travel buffs, 109
Victorian, 109
wedding weekend, 118–19
tipping, 33, 380
toasting, 41, 100–1
how to write a toast, 42
Irish toasts, 114–15
origin of word, 103
special guest at table, 46–47
transportation, 278–83

alternatives to limos, 281
budget and costs, 279–80
captain, 46
contract, 279, 280
cost-cutting tips, 36, 280
decorating-the-car caution, 282
emergency remedies, 306
getting to the ceremony, 281
getting to the party, 281–82
for guests, 282
limousine rental, 279
for parents, 283
photographer and videographer on rides, 282
post-honeymoon, 282
preparation call sheet, 280
reservations, 280
treats/wedding packages, 281

United States Tour Operators Association, 373
Universal Life Church, 70
ushers, 46
junior, 44
seating of guests, 75
See also groomsmen

vendors, 32–34
baker, 238
band, 266–67
bridal gown, 177–78
bridesmaid dresses, 202
cancellations, 157
caterer, 224–27
choosing, 32
Cindy & Wayne, Livingston, NJ, 302, *302*
contracts, 32, 33, 150, 158, 202, 216, 245, 252, 262, 267, 270, 280
credit cards for deposits, 35
deposit and receipt, 32
DJ, 267, 268–69
finding photographers, 244, 245
finding reception sites, 145
finding stationers, 133
florist, 215–17
keeping in contact, 32–33, 300–1
last-minute problems, 305–6
last-minute questions, 300
limo, 279, 280
meetings with, 32
men's formalwear, 197
musicians, 262–63
negotiating with, 32
photographer, 244–47
reception site, 150, 156, 157–58
rentals, 158
stationer, 132–34, 137
videographer, 254
written estimates, 32
Victorian wedding, 109
videography. *See* wedding video
vows
exchange of, at ceremony, 76
reading or memorizing, 80
samples of vows, 80–81
writing your own, 78–80

Wade, Paul, 229
wedding cake, 234–39
baker for, 238
contract, 238
cost, 238
cost-cutting tips, 35, 238
cutting the cake, 103, 237–38
flavor combinations, 237
frosting, 236
groom's, 239
saving, 237
style, 235–36
taste, 236
toppers, 236
wedding consultant, 22–23
cost, 22, 31
finding your wedding site, 146
money saved by using, 29
for out-of-town wedding, 20
pros and cons, 22
referrals, website, 22
tip on hiring, 22
what a consultant can do, 23
wedding day
breakfast with fiancé/e, 304
early preparations, 303–4
emergency remedies, 304–5
having a ball, 306–7
last minute preparations, 304
night before to-do list, 303
punctuality, 303
vendor problems, 305–6
ways to savor the day, 307
wedding decorations, 217–19. *See also* flowers
wedding night, 307–8
wedding planning (overview)
attendants and other participants, 39–47
bridal gown and attendant attire, 161–70, 195–202
budget, 25–31
ceremony, 66–93
consultant, 20, 22–23
date and time, 14–16
family at ceremony, 47–50
favors, 272–77
food and drinks, 221–39
gifts, 285–94
guests, care of, 50–52
invitations and other stationery, 123–43
last-minute business, 297–306
music, 257–71
organizing tools, 14, 26
photography, 240–54
reception, 94–104
second weddings, 90–92
setting priorities, 13–14
site, 19–21, 112, 145–58
size, 17–19
style, 20, 22
themes, 107–20
transportation, 278–83
vendors, 32–34
volunteers, 47
wedding cake, 234–39
See also specific items
wedding program, 81–82
wedding stationery
announcements, 140–41
cancellation card, 141
ceremony programs, 138

earth-friendly, 139
escort and place cards, 139
glossary for paper and printing, 125
invitations, 123–34
map-hotel info cards, 137–38
menu cards, 139–40
name-change cards, 142
pew cards, 138
printing techniques, 123–25
reception or ceremony cards, 135–36
response cards, 136–37
save-the-date cards, 134–35
selecting a stationer, 132–34, 137
thank-you notes, 142, 291–92
weekend wedding program, 140
See also invitations
wedding video, 250–54
ceremony limitations, 251
contract, 252
emergency remedies, 306
friend/relative handling, 252
hiring a pro, 252–54
storage tips, 254
style, 251–52
wedding weekend, 118–19
itinerary or program for, 140
schedule of events, 118
What People Wore (Gorsline), 108
Wild Geese and Tea: An Asian-American Wedding Planner (Costa), 113
word origins
betrothed, 3
fiancé/e, 3
honeymoon, 349
husband, 3
toast, 103
wife, 3

PHOTO CREDITS

Pages ii, 24, 38, 94, 121, 144, 225, 234, 256, 272: Karen Zieff, Zieff Photography, www.zieffphoto.com
Pages 2, 66, 278, 296: Missy McLamb Photographers, www.missymclamb.com
Page 5: AP/Wide World Photos
Pages 12, 240: Elizabeth Grubb, E Photography, www.elizabethphotography.com
Pages 15, 213: Philippe Cheng, Philippe Cheng Photography, www.philippecheng.com
Page 21: Cappy Hotchkiss, Cappy Hotchkiss Photography, www.cappyhotchkiss.com
Page 31: Phil Cantor Wedding Photography, www.philcantor.com
Page 34: Jeannine A. St. Marie-McCutcheon, Photography by Jeannine, www.photosbyjeannine.com
Page 51: Greg Hark Photographics, www.greghark.com/aboutus.htm
Pages 54, 106, 160, 206, 220, 284, 310, 334: Elizabeth Messina Photography, www.elizabethmessina.com
Page 64: Lisa Lefkowitz Photography, www.lisalefkowitz.com
Page 82: Manuel Llaneras Photography, www.mlphotography.com
Pages 90, 324: Willi Wong Photography, www.williwongphotography.com
Page 98: Oakley Photography, www.oakleyphotography.com
Page 102: Christopher Smith, 212-219-8862
Page 110: Documentary Photo, www.adocumentaryphoto.com
Pages 117, 327: Louis Felix Photography, www.louisfelix.com
Page 135: Theo Wargo
Page 149: Kristen Alexander Photography, www.kristenphoto.com
Page 151: Solas Gallery, www.solasgallery.com
Pages 172, 199, 314, 329: Karen Hill, Karen Hill Photography, www.karenhill.com
Page 192: Angie Silvy Photography, www.angiesilvyphotography.com

Page 243: Rob Fraser, Rob Fraser Photography, www.robfraser.com
Page 264: David Bates Photographics, www.dbphotographics.com
Page 268: Joshua Zuckerman Photography, www.jzweddings.com
Page 302: Jared Bernstein Photography, www.jaredbernstein.com
Page 341: Phil Kramer Photographers, Inc., www.pkphoto.com